CAUSES OF INDUSTRIAL PEACE

UNDER COLLECTIVE BARGAINING

CAUSES OF
INDUSTRIAL PEACE
UNDER COLLECTIVE BARGAINING

Edited by CLINTON S. GOLDEN
and VIRGINIA D. PARKER
for the CIP Committee of the National Planning Association

HARPER & BROTHERS, PUBLISHERS
NEW YORK

This book is developed, with additions, from materials originally
published by the National Planning Association.

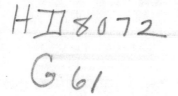

CONTENTS

MEMBERS OF THE COMMITTEE ON THE CAUSES OF INDUSTRIAL PEACE UNDER COLLECTIVE BARGAINING

The *Final Report* won unanimous approval of the Committee on the Causes of Industrial Peace. Its members—all of whom served from the Committee's creation in 1947 to issuance of the *Final Report*—are:

CLINTON S. GOLDEN, *Chairman:* Executive Director, Trade Union Program, Harvard University

E. WIGHT BAKKE, Director, Labor and Management Center, Yale University

J. DOUGLAS BROWN, Director, Industrial Relations Section, Princeton University

EUGENE BURGESS, Business Economist, Des Plaines, Illinois

STUART CHASE, Author and Consultant

WALTER L. CHRISTON, Retired, Largo, Florida

PHILIP J. CLOWES, Director, Gulf States Organizing Area, United Steelworkers of America

WILLIAM H. DAVIS, Attorney, Davis, Hoxie and Faithfull

JOHN T. DUNLOP, Associate Professor of Economics, Littauer School of Public Administration, Harvard University

SANDER GENIS, Vice President, Amalgamated Clothing Workers of America

FREDERICK H. HARBISON, Executive Officer, Industrial Relations Center, University of Chicago

MARION H. HEDGES, Washington, D. C.

L. CLAYTON HILL, Professor of Industrial Relations, School of Business Administration, University of Michigan

LAWRENCE E. JOSEPH, Pittsburgh, Pennsylvania

CLARK KERR, Chancellor, University of California, Berkeley

WILLIAM M. LEISERSON, Director, Labor Organization Study, Johns Hopkins University

DOUGLAS MCGREGOR, Professor of Management, School of Industrial Management, Massachusetts Institute of Technology

EARLE D. MCKAY, Short Creek, West Virginia

ERIC A. NICOL, Partner, Rogers, Slade & Hill

ERIC PETERSON, General Secretary-Treasurer, International Association of Machinists

ANNA M. ROSENBERG, Anna M. Rosenberg Associates, Business, Industrial and Public Relations Counsellors

JOSEPH N. SCANLON, *Project Co-Director:* Industrial Relations Section, Massachusetts Institute of Technology

vii

GEORGE W. TAYLOR, Professor of Industry, Wharton School of Finance and Commerce, University of Pennsylvania

CHARLES R. WALKER, *Project Co-Director:* Labor and Management Center, Yale University

Other charter members of the Committee, whose counsels were deeply appreciated, served until their deaths: *Alvin E. Dodd, Fred A. Krafft, Herbert W. Payne, Louis Stark,* and *R. B. Wolf.* Mr. Stark and Mr. Wolf were signers of the Committee's *Final Report.*

NPA's series of reports on the Causes of Industrial Peace Under Collective Bargaining grew out of a statement made by Clinton S. Golden at an NPA meeting in 1946—"In my opinion, the time has come when, instead of looking into the causes of conflict that we know and hear so much about, we ought to try to discover *how much peace there is and what makes peace.*"

Following immediate and enthusiastic endorsement of this idea by the NPA Board of Trustees, the Committee on the Causes of Industrial Peace was established, under Mr. Golden's chairmanship, in 1947. Since then, Committee members—experts in industrial relations drawn from business, labor, universities, and the professions—have given freely of their time and talents in carrying out this project.

The Committee set itself a difficult assignment. It decided to survey in some detail the labor-management relations of twelve to fifteen firms and unions which had experienced successful and peaceful industrial relations, in an effort to discover whether what makes peace in some companies can be extended to others.

From the start, the Committee's job was made more difficult by the fact that there are so many cases of industrial peace. It was necessary to set up criteria for selection of the companies, and then to select only a few companies from the many which met those criteria. Once the selections were made, the Committee faced numerous, continuing tasks: arranging for top-flight scholars, who could be counted on to keep an open mind, to make on-the-spot investigations, and write objective reports; reading and commenting on all the reports in the series before publication; agreeing on a Committee Statement for each report, which pointed out the important elements within the individual situation and significant parallels found in all cases; and, finally, putting together the facts brought out in independent studies and evaluating their meaning for labor and management in many other situations.

The first section of this book presents the Committee's study, *Fundamentals of Labor Peace, a Final Report,* which was issued by NPA in December 1953. In it, the Committee members present their views on the principles and policies followed at the companies studied which could be applied profitably to the development of industrial relations elsewhere. And they raise a number of questions which require future intensive study. In line with usual NPA procedure, members of the Committee who signed the report were asked to express their opinions in footnotes where they disagreed with or desired to comment on details in it. Only one such footnote was submitted. Based on discussion at a number of Committee meetings, the report itself was prepared by several authors.

Clinton S. Golden, Chairman of the Committee, explains the reasons for the project, the Committee's approach to its work, and the Committee's conception of industrial peace in Chapter 1.

Clark Kerr, Committee member and coauthor of *Case Studies No. 1* and *No. 6,* wrote Chapter 2, "The Collective Bargaining Environment."

John T. Dunlop, Committee member, is author of Chapter 3, "The Growth of the Relationship."

Douglas McGregor, Committee member and coauthor of *Case Study No. 3,* not only wrote Chapter 4, "The Influence of Attitudes and Policies," but served ably as editor for the entire Committee report.

Frederick H. Harbison, Committee member and coauthor of *Case Studies No. 2* and *No. 13,* and John R. Coleman, coauthor of *Case Study No. 13,* describe "Procedures and Methods" in Chapter 5.

Charles A. Myers, coauthor of *Case Study No. 7,* presents "Conclusions and Implications" in Chapter 6.

The book's second section includes condensations of thirteen *Case Studies* in the Committee's series. Appendix A briefly summarizes a report on *The Development of a Policy for Industrial Peace in Atomic Energy,* which was prepared under the Committee's sponsorship. Appendix B is an NPA staff summary of responses to questionnaires sent out to union and management officials in companies nominated for study by the Committee.

We hope that publication of this book—edited by Clinton S. Golden, who has had primary responsibility for the project's success, and Virginia D. Parker, editor of NPA's publications throughout the series—will carry forward and intensify the usefulness of the Committee's work. We have been gratified by the growing body of evidence that the *Case Studies* have had an impact on thinking both at home and abroad. Management and labor have put them to practical use in their daily decisions; they have been used as classroom texts in colleges and universities; many labor-management forums have been built around them; new research projects have been patterned after them; and they have been popular subjects in newspapers, magazines, and trade and professional journals. It is our hope that this activity is but a start in an ever-widening attempt to answer the important question: "What makes labor peace?"

This series has been made possible through the generosity and support of John Hay Whitney. Early in the project, Mr. Whitney described the undertaking this way:

"This is the first big-scale attempt in the area of labor-management relations to find out the truth from facts derived from case studies. It has a positive approach. The direct achievement of production and distribution in American business is itself a very positive quality, and I feel that the successful labor-management relationships which are so importantly behind the achievements of industry deserve at least as much study as those cases in which relationships have failed.

"The improvement of contractual relationships presents a real challenge in establishing the validity of our democracy."

The findings in this series, in our opinion, provide clear evidence that American men and women are meeting that challenge.

NPA is deeply indebted to all who have contributed to this project—especially to Clinton S. Golden, originator of the idea and leader in developing it; to John Hay Whitney; to Committee members and the project's codirectors, Joseph N. Scanlon and Charles R. Walker; to the authors of the *Case Studies;* and to management and union representatives at the plants studied.

> H. Christian Sonne
> *Chairman of the Board of Trustees*
> *National Planning Association*

PART I

FUNDAMENTALS OF LABOR PEACE

A Final Report

CHAPTER 1

Introduction

CLINTON S. GOLDEN
Executive Director, Trade Union Program,
Harvard University

The history of workers' attempts to extend union organization and to secure employers' recognition and acceptance has been characterized by resistance and conflict. Throughout the evolution of our industrial society, these conflicts have been closely scrutinized and widely publicized. But little attention has been given to the vast number of employers and union members who have achieved peaceful relationships.

EVOLUTION OF INDUSTRIAL RELATIONS

The great railroad strikes of the 1870's and 1880's; the Homestead Steel strike of 1892; the anthracite coal strike of 1902; the textile strikes of 1912–14; the great steel strike of 1919; and the nation-wide railway shopmen's strike of 1922 marked the period of conflict. These strikes produced two distinctive by-products:

1. Inquiries as to their cause by some agency or instrumentality of the federal government; and

2. The creation of workers' fear of the vast power and influence of corporations and industry. This heritage of fear has become a part of the folklore of the labor movement which has been bequeathed to the present generation of union members.

In spite of this background, a remarkable change in the climate of industrial relations has occurred over the past eighteen years. There has been a steady growth of mutual confidence between management and organized labor coupled with the discovery of new techniques for peaceful settlement of disputes. Even during this period, however, students, editorial writers, and the public have focused most of their attention upon disturbances of industrial peace or upon the formidable difficulties faced by both sides in learning to live together.

Membership in labor organizations began a period of significant growth in the early thirties, but the unions' greatest momentum came in the years after the passage of the National Labor Relations Act—the Wagner Act —of 1935. The following decade saw an increase from three million to fifteen million union members.

The Wagner Act legalized and safeguarded the right of workers to join and form bona fide labor organizations for purposes of collective bargaining. It also placed an affirmative obligation upon employers and industrial management to bargain with union representatives designated by the employees and to reach mutually satisfactory collective bargaining agreements. The advent of these new rights and obligations brought problems of readjustment to both management and labor, especially during the war years.

America entered World War II with a greatly expanded labor movement, which meant that in a period of national crisis thousands of obscure, inexperienced, rank-and-file workers were catapulted into positions of organizational leadership at local and regional levels.

Management was similarly unprepared to make the required shifts to unfamiliar forms of relationship with organizations representing the individual employee. Historically, management had, in the main, operated on authoritarian principles. It was therefore unprepared for adjustments because as long as its principles were not effectively challenged, there was little evident need to prepare for anything else. The expanding labor movement, operating basically on democratic principles, did not have to overcome this obstacle. It was dedicated to recognizing and serving the needs of people rather than property.

In an older and less resilient society, a movement involving millions of organized workers, intent upon having a voice in determining the conditions under which they would be employed, would have had profound revolutionary implications, if not consequences. Yet the presumably immovable object symbolized by industrial management and the seemingly irresistible force of millions of newly organized workers met without a violent and shattering collision.

Beginning in 1937, thousands of collective bargaining agreements were negotiated for the first time between representatives of the unions and management. In spite of the heritage of fears and suspicions and the unpreparedness on both sides, with notable exceptions, agreements were reached without interruptions to production. As time passed, management and union representatives were brought into closer personal contact and gradually faced their new responsibilities.

Many newly negotiated agreements covered a comparatively short period—usually one year. In retrospect, it is obvious that management had not yet come to believe that the unions would be enduring and permanent institutions. And union leaders, particularly in the new and rapidly expanding organizations, were not too confident of the cohesiveness and solidarity of their own organizations or of the good faith of management in the new relationship.

Inside influential management circles, many held that the new relationships were the result of a "shotgun marriage" rather than of logic, reason, or intellectual conviction. Nevertheless, the frequently unwilling partnerships continued. Expiration dates of the initial agreements, although approached with apprehension on both sides, did not terminate relationships. In most instances, contracts were renewed and continued on the basis of mutually acceptable revisions and with a minimum of interruption to production.

The phenomenon, ever more general, of widespread contract renewal and progress toward understanding still remained largely unnoticed by the public and even by labor "experts." For whenever strikes did result from inability to reach agreement, they were widely dramatized and their significance frequently exaggerated and misinterpreted. For example, in 1946, when the American public heard or read about more strikes than ever before in our history, more than nine out of every ten contracts between employers and unions were negotiated peacefully. Another significant aspect of that year's record to which little attention was given is that the strike wave following World War I—when a far smaller percentage of workers had been organized into unions—actually affected a larger percentage of the work force than the 1946 strikes. Furthermore, there was comparatively little violence in the strikes of 1946 as compared with the big strikes in earlier American labor history.

The extensive dramatization of the comparatively few strikes that occurred following V-J Day unfortunately served to renew in the minds of workers the old fears of employers' power and hostile intentions. At the same time, there was rapidly accumulating evidence that for the most part the new industrial relationships were evolving on an orderly, peaceful basis, with strikes diminishing as relations matured. If this proved to be the actual and prevailing pattern of industrial relationships, it seemed that the evidence should be made known to the American people.

THE COMMITTEE AND ITS PROCESS

By 1946, an inquiry to determine the extent to which employers had entered into one or more successful agreements with unions without encountering conflict seemed urgent and useful.

Woodrow Wilson once observed that: "Everything I know about history, every bit of experience and observation that has contributed to my thought has confirmed in me the conviction that the real wisdom of human life is compounded out of the experience of ordinary men." [1]

With this cogent observation in mind, it seemed that much of value might be gained by ascertaining factually the nature of the experience of both management and union people at the company or work-place level, who had made a success of their new relationships.

The proposal that a study of instances of peaceful and constructive relations, rather than of industrial conflicts, be undertaken won the approval of the National Planning Association's Board of Trustees and Committees. A new special committee, composed of twenty-nine business and labor leaders and professional consultants, was appointed and charged with the task of formulating an approach and establishing the necessary criteria to be used in selecting the obviously limited number of companies and unions to be studied.

To bring the inquiry within workable limits and to sharpen the focus of research, the Committee on the Causes of Industrial Peace Under Collective Bargaining set up these criteria for the selection of companies and unions to be studied:

1. The cases should be from industries important to the country's over-all economic health.

2. There should be geographic distribution so that no one section of the United States would be overrepresented.

3. Companies should be of substantial size, with at least one thousand employees.

4. A reasonably competitive situation should exist to assure that management had not bought peace at a price.

5. The studies should be made where peace as a constructive relationship could not be explained in terms of a personality or some other unique factor, whether on the union or the management side of the bargaining table.

6. The problems tackled and solved by company and union should be representative of important industrial relations questions.

7. Industrial warfare was absent.

This last criterion did not mean that companies and unions which had been involved in strikes would not be selected. The absence of strikes is not the only criterion of good industrial relations, nor is their occasional occurrence a proof that relations are bad. To the Committee, "How

---

[1] Woodrow Wilson, *The New Freedom,* Doubleday, Page and Company, 1913, p. 7.

many strikes?" was as a rule less crucial than such questions as: "How much and what kind of freedom does the employer enjoy in his relationship with the union? How much mutual confidence have both parties in each other? Have the company, the union, the public gained or lost from the collective bargaining relationship?"

After establishing these criteria, the Committee turned to industry, labor, and the public for help. Ten thousand leaders in industry, labor, and in public service were asked, "What company or union would you nominate as representative of a successful collective bargaining relationship?" Suggestions were invited through radio and newspapers.

Over a thousand nominations were made. To those who came within the requirements of the Committee's criteria, questionnaires were sent requesting more information and asking whether the company or union would be willing to be studied. The final list of cases for study was chosen from several hundred replies.

Well-known scholars made on-the-spot investigations of the cases selected; and Committee members carefully read and advised on each study before publication, evaluating as the work progressed significant parallels found in the different cases.

WHAT IS INDUSTRIAL PEACE?

In tackling the basic problem of how industrial peace of a constructive character can be won, the Committee made no claim that it would record all the causes or conditions of a good labor-management relationship. As the work progressed, however, there emerged an ever clearer definition of "industrial peace" and "good union-management relations."

The Committee's studies re-emphasize the conclusion that peace is something more than the mere absence of conflict.

Two principal elements exist in the industrial relationship—the employer and the employee. Their interests are not completely mutual. The employer represents, and is concerned primarily with, a property interest which in turn is directly related to the financial interests of a *limited* number of stockholders or owners. The interest of the employees' organization or union is primarily that of people—a greater number in most cases—and is concerned with their material as well as their spiritual and psychological interests and needs. In modern society each of these elements is interdependent rather than completely identical.

Under these circumstances, the Committee's concern has been to ascertain how historically hostile groups can coexist on a basis of reasonable equality of position in the enterprise, and at the same time participate in a common endeavor from which both seek security, opportunity, and sustenance.

There are relative degrees of industrial peace. These range from a precarious equilibrium of mutually hostile forces for a stated period of time —the life of an agreement—to an enduring, harmonious, and cooperative relationship of a really creative character. Under present conditions, neither extreme represents the typical. There is some evidence, though, that we are moving from the first *in the direction* of the second, which may be thought of as the ideal.

For the purposes of its studies, the Committee defines industrial peace as the product of the relationship between two organized groups—industrial management and organized labor—in which both coexist, with each retaining its institutional sovereignty, working together in reasonable harmony in a climate of mutual respect and confidence.

Within the framework of this definition, wide variations may be observed in the *quality* of the relationship. A greater measure of mutual confidence and respect can be discerned, for example, in the relations described in *Case Study No. 1* of Crown Zellerbach Corporation and in *No. 4* on Hickey-Freeman Company than in *Case Study No. 2* of Libbey-Owens-Ford Glass Company and *No. 6* on Lockheed Aircraft Corporation. Yet in all four situations the relations are peaceful and considered good by the parties.

The variety of relationships encompassed by the studies illustrates the dynamic quality of our democracy. Democracy, as known and practiced in the United States, is not a static concept of a way of life narrowly limited to the participation of citizens in the political processes of government. To be purposeful, democracy must be an ever-expanding and growing process that will meet the needs and provide the opportunities for personal growth and recognition required by free people. All the studies indicate the expanding nature of our democracy. They indicate the willingness of workers, while deeply dedicated to individual freedom, to subordinate *voluntarily* in varying degree the individual interest to that of the work-place group.

The growing awareness of management that if managerial policies and decisions are to have meaningful and ready acceptance by the employees, they must be the product of broad consultation and understanding rather than unilateral imposition, is of profound significance.

The idea has been advanced [2] that, as the industrial revolution continues, the mass-production system evolving out of it is producing a new type of community built around the work-place unit of enterprise. The

[2] Peter Drucker, *The New Society*, Harper & Brothers, 1950.

question of the type of government of such a community is bound to arise. Is it to be governed in accordance with authoritarian or democratic principles?

The trend indicated by the *Case Studies* is in the direction of introducing increasingly familiar democratic processes into the management or government of the enterprise. Attention is being directed to the conduct and behavior of the individual as a member of the large, impersonal organization that makes large-scale production possible. The frustrations that result from the loneliness and lack of recognition of the individual in such an environment no doubt can be overcome by conscious democratic participation in a community of purposeful and meaningful effort.

Certain new, but not immediately recognized, values emerge from the conditions of industrial peace described. These are moral and ethical in nature. If as a result of organized group relationships, as distinguished from individual relationships, employees have acquired greater self-confidence and self-respect, the chances are that new, heretofore untouched, resources of skill and ingenuity can be released.

The worker, who in a new climate of relations is aware that his personal usefulness to the enterprise is valued, is prepared to share freely his knowledge of work methods and processes with fellow workers and management. Thus a democratic industrial environment forms wherein the desire for personal participation finds fulfillment. The employees are not the exclusive beneficiaries. The morale of the management group which enjoys the confidence and respect of the employees is significantly improved.

The *Case Studies* have been directed toward ascertaining the elements contributing to peaceful or good union-management relations. They necessarily deal with the realities of existing relations. It is doubtful whether the parties will be content to accept the current status of relationships as final and enduring. Further improvement and greater satisfactions will be sought. A goal possible of attainment by conscious effort might well be a relationship in which—because of complete mutual respect and confidence, complete absence of fear of each other, excellent two-way communication, and wide mutual consultation on possible solutions to problems of common concern—both institutional groups have largely, but voluntarily, become integrated into an increasingly democratized enterprise.

In the absence of external forces beyond the control of either or both parties, the peaceful relations found in these studies may be slowly, though perhaps unconsciously, evolving toward such a goal.

CHAPTER 2 —————————————————————

The Collective Bargaining Environment

CLARK KERR *

Chancellor of the University of California at Berkeley

The environment of a collective bargaining system is the aggregate of external forces which affect its development and its character. External forces are those which are largely outside the influence of the parties. We are here concerned with how the environment relates to the prospects for industrial peace; and by "industrial peace" we mean a continued state of mutually agreeable but nonconclusive relations freely and amicably negotiated by parties of relatively equal strength. We shall be concerned with these questions: What are the more important external forces? How do they separately affect the likelihood of peaceful relations? What combination of environmental elements is most conducive to industrial peace? Does this combination cause industrial peace or only create a situation in which peace can be more readily achieved by other means?

As we go along, reference will be made to the individual collective bargaining relationships covered in the Causes of Industrial Peace series, and at the end the environmental forces typically at work on these relationships will be compared with the combination of elements deemed favorable to industrial peace. Were these records of industrial peace accomplished with the aid of their surrounding environments or in the face of hostile outside forces?

External factors do not necessarily predetermine the nature of a collective bargaining relationship. Environmental factors set limits, but within these limits the parties normally are free to create a bad relationship or a good one. Analysis of the external factors, therefore, contributes primarily to an understanding of (1) the limits within which the parties must operate, and (2) the influences which may aid or hinder them in achieving a healthy relationship.

* Abraham Siegel, Research Assistant in the Institute of Industrial Relations, University of California at Berkeley, aided in preparation of this chapter.

10

THE INDUSTRIAL ENVIRONMENT

Collective bargaining relationships are influenced by the nature of the industries and plants in which they take place. Here we will consider some of the factors which are important in the industrial environment.

Size of Plant and Company

The difference in industrial relations in a two-man shop as against a mass-production industry is one of kind rather than degree. Size is an important determining condition. Among other things, the growth of the large corporation brought modern industrial unionism.

Size affects the nearness of managers and of union leaders to the workers; the identity of interest or lack of it among the three groups; and the amount of knowledge held in common. It usually establishes who is the boss—the owner, the manager, the superintendent, or the foreman. It decides the extent to which formal substitutes are required to replace informal and more spontaneous relationships.

Among the *Case Studies* none is concerned with a really small plant or a great industrial giant. Most are important in their industry and area but we did not study Ford or Swift or U.S. Steel or Standard Oil, or the corner grocery store or barber shop. The series might, in fact, be entitled: "Industrial Peace in Medium-Sized Companies." This is not an accident. In the selection of companies the large may have been avoided as too unique and the small as too insignificant to attract attention; but beyond this the causes of industrial peace are more likely to be discovered in the middle range. The large are often chosen by the unions or themselves or by fate to battle through the general lines of development of collective bargaining. In the process of setting patterns, they do not set records for industrial amity. Moreover, their size may make it difficult to adjust quickly and flexibly to collective bargaining, and to substitute good personnel practices for the friendly personal contacts of the small firm.

At the other end, the small companies have their special problems. Their collective bargaining relationships are subject to the personalities of the people involved and, conversely, to the patterns set by others. Small-scale enterprise also is the area in which union-management collusion on the one hand, and the union price list on the other, have on occasion developed.

Medium-sized firms, by contrast, are less compelled to set or to follow specific patterns, and are in a better position to achieve a successful balance of policies and personalities.

Production Patterns

Most industries have a steady flow of production throughout the year. Notable exceptions exist, however, and have an impact on collective bargaining. Industries marked by seasonal cycles present special problems for collective bargaining, such as layoff policies and programs for division of work. Some production depends on the hiring of casual workers and this occasionally raises difficulties, deriving from the meager community of interest between employers and employees or from union insistence on control of access to jobs. A number of industries experience production crises related to availability of raw materials or consumer demand during restricted periods of time. Union power tends to rise and fall with such crises, and bargaining tends to be timed to correspond with their peaks. Consequently, production crises and bargaining crises frequently go hand in hand.

The industries we studied have a relatively steady production flow from day to day and month to month throughout the year. They are not plagued with the casual nature of employment, as in longshoring; or pronounced seasonal swings, as in construction; or production crises, as in the Alaska salmon industry. The smooth flow of production has smoothed the path of the parties in their joint industrial relationships.

Technical Advance

Each new machine or method affects job assignments or the volume of work. The larger the volume of technological changes and the more basic their character, the greater problems they pose for management and unions in collective bargaining—problems of promotions, transfers, retraining, and rate setting among others. The severity of these problems depends largely on whether the changes open or close opportunities.

Most of the companies included in these *Case Studies* are in moderately progressive industries and the parties have had special problems in adapting to technological changes. Only one has been faced with an overwhelming problem of this kind. At Lockheed, the shift back and forth from custom building of aircraft to mass production has been one of the severest problems for the parties, and their record of peace has only narrowly survived difficulties over new jobs, new rates, new personnel.

Related to technological improvements is dollar investment per worker. Generally, as investment per worker increases, management becomes more concerned with the consent of the employees who work with this investment. Again, most of the companies studied in this series have a substantial investment entrusted to their employees. Thus they are, perhaps, less inclined to dismiss their employees' welfare thoughtlessly than if these employees wielded picks and shovels.

The Nature of the Jobs

The quality of jobs varies enormously—from the relatively unsupervised responsible job all the way to monotonous repetition of minutely set tasks. The composition of jobs in a plant influences the type of worker attracted and the attitude of workers toward their work and employer. Even in our fluid society, a man is, to an extent, his job; and the employer, to the worker, is the job the employer makes available. The "good job" and the "good employer" are not carefully distinguished; nor the "bad job" and the "bad employer." A "good job" consists, of course, of more than the total task performed; the concept includes good supervision and good working conditions. Satisfaction or dissatisfaction with jobs *per se,* however, affects worker attitudes toward the employer, the volume of grievances, and the propensity to strike.

By and large, the jobs in the plants under review are semiskilled or skilled, and frequently interesting and responsible. At Lockheed, they even carry with them some romance; and in another case, Hickey-Freeman, the high quality of the work required creates a special bond between worker and employer. Plant conditions are generally reported to be pleasant. Assembly-line operations, with their problems of slow-down and speed-up, do not dominate most of the plants. This is noted as a favorable factor in the study of The Nashua Corporation.

Cost Factors

A bargaining relationship can be materially influenced by the comparative cost position of the employer. If the employer, because of high efficiency, low raw material expenses, or some other reason, is in a favorable cost situation, he is more likely to be willing to pay adequate wages and provide good conditions; a high-cost producer is likely to resist more vigorously. High costs, it is true, sometimes lead to union-management cooperation aimed at preservation of investment and jobs; but often also to strained relations.

The companies here included are in no case marginal ones. They are among the most efficient. Because of greater efficiency and other cost savings, the West Coast pulp and paper industry, for example, is able to pay wages substantially above the rest of the industry. Generally these companies are not only comparatively efficient, but they have also been steadily increasing efficiency, as at Sharon Steel, Libbey-Owens-Ford, and the Minnequa Plant of Colorado Fuel and Iron.

Similarly, firms and industries where labor costs are a relatively small percentage of total costs are in a better position to "buy" industrial peace than those where the percentage is high. For a majority of the companies studied in this series, labor costs are a small or moderate percentage, but not for all. Labor is an unusually large cost factor for Lockheed and Hickey-Freeman, yet they have established favorable industrial relations histories.

Market Factors

An expanding market, such as most of these companies have, generally means a sufficiency of jobs, promotional opportunities, and many adjustments to increasing size. A contracting market, on the other hand, raises problems of layoff policies and attempts to make work.

The sensitivity of the market to cyclical fluctuations affects the degree of employment security and, to a lesser extent, wage adjustments, both of which affect the workers' attitudes and the policies of the union. The greater the insulation from swings of the business cycle, usually the greater the stability of the relationship. Only one of the relationships studied—Hickey-Freeman—has gone through a severe depression. Its industry, clothing, is particularly sensitive to the swings of the cycle. Here the parties have made a provision for sharing the work in order to break the direct connection between volume of sales and volume of employment. The Lockheed relationship, however, is subject to a special kind of a cycle—the fluctuations in the military demand for its products—and in this case the gyrations in demand have constituted a heavy burden on collective bargaining. The feast-and-famine nature of demand for machine tools has similarly created problems to which the Lapointe relationship has had to adjust.

The responsiveness of market demand to changes in price has a further effect on collective bargaining. The less the relation of demand to price, the easier it is to pass on higher costs, including higher labor costs, to purchasers. The greater the relation, the less elbow room the parties have to work out their economic settlements. While none of these companies has a monopoly over supply, neither is any faced with cutthroat price competition. The standard situation is one of some form of administered prices.

None of the relationships in the cases studied is specially subject to governmental surveillance.[1] Several of the parties, however, are under

---

[1] An exception to this, as well as to the situation with regard to monopoly and

pressure to avoid strikes because of the fickleness of their customers, as in the case of Marathon. If customers not served during a strike take their trade elsewhere permanently, the cost of a strike is greatly augmented. Consequently, there is more pressure on the parties to maintain peace.

Locational Factors

The degree of attachment of a plant or an industry to a locality plays its part in collective bargaining. Mobile plants, capable of escaping from union-organized areas, create special organizing problems for unions and for their competitors who do not move. An industry, such as the women's garment industry, which is not tied to a locality by markets, raw materials, or investments, generally displays a special bargaining pattern of union-management cooperation in organized areas, constant organizing drives in unorganized areas, and supremacy of the national union in an effort to standardize labor costs among areas. Conversely, the more restricted the geographical area of movement and of product competition, the greater the autonomy of the local parties and the less the standardization of contractual terms. Most of these companies are rooted in their localities, and no one is of the fly-by-night variety. At the same time none is insulated from outside forces and each must keep an eye on the costs and prices of its competitors.

THE COMMUNITY ENVIRONMENT

Physical location can make an appreciable difference in bargaining relationships. The surrounding community, whether pre-existing or created to serve the plant, is characterized by workers, attitudes, and comparative wage levels which variously affect the parties and their dealings.

The Work Force

Work forces vary in available skills, their acceptance of industrial discipline, and their social and religious composition. The choice of workers by the company or the union—and the choices made are not unrelated to the supply of workers in the community—can influence plant efficiency, the quality of individuals available for positions of leadership in the company and union, and the harmony of working relationships. A western mining town turns out a working force different from that in a rural area in the South, and the fur working community of New York City from a Mormon town in Utah.

Only one of the companies here surveyed has had special problems

prices, is the Committee's special report on labor policy in the atomic energy industry, summarized in Appendix A.

connected with the composition of the available work force. At Lockheed during the war the many untrained women and the many other workers employed on a walk-through basis created an element of instability for union and company. In another of the *Case Studies,* Atlantic Steel in Georgia, the impact of the homogeneity of the work force's customs, attitudes, and moral precepts has been significant in shaping the bargaining relationship.

The Plant and the Labor Market

The percentage of the area's labor force employed in the plant is important in several ways. When the percentage is small, the plant can pull in and push out employees without great concern; but when it is large, the pulling in is more likely to strain the capacity to supply and the pushing out to dislocate the community. Both situations have repercussions on collective bargaining. Lockheed was able to expand and contract its employment so phenomenally in World War II only because it was located in a large metropolitan area.

When the percentage of employment is high, the worker is more dependent on the one company; when low, considerably less so. When the percentage is high, industrial disputes are likely to involve the entire community; when low, to be absorbed and dulled by the presence of comparatively large numbers of noncombatants. The one-industry town, historically, has been particularly subject to violent strikes. Historically, it has also been the scene of excellent industrial relations for, when the circumstances are otherwise favorable, the one-industry small town creates an opportunity for the social mingling of the various strata in the plant hierarchy. The pulp and paper plants studied are happily situated in their small communities.

Local Wage Levels

Wage comparisons are more relative than absolute. Local wage levels influence the rates paid by a plant by affecting recruiting, turnover, and morale, as well as the expectations of union members. A high-wage community virtually insists on a high-wage plant; while a low-wage community at least permits a low-wage plant. Generally, the lower the level of wages in the community the greater the latitude of the parties in making their wage settlements; and the lower the level of wages in the industry, the more restricted it is in its location.

The firms studied are generally in relatively well-paying industries and are able to match or surpass community wage levels. The Dewey and

Almy Chemical Company, for example, operates in a high-wage industry but its Cambridge plants are located in a relatively low-wage community.

Industrial Climate

In a "union town," the workers are more likely to desire organization, the trade-union movement to support it effectively, and the employers to accept it as a natural development. The reverse is true in an "open-shop town." Individual bargaining relationships, unless unusually well insulated, are likely to be influenced by the local attitudinal patterns.

The West Coast pulp and paper industry started its bargaining history more smoothly than some others because collective bargaining was comparatively well accepted in northern California and the Pacific Northwest where it operated. Conversely, Sharon Steel broke away from the pattern of "Little Steel" resistance to unionization in 1937 and Lockheed from the open-shop atmosphere of Los Angeles. Even in the South, where, except for restricted trades and areas, collective bargaining has never been fully accepted as standard practice, Atlantic Steel departed from its community pattern. All three companies gained union gratitude for their willingness to break away from the surrounding industrial climate.

THE "POLITICAL" ENVIRONMENT

Actions of unions and management are governed to some extent by their forms of organization. Both are affected by their "political" environments. Unions must be alert to the desires of members in order to hold support, to the behavior and achievements of rival unions, to the threats of factional splits within the union, to the attitudes of government and the public. Management analogously is influenced by industry patterns and by going practice, as well as by owners.

The Union

The union, being primarily "political," is subjected to more pressures than management. Of the pressures affecting bargaining relationships, perhaps rival unionism without and factionalism within the union are most compelling. Both create insecurity in current leaders, and this encourages aggressive actions. Bargaining demands and settlements are both likely to be somewhat elevated above the levels which would otherwise prevail, just as grievances are more likely to be indiscriminately prosecuted. Stability on the union side does not guarantee industrial peace, but instability makes its achievement more difficult.

The West Coast pulp and paper relationship has been closely geared in its wage adjustments to developments in the adjacent lumber industry through potential and, on at least one occasion, actual rival unionism. This is also a factor at Lockheed, where the International Association of Machinists has to be constantly on the alert to match or surpass the gains of the rival United Automobile Workers in nearby plants. In the case of Nashua, however, despite the existence of seven unions, there has been no evidence of rival unionism or jurisdictional conflicts.

Factionalism has been a disturbing force in at least two of the situations. Good relations did not finally develop at Libbey-Owens-Ford until the Glass Workers resolved internal difficulties. Factions may be differently oriented. Their orientation, whether to the personality of a leader or to communism or catholicism, affects greatly how they operate. At Lockheed, during the war, factionalism caused by the left-wing character of opposition in the union caused trouble.

Related to factionalism is a heterogeneity of membership interests. In the industry-wide bargaining system in West Coast pulp and paper, the interests of pulp locals in Washington and paper locals in California on occasion have been sufficiently diverse to threaten a breakdown in bargaining relationships; and in this situation and one or two others, skilled workers have had separatist tendencies and demanded special treatment to avoid going off in their own directions.

The upsetting effects of rival unionism, factionalism, and heterogeneity of interests can be greatly mitigated by the actions of the parties in collective bargaining, as in the Hickey-Freeman case. The contract there gives security to the union, disciplinary powers to its leaders, and special treatment to special groups.

The location of power within the union is likewise significant. This power locus (which can change and may react especially to fluctuations in business activity) may be concentrated at the local, regional, or national level; and the point at which it becomes centered influences with whom the employer deals, the considerations which will be uppermost, and the degree of flexibility in reaching an agreement. In several cases, as at Dewey and Almy and at Lockheed, the local union has almost complete power to make its own arrangements, and this authority is said to be most important in working out locally satisfactory arrangements. Where the greatest authority is concentrated at the national level, as in the Steelworkers Union, the formal policies of the national union become quite important. Fortunately for the relationship at Atlantic Steel, Sharon Steel, and at the Minnequa Plant of Colorado Fuel and Iron, the Steelworkers Union, while negotiating a pattern-making contract nationally, permits and even encourages adjustments to local conditions and strongly favors peaceful relations with employers. Did it not, there would be little that any one of these companies could do to get policies changed. The more power at the local level, the more influence the ideas of the local workers and the attitudes of local management can have on the relationship—for better or for worse.

Important "political" forces may arise outside the individual union itself. While some unions help set patterns and others are isolated from them, many follow the patterns set by others. Although the existence of a pattern may help resolve disputes, it does so by reducing independence of action. Few of the relationships here described fall outside the influence of other people's wage decisions.

The situations which further local democracy and autonomy seem to work against peace. Rival unionism gives the workers a choice of organizations to represent them, rather than confining them to one agent. Factionalism is often the only vehicle for protest against the incumbents under the one-party system which characterizes most unions. Pattern setters make peaceful settlements easier elsewhere by supplying a decision which the local parties would otherwise have to battle out for themselves. A cost of industrial peace is often the loss of freedom of choice for the workers and freedom of action for their local officers. In some of the cases studied, a reduction in independence has been accompanied by an increase in peace—a triumph of union-management fraternity over worker liberty.

The Employers

The employer is not free from the direct, as well as the indirect, influence of patterns. Acceptance of them often removes troublesome problems from the bargaining table and the risks that accompany independent decisions. This is the experience, for example, of Sharon Steel, which follows the United States Steel pattern, and Libbey-Owens-Ford, which (along with Pittsburgh Plate Glass Company) follows the steel and automobile patterns. Fortunately, both Sharon Steel and Libbey-Owens-Ford are able to afford the pattern, for, while following the pattern solves problems when you can meet its costs, it causes problems for firms whose unions want to match it but where the ability to pay it does not exist.

When an employer belongs to an employers' association, his sovereignty is subordinated to that of the group; and group desires are ascertained through "political" processes.) The task of satisfying diverse company interests, as in the case of the West Coast pulp and paper industry, can be arduous. If the association can be held together, the prospects for peace may well be enhanced. The cost of striking an entire association is a sobering consideration to unions. The employers by banding together can better resist union demands, but they can also better grant them, since by acting as an industry they can benefit from a more inelastic demand for their products than if they acted individually. If one employer raises prices to offset higher wages, he may lose his market, but if all the competitive employers do so together, the loss to each will be minimized. In the case of the clothing industry, where wages are a high percentage of costs, Hickey-Freeman would be less anxious to grant wage increases by itself than jointly with all the other manufacturers of men's clothing. Beyond this, equality of wages among companies, as in the West Coast pulp and paper industry, has a quieting effect on the workers just as the greater security through uniformity of costs has on the employers.

Even without formal association, the employer may be sensitive to the opinions of other employers and adjust in response to them. The going practice can be almost as much of a ceiling for the employer as it is a floor for the union. Depending on the content of the group feeling, the prospects of peace for the individual employer may be aided or impaired.

Further, when the local plant is a branch of a larger concern, the local manager may be subject to strict policies and close supervision. Under these conditions his contribution to peace or warfare is minimal. In none of the plants here reviewed is local autonomy so reduced.

TIME AS AN ENVIRONMENTAL FACTOR

Time can be as constraining as the industry, community, and "political" environments. Collective bargaining systems do not consciously pick the year in which they are to be born and first develop their personalities, although they might wish to do so were they conscious of the potential effects. Systems started during the first flush of the New Deal, or the era of the sitdown strikes, or the war period of government tutelage, or the time of the Labor-Management Relations Act of 1947 (Taft-Hartley) frequently bear marks of national developments which coincided with or caused their origin.

Time in other senses is influential. The old union tends to be more peaceful than the young. The old collective bargaining relationship tends to be less hectic, as in several of these cases, than the new, since the parties have had time to adjust to each other and develop the basic aspects of their contract. Nor is the old industry quite like the young. It is less likely to be experiencing rapid technological change and more likely to be lay-ing off long-service workers; and bargaining relationships will reflect the different types of problems.

While the parties cannot control the passage of time, they can anticipate its normal results, which are improved relationships; and, by study of the experience of others, achieve them more promptly.

Favorable and Unfavorable Factors

We have reviewed the environmental circumstances which are normally favorable to the development of industrial peace. By and large they are the circumstances surrounding the collective bargaining systems here analyzed. The description of a typical environment for these systems reads somewhat as follows:

A medium-sized company with a steady production pattern and subject to moderate technological advance; interesting and responsible jobs; an efficient company with an expanding market and administered prices; a company firmly established in a multi-industry community containing a tractable labor force and paying wages which can readily be met in accordance with industry standards; a community which is accustomed to collective bargaining; a secure union with stable leaders and a homogeneous membership; a wage pattern which the parties can use as a guide; some local autonomy for both parties; a system which is well-established, and leaders on both sides who are experienced.

There are important exceptions in individual cases to this omnibus description, but, in general, it fits.

These environmental forces, individually or collectively, do not, by themselves, cause peace, but they give the parties the opportunity to develop it. The attitudes and policies of the parties, the personalities of their leaders, and their techniques bring about the good relations—with the permission of a favorable environment.

We do not find in this series of cases any of the following:

Small, competitive employers and a dominant union which take advantage of an inelastic demand for the product or service to organize a collusive system to gouge the consumer; or a group of miscellaneous or minor or occasional purchasers of a type of skilled labor who hire this labor according to a price list announced by the union; or a union torn with internal factionalism or facing a life-or-death struggle with a competitive union; or a casual labor market organized through a hiring hall; or highly marginal firms; or an industry of such importance to the public that its industrial relations are dominated by government boards;[2] or a national pattern-setting relationship.

[2] Here again, the Committee's report on labor policy in the atomic energy industry is in a special category.

In such situations it may be said that environmental pressures are so strong that the parties are almost driven into or impelled toward a certain type of relationship. More fortunate, however, are those bargaining systems for which the environment is not so compelling and where, in consequence, the parties have an opportunity to develop for themselves the quality of their relationship.

ENVIRONMENTAL FACTORS AND INDUSTRIAL PEACE [a]

Factors	Frequently Favorable Circumstances	Frequently Unfavorable Circumstances
Industrial Environment		
1. Size of company	Medium-sized	Industrial giant
2. Production pattern	Steady	Seasonal; intermittent; production crises
3. Technological advance	Moderate	Severe
4. Nature of the jobs	Skilled; responsible	Assembly-line type
5. Cost factors	Inframarginal plant	Marginal plant
6. Market factors	Expanding; cyclically insensitive; inelastic demand	Contracting; sensitive to cycle; elastic demand
7. Locational factors	Relatively immobile plant	Relatively mobile plant
Community Environment		
1. The work force	Steady; tractable	Inconstant; combative
2. Plant and labor	Metropolitan area	One-industry town
3. Local wage levels	Low-wage community and high-wage industry	Low-wage industry and high-wage community
4. Industrial climate	Union town	Open-shop town
"Political" Environment		
1. The union	Secure union; secure leaders; homogeneous membership; local autonomy; pattern following	Insecure union; insecure leaders; heterogeneous membership; external domination; pattern setting
2. The employer	Pattern following; in employers' association; local autonomy in noncontractual matters	Pattern setting; lone bargainer; strong central domination of local plant
Time as an Environmental Factor	Origins in peaceful period; old relationship	Origins in warlike period; new relationship

[a] Reference is made here to "industrial peace" developed by parties of relatively equal strength, not arising from domination by one side or by government.

CHAPTER 3

The Growth of the Relationship

JOHN T. DUNLOP
Associate Professor of Economics,
Littauer School of Public Administration,
Harvard University

The relationship between a company and a union is not predestined. A constructive relationship may deteriorate and a poor start may be overcome. Indeed, in some situations, mutual respect and peace are born out of conflict, as illustrated by the beginning of the era of industrial peace at American Velvet following a sixteen-month strike. The quality of the relationship, however, is often materially influenced by the early associations of the parties.

IMPORTANCE OF THE FORMATIVE PERIOD

In all of our *Case Studies* the relationship got off to a comparatively good start. There were no strikes for recognition. There were no unfair labor practice charges, except during the transition from the Employee Representation Plan to the United Steelworkers at the Minnequa Plant of C. F. & I. There were only three NLRB elections out of twelve and one of these was a consent election with an agreement in advance to sign an exclusive bargaining contract if the union won the election.

These *Case Studies* show that investigations of the quality of industrial relations should be planned to examine the organizing stage, the first contract, and the initial experiences of the parties. Insight into current problems and relations is enhanced by study of these formative periods. The following quotations from the *Case Studies* substantiate the conclusion.

In contrast to the strife over initial recognition in other mass-production industries, collective bargaining started in glass gradually and relatively peacefully.—*Case Study No. 2.*
Lockheed was the first airframe company to agree to collective bargaining

in Southern California. Its acceptance was voluntary, not forced by a strike or by action of the National Labor Relations Board. This not only involved going against the predominant policy of the local business community, but also it required a reorientation in the thinking of Lockheed management —*Case Study No. 6.*

The Sharon management's willingness to accept the outcome of the NLRB election and to work constructively with union officials in seeking to develop a peaceful relationship made a deep impression upon the employees—an impression shared today by new as well as old employees. . . . the Company was willing to go farther than almost any other important steel producer had gone up to that time.—*Case Study No. 5.*

Thus the relationship [at Marathon Corporation] which has existed ever since came about. It was accomplished without violence or the opening of wounds which would be long in healing.—*Case Study No. 8.*

Similar statements are found in the *Case Studies* of Crown Zellerbach, Dewey and Almy, Hickey-Freeman, and Nashua. The relations between parties typically begin even before recognition or the start of negotiations over the first contract. The attitude of the company is certain to be influenced by many aspects of the organizing campaign conducted by the union: the principal appeals made to the workers, the way in which the company is portrayed, and the extent to which personalities are made the target of attacks. The union may conduct a bitter and personal assault against the company and its top officers, depicting them as "bloated capitalists" or as "grasping, miserly, and dictatorial." On the other hand, the union may develop a campaign seeking primarily to sell the employees the benefits of organization and to promise responsible collective bargaining to the company, as was the case at Lapointe. The initial attitudes of the company toward the union and the prospects of industrial peace are affected by early impressions.

In the same way, the union will be influenced by policies adopted by the company during the organizing stage. Most management reflects in a variety of subtle ways its basic attitudes toward a union at such times. A paternalistic management may be "shocked" that its employees appear "ungrateful"; a hostile management may skirt the limits of law as defined by counsel. Most supervisors will show resentment at a challenge to their authority, despite unequivocal orders from top management. The workers are certain to be keenly perceptive of management's reaction to the union. A farsighted management recognizes that at the organizing stage it is shaping union reactions and attitudes which will affect the quality of later bargaining.

Other associations prior to the first contract may also set the tone of the later relationship. A choice was possible under the Wagner Act between an election and a card check of membership in securing NLRB certification. Voluntary recognition was also possible without NLRB intervention. In the Lockheed and Marathon cases, voluntary recognition was afforded. In the Dewey and Almy case the card check was deliberately chosen by management. These methods mitigated conflict and name calling which are difficult to avoid in getting out the vote. Even when an election is necessary, the parties have the opportunity to consent to the election with an agreed-upon election unit instead of becoming involved in a contested NLRB proceeding.

The relationships between the parties may also be affected by grievance handling before negotiation of the first contract. Moreover, after certification, organizing activities will ordinarily continue as the union seeks to induce nonmembers to join. This will create problems for management. The union in turn will be faced by incidents which reflect the need for adaptation in company supervision to the new order. These threshold problems can aggravate or ameliorate the task of negotiating the first contract and starting the collective bargaining relationship on its course.

MANAGEMENT ADJUSTMENTS

The accommodation of management to a union at the outset of collective bargaining typically requires substantial changes in the management organization. Many years may be required before the many aspects of this adjustment process are completed. But the most dramatic changes are likely soon after recognition of the union. These changes do not relate primarily to management prerogatives but concern the internal organization and procedures of management—communications, personnel policies, role of the foremen, and decision making generally. Often attributed to "progressive management," such changes are also in substantial degree a response and an accommodation to unions.

In confronting their opposite numbers in the union hierarchy, management representatives need to be certain that they are informed of developments in the shop. Superiors must carefully appraise information from subordinates in ways which were never necessary prior to the union. They must be certain that company representatives down the line know about labor relations developments, and that they learn of changes in policy and bargaining results from the company rather than the union. Only then can supervision deal competently with corresponding union representatives. A union thrust on a management almost invariably requires the company to overhaul its methods of communication.

All personnel policies, even those outside the scope of the agreement, must be made more explicit with the advent of a union. There develops a greater centralization of policy making in management and less is left to the discretion of immediate supervisors. The union is quick to discover inconsistencies in company policies between departments and to utilize whipsaw tactics to spread the most favorable conditions. Top management soon learns from the union about unsuspected past practices in the company which the union proposes to extend. Management's only possible defense is to reduce policies to writing with more formal directions for uniform enforcement.

Partly as a consequence of changes already noted, the introduction of a union tends to alter the role of the foreman. The union is a challenge to his authority on the working level. The simple boss-worker relationship is now the complex triangle: boss-worker(member)-steward. A new and significant factor enters into the selection of foremen and other supervisors—their ability to deal with the union. It may take many years before a management has retrained its foremen or removed those who are incapable of adapting to the new system of bargaining.

The company's top officers cannot ignore possible effects of every decision on collective bargaining, nor the impact of labor relations on all other decisions. Internal procedures must be developed to assure such consideration. A declaration of dividends or the timing of a financial statement, for instance, may be revised in the light of bargaining results. The selection of plant managers may be affected by their capacity to deal with union representatives.

These do not exhaust the full range of consequences. They do indicate, however, that a union necessarily compels a marked readjustment in management's decision-making process and that these changes cannot long be delayed. The ways in which these initial adaptations are made in a company may have long-run effects on the quality of its collective bargaining relations.

Union Adjustments

Analogous changes are made in a local union when it leaves the organizing campaign and enters upon the negotiation and administration of an agreement. The organization of a union designed to get out the vote and persuade the electorate may not be ideally adapted to the administration of an agreement. Frequently an effective organizer does not possess the capacities required for day-to-day operations of the union.

At the organizing stage, the union asks the employee simply to sign a card or cast a vote. Only later does it seek to instruct the individual member in his responsibilities, and such education is a slow process. All the promises of the campaign cannot be immediately delivered. Individual members must come to realize that they cannot take matters into their own hands. Most early collective bargaining relationships must contend with the wildcat strike; these *Case Studies* showed no exception. The development of respect for the contract and the sanctity of an orderly grievance procedure requires a major transformation in workers. They may have just "organized," but the real organization is still ahead. The union leadership is just as much, if not more, interested in this discipline as management. The union leadership can be effective, for either industrial war or peace, only if there exists an organization through which the conduct of the individual members can be controlled.

Since the type of organizing leadership is at times ill suited for the task of collective bargaining, the local union at the outset frequently changes shop stewards and other elected officers. Unlike the problem in the company, where top management may select new foremen, a union utilizes a process which is political in form. While top officers of the local and the international union often may exert some influence, the choice lies with the individual members. In the choice of local union leadership lies one of the most unpredictable factors affecting a collective bargaining relationship.

An Evolving Relationship

In negotiating their first contract and in the period immediately thereafter, the parties are required to make decisions which have a lasting impact on their relations.

The parties must determine the form of their first agreement. They may negotiate a simple contract, deliberately leaving many problems to be worked out, or they may attempt a more comprehensive agreement. This choice is itself a reflection of competing views of the nature of the agreement and of collective bargaining itself. Experience from our *Case Studies* suggests that simple agreements at the outset permit the parties to develop more complex provisions as they gain experience.

The grievance procedure and its early administration are significant. Some grievance procedures narrowly confine a grievance to the interpretation of the agreement while others permit any dispute or difference between the parties to be handled. Regardless of the form of the agreement, the parties must soon decide whether to have a legalistic view or whether to use the grievance steps to solve problems and difficulties. Each side must early decide whether its negotiations will be conducted by principals or whether reliance will be on outside lawyers. In our *Case Studies,* negotiations have been conducted without outside legal talent.

Decisions on the use of arbitration, and the choice of permanent or *ad hoc* arbitrators, are likely to influence the development of relations. The Hickey-Freeman study illustrates the influence which an impartial chairman had upon the evolving relations.

No bargaining relationship can develop in all directions at the same time. There are a limited number of problems to which the parties can direct their attention, at least at the outset. There may be special joint interest in: safety, job evaluation, incentives, apprenticeship, merit rating, or a production committee or Scanlon Plan. There may be no such special interest. The areas of joint interest give each collective bargaining relationship a distinctive cast.

As the relationship between two parties develops there are crucial tests of the relationship. Business may fall off as in Lockheed after the war, creating mutual problems. A rival union may emerge. There may be tests of leadership internal to the union. The parties may complete a job-rating or evaluation plan after much hard work and much give and take; or their safety program may win national recognition as a result of mutual persistent effort. There may even be a strike over the terms of a new contract. As the parties look back upon these events, the successes and the failures themselves become an important factor in their relations. Their past experiences and judgments of the other side have a decisive influence on current collective bargaining practices of the parties.

The improvement of collective bargaining relations in the country, our studies suggest, must recognize the significance of the earliest stages in the relationship. Between five and ten thousand new relationships begin each year. If these could be started on a more constructive foundation, their quality would doubtless be improved. To this end unions would do well to consider more carefully the effects of organizing campaigns upon eventual collective bargaining. Members of management might find much to change in their initial reactions to a union campaign if they were to consider seriously the consequences of their policies for later collective bargaining.[1]

[1] *Comment by Committee member George W. Taylor,* Professor of Industry, Wharton School of Finance and Commerce, University of Pennsylvania: "In this chapter, reflecting the studies, the 'advantages of a good start' are emphasized and I believe they are overemphasized. This could serve to develop a defeatist attitude in some quarters where the start of the relationship was stormy. Nor is the emphasis justified. There are many cases where a stormy beginning served to convince the parties of the stark necessity of developing cooperative relationships. From bitter experience, they are aware of the adverse consequences of a failure to solve their mutual problems by agreement."

CHAPTER 4

The Influence of Attitudes and Policies

DOUGLAS McGREGOR

Professor of Management, School of Industrial Management,
Massachusetts Institute of Technology

The important psychological factors influencing the quality of a collective bargaining relationship are certain broad attitudes and beliefs possessed by the parties. Policy decisions as well as day-to-day actions reflect such attitudes. We will be concerned with an outline of these attitudes—with what may be called the "philosophy" of key members of management and union.

A manager who believes that people are lazy, untrustworthy, and antagonistic toward him will make different decisions from those of a manager who regards people as cooperative, honest, and friendly. A union leader who hates and fears those in authority will deal differently at the bargaining table from one who regards managers as decent people. Such underlying attitudes are acquired bit by bit, on the basis of day-to-day experiences over long periods. Ultimately they become generalized and firmly fixed. Thereafter, each situation or problem is interpreted and acted upon by the individual within the context of such generalized attitudes. They comprise his philosophy of human relations. Despite our pride in being rational, humans do not actually respond in general to the facts. We respond to our perception of the facts as they are filtered through the screen of our attitudes and fears and hopes. Objectivity in human relations is a desirable trait never perfectly achieved.

One of the criteria used in the selection of these cases was that the relationship should not be the product of a dominant personality. The Committee felt that such relationships were exceptions which could not serve as useful models. Nevertheless, we are struck by the evidence from virtually every one of the *Case Studies* that the philosophy of the key people in the relationship is a dominant causal factor. Personality factors are important in influencing the quality of the collective bargaining relationship.

A philosophy—a complex of attitudes, values, and emotions—is not the whole of a personality, even though it is central. It is foolhardy to try to describe the "personality type" of the successful manager or the successful union leader. Many differing personalities are successful. However, among the different personalities of management and union leaders whose influence has been critical in the organizations studied, we detect common attitudes.

Management Philosophy

Four significant attitudes on the part of management were found to have a profound effect on industrial peace.

On the Union and Collective Bargaining

First among the significant attitudes of management is an acceptance of collective bargaining, and of the union institution, as permanent factors in the success of the enterprise. Moreover, this attitude is one which in collective bargaining is felt to have positive values (even though it may have liabilities also) for the company.

If management regards collective bargaining negatively, a variety of crucial management decisions will be made in one way rather than another. Almost inevitably, there will be a strong defensive flavor in management's actions—secrecy, antagonism, reliance on legal technicalities in negotiation, a readiness to perceive a threat in any union demand or action—and in consequence a failure to acquire the understanding of human behavior which is a prime essential for good relations. The observer learns to expect symptoms of conflict and unhealthy relations in a firm whenever he detects within management evidence of an underlying antagonism to collective bargaining. When management's attitude, on the other hand, is one of belief in bargaining, the observer expects a healthy relationship, no matter how serious the problems of the moment. Acceptance of collective bargaining involves far more than mere recognition of the union. In all the cases the employers saw positive advantages in bargaining with a strong and well-disciplined union, and were convinced that they should take steps, directly or indirectly, to encourage workers to join and support their union.

In some cases, management felt it sufficient to instruct supervisors to let it be known that the company favored membership in the union. In other cases, it agreed in the contract to enlist employee support of the union, as in a clause of this type:

In order to maintain a spirit of cooperation among all employees so that mutual relations between the company and the union may be improved, the company agrees to use its moral force, with the cooperation of the union, to assist in obtaining and retaining membership in the union on the part of all eligible employees.—*Case Study No. 13.*

In another instance, the president of the company on occasion would write letters to employees pointing out the advantages to workers of participating in the union. Finally, in many cases, the contract provided for maintenance of membership or the union shop, and union membership was made a formal condition of employment by mutual agreement.

Encouragement of union membership by the employer is one of the causes of industrial peace. If an employer accepts the union as a potentially positive force in industrial relations, he is necessarily concerned with the problems which union leaders face in developing a responsible and well-disciplined union. Consequently, he is usually convinced that measures must be taken to build worker loyalties to the union as well as to the company.

On the other hand, the evidence refutes the contention that a formal union shop or closed shop is necessary for harmonious relations. When the employer indirectly encourages union leadership, and where the vast majority of eligible workers support the union, the union shop usually ceases to be a really vital issue in collective bargaining. The union may ask for the union shop in each new contract as a bargaining point, and management may oppose it in principle. Yet, where management goes beyond mere recognition of the union to genuine acceptance of collective bargaining, the question of union security is usually not difficult to resolve.

On the Union as a "Political" Organization

Related to management's acceptance of collective bargaining is a willingness to adjust to the characteristics of a union that differ from those of a management organization. The influence of the members of a union upon its leadership tends to be more direct than the influence of the employees upon company leadership. In the negotiation of an agreement, for example, most unions require ratification by the membership. Top management usually has authority to enter into binding agreements.

Unions, to a greater extent than the management of companies, are "political" organizations. If the manager approaches the collective bargaining relationship with the belief that the union must logically deal with him as a supplier or a customer would, he is heading for disillusionment, and he will force the union into defensive reactions of an unhappy character. Since the union is primarily a "political" organization, the rank and file is in some respects more important than its leadership. If management does not realize this, a gulf may open between the union leaders and their members, and the leaders are likely to be replaced at the next election because they have "sold out to management."

Management's appreciation of problems of this kind will influence the whole character of negotiations, of management's relations with union leaders, and, most importantly, of relations between management and its union-member employees. In most of our evidence, management has dealt successfully with these problems.

On Responsibility for Personnel Administration

A third fundamental attitude is top management's acceptance of personnel administration as top-drawer responsibility of every member of line as well as staff management—having equal importance with problems of finance and technical operation. This point is clearly brought out in several of the *Case Studies*. Examples are found in quotations from management in the Crown Zellerbach study, the account of the shift in attitude which occurred at Dewey and Almy, the statement on line-staff relationships at Sharon Steel, and the discussion of management responsibility at Nashua.

Successful human relations cannot develop so long as top management is willing to say of some line subordinate: "He'll never learn how to handle people, but he gets out the production." Nor can healthy relations develop if management expects to dispose of the problems of personnel administration by delegating them to a staff department. An interesting apparent exception to this statement is the organizational structure at Hickey-Freeman. However, the labor-relations manager is in fact the manager of production in this situation. The necessary attitude is one in which a high level of competence is demanded from all members of management in dealing with people, and in which those who cannot develop this competence are replaced.

On the Workers as Individuals

A fourth important set of management attitudes are those toward people generally, and toward subordinates in particular. These include a concern for the welfare of workers, and a recognition of their needs and feelings. Such attitudes are reflected in deep-seated habits: the avoidance of arbitrariness, regular consultation with subordinates and with the union before actions affecting them are taken, skillful handling of problems involving management prerogatives, a clear recognition that workers are people, and that labor is not a commodity which can be purchased and manipulated as can the other elements of the production process.

Even more is involved. Healthy human relations require of management a genuine confidence in the potentialities of ordinary people. While management seldom directly expresses this attitude, there is sometimes a tendency to regard management's competence as a result not of experience and training, but of inherent superiority. This tacit conviction may be carried to the point where employees are believed to be incapable of understanding management's problems and point of view, and, therefore, incapable of contributing more than their physical effort to achieve the company's purposes.

Such an attitude fosters not only a "we and they" philosophy, but the development of opposed groups with different characteristics. It prevents workers from identifying themselves with the company; it breeds distrust, antagonism, and misunderstanding. Healthy human relations can develop only when members of management are willing to accept all levels of employees as members of the company team, as people like themselves with similar abilities and potentialities. Evidence of the presence of this attitude on the part of management is found, for example, in our *Case Studies* on Crown Zellerbach, Libbey-Owens-Ford, Dewey and Almy, Hickey-Freeman, and Colorado Fuel & Iron.

These attitudes are closely tied to a central personality variable: the degree of the individual's need for power. The manager whose personal security rests (usually unconsciously) upon his ability to dominate others —the man with an extreme authoritarian character—cannot develop the necessary attitudes toward his employees. He may appear to be a benevolent paternalist, vitally interested in the employees; but if his need for power is strong this façade will last only so long as they remain docile. The subordination of the power drive to other more humanitarian motives is an essential basis for healthy industrial relations.

Union Philosophy

Now turn to attitudes of union leaders and members which influence the relationship.

On Management and Union Roles

Union leaders may view their organization's role in collective bargaining in different ways. They may think of the union's function primarily as that of a *protest organization* designed to fight the company and to contest all kinds of managerial authority. At the other extreme, they may conceive of its role as almost that of a *partner with management* in raising output and improving efficiency for the mutual gain of both company and employees. More commonly, however, union leaders believe the union's main function to be that of *policing or "regulating" the company.* In most of the situations we studied, the union leaders take this middle view—they conceive their role to be that of protecting the interests of the workers they represent.

This attitude implies acceptance of the company and a recognition of management's objectives in running the business profitably. Conceiving of its role as a regulator of management, the union necessarily has a stake in the economic welfare of the enterprise. In particular, it is anxious for the company to remain competitive and to make profits to safeguard members' jobs and employment opportunities.

There are many evidences of this attitude in the operation of our cases of collective bargaining. They are found, for example, at Hickey-Freeman, Lockheed, Nashua, Lapointe, American Velvet, and Atlantic Steel. As one union officer put it, in making an urgent appeal to workers to give a fair day's work for a fair day's pay:

You just can't loaf yourself into prosperity. You must work yourself into prosperity. If you want higher wages, better vacations, more security, a health and welfare fund, you must, of necessity, recognize that your company cannot give it to you unless it can meet its competition and make a profit. You've got to put production in the barrel if you expect me to get money out for you.—*Case Study No. 13.*

There is evidence that the unions involved were concerned with the economic welfare of the companies. Yet their acceptance of the necessity for profitable operations is not vaguely grounded in belief in private enterprise. It seems to stem much more realistically from a hard-boiled recognition that the union as an institution and the job interests of its membership are dependent upon the economic success of the business and that, under prevailing competitive conditions, there is no practical means for workers to get more except by bargaining with a company which keeps itself in a condition to provide more.

On Management Rights

The realistic acceptance of management's objective of industrial enterprise implies also an acceptance of management's responsibility for its achievement. This is a ticklish point, and one which often arouses heated feelings. If management's attitude is to consider this responsibility a sacred right, to refuse to discuss or bargain about anything connected with a rigidly defined "management right to manage the business," union suspicion and antagonism will be generated. The absence of union knowledge and understanding will stand in the way of successful relations. On the other hand, management cannot escape its responsibility for the economic welfare of the company.

Our studies point toward a middle course. Management gains by being willing to discuss anything, by being willing to state its position frankly, by putting its cards on the table, while insisting upon its responsibility to the owners for the conduct of the business.

There is little or no difficulty along these lines among the companies represented in these studies. Most of the studies point out that the question of management prerogatives has not been an important issue. Honest desires to have the union know the facts seem to minimize conflict and to promote acceptance by the union of the importance of the profit objective and of management's responsibility for achieving it.

On Confidence in Management

In discussing management's acceptance of collective bargaining, we stressed that there is more involved than mere recognition of the union. Similarly, there is more involved for union leaders than recognition of management. Confidence in management seems to be an essential ingredient of good human relations.

Union leaders in healthy union-management relationships do not fear arbitrary action by management, or management indifference to worker welfare, or management antagonism to collective bargaining. If union leaders fear management in any of these respects, their behavior will be defensive and often hostile. While it may be argued that the very development of unionism is itself a symptom of worker fear of management action, the continuation of this attitude does not bring healthy relations. Certainly it is characteristic of those situations comprising this volume that, generally speaking, fear was not present.

It is not sufficient, however, to characterize this attitude with the phrase "absence of fear," because a union may be so powerful that it can dominate management in a contemptuous fashion. This obviously does not lead to industrial peace. Hence, the use of the term "confidence," which implies a genuine belief in management's good intention and competence.

COMMON ATTITUDES

The success of any human relationship depends upon existence of some attitudes common to the parties. In our studies, a few such common attitudes seem to have special significance. We found mutual security and predictability, satisfaction with the relationship, and a preference for intelligent compromise.

Throughout the various studies, repeated references have been made to feelings such as good faith, sincerity, good will, mutual trust, confidence, and fair play. In a healthy union-management relationship, these are not abstractions, nor are they primarily moral pronouncements. They are manifestations of a feeling of security which grows out of the operation of a successful relationship.

When directly asked what he meant by the terms "mutual trust," "confidence," and "sincerity," a union leader said:

I hear people in the union talking about the sincerity of the company. Now, most people are honest, and that goes for most of the company executives, too. The real basis of our respect for LOF people is that they think out labor relations in a logical way. You know what to expect from them; you know how they will act because they usually take the trouble to find out what the problem really is. We aren't getting along just because they are "sincere" or because we like each other. Our confidence and trust in LOF is a result of our ability to anticipate this kind of management thinking.—*Case Study No. 2.*

On the management side, as well, we found evidence that confidence, trust, and good will were closely connected with the ability to predict with reasonable certainty the actions and reactions of the union leadership. When a company accepts the union and acts accordingly, the union leaders may have confidence that management will not try to destroy the organization or undermine the workers' loyalty to it. The same thing applies to confidence which management has in union leaders who recognize that their interests are dependent upon the economic welfare of the enterprise. Bargaining in good faith, mutual trust, and sincerity, therefore, are tangible results of a relationship in which experience has given both parties a feeling of certainty and predictability.

An essential to continuing industrial peace is a feeling of satisfaction by both parties that their relationship is productive—that it benefits each side. References have been made to the good earnings made by the companies. In practically every case, furthermore, the workers appeared to be receiving wages at least average for either their community or industry. In most cases, also, the unions appeared to be getting benefits for their members which compared favorably with those secured in other companies by rival unions. There were one or two examples of unusual, if not phenomenal, wage and profit records achieved through union-management cooperation.

Cooperation may also develop where a company is faced with a serious economic crisis. But, it was apparent in our studies that each side was getting some tangible economic benefits or avoiding real economic disasters. To be sure, the ability to get benefits depended to a great degree on the nature of the industry, the sustained demand for the product, and the general economic climate of the country. However, the parties attributed their success, also, to the type of bargaining relationship which existed. And, even under adverse economic conditions, it is logical to expect that the experience gained in the process of successful collective relations will enable both parties to face new problems with greater realism and keener insight.

The use of force in the event of failure to agree has been potentially present in every relationship we studied. The ability of a union to conduct a strike and the freedom of the employer to shut up his shop may well be necessary conditions for effecting industrial peace. In the more successful kinds of relationships there are fewer strikes, but the absence of industrial warfare does not mean that differences no longer exist. In fact, the very essence of collective bargaining is the resolution of differences. In healthy relationships both parties are opposed to the use of force except as a last, unlikely necessity. The sincere desires of both lead them to rely heavily on realistic compromise. In the harmonious types of relationships which we have described, the parties apparently have become skillful in reaching intelligent compromises which are acceptable to both.

ARE ATTITUDES CAUSES?

It may be argued that attitudes and beliefs such as those here described are not causes but consequences of healthy industrial relations. There is no doubt that the development of these attitudes is part of a circular chain of circumstances. A member of management or of the union acquires his attitudes through his experiences. Given certain attitudes, he behaves in certain ways. His behavior is subsequently observed by others in the relationship. It becomes part of the events on the basis of which the others acquire and modify their own attitudes. In turn, the behavior of those others reacts back upon him.

In this sense attitudes are both causes and effects. However, attitudes and beliefs are acquired over a lifetime. Moreover, changes in them may result from experiences outside and inside the immediate industrial relationship. The attitudes held by management at the time that relationships we studied were established were important in determining whether the relationship got off on the right foot. Many subsequent events which aided the healthy development of the relationship were materially influenced by this original constructive management attitude. Moreover, in some cases the character of the relationship changed materially because of the entrance into the picture of a key person who possessed certain definite attitudes.

It does not seem incorrect, therefore, to attribute important causal significance to management and union attitudes, even though the circular process of development is apparent.

CHAPTER 5

Procedures and Methods

FREDERICK H. HARBISON
Executive Officer of the Industrial Relations Center,
University of Chicago

and JOHN R. COLEMAN
Industrial Relations Section,
Massachusetts Institute of Technology

No ready-made or sure-fire techniques exist for achieving industrial peace. In each of our studies, the techniques and methods of bargaining have been different from the other studies in many respects.

At Crown Zellerbach and Marathon, for example, the parties conducted their contract negotiations in a "goldfish bowl" before large gatherings of company and union members. Most of the other studies demonstrate that realistic trading can be carried on just as successfully by a small number of competent and sophisticated bargainers who share broad understanding of internal "political" forces in both the company and the union.

Again, some studies stress that the operating executives of the company have been responsible for bargaining, while others credit the industrial relations specialists. In some cases, management-union communications are formal. Dewey and Almy, for example, places emphasis on a policy manual, whereas Nashua and Atlantic Steel have an aversion to putting anything on paper unless absolutely necessary.

Yet, certain tactics, methods, and procedures, used repeatedly in many of the cases studied, appear to have promoted industrial peace. Although methods and procedures are as often manifestations as they are causes of harmonious relations, a few techniques will be reviewed here which appear to be associated with constructive relationships.

In practically all cases both management and labor were primarily

interested in solving specific problems rather than in defining prerogatives. Both parties seemed to avoid talking about "management's right to
do this" or "the union's power to do that." Rather, the approach was,
"Here is a problem; what will it take to get it settled?" Inherent in this
approach was the absence of legalism. This does not imply, however, that
the parties cast principles aside and resorted to expedient or haphazard
compromises. Instead, the problem-solving approach is based upon a
sound principle—management and union policies in collective bargaining
can be developed better by thrashing out concrete issues than by arguing
about abstract concepts of managerial prerogatives and union job control.

Another generally cited cause of industrial peace was the development
of effective union-management communication on an ever-increasing
range of issues in which the parties had both common and conflicting interests. In many instances, the success of a relationship appeared to depend upon the ingenuity of the parties in developing effective methods of
union-management communication.

Managerial Functions and Union Job Control

In almost every collective bargaining relationship, management's concern with retention of its function and the union's quest for greater job
control present difficult issues, because the objectives of the two parties
are, in most respects, in conflict. The quality of industrial peace in any
situation is largely dependent, therefore, upon the manner in which the
parties are able to resolve these troublesome issues. Management was concerned with retaining its control over the operation of the enterprise in
every case we studied. In other words, management wanted freedom to
exercise managerial functions and sought, in nearly every instance, some
recognition by the union of managerial prerogatives. The union, for its
part, was almost invariably concerned with getting more control over jobs
and acquiring a greater degree of participation in making decisions which
might affect the conditions and opportunities for employment of the
union members.

In many instances, management made a practice of consulting the
union before taking any action which might have a bearing on jobs. It
would seek the advice of union leaders before taking a serious disciplinary
action, making a revision in a wage rate, installing new equipment or
processes. This was done even though many contracts specified that management could act unilaterally on such matters. In taking this course,
management's aim was to exercise its functions with the concurrence and
if possible the positive cooperation of the union.

The union's quest for control over jobs is achieved, in part, when it is in the know about managerial actions. If, for example, the company sounds out the union on its reactions to the introduction of a new conveyor system, the union is, in effect, given a chance to participate in making a managerial decision. It can voice objections to the contemplated change; it can make suggestions on procedures for the system's introduction; or it may negotiate the new rates of pay which will be applicable. From the standpoint of the union, discussions of this nature can be tantamount to negotiations. Under such circumstances, the union leaders are in a position to claim that they are sharing control with management over vital issues affecting jobs. In most of our *Case Studies,* the companies and unions involved approached the touchy problems of managerial functions and union job control in this way.

GRIEVANCE MACHINERY

One function of a collective agreement is to provide a means for draining off grievances. The grievance machinery establishes orderly procedures for hearing complaints of workers and for settling disputes over interpretation of the contract, thus providing a lightning rod that drives to ground dissatisfactions and resentments which might otherwise cause serious damage. An efficient and well-functioning grievance system is vital for good labor-management relations, but it is a contributing rather than a main cause of industrial peace.

In most of the companies studied, the parties used the grievance machinery to perform more than one function—they made it operate as a fire-prevention as well as a fire-fighting device. Important grievances were viewed as symptoms of underlying problems, and the parties attempted to work out satisfactory solutions for such problems in order to prevent the future occurrence of similar grievances.

In several cases, moreover, the parties used grievance settlements as a point of departure for discussion of an ever-broadening range of mutual problems. At both Libbey-Owens-Ford and Atlantic Steel, for example, formal grievances were disposed of as rapidly as possible at the beginning of joint meetings, and then the parties customarily used the grievance meetings to feel each other out on all kinds of issues, many of them lying beyond the scope of customary collective bargaining—such things as the economic position of the company, proposed new machinery and processes, issues in forthcoming contract negotiations. This meant, in effect, broadening the grievance machinery into a semiformal system of two-way management-union communication.

Special Joint Committees

Special joint committees were set up in some of the cases to deal with such problems as safety, time study, job evaluation, seniority, production, or just matters related to "the good of the order." Their underlying objective was to broaden the base of joint determination of matters which traditionally had fallen within the area of exclusive managerial authority. In this category, joint safety committees were by far the most common, although there were some instances of successful joint time-study and joint production committees.

It is difficult to measure the direct contributions of such joint committee to industrial peace. In general, the safety and time-study committees facilitated reasonably satisfactory solutions to specific joint problems in these areas. The indirect effects of joint committees, however, appeared to be more significant. By providing additional opportunities for periodic and systematic communication between company and union officials, these committees frequently had a profound effect on the general tone of the relationship and made it easier for the parties to understand each other's thinking in discussing key bargaining issues.

On the other hand, effective communication was also found where no such committees existed. It can be concluded that special joint committees are not in themselves causes of industrial peace, although they are likely to be indicators of the presence of harmonious and constructive relations. The underlying cause of industrial peace is the basic desire and intention of the parties to share information and make joint decisions rather than the type of machinery which they employ to achieve such ends.

Cooperation in Communication

In addition to problem solving and joint consultation, cooperation in communication is an important, closely related cause of peace. In most medium-sized or large business establishments, the problem of keeping employees informed about company policies and objectives is difficult. Workers may form their opinions of the company through official communications, statements of the foremen, or through the grapevine. The larger the organization, the more difficult are the problems of communication. The same situation prevails also within the union organization. The members may get information from union meetings, from the steward, or again simply from the grapevine. It is also a well-known fact that workers may have loyalties to both the company and the union.

In relationships which are fraught with conflict, there is usually bitter rivalry between company and union officials for the support and allegiance of workers. Often the struggle to win loyalty degenerates into a name-calling and mud-slinging contest aimed at destroying the workers' confidence in the other party. Such competition, with the management and the union communications systems in conflict, causes employee discontent, general suspicion, and strained relationships.

In contrast, we found a great deal of management and union communication. Attempts were made in negotiations to thrash out a problem, to agree upon a solution, and then to sell the same ideas within both communication systems. Indeed, the companies involved were convinced that the union, to the extent that it could communicate information about company plans and problems to employees, might be of great assistance in the exercise of managerial functions. Likewise, the union had much to gain from open company encouragement of membership in the union. Thus the various techniques and procedures used by the parties to get the same story across to the workers were probably important causes of peaceful relationships.

Negotiation Procedures

The most spectacular aspect of collective relations is the negotiation of the labor agreement. In effect, this is a treaty-making process where both sides may resort to force if necessary to achieve their ends. From the variety of strategies employed by companies and unions in the cases studied, it was possible to single out certain procedures which appear to be at least partially responsible for peaceful relations.

First, relationships were generally most successful where the negotiators on both sides had authority to make commitments. Mere discussions between "messenger boys" almost invariably led to prolonged negotiations, misunderstandings, and confusion. On the other hand, if the company representatives had the authority to bargain, it made little difference whether they were staff representatives, that is industrial relations directors, or line representatives in charge of operations. On the union side, local officers appeared to be successful bargainers but so were international representatives and top union officials provided one person had responsibility for leading the talks. There was substantial evidence to indicate that lawyers could make negotiations more peaceful by staying away than by injecting themselves into the negotiations.

There was wide variation from case to case on the matter of selecting negotiators. Dewey and Almy made a strong effort to bring more and more levels of management into the bargaining process, even where this meant sacrificing a united management front. Nashua Corporation was represented in its negotiations with seven AFL unions by the industrial relations manager; the company president had delegated to him the authority necessary to reach an agreement. On the union side, there was similarly a difference in the roles played by the union's international representatives. Their role at the steel companies was fairly prominent, although more so at Sharon Steel and the Minnequa Plant of C.F. & I. than Atlantic Steel; it was much smaller in the AFL unions at Nashua Corporation; and at Dewey and Almy it was not unusual for the international representatives to play no part in the negotiations.

But there was one point on which virtually all companies and unions agreed in regard to the make-up of the negotiating teams: the exclusion of lawyers. The lawyer may plead in his own defense that he is being made the whipping boy for all the troubles that labor and management had in the past. Whenever the parties did not trust each other, their lawyers were called in to put the agreements into legal jargon; but frequently this jargon merely spelled out the basic conflict of the parties—a development which could not justly be blamed on the lawyers.

The aversion to lawyers, however, goes beyond this reasoning. It seems to grow out of new independence on the part of the bargainers, a feeling that they understand each other and can say what they want to without the help of an outsider, and without the fear that the agreed-upon words subsequently would be stretched to mean things not mentioned at the negotiations. This attitude was best summed up in the words of Sharon's president to a union official, "I know the steel business and you know the union business, so let's keep lawyers out of this so they won't obscure our mutual objectives."

Second, some kind of prenegotiation in advance of formal conferences on final contract terms contributes to peaceful relations. Surprises of any kind are likely to upset negotiations. Each party has greater confidence if it has a thorough understanding of the issues to be raised by the other as well as of the social, "political," or economic background of the various demands. Where the parties had been successful in solving problems and in developing effective communications, each was likely to enter contract negotiations with a fairly sophisticated awareness of the other's needs and with a reasonably good idea of the probable reactions to any given demand.

It made little difference, however, whether the preview of issues stemmed from day-to-day relationships under the contract or resulted from informal prenegotiation sessions. The important thing was that both parties sat down to contract bargaining fully cognizant of all ramifications connected with each issue.

Third, peaceful negotiations were facilitated when both parties came to conferences armed with facts pertinent to the issues being negotiated. This meant that the negotiators had to be thoroughly briefed on the reasoning underlying positions to be taken. Even more important, management representatives appeared to have a clear idea of how far they could go, of the stage at which they would prefer a strike rather than agree to the union's terms; and the union negotiators had a good idea of what they could settle for without asking the membership to walk out. There is no substitute for hard-boiled realism even in the most peaceful union-management negotiations.

Fourth, in the most successful relationships the negotiators saw themselves as seasoned traders rather than as belligerent table pounders. The negotiators took pride in their skill in striking bargains which were good for both sides, rather than in forcing their counterparts to give in. Thus, the *Case Studies* showed little maneuvering in the form of delaying tactics, deliberate needling or name calling, or strategies designed to split the ranks of the opposing party. This attitude in bargaining, combined with sophisticated awareness of all issues involved, adequate knowledge of facts, predetermined positions, and authority to make final settlements, all helped build the mutual respect and confidence so important in successful bargaining relationships.

Finally, negotiations were always marked by the union's specific awareness of its responsibility to the membership. The techniques by which this sense of responsibility was introduced into the negotiating sessions varied. At one extreme, there was the "goldfish bowl" bargaining which permitted the membership to have large numbers of representatives attend negotiations. At the opposite extreme, perhaps, was the Dewey and Almy situation in which the members were asked only to accept or reject a tentative agreement as a whole. In virtually all cases, however, the rank and file were brought in on the negotiations. Management and union leaders alike were made aware that they bargained not for themselves alone, but for the whole worker group. This meant, in turn, that the hard-won results of several days of negotiating were seldom lost through subsequent rejection by a dissatisfied membership.

CHAPTER 6

Conclusions and Implications

CHARLES A. MYERS *
of the staff of the Industrial Relations Section,
Massachusetts Institute of Technology

In the preceding chapters we have seen how favorable external environmental factors give to management and the union an opportunity to develop peaceful relationships; and how certain attitudes, approaches, policies, and procedures make it possible to achieve these relationships in specific situations. The importance of historical factors influencing the relationship, particularly in the initial period, has also been stressed. The individual *Case Studies* from which these conclusions have emerged constitute the most complete and detailed record available of peaceful union-management relationships. What is their significance? Is it limited to the specific situations studied, or are the findings applicable to a wide variety of firms and unions? These are the central questions which this chapter will attempt to answer.

WHAT ARE THE BASIC CAUSES?

Environmental factors, as pointed out in Chapter 2, do not by themselves cause peace. A favorable combination of various environmental factors may make it easier for management and a union to achieve a mutually agreeable and noncollusive peaceful relationship, but the parties still have to desire peace and work to achieve it. Not all the environmental factors themselves are fixed in the sense that management and union representatives can do nothing about them; rather they establish a range within which management and the union can largely determine their own relationship.

In the Committee's statements introducing each *Case Study* some basic causes of industrial peace have been listed. The list has varied and been expanded as the studies accumulated. It has one distinguishing

* Otto Lerbinger, formerly assistant in the Industrial Relations Section, MIT, aided in preparation of this chapter.

characteristic. Each cause on the list refers to attitudes and approaches which the parties themselves have consciously adopted or helped to achieve. Furthermore, each was important in explaining the degree of industrial peace found in the specific case. It is worth repeating the complete list here.

1. There is full acceptance by management of the collective bargaining process and of unionism as an institution. The company considers a strong union an asset to management.

2. The union fully accepts private ownership and operation of the industry; it recognizes that the welfare of its members depends upon the successful operation of the business.

3. The union is strong, responsible, and democratic.

4. The company stays out of the union's internal affairs; it does not seek to alienate the workers' allegiance to their union.

5. Mutual trust and confidence exist between the parties. There have been no serious ideological incompatibilities.

6. Neither party to bargaining has adopted a legalistic approach to the solution of problems in the relationship.

7. Negotiations are problem-centered—more time is spent on day-to-day problems than on defining abstract principles.

8. There is widespread union-management consultation and highly developed information sharing.

9. Grievances are settled promptly, in the local plant whenever possible. There is flexibility and informality within the procedure.

Some of these may be termed psychological causes; others involve techniques and procedures. Some also reflect the initial attitudes in the formative period of the relationship. We have said that the external environmental factors must be at least permissive, so that these causes of peace can be effective. In Chapter 2, we have outlined the typical environment for the peaceful situations which have been studied in this series. The broad applicability of the causes of peace found will depend on two factors: first, the extent to which this favorable or permissive environment is found in American industry and, second, the extent to which the individual management and union can change or modify the impact of unfavorable environmental factors. We need to examine these points in more detail.

TRANSFERABILITY OF OUR CONCLUSIONS

The situations studied are generally regarded as outstanding instances of industrial peace. This characterization tends to lead to the conclusion that they are exceptional or even unique. But there is nothing exceptional in the favorable environmental factors. There are many medium-sized companies with a steady production level and subject only to moderate technological advance. Many firms have jobs which are no less interesting or responsible than those in the cases studied. These are not the only efficient firms in the particular industries, nor the only ones with expanding markets and administered prices. Well-established firms in multi-industry communities are more characteristic of the American industrial scene today than are new firms or one-industry towns. Casual, intermittent, migratory, or irresponsible labor is not the usual type of labor force. Increasingly, many firms are attempting to keep their wage levels in line with community or industry standards.

More and more communities in America, especially in the industrialized areas, are becoming accustomed to unions and collective bargaining. National and local union stability is certainly greater, on the whole, than it was a decade ago and earlier. Wage patterns are getting increasing attention, as many firms and unions adjust to the "leaders" (although in many industries there is still no clear-cut pattern or wage leader). Local autonomy seems to be declining in some unions, but remains strong in others. Four of the cases studied involved a strong centralized union, the Steelworkers, yet local adjustments were possible. Finally, there are many union-management relationships which have been accumulating experience and skillful leaders on both sides.

In short, the environmental factors typical of the cases studied are also found in many other situations, some of which undoubtedly have at least as good relationships as those studied. But the working harmony typical of these instances is not the dominant pattern in all companies with comparable environments. "Orderly armed truce" is still frequent in American industry.[1] Many of these cases are found where external environmental factors are permissive or favorable for industrial peace or working harmony.

It is a fair conclusion, therefore, that the nine basic causes of industrial peace listed by the Committee could apply to many more labor-management relationships. These studies represent an important fund of knowledge on how to achieve industrial peace and this fund could be drawn upon by many firms and unions which operate within a similar environmental setting. As Clinton Golden has said in the statement "A Positive Approach to Peace," reprinted in each *Case Study:*

Health in the individual, as recent studies have shown, is essentially not the result of mere passive submission by the organism to an environment, but

[1] Frederick H. Harbison and John R. Coleman, *Goals and Strategy in Collective Bargaining,* Harper & Brothers, 1951, pp. 49–51, 144.

of *active striving* with material and social surroundings. So health in the industrial body is the conscious and laborious creation of men.

What about firms whose existing environment is not so favorable? Can they do nothing to achieve industrial peace? Are the causes—the philosophies, attitudes, and approaches of both parties—of no significance in helping to shape the environment itself? Can either management or union leaders do anything to achieve a more favorable environment in which to develop peaceful and constructive relationships?

A glance at the table of "Environmental Factors" in Chapter 2 suggests that, in fact, the "frequently favorable circumstances" are not necessarily and irrevocably fixed. Some are more subject to conscious control than others, but in nearly every one there is a range of possibilities. Within this range, where a particular firm or union finds itself is, at least in part, the result of conscious decisions and policies by management and the union.

THE RANGE OF FIXITY IN THE ENVIRONMENT

During a short period many of the industrial environmental factors are fixed. But a resourceful management, anxious to secure a favorable environment for industrial peace, can change some of these so-called "fixed" factors over a longer period.

The size of plants in a multiplant company, for example, is affected by a decentralization policy as the firm expands. A seasonal production pattern may be regularized by various well-known employment stabilization methods, as in several of the cases studied—Crown Zellerbach, Hickey-Freeman, and Marathon Corporation, for example. The rate of technological advance is partly within the control of individual management, particularly in the less competitive industries. And the manner in which even fairly rapid technical changes are introduced can certainly help shape labor-management relationships.

The nature of the jobs is again partly a result of management's production planning and layout; minute specialization of labor is not necessarily inevitable. Unfavorable market factors, such as contracting or elastic demand and cyclical sensitivity, may be offset at least in part by product diversification—as illustrated by Dewey and Almy and Nashua. Finally, the location of plants is fixed in the short run, but an unfavorable location can be overcome by expansion in other areas.

The community environment also is largely fixed in the short run, but can be modified over a longer period through decentralization and relocation of plants. The quality of the work force can be improved by good selection methods and in-plant training. The nature of labor-management relations is partly the cause, and partly the result, of the quality of the work force. Whether the plant is in a metropolitan labor market or in a one-industry town will not necessarily predetermine industrial peace. Community wage levels may be taken into account in management's decisions on location, and may even be a decisive factor as expansion takes place. And industrial climate is affected by management's own attitude toward labor-management relations and its influence upon other management and union representatives in the community.

Factors in the "political" environment of the parties are partly fixed in the short run and partly within the control of management and union officials. The basic causes which were listed earlier include attitudes and approaches which really help to determine the "political" security of the union and management. To be sure, if the local union is permitted considerable local autonomy by the national officers, or if it follows patterns established elsewhere, conditions may be more favorable for industrial peace. At Nashua Corporation, however, there was an increase in local autonomy as relationships matured. When companies are differentiated from widely scattered competitors, as in this case, there is no real problem of pattern setting or pattern following. The extent to which management will feel itself bound by patterns established elsewhere or suggestions by an employers' association will be, at least in part, a matter of conscious decision. Local management autonomy in a multiplant company also varies, in part because of different top management attitudes and policies, as in the Libbey-Owens-Ford case. Industry-wide bargaining, which reduces local autonomy, has been an instrument of industrial peace in the Pacific Coast pulp and paper industry, as well as in the New York ladies' garment industry,[2] and in a country like Sweden.[3]

Finally, time, as an environmental factor shaping the relationship, is not outside the control of management or union. A realization of the importance of time in maturing a relationship suggests a different approach than if the parties were unaware of its significance. Relationships born in strife may be more difficult to develop into peace, but with conscious efforts this initial handicap can be overcome, as it was in the Colorado Fuel and Iron Company and in the Inland Steel Container Company.[4]

[2] Dwight E. Robinson, *Collective Bargaining and Market Control in the New York Coat and Suit Industry*, Columbia University Press, 1949.

[3] Charles A. Myers, *Industrial Relations in Sweden: Some Comparisons with American Experience*, Technology Press, 1951, Chap. II. For further evidence on industrial peace under city-wide employer association bargaining, see Jesse T. Carpenter, *Employers' Associations and Collective Bargaining in New York City*, Cornell University Press, 1950; and under regional bargaining, see Richard A. Lester and Edward A. Robie, *Wages under National and Regional Collective Bargaining*, Industrial Relations Section, Princeton University, 1946.

[4] William F. Whyte, *Pattern for Industrial Peace*, Harper & Brothers, 1951.

To summarize, even unfavorable environmental factors can be changed by management and labor over a period if they wish to achieve industrial peace. Some are more fixed than others, and the existence of several relatively fixed unfavorable environmental factors may predestine the parties to a certain type of relationship. But we cannot say this with certainty, for the environment itself can be changed over time. One of the unanswered questions is: Are there *any* cases of peaceful and constructive labor-management relations in industries or communities where the external environment is largely unfavorable? It would be surprising to find none whatever.

THE IMPACT OF THE *Case Studies*

Another way of judging the transferability or general applicability of the findings of the *Case Studies* is to evaluate their impact on industrial relations in this country. Here we lack any specific proof of the extent to which management and unions in other companies have been influenced in their relationships by reading, discussing, and reflecting upon the published reports. But there is some evidence that the wide publicity and distribution given to these studies have made an impact upon industrial relations in America, and even in Western Europe.

The studies have been widely reported in newspapers, magazines, and trade and union journals. They have been used at many of the country's leading colleges for classes in industrial relations and personnel and business administration; and have formed the basis for labor-management forums and workers' education programs. A number of companies have distributed copies of the studies to stockholders, customers, or employees, as have unions to their members. They have been read and discussed by many union and management representatives in the seventeen Marshall Plan countries. Since their distribution has been more extensive than previous studies of industrial relations, our presumption is that they have had some favorable impact on other labor-management relationships. We should expect to find the greatest improvement in those situations where both management and labor desired better relationships, but needed suggestions on how to achieve them. However, the reservoir of experience which the studies represent has certainly not been tapped to the full. Many more management and union representatives could draw upon the findings to improve their own relationships.

WILL THIS PEACE CONTINUE?

The lasting significance of our conclusions will be affected by whether industrial peace continues in these specific labor-management relationships. The available evidence indicates that to date each has remained peaceful. With few exceptions, there have been no strikes or other indications of strife in the cases described in our series, and even in those situations the relationships are still reported good. One important reason is undoubtedly the past history of good relations, which itself helps the parties to continue such a relationship. A good example is Lockheed, in which a prior history of good relations helped the parties to meet the difficult problem of rapid expansion from 1942 to 1945. Management and union officials in these firms understand the pressures on each other, and how the relationship must accommodate itself to these pressures. Such understanding is a good guarantee that industrial peace will continue, even in the face of changes in the external environment.

Nevertheless, some follow-up studies of the NPA cases would be helpful. That would show in more detail how a relationship evolves, how it meets new problems, and adjusts to new conditions. Our economy is dynamic, and its state at any one time is also affected by conditions of world tension through our military expenditures. Some of the firms studied expanded during the past few years, while others were affected by material shortages or declining demand. Collective bargaining has had to adjust to both expanding employment and declining employment, along with product and process changes. The political environment may have changed the mood of some sections of American management and unions, and this change may affect the situations studied. Expectations on the future level of business activity will also have an important bearing on the prospect of industrial peace.

We have seen in *Case Study No. 13* how working harmony can deteriorate. Management may want peace so badly that it pays a price (such as loose production standards during a labor shortage) which costs more in terms of strife later when competitive conditions force a revision. Or, management may become so closely identified with the union leaders that subsequent changes required by economic conditions may discredit the union leadership and the whole labor-management relationship.[5] This, in fact, is a serious problem for union leaders under working harmony. They cannot afford to become known among the union members as management boys or stooges. They need to continue to show some gains or constructive activity which benefit the membership if they are to continue in office. Management in some of the cases was as concerned about this problem as union leaders. One answer lies in broadening the

---

[5] See, also, R. C. Nyman, *Union-Management Cooperation in the "Stretch-Out,"* Yale University Press, 1934. For another account of this case in which a cooperative plan deteriorated, see Sumner H. Slichter, *Union Policies and Industrial Management,* Brookings Institution, 1941, Chap. XVIII.

problem-solving activities of management and union jointly, and encouraging wider participation by employees who are also union members. Only Lapointe, of all the companies and unions we studied, however, had developed formal union-management cooperation on production problems.

There are other reasons why good relationships may deteriorate. First, if key management or union officials are replaced by newcomers who have other motives or objectives than continuing the past relationship, a change is inevitable. In one firm, not included in the published series, a good relationship grew worse when a rival faction in the local union got control. Factional rivalries that arise within a union, in fact, can make the task of maintaining a good relationship very difficult.

A second reason why industrial peace may deteriorate in the cases studied is that both management and union leaders may slacken their efforts and fail to provide continuing opportunities for progress in the relationship. An enlightened management tends to neutralize the militance of the union's program. For example, if grievances fall off because plant problems are being handled better by foremen and superintendents —if contract administration is improved—there is probably less for the union to do. This is the problem mentioned above, and discussed in the Dewey and Almy study, when the need to broaden joint problem-solving activities was stressed.

Third, none of the cases studied had really weathered a severe economic crisis, such as the one confronting the cotton textile industry in the North, for example. It should be noted that at least four of the companies in the *Case Studies*—Lockheed, Lapointe, Hickey-Freeman, and American Velvet—did have economic difficulties during the course of the relationship, although good relations did not deteriorate. In the northern hosiery industry, such severe crises have apparently been met without strikes or bad relationships,[6] but the task is certainly more difficult than when business is good and employment is stable or expanding.

Finally, industrial peace or working harmony itself may have costs which need to be weighed against the gains. It has been suggested that an orderly armed truce relationship may be more conducive to the protection of individual employee rights and the advancement of economic progress —both important goals in a democratic society.[7] In at least one of the cases studied, the regional bargaining system has been criticized as reduc-

[6] Thomas Kennedy, *Effective Labor Arbitration*, University of Pennsylvania Press, 1948. An arbitration board ordered a substantial wage reduction in this industry, and the award was accepted by the union.

[7] Harbison and Coleman, *op. cit.*, Chap. VI.

ing the degree of participation of the local unions in labor-management relations. To the extent that management and a dominant union keep out rival factions and rival unions, individual employee rights may be limited. But there have been no other charges that the firms and unions studied were neglecting individual rights or economic progress in their search for industrial peace. These goals of a democratic society need not be conflicting, and there is a further positive gain when management and the union are able to resolve their differences and accommodate conflicting objectives without resort to the intervention of government or third parties.

Some Unanswered Questions

The points at which more study is needed to answer some of the questions which have been asked about the causes of industrial peace under collective bargaining have been indicated in the preceding sections. These can now be summarized:

1. What happens when industrial peace continues for a long time? Do management and the union find new areas for joint activity, or does the relationship stagnate and even deteriorate as a disillusioned union membership rejects the peaceful leadership?

2. How do employees, who also constitute the union membership, view the relationship which union and management officials characterize as "good" or "peaceful"? Are they equally enthusiastic or are they apathetic? One weakness of the NPA *Case Studies* is that few reported on how the employees and rank-and-file union members felt about the relationship.

3. What happens to cases of industrial peace when favorable external environmental conditions change for the worse? Can the relationship stand this test of adversity?

4. Is industrial peace of the type found in the *Case Studies* possible only when companies have an equally favorable environment? Can we expect industrial peace only in relatively stable industries like pulp and paper, or in medium-sized, pattern-following firms? Are there no cases of good labor-management relations in industries like longshoring, coal mining, or in the giant pattern-setting firms? The 1948 and 1950 General Motors-United Auto Workers' collective bargaining agreements cast some doubt upon generalizations about the impossibility of securing industrial peace in the so-called "power centers" of American industry. Yet we need to know more about the prospects of good relationships in these situations.

PART II

CONDENSATIONS OF THIRTEEN *CASE STUDIES*

CHAPTER 7

Crown Zellerbach Corporation and the Pacific Coast Pulp and Paper Industry

and Two AFL Unions— the Pulp Workers and the Paper Makers

CLARK KERR, *now Chancellor, University of California at Berkeley, and* ROGER RANDALL, *Institute of Industrial Relations, University of California at Berkeley, are authors of* NPA Case Study No. 1. *Their full report, condensed in this chapter, was published in September 1948.*

The quality of peace achieved by region-wide bargaining in the West Coast pulp and paper industry is high. The explanation of how that peace has developed offers no easy cure-all, but it does indicate certain fundamental requirements for industrial peace.

Although it is not a basic measurement of quality, the industry's record on work stoppages and intervention by third parties since it began bargaining as a region-wide unit in 1934 has been remarkable. During the fourteen years studied, not a single day's interruption of work has been experienced by any paper mill on the Pacific Coast and only two grievances have been submitted to arbitration. Only one unfair labor practice charge was processed under the National Industrial Recovery Act; none under the National Labor Relations Act; and only one dispute was presented to the War Labor Board.

The workers are adequately represented in the West Coast pulp and paper industry. The unions are not dominated by the employers, and the employers are not subjected to unduly burdensome conditions. There is no labor-management collusion to raise prices. Workers have benefited from standardized and relatively good wages and working conditions.

The unions have obtained basic institutional protection. Management has gained from low turnover and absenteeism. The industry has been expanding, with relatively satisfactory profits and high productivity. Pacific Coast pulp and paper mills probably have the highest man-hour output in the nation. While the exact contribution of the workers to productivity cannot be measured, the majority of mill managers stated their belief that man-hour output and general employee cooperation in increasing production have shown a substantial and continuing improvement since unionization of the plants.

Another indication of sound industrial relationships is the speed with which the annual region-wide negotiating conference is completed. Differing points of view on contract changes of representatives of management and workers brought together from over thirty mills have to be reconciled, yet these conferences are concluded in three to ten days with a minimum of acrimony. This suggests that the parties come together with the intent of reaching agreement rather than maneuvering. Almost every conceivable phase of employer-employee relations has been a subject for joint deliberation. The consistent record of contract observance, upon which both employers and unions in this industry justifiably pride themselves, and the complete absence of charges of bad faith, indicate a careful weighing of the consequences of actions.

A final indication of industrial peace has been the high mutual regard of the representatives of the parties for each other. Personal animosities, natural results of differences during negotiations, have not been carried over from the annual negotiations to becloud next year's day-to-day administrative relationships. The parties to bargaining frequently have expressed mutual trust and confidence. (Examples of such statements are given in *Case Study No. 1.*) The strongest impression obtained from interviews is the conviction of union leaders that local management has been carrying out the terms of the uniform labor agreement in good faith; and the sincere concern of local managers that the unions remain strong and capably led so the workers may be effectively represented as an aid to management in carrying out a constructive personnel program.

THE PARTIES AND THEIR ENVIRONMENT

Management and unions in the West Coast pulp and paper industry are in an environment generally favorable to realization of good relationships, although they have been operating adjacent to centers of industrial unrest. Special attention has been given to Crown Zellerbach Corporation in this study because it has been one of the principal architects of the peace, and also because it was the largest in the group and the second largest pulp and paper company in the United States. Founded in 1870, Crown Zellerbach has over 50 per cent of the Pacific Coast newsprint capacity, and about 50 per cent of the coarse paper capacity. It has large timber reserves, operated on a sustained yield basis, and the world's largest integrated pulp and paper mill at Camas, Washington. The isolated study of a single firm within this system, however, would not permit a complete or valid analysis, since the particular qualities of the employer-union relationship have been so greatly influenced by the region-wide approach.

This complex bargaining system includes 32 primary pulp, paper, and converting mills in the states of Washington, Oregon, and California. Some of them are more than 1000 miles apart. Eighteen individual companies, through the Pacific Coast Association of Pulp and Paper Manufacturers, make up the bargaining group. (Only three pulp and paper firms of any size, with one plant each, do not belong. While some paper converting plants in the West Coast industry have belonged, the large majority have not.)

Locational Factors

Certain economic characteristics vary according to the geographic location of the 32 mills. Seven plants in central and southern California are exclusively paper converting and paper products mills producing no pulp of their own. Of seven Oregon plants, five are integrated pulp and paper products mills, one is a commercial pulp producer, and one is engaged in paper converting. In Washington, out of eighteen mills, seven produce only pulp, nine are integrated plants, and two are paper converting plants. The industry is not mobile. Its original location is largely determined by the available supply of raw materials, and once located, it is difficult to move equipment.

The Pacific Northwest, where most of the mills are located, has been known historically as an area of industrial strife. There have been difficulties, particularly, in the industries most closely related to pulp and paper—lumbering, longshoring, and shipping, which also are geographically adjacent to many of the mills. But despite difficulties, collective bargaining was more of an accepted practice on the Pacific Coast in the early thirties than in any other part of the United States. Union representatives say that firms, including Crown Zellerbach, with their main offices on the Coast accepted unionism more readily than firms directed from the East.

The Work Force and Their Jobs

Approximately 15,000 workers, production and maintenance, are employed in the 32 pulp and paper mills, ranging from plants with fewer than 200 to the Camas plant with fewer than 2000 workers. Over 98 per cent of eligible workers belong to the two AFL unions—the International Brotherhood of Pulp, Sulphite and Paper Mill Workers and the International Brotherhood of Paper Makers—which jointly possess exclusive bargaining rights. On the West Coast, the unions have joined for purposes of contract negotiation and administration as the Pacific Coast Pulp and Paper Mill Employees' Association. The Paper Makers, much the smaller of the two unions, exercises jurisdiction principally over the paper machine operators, the industry's highly skilled craftsmen. The industrial-type Pulp Workers has jurisdiction over all other production and maintenance workers.

Although the two unions have constituted practically a single industrial union for purposes of collective bargaining, the autonomy of each has been carefully preserved. They have their own separate officers and internal life. Both unions are long-established and relatively conservative, and their national officers had a reputation for integrity and contract observance long before organization of the Pacific Coast mills in 1933.

The workers are drawn from a population that is unusually homogeneous, particularly in the smaller cities of the Pacific Northwest. There is no management or union policy of segregation of minority groups, but inconsequential numbers work in the mills. Consequently, there have been no social conflicts of community origin. Many persons in the industry stressed the high caliber and steadiness of the work force.

The percentage of workers in the skilled and semiskilled classifications is fairly high. The industry's extensive mechanization has not resulted in substantial creation of monotonous tasks, except in the converting and finishing departments where women principally are employed. The average worker supervises a machine or a process, rather than manually operating it or participating in it. This stimulates a sense of responsibility and pride in the individual's work and in the operation as a whole. The individual employee worked with an average investment in 1940 estimated at $15,000 in the Pacific Coast pulp and paper mills ($25,000 for Crown Zellerbach) as compared with approximately $6000 in all manufacturing industry. The control vested in each worker over the quality of the product strongly affects the efficiency with which that investment is used. Management, consequently, is encouraged to act responsibly toward the worker. The employers cannot afford to tolerate or create plant conditions which breed worker contempt for management or indifference to the job.

Production Patterns and Markets

The exceptional stability of employment in the pulp and paper industry has attracted workers to whom security is especially important—the family type rather than floaters. A small fringe of casual and seasonal jobs exists, but careful scheduling of production has minimized them, and fluctuations seldom affect the bulk of employees beyond the requirement of overtime work. Although pulp and paper prices have seemed to be moderately sensitive to cyclical changes in general business activity, employment has remained relatively stable even in the face of drastic cyclical fluctuations in the general economy. This is illustrated by experience in the depression years. The demand for newsprint, food containers, and other items continued more steadily than for steel, or automobiles, or clothing. Whereas the lumber industry experienced many bankruptcies and layoffs, not a single pulp and paper company in the Pacific Northwest ceased operations. Work-sharing arrangements were developed so that few pulp and paper employees were completely unemployed.

Other Favorable Factors

Continued growth and expansion of the industry on the Pacific Coast have offset the fear of technological unemployment which often underlies employee resistance to the introduction of new laborsaving methods or machinery. New machines, rather than being feared as rivals or threats to job tenure, have presented positive advantages in higher pay and more responsibility as workers have moved up all along the line. The number of wage earners in the industry in the Pacific Northwest went up from 7000 to over 11,000 between 1929 and 1940, and Crown Zellerbach raised its output in tons by 40 per cent from 1939 to 1947.

The "curse of bigness" has not troubled this industry. Since the average mill has fewer than 500 production and maintenance workers, local managers can know all or nearly all the employees, and even top management in a number of companies has remained in touch with individual workers. This gives the workers a sense of belonging and an opportunity to comprehend the over-all operations. The medium size of the plants may have abetted the initial establishment of peaceful relationships, since companies may have felt they did not have enough strength successfully to resist unionization by force, as some of the eastern giants did at the time. Most of the plants are located in medium-sized or small towns. In this case good relations seem to have been made better by greater mutual interdependence and social contact in the communities where the plants are located.

Two other environmental factors seem to have helped. The industry has no periodical production crisis. Thus there is no one time when one party can put undue pressure on the other. With no deadline for the completion of negotiations externally imposed, the bargains can be surveyed and consummated without duress. Also a favorable factor is the neutrality of purchasers. Apparently no pressure has been exerted by buyers of the products either for or against certain industrial relations policies.

MANAGEMENT'S APPROACH TO EMPLOYEE RELATIONS

An important aspect of the company's personnel policy is that of having *no rigid policy*. Although practices are formalized, Crown Zellerbach's approach is more of a state of mind, a point of view. A conscious opposition to the development of categorical answers exists. This does not mean that management does not consider employee-employer relations of crucial significance, as a typical comment by J. D. Zellerbach, president of the company, makes clear. In the *American Magazine* of May 1947, he said: "No one aspect of modern industry is more directly important to the executive head of a company than labor relations."

An outline of Crown Zellerbach's personnel policies and practices indicates also the way policies of the other firms in the industry have evolved under region-wide bargaining. And one of the management leaders primarily responsible for the West Coast industry's good industrial relations underscores Mr. Zellerbach's views. R. B. Wolf, former manager of the Pulp Division of the Weyerhauser Timber Company and vice-president of the Pacific Coast Association of Pulp and Paper Manufacturers, has pointed out on many occasions that management gets the kind of labor leader it deserves from the way it deals with men.

Selection of Employees

The company pays special attention to proper selection of employees and the way they fit into the human relations system of the plant. In general, when an employee is hired, he goes in as common labor. This makes the selection process more difficult because work histories disclose relatively little about common labor. Further, under a system which relies predominantly on seniority as the basis for promotion, the individual must be visualized as he will progress through the mill's job structure.

When employees with over five years of seniority leave, exit interviews are held to find out why.

Giving and Getting Information

In its efforts to get information to the man who works, the company relies partially on such standard procedures as the distribution of the annual report to the employees and the provision of an employee hand-book, *Partners in Industry*. Primary attention, however, is directed to less conventional channels. The general theory is that the employees will not be interested in the enterprise unless they know something about it. There should be an "aggressive willingness to share" any information in which the workers indicate an interest, according to Alexander Heron, vice-president in charge of industrial and public relations. Data should be made available on such subjects as finances, profits, expansion plans, the outlook for the industry, the production processes, and the products and their uses.

Periodic joint meetings are scheduled between the unions' shop stewards and the foremen to discuss problems of mutual interest, such as safety questions, seniority status of returning veterans, first-aid classes, and open-house programs. In addition, union officials are consulted on unforeseen problems affecting quality or production, in order to work out procedures which otherwise might create misunderstanding or friction. Such discussions, which bear little or no relation to the collective agreement, have been referred to by Mr. Heron as a step toward "collective planning" for the industry. Crown Zellerbach encourages workers to ask questions and discuss situations as well as to receive facts. It has found the foremen and union representatives to be the essential links in the chain of upward as well as downward communication, because they are likely to know what the employees want. The fact that the foreman has been well informed increases the employees' confidence in him. And the status of union leaders is heightened by their responsibility for relaying information to the employees.

The union is encouraged to bring questions and suggestions to the attention of management through a union advisory committee which meets regularly with management, informal and irregular meetings between management and union officers, and union committees dealing with specific problems. Mr. Heron believes, however, that it is essential that such committees or groups be kept separate from grievance committees and stay away from grievance problems. Such channels of communication have brought into play nonfinancial incentives, such as interest in the product and its uses, the attainment of production records, the success of safety efforts, and the importance of the individual job. Another channel, the suggestion system, has resulted at the largest mill in 60 to 100 suggestions a month, of which about 40 per cent have been used.

The Foreman's Role

A major step in making constructive use of foremen is the employment of a high ratio of foremen to workers, which permits constant personal contact between the workers and the first layer of management. There is a working foreman or leadman for an average of seven employees, and a nonworking foreman or supervisor for every fifteen to twenty.

The company's general policy is to delegate responsibility as completely as possible to the local plant manager, from there to the individual foreman, and ultimately to the worker, particularly in the more skilled classifications. The foremen are consulted on almost every conceivable operational problem and are given considerable responsibility. While applicants are pretested and screened by others, the foreman of the work group makes the ultimate decision to hire. He has the power to settle grievances, except where a matter of policy is involved.

Other ways in which the foremen are identified with management include: (1) weekly meetings of foremen in each division to discuss operating, maintenance, and cost problems; (2) monthly dinner meetings of each division manager with his foremen; (3) an annual management conference attended by a limited number of senior foremen and department heads; (4) conferences of mill managers and their foremen; and (5) higher pay per hour than the highest skilled worker under them.

Since foremen tend often to resent the intrusion of the unions into their domains, an effort has been made to give the foremen an appreciation of how unions can aid in their work. Union representatives are often consulted on the selection of foremen; and the unions permit foremen to return to their old jobs without loss of seniority. The company recognizes that good relations with tomorrow's foremen start with good relations with today's union members, who may be expected to graduate into supervisory jobs.

Labor Relations: A Line Job

The line organization has sole responsibility for handling personnel and industrial relations problems; staff specialists serve in an advisory capacity only.

An important test of mill managers, particularly in the larger mills, is their ability to get along with the men under them. Outside experts can be hired to solve engineering or chemical or accounting problems, but it is far more difficult to find a man capable of solving touchy human relations problems once the good will of the employees is lost. Foremen and other line supervisors are trained to understand some of the more technical subjects, like job evaluation and time and methods study, so that they may work more closely and cooperatively with industrial engineers and other experts. The general policy is to place the responsibility for leadership on the next man above, where it can be exercised in the most personal manner. Staff personnel stays out of specific conflicts in administering the contract; the personnel man is not ordinarily an active participant in the grievance adjustment machinery.

Providing Security to Workers

New workers are assured in the employee handbook that "Every effort is made to insure steady employment for those who go to work for Crown Zellerbach." Provision for a permanent source of pulpwood and advance planning to even out production throughout the year help to assure a steady flow of job opportunities.

The collective agreement provides for promotions on the basis of seniority, if other things are equal. In fact, partly through careful selection and training, over 95 per cent of Crown Zellerbach's promotions have been made in accordance with seniority. The company has a voluntary retirement plan, to which employees contribute, for all workers with five years or more of service. The company contributes rather more than half and pays the costs of administration. Over 98 per cent of the eligible employees participate.

Crown Zellerbach makes careful preparations for changes which might threaten the sense of security of employees and thus lower morale and productive efficiency or result in conscious or unconscious sabotage of the new process or equipment. By never taking the employees by surprise, the company has gained their constructive participation.

For example, the company decided to make major technological changes at one mill. Some old machines were to be moved and new ones, demanding different skills, were to be installed. Six months before the time-consuming change was to start, the company began talking with the union about the nature of the change and the need for it, and the parties began working out ways to minimize any unfavorable effects on the employees involved. No one was fired or laid off. The cooperative approach, in what might have been construed as an area of management prerogatives, secured complete worker acceptance, and it strengthened employer-union-worker understanding and mutual confidence.

Paternalistic practices are avoided because of the belief that the employees desire the maximum freedom of self-determination. The company, however, assists the employees in developing their own programs, such as group life insurance, hospital and medical plans, credit unions in the mills, and athletic teams, but not "company teams."

"Political" Compatibility of the Parties

A sharing of power and rights mutually acceptable to both parties has been worked out by the companies and unions in the West Coast pulp and paper industry. This "political" compatibility is prerequisite for industrial peace.

The president of Crown Zellerbach, speaking as a representative of "progressive employers," has stressed that, although some of the employers were negative in their reaction at the start, most of the employers now not only believe in the principles and practices of true collective bargaining, but also believe that it "promotes stability in our economy" and "is a wholesome exercise in real democracy." Collective bargaining, according to his view, is a worth-while process subject to gradual extension to cover more and more aspects of the employment relationship and of the operation of the enterprise.

R. B. Wolf, who had dealt with these same pulp and paper unions in the East, was one of the most forceful early advocates of dealing with the unions on a positive, constructive basis. He consistently viewed them as a natural development, as an instrument for freeing the employees from domination or fear of domination, and even as a positive advantage to management in the effective operation of the enterprise. (A number of direct quotations by management representatives, spelling out these and similar points of view, appear in *Case Study No. 1.*)

The two pulp and paper unions, by 1933, had forty years of collective bargaining history behind them. As old-line AFL unions they were conscious of the problems of the whole industry, rather than of the craft or trade which their members pursued. They had gone through war and peace, prosperity and depression, and had signed contracts with many different companies. They had found that the unions and workers could not prosper unless the industry and companies also prospered, and were generally familiar with the maximum concessions that could be obtained peacefully at any given time. (The general outlook of the unions is indicated in a remarkable document prepared by a research committee appointed by the president of the Paper Makers in 1943. Excerpts from this appear in *Case Study No. 1*.)

A great deal of credit for the good relations on the West Coast is due the presidents of the two unions, John P. Burke of the Pulp Workers, and Matthew Burns of the Paper Makers. Under their guidance, excesses which sometimes embitter relations were avoided. Stable local leadership was encouraged from the outset. On the West Coast, John Sherman has been the principal union leader and his policies have been influential in building the record of peace.

The internationals have retained some control since the start of organization on the West Coast. The West Coast companies favor participation by international officers in local negotiations because of the internationals' objective and long-run approach made possible by freedom from personal pressures exerted by the local workers, from passions aroused by constant local contact with real or fancied grievances, and by the habit of relating the local scene to national developments. The two internationals not only retain the right to sign collective agreements on behalf of the union locals, but also the authority to suspend, expel, or administer the individual locals; to expel members for "subversive activities"; and to pass on the validity of strikes before they are called.

Even so, both unions are democratic, with authority retained to an unusual degree by the membership. A particular point is made of avoiding a bureaucracy of paid officials. Only six full-time salaried officials are currently employed by the two unions for the Pacific Coast (including British Columbia) and all of these have held jobs in the mills. Day-to-day relations with management are conducted on an unpaid, volunteer basis by the local officers and committeemen. There are no local business agents.

The Initial Contact

When the unions first started organizing the West Coast workers, the mills were neutral; their lack of opposition discouraged any aggressive militancy by the local union leadership. There was no need for a strike or NLRB intervention. In August 1934, the unions formally approached the industry to negotiate a contract. Within three days, a uniform region-wide agreement had been signed, covering most of the industry.

Organizers conducted themselves intelligently. In advance of negotiations, they called on management representatives in each firm to allay such fears as they could. This preparation of the employers for the inauguration of bargaining relationship displayed a keen understanding of the difficult psychological and organizational adjustments required of management when a union first enters its plant. The shock was greatly cushioned.

Management had been prepared in other ways. Under the National Industrial Recovery Act, the government encouraged unionization and collective bargaining. Mr. Zellerbach, who served on the NRA pulp and paper code authority in 1933 and 1934 with two international union leaders (Mr. Burke and Mr. Burns), had formed a high opinion of their statesmanship and knowledge of the industry. Mr. Wolf pointed out that he had gone through the stage of fighting labor organizations before World War I, and when he was compelled to work with them during that war discovered there were many advantages in doing so. In addition, violent conflicts in the maritime and lumber industries in the early thirties had demonstrated the strength of unionism and the costs of open conflict.

The first contract was simple. It recognized the unions, provided for wage increases and standardization of wages among the mills, and established a formal grievance machinery. At the suggestion of union leaders, the employers joined together for negotiating purposes. The contract was uniform for all members of the bargaining group, although individually signed. Concessions by management, although equalling or surpassing those following real struggles elsewhere, met some criticism from local union leaders—particularly the absence of a union security clause. President Burke of the Pulp Workers is said to have reasoned with these leaders in this way: "Of course, it's not all we want; but look at this clause. It says 'recognition'—the very thing other unions all around us at this very time are having to fight and strike for; and here it is given to us at our first meeting by the employers."

Management Rights

Management had all the rights originally, and the unions had none; then the unions penetrated the bundle of rights. A general line has been drawn which is sufficiently acceptable to both parties so that there have been no strikes or lockouts in a battle over prerogatives. Decision making is now shared on many subjects and there is constant management consultation with union leaders on a wide variety of operating problems.

The basic clause which has served to break several deadlocks over managerial rights, and still stands as the essential outline of them, was proposed by the unions as part of the 1934 agreement. It points out as a mutual purpose of the employer and employee, "the operation of the plant (or plants) . . . under methods which will further, to the fullest extent possible, the safety, welfare, and health of the employees, economy of operation, quality and quantity of output, cleanliness of plant, and protection of property."

A no-strike clause in the contract has been a source of contention. At first, because management feared quickie strikes like those then prevalent in shipping and lumbering, it listed situations under which strikes were not permissible. Since the clause was unwieldy and the list could not cover all possibilities, it was dropped in favor of a simpler clause stating that there would be "no strikes, walkouts, or other interruptions of work" during the period of the agreement or upon its expiration without the specific sanction of the signatory unions—the internationals; and stating also that there should be no lockouts by the signatory company during the period of the agreement.

This caused no trouble until 1946 when a local union conducted a strike vote. While the dispute was peacefully settled, the international officers defended the right of the local to take a vote provided no strike actually occurred, pointing out that the vote was a method of indicating the strength of feeling on an issue. Management, however, was uncertain whether a strike was actually intended, and in reaction to this, proposed a new clause in 1947 banning strikes absolutely and unconditionally during the life of the contract. Its wage offer, for a time, was made contingent upon union acceptance of this proposal. The internationals pointed out the impossibility of absolutely controlling the actions of thousands of individuals in connection with strike votes or unauthorized strike action, and said such actions would not constitute violation of the agreement unless the internationals were remiss in trying every means to end quickly any local repudiation of contractual obligations. The internationals held, further, that they must reserve the ultimate right to conduct an authorized strike in the event of willful, flagrant violations or repudiation by the employers. At the same time, they pointed to their long record of complete absence of work stoppages.

The clause remained unchanged, but only after the official record made it clear that the employers had the essential protection they requested. The unions stated that the clause had the same effect as an unqualified no-strike provision. (This illustrates a standard practice of the parties. Each year following negotiations, they develop a *Statements of Policy*, based on a transcript of proceedings, which sets forth understandings and accords as to the intent of various contract provisions. It has the same validity as the written agreement, but safeguards the simplicity of the agreement.) In 1948, to avoid possible law suits over wildcat strikes under the Taft-Hartley Act, provision was made to absolve the union from responsibility for such strikes.

Management is protected by a listing of causes for immediate discharge of employees. Such rules may not conflict with the agreement and are subject to local discussion with the union. Grievances may be filed when workers are disciplined. Explanations in writing of reasons for discharge are required and an elaborate code of what constitutes evidence has been built up. The unions are cautious in protesting discharge cases, refusing to defend members when the evidence is obviously against them.

The agreement provides that employees must be at their post of duty as required by the operations—particularly important since many continuous operations cannot be readily stopped or started. The contract formally recognizes the worker's responsibility not only to his own shift, but also to the continuing operation of the plant.

The grievance machinery includes the standard steps at the company level, and proceeds from there to a regional Joint Relations Board, which processes grievances not settled earlier arising in any mill covered by the uniform agreement. (Only ten grievances have reached the region-wide Board. Eight of them were settled by the unanimous action of industry and labor members, and two went to arbitration.) Expeditious settlement at early steps of the procedure is emphasized.

Since 1937, the contract has provided that, other things being equal, seniority shall govern promotions, but management may determine whether other things are equal. Advance consultation with the local union, however, is required; and the union's recommendation is secured before action is taken, except for emergency situations. Union committeemen, at the same time, have been quick to recognize a misfit and to set aside seniority. The cost to a seniority-laden employee who leaves his job and starts at the bottom elsewhere is great. Because of this, the Paper Makers Union has proposed that every fourth vacancy in the skilled machine operators' jobs may be filled at management's discretion by a qualified employee who has gained his experience in another mill, rather than by in-plant promotion.

The most critical conflict over management rights came in the 1947 negotiations over the right to direct. Starting in 1934, the contract had provided for the settlement of grievances with work continuing "as per the conditions existing prior to the time of the dispute." As grievance procedure was followed, management sometimes deferred actions to which the union objected, or the unions acquiesced to the continuation of objectionable arrangements, but the parties always complied with the grievance settlement. In 1946, however, management orders caused two incidents, both at the same mill, which led to union grievances. One of these had to do with an extra day's work for a department, and the union argued that "conditions existing prior to the dispute" included the normal 40-hour week. The issue was still hotly fought at the time of the 1947 negotiations, when the unions proposed a formal amendment to the contract requiring local union approval before overtime work could be ordered, except in case of an emergency.

Both issues could have been avoided by more careful advance explanations; but management's right to direct had been bluntly challenged. The employers sought a clause which would clearly provide that employees should "work as directed by management" pending settlement of the case; the union delegates vehemently resisted this. They feared restoration of autocratic power in the hands of supervisors, particularly during the time it took to process grievances.

The companies' position, as set forth in the transcript (which the union in the end reluctantly accepted), made clear management's recognition that "some unwise signals" would be called from time to time, and stated its desire for "the tightest possible assurance in the agreement that will correct any such decision when it works a hardship or an injustice on the employee." However, management still was unwilling to surrender its "responsibility for calling the signals and issuing directions."

The unions secured, in return for acceptance of the proposed clause, further guarantees for speeding up grievances. A union spokesman, commenting on the decision, made clear that the union was somewhat fearful of what might happen in the future, and expressed a determination to watch "very, very carefully the position of supervision regarding this particular question." If supervision should take undue advantage of the employees, he said, the union, at the next conference, would "come in here fighting mad," and "clear the thing once and for all."

Management, keenly aware of the explosive potentials of the situation, bluntly warned all its supervisors and foremen that it would tolerate no abuses of this right to direct and that the new clause was not to be regarded as representing any basic change in the relationship with the unions.

The unions still smart from what they consider a major sovereignty concession. This dispute brought the parties closer to "political" incompatibility than they had previously come. The issue of management's right to direct, subject to subsequent protest, as against the union's right to veto in advance may not be settled permanently if other incidents develop.

The West Coast pulp and paper industry has yielded at least one right which is normally retained by management in manufacturing plants— sole control over the safety program. In addition to joint local committees, which meet at least monthly, state-wide conferences on safety are held. Accident rates, partly because of the program, have been cut in half since 1934.

The unions have not challenged management's right to bring in new machinery or methods or to set the speed of work. Most of the improvements have made the work easier and some have resulted in higher job rates. Management has also retained the right to hire, partly because the slow inflow of new workers has constituted no threat to the unions. Nor have the unions sought to represent the foremen. Certainly, management in pulp and paper no longer enjoys unrestricted powers, but if sovereignty of management means retaining those powers essential to the achievement of quantity and quality of production little if any real impairment has taken place.

Security of the Unions

The unions secured recognition in the 1934 contract. In 1936, the parties negotiated a maintenance-of-membership clause which became a model for the standard federal policy on union security. It provided that "Any employee who now is or at any time since June 1, 1936, has been a member in good standing or who after this date becomes or is reinstated as a member of either of the Signatory Unions shall, as a condition of continued employment, maintain such membership in good standing." Further, the company through its local management "will cooperate with the Local Union in every proper and lawful way to assist in obtaining and retaining members."

Management at each mill actively assisted the unions in securing new employees as members in a variety of noncoercive ways, and nearly all workers in the bargaining unit became members of the two unions. At the same time, the 1936 clause also provided that local mill managers be notified of disciplinary measures against members, and gave management an opportunity to intercede on behalf of any employee subject to union discipline, although final authority was reserved by the unions.

These arrangements, and the generally favorable attitudes of the industry, gave the unions a sense of security from attack by management and from mass withdrawals by the membership. But a major source of insecurity still remained—rival unionism. The principal threat came from the International Woodworkers of America (CIO), which had locals in many of the same towns and was an aggressive union, anxious to expand its jurisdiction. The IWA's major effort to infiltrate the pulp and paper industry came in 1943 when it apparently secured the support of a majority of the members of the Pulp Workers local at the Rayonier plant in Hoquiam. The IWA claimed bargaining rights, but the NLRB held that the region-wide bargaining system was the "appropriate unit"—not a single plant. The rival union could not organize the entire industry, and the jurisdiction remained intact. The chief leaders of the IWA faction were expelled.

The unions have sought the union shop since 1934, vigorously at the 1943 negotiations. Turnover, greatly increased under wartime conditions, made maintenance of membership less satisfactory, and the IWA issue was still unsettled. Under War Labor Board rules, little could be expected in the way of wage increases, and nonwage demands such as the union shop were pushed instead. Too, the unions argued, their responsible behavior had earned the union shop.

The employers countered with a proposal for a check-off. They contended that compulsory union membership might cause the loss of some of their most valuable employees, critically needed during the war. The employers have at all times abhorred the possibility in their complex industry of having to deal with the fifteen to twenty individual craft unions, because of the need for conducting many negotiations, the prospect of jurisdictional rivalries, and greater possibilities of strikes. The employers preferred what amounted to industrial unionism. The difficulty lay in the vulnerability of the two pulp and paper unions under their AFL charters to disastrous jurisdictional awards if the craft unions ever claimed effective jurisdiction. On their part, the craft unions had tolerated the infringements on their claimed territory only so long as the door to organizational efforts remained open. They indicated that they would consider the union shop a hostile act and would begin to organize actively. Settlement in 1943 was long delayed because of this issue and negotiations nearly broke down. The final agreement provided for the voluntary check-off and renewed efforts by management to encourage universal membership in the two unions.

A new uncertainty appeared in 1947 with passage of the Taft-Hartley Act which gave a clear preference for craft bargaining units. The unions were dependent on management to make the maintenance-of-membership clause work. The employers were dependent on the unions to keep out the rival CIO union and craft organizations. Although the two unions had achieved a measure of security, they were still faced with two threats. The craft unions, through their influence in the AFL executive council and aided by the provisions of the Taft-Hartley Act, could move in on a large scale; and management might attack the unions—although this seemed highly unlikely.

In their 1948 negotiations, the parties adopted a clause providing for the union shop to take effect on June 1. This reversal of the employers' position followed an election requested by the unions under the provisions of the Taft-Hartley Act. The election was held on a coast-wide basis, thus solidifying the region-wide unit. Of those eligible to vote, over 95 per cent cast callots and over 95 per cent of those voted for the union shop, including many of the craft workers. The unions also pointed out that their relationships with craft unions were cooperative enough to avoid having craft unions take offense at the union shop and, in any event, they were in a strong position to defend themselves.

The specific union-shop clause adopted in 1948 has two important qualifications. First, it applies only to new employees. Employees on the payroll continue to be covered by the maintenance-of-membership provision. Second, by mutual agreement, the parties are permitted to extend the 30-day period within which a new employee may join. This permits the unions not to press a craft worker too hard to join by threat of immediate dismissal.

Negotiating Sessions

Annual negotiations between management and the unions, held in Portland, are popularly known as the Goldfish Bowl. The employers convene ahead of time to discuss their own demands and plan their response to union demands. A negotiating committee of eight members is selected. Representatives of each union local also convene ahead of time. They formulate their requests and select a bargaining committee also composed of eight persons. When the negotiations are undertaken, the two committees face each other across the table. In the background are 100 to 150 representatives of the local workers in the mills and 50 to 100 members of local mill management. The sessions are conducted with some formality. The chairmanship rotates from year to year between a union man and an employer. A court reporter keeps a verbatim transcript. The parties present their arguments and factual data back and forth; and caucus from time to time on the submission or acceptance of proposals.

When the two committees reach an agreement it is only tentative. Before becoming final, it must be accepted by a majority vote of the mills, with one vote per mill; and approved at several levels on the union side:

the elected delegates to the negotiating session, the international officers, and by referendum vote of a majority of the union members up and down the coast.

Mill managers and union leaders have learned more about collective bargaining, about each other, about the industry, and about the contract, than if more customary bargaining methods had been pursued. The Goldfish Bowl, while useful, has not basically caused the good relations. Had relationships for other reasons been bad, the large negotiating sessions, with a tendency to play to the gallery and a disinclination to withdraw from publicly stated positions, might have made them worse.

Economic Compatibility of the Parties

Matching of the unions' requirements for wages and fringe benefits with the industry's ability to pay in West Coast pulp and paper has been achieved at all times, but on several occasions by only a narrow margin.

Union Needs

Three requirements had to be met in order for the unions to be able to conduct themselves peacefully and to live harmoniously with the industry. Wages had to be higher than for the rest of the pulp and paper industry, because the Pacific Coast is a high-wage area nationally, but particularly so in comparison with areas where many of the other pulp and paper plants in the United States are located. The common labor rate had to approximate that in lumber, which accounted in 1940 for half of manufacturing employment in Oregon and Washington and serves as the key rate in the Pacific Northwest. Craft rates had to equal or exceed those generally prevailing on maintenance jobs in the area. Failure by a small margin to obtain these needs would have resulted in industrial warfare. Failure by substantial margins probably would have resulted in the destruction of the two unions by rival organizations and internal dissension.

The common labor rate in sawmills has influenced the needs of the pulp and paper unions in several ways. If the rate in pulp and paper were significantly below that in sawmills, many workers might be tempted to change jobs or at least withdraw their membership and shift allegiance to the unions' major rival, the International Woodworkers of America. But even more, the comparison of these rates has provided a test of the success of top leadership in the union. The wage rates, however, have not had to be identical in pulp and paper and in lumber, chiefly for two reasons. Employment in pulp and paper is seasonally and cyclically more stable than lumber, and the workers have given this stability some weight in making comparisons. Further, a greater proportion of the employees have been above the common labor rate in pulp and paper than in the sawmills, so that the average rates have been higher, even when the common labor rate has been the same or somewhat lower. Despite these off-setting factors, difficulties have arisen whenever the common labor rate in pulp and paper has fallen below that in lumber and have increased in a geometrical ratio with the increasing magnitude of the gap.

The needs of the two unions in the area of craft rates have been even more specifically defined than for rates in general, and the test of adequate performance has been more stringent. The more highly skilled workers have been the most influential in the unions, and have had a freer opportunity to move into a variety of other employments, since job content for craft workers is highly standardized. The craft unions have never formally relinquished their asserted rights to represent these craft workers. Were the craft rates to fall below those in other major industries for any substantial period of time, the craft unions could readily obtain the allegiance of the craft workers and promise equalization with rates elsewhere. Many craft workers in pulp and paper have also carried craft union cards, and transfer of the bargaining agency could take place within the framework of the AFL—possibly even with its support because of the influential position of the craft unions.

The Industry's Capacity to Pay

The industry has been able to satisfy the unions' needs, although its capacity has been strained at certain times and in certain mills.[1] The West Coast segment is less than one-fifth of the national industry and has had to keep its over-all costs and prices generally in line with the rest of the industry. It also has been faced, particularly in newsprint, with competition from Scandinavian and Canadian producers. Because of a number of factors in the industry which could lead to severe price cutting, the price situation, with the exception of some segments of the industry at some times, has not been particularly conducive to the establishment of moderately high or relatively stable wages.

[1] For information on costs, productivity, prices, and profits in the pulp and paper industry, see: Reports of the U.S. Bureau of Labor Statistics and U.S. Bureau of the Census; annual review issues of *Pulp and Paper Industry;* Office of Price Administration, *Survey of Paper and Paper Products Manufacturers,* OPA Economic Data Series No. 25, May 1947; John A. Guthrie, *The Newsprint Paper Industry, An Economic Analysis,* Harvard University Press, 1941; Guthrie, "Price Regulation in the Paper Industry," *Quarterly Journal of Economics,* February 1946; and W. Rupert Maclaurin, "Wages and Profits in the Paper Industry," *Quarterly Journal of Economics,* February 1944.

The West Coast industry has met the unions' requirement for the highest wage rates in the pulp and paper industry in the United States. West Coast average hourly earnings in the industry have generally exceeded those in the rest of the United States by about 30 per cent, with the excess rather greater in more recent years than at the start in 1934. (For comparative hourly wages for selected years, see *Case Study No. 1.*) Several factors have created the capacity to absorb higher wage levels. The Pacific Coast industry has been expanding both absolutely and relatively. In 1924, it produced 8 per cent of the pulp in the United States; by 1946, it was turning out 17 per cent. The mere fact of expansion indicates profitability. The industry has been highly and efficiently mechanized; most of the Pacific Coast mills have been built since World War I and have the latest and best manufacturing processes in a relatively old industry. Only in the South is the industry's development more recent. The Far West industry has a comparative advantage in pulpwood costs and abundant, good quality pulpwood. Since pulpwood costs are the largest single cost item for the industry, this advantage has been a major one. Fuel costs, also, have been lower. However, transportation costs, despite the tidewater location of most mills, on the average have been higher per ton on the West Coast. Although wage rates have been higher, labor costs per ton of newsprint and pulp and wage costs per manufactured unit have been generally lower than in other parts of the United States.

Profits for the nation-wide industry have been lower than for manufacturing industry generally; and prices have been relatively flexible, although the tendency toward severe price cutting seems to have been avoided. Free entry into the industry may have helped keep down the general level of prices and profits. Much of the Pacific Coast raw pulp has been sold in the East, and West Coast prices for standard items have been almost identical with those on the East Coast. (This is illustrated by checks of prices of newsprint and kraft wrapping in San Francisco and New York for selected periods from 1939 through early 1948, which are shown in *Case Study No. 1.*)

The over-all result apparently has not been payment of higher prices by West Coast consumers, but perhaps some stabilizing of prices—involving not only some standardization of prices and the avoidance of cutthroat competition, but also some informal price control in periods of excessive demand, such as efforts to keep newsprint out of the black market after the end of OPA controls. The restrictive devices, to the extent that they have been effective at all, have been more defensive measures than offensive methods to exploit the consumer.

While profit comparisons are notoriously difficult, an examination of reports on a number of East and West Coast firms showed that profits before taxes as a percentage of net fixed assets were at about the same general levels on both coasts, but with some advantage for the Pacific Coast firms during the period 1939 to 1946. Profits for Crown Zellerbach Corporation, at least, have been relatively stable. Net profits after taxes for selected years have been: 1937, $6.2 million; 1939, $8.1 million; 1941, $11.1 million; 1943, $7.6 million; 1944, $7.1 million; 1945, $7.8 million; and 1946, $9.8 million. Profits for the smaller companies, however, appear to have fluctuated more widely.

The History of Wage Rates

The record of wage rates in the West Coast pulp and paper industry generally parallels lumber rates in the Pacific Northwest. (Entrance rates of male common labor for sawmills and for pulp and paper mills from January 1937 through June 1948 are given in *Case Study No. 1.*) From 1934 to 1937, the pulp and paper rate led the general level of lumber rates. The base rate was set at 45 cents in 1934; 47.5 cents in 1935; and 52.5 cents in 1936. Between 1937 and 1942, pulp and paper led in as many months as it followed. Lumber has been the steady leader since 1942. No gap in either direction has been more than 5 cents per hour, following the parallel adjustment. The delay in making such adjustment has usually been three months. The base rates were identical during two-thirds of the elapsed period.

Three recent adjustments are interesting. The lumber rate was raised to 16 cents more than the pulp and paper rate in November 1946. Although the pulp and paper contract could not be opened until June 1947, in January the employers voluntarily, though with union knowledge and encouragement, raised the rate to $1.20, closing the gap to 5 cents. In April 1947, the lumber rate was raised by 7.5 cents to $1.325. In the June negotiations, the pulp and paper rate was increased to $1.275. The employers viewed this as an increase of 18.5 cents over the last negotiated rate; the unions as a raise of 7.5 cents over the existing rate. This was the first time the parties had negotiated a rate more than 1 cent per hour below the lumber rate; this time it was 5 cents less. In the late spring of 1948, to be effective June 1, the parties in the pulp and paper industry negotiated a 9 per cent wage increase with a minimum raise for men of 15 cents per hour. Since the increase in the lumber industry had previously been set at 12.5 cents, the gap for male common labor was narrowed to 2.5 cents.

It does not appear that much larger disparities would have been accepted peacefully by the unions and workers. Since some of the pulp and paper increases were on a percentage basis and some on a percentage and cents-per-hour basis, the wage levels of the more highly paid workers in cents per hour rose more than those of the lower paid workers, giving greater gains to the average pulp worker than the average lumber worker. Steadier work and the higher average rate than in the sawmills, because of less concentration of employees at the lower end of the scale, have helped to make differences bearable. Furthermore, several nonwage fringe provisions of the pulp and paper agreements have been more favorable than those in lumber agreements, and this has been an additional compensatory factor. The workers in the West Coast pulp and paper industry who fell behind the lumber wage rate were generally the women and the unskilled men. The workers who moved ahead of lumber were the more skilled men who are more in demand in the labor market, potentially more sought after by rival craft unions, and more powerful in union circles.

The history of pulp rates has led, since 1942, to the charge that the pulp and paper unions have been "coattail riders," following the lead of the more militant unions in lumbering. This has conformed with the typical postwar pattern of American industrial relations. A few key bargains in strategic industries have set the pace and a multitude of contracts followed the results, reducing the attention paid to conditions in the other labor and product markets, at least temporarily. It has, however, involved an economy of means. The pattern, having been established, usually after a conflict, has been followed by others with a minimum of controversy. In the pulp and paper case, the lumber settlement has served as a ready and objective test for the union negotiators. If they could get as much as lumber, they did not have to fight to prove that they did all right.

While matching lumber rates generally, Pacific Coast pulp and paper rates at the craft level have generally kept ahead of prevailing rates in the area. Some crafts, such as the sawyer, are common only to pulp and paper and lumber, and the parties in pulp and paper have been careful to keep the sawyer rate at or above the rate in lumber. Craft rates have been lower than in construction work, but the more urgent comparison has been with maintenance work. A comparison of rates in pulp and paper, as of May 1947, with prevailing craft rates for factory maintenance in Portland industries (*see Case Study No. 1*) shows that with one exception the rates in pulp and paper were about 10 cents higher. Furthermore, the pulp and paper rates were increased 7.5 cents in June

1947, and most of the mills were located in smaller towns, with a tendency toward lower craft rates than Portland.

Averages Are Deceptive

The averages given here which make it appear that the industry's maximum capacity to pay was always equal to or in excess of actual payments do not tell the complete story. The question has been not only whether on the average the mills in this bargaining unit have had the capacity to meet the average needs of the unions—which they have—but also whether the capacity of the least able mill has been adequate to meet the needs of the union local with the highest requirements. The occasional excess of these needs over these capacities was the source of some of the greatest difficulties to the parties in their bargaining relationships.

The uniform agreement negotiated in this region-wide bargaining sets up identical wage rates. Not only basic rates, but also individual job rates, have been largely standardized by a uniform job-evaluation system adopted in 1936. Both parties have insisted on this uniformity, even though basic situations in the mills and local unions have not been uniform.

The most severe problems have resulted from the high level of needs of union locals in certain towns in the state of Washington, where most of the mills produce pulp, and the low capacity of certain mills in Southern California which are primarily paper converters. Occasionally pulp prices have been very favorable compared with prices for paper and paper converting products, making the pulp mills by comparison highly profitable. Traditionally, both general wage rates and the cost of living have been higher in Washington than in Southern California, so that the real level of pulp and paper wages has been lower than in Southern California. Also, Washington pulp and paper mills are next to lumber mills; none is so located in Southern California; and the woodworkers' and longshoremen's locals—such active rivals in several Washington communities—do not trouble the locals in southern California.

There is more competition in paper products converting than in pulp and paper making. Most of the numerous paper converting firms located in Southern California—many with fifty or fewer employees—are not members of the Association of Pulp and Paper Manufacturers, and they have been less unionized and have paid lower wage rates than in pulp and paper. Prices have been more directly subject to supply and demand forces, and labor is a higher percentage of total cost in paper converting than in pulp manufacture. Profitability of the paper converting mills has varied greatly. Sometimes commercial pulp mills have been unprofitable while paper converting was profitable, or both unprofitable while newsprint production was profitable, or vice versa. The strain on the relationship has tended to be least when Southern California mills have been profitable and Washington mills unprofitable, because this has led to the greatest uniformity of outlook on both sides.

Each mill has committed itself prior to each negotiating session to be bound by majority decisions. Settlements have been reached which were unsatisfactory to some mills, and these mills have voted against acceptance. None, however, has ever failed to fulfill the commitment to accept the end result (although the manufacturers' association had to use strong persuasion to keep at least one Southern California member from withdrawing).

The difficulties on the union side have been more intense. This is particularly true of Washington locals which have had to contend with rival unionism from the CIO. Some Washington locals have voted against the terms of the new contracts, and even refused to sign; but the Oregon and California locals have always voted to accept. Through the international union's power to execute agreements and expel or reorganize recalcitrant locals, and through use of the maintenance-of-membership clause to discipline dissident leaders and members, the uniform coast-wide wage structure has been maintained. Only appropriate action by both sides has maintained this peaceful relationship on those occasions when the excess of needs felt by some Washington locals over the expected capacity of certain Southern California mills has threatened disruption.

The achievement of industrial peace in the West Coast pulp and paper industry has not been cost-free. But the advantages have outweighed the costs in all the relevant balance sheets—those of the industry, the unions, the workers, and the public as a whole.

A POSTSCRIPT

A review of industrial relations in the pulp and paper industry reveals that there has been no significant change in the relationship of the parties. The analysis and the conclusions remain unaffected by whatever minor changes have occurred. The parties continue to resolve their problems in a peaceful manner. The 1949 recession, for example, was smoothly hurdled; and the problem of matching sawmill labor rates was amicably adjusted in 1950 when the pulp and paper industry negotiated a health and welfare plan in lieu of the wage increases achieved in the sawmills. The parties, in brief, continue to coexist in harmony, "politically" and economically.

CHAPTER 8 _____

Libbey-Owens-Ford
Glass Company
and the Glass Workers (CIO)

FREDERICK H. HARBISON, *Executive Officer of the Industrial Relations Center, University of Chicago, and* KING CARR, *then on the staff of that Center and now with the Bureau of the Budget, are authors of NPA Case Study No. 2. Their full report, condensed in this chapter, was published in October 1948.*

Since the early thirties the Libbey-Owens-Ford Glass Company has been bargaining with the Federation of Glass, Ceramic and Silica Sand Workers of America (CIO) and its predecessor. During these years there have been sitdowns, slowdowns, work stoppages, and two prolonged and costly company-wide strikes. In an over-all view, the pattern of labor-management relations in the flat glass industry is the same as the pattern in other mass-production industries, where the struggle for power between labor and management has not been free from conflict.

Certainly, the Libbey-Owens-Ford case is no model of the perfect relationship. Nor were there any spectacular conversions of individuals in either the company or the union. Neither side boasts of success or claims to have set a new standard of industrial harmony. This case portrays a collective bargaining relationship which seems to be growing away from its era of strife and rivalry. Both the company and the union appear to be maturing—each acquiring a seasoned understanding of its respective objectives and each looking at the collective relationship in a practical and reasoned, rather than emotional, frame of mind. Representing progress rather than perfection, this case seems a possible pattern for the future—one that may have an appeal to practical leaders in labor and industry alike.

The Parties to the Relationship

Libbey-Owens-Ford Glass Company and the Pittsburgh Plate Glass Company together produce about 95 per cent of the nation's plate glass, including about 55 per cent of the window glass, and over 90 per cent of the safety plate and safety sheet glass used in the automotive industry. While Pittsburgh Plate also manufactures a variety of other products, LOF is primarily a producer of flat glass. Libbey-Owens-Ford operates eight flat glass plants with about 7500 hourly-paid workers. All four plants in Toledo, Ohio, employ 3900 workers; one in Shreveport, Louisiana, employs 767 workers; one in Charleston, West Virginia, 1519; and two in Ottawa, Illinois, 1107.

Glass workers, like auto, steel, and electrical workers, are semiskilled production employees working in fairly large plants with highly mechanized operations. Because they have much the same environment as other mass-production workers, they are a fair cross section of America's working class.

From the standpoint of labor relations, the important economic factors in glass manufacture are:

1. Capital investment per worker and labor costs in the flat glass industry closely resemble those in other mass-production industries. Libbey-Owens-Ford tries to keep labor productivity high in order to spread fixed costs over a large output volume, and so continually extends an incentive system of wage payment.

2. Constant changes in technology and processes, required to meet changed demands of automobile producers, have a far-reaching effect on work assignments and wage rates.

3. Safety glass is sold mainly to the automobile manufacturers. Because it is usually furnished on a fixed-price basis for a year at a time, the variable element is the quantity sold, and this is geared to volume of automobile production.

Management at LOF

The management structure of Libbey-Owens-Ford is compact. The top executive group and practically all the plant managers have had long service with the company, and are to a large extent home-grown. In LOF's top management group, the four executives who have shaped labor policy are John Biggers, the president; D. H. Goodwillie, the executive vice-president; L. G. Bryan, vice-president in charge of production; and C. W. Davis, general factories superintendent. The result of their teamwork is a remarkably consistent approach and policy on labor relations at the top management level, which is well understood and accepted without question by those in charge of operating the plants.

Throughout the LOF organization, operating executives develop, determine, and administer labor relations policy, which they consider perhaps their most important production problem. The industrial relations department serves in a staff and advisory capacity to executives and plant managers.

Top management believes strongly in the principle of decentralized management and in its corollary, interplant competition, as a means of developing efficient management. In a basic expression of this belief, LOF gives its plant managers responsibility and authority and pays them a fixed salary and substantial bonuses commensurate with plant production and costs.

The LOF management, like that in other enterprises, is in business to make a profit. But beyond that, the top executives feel that they have a broad responsibility and obligation to provide steady employment at good pay for their workers and at the same time to provide better glass at reasonable prices to their customers.[1] Their ability to discharge these responsibilities is dependent on production of a large volume of glass at low cost, improvement of its quality, and maintenance and expansion of markets for the various kinds of glass that the company manufactures.

The Union

The organization of the Glass Workers, like the LOF management structure, is compact. The Federation of Glass, Ceramic and Silica Sand Workers is a small union compared with its sister organizations in the CIO. Of its 30,000 members, 10,000 work at Pittsburgh Plate and 7500 at Libbey-Owens-Ford. Thus its backbone is in "Big Glass." White-collar

[1] The sales and marketing problems of LOF lie beyond the scope of the study, but one aspect of these problems bears on labor-management relations. Libbey-Owens-Ford and Pittsburgh Plate are often cited by textbook writers as a dual monopoly. In 1948, they were both involved in suits brought under the Sherman Antitrust Act in the Government's drive against "virtual monopolies." Some people will undoubtedly feel that the relationship described in this study is made possible mainly by the favorable position of this company in its industry, and thus by its favorable price situation. With respect to this contention, two facts should be considered: (1) Most mass-production industries during 1947 and 1948 were in the same favorable price situation, i.e., a sellers' market in which they could set their own prices. (2) If the monopoly factor were controlling in making good relations possible, then the relationship at Pittsburgh Plate Glass should be about the same as that at LOF. Such is not the case. The LOF relationship is generally considered to be much more harmonious than that at Pittsburgh Plate. For these reasons, it is felt that the Committee's criterion in regard to a monopolistic condition does not disqualify LOF for study. This report is devoted primarily to labor relations at the plant level.

workers are members as well as production workers. In spite of its small size, the union enjoys a remarkably secure position.

After a hectic history of internal dissension and factionalism, the union now has a closely knit and stable group of international officers and local union presidents. The international president, Joseph Froesch, its first vice-president, Leland Beard, and Lewis McCracken, its secretary-treasurer, have served continuously since 1942; Ralph Reiser became second vice-president in 1943 and the head of the largest local, in Toledo, William Akos, has served since 1943. With all its security and with these and other examples of the continuity of service of officers, the Glass Workers is a democratic organization. The rights of the locals are rigorously safeguarded. International officers are elected by referendum vote every two years. There is substantial participation in local elections, partly because voting is in the plants rather than in the union hall. The union staff's payroll is kept to a minimum; there are only four international officers, five district presidents, and eight organizers; and the local's only full-time officer usually is the president.

Bargaining in Perspective

The history of this LOF-Glass Workers relationship goes back to 1917, when the present company's predecessor signed a contract with the Window Glass Cutters' League of America covering highly skilled craftsmen in its Charleston plant. Gradually, collective bargaining with the craft union was extended to other LOF and Pittsburgh Plate plants, and in 1933, the Cutters' League started organizing the unskilled and semi-skilled workers into the Federation of Flat Glass Workers. Locals at LOF's Toledo and Ottawa plants were quickly and easily organized, and within a year the Federation had signed up 10,000 members. Thereafter, the 1500 craft-minded members of the Cutters' League became fearful of being swallowed up by this new industrial union they had organized, and in 1934 they severed relations with the Federation. The Federation was affiliated with the AFL in 1934, but in 1936 joined the CIO. In 1940, its name was changed to the Federation of Glass, Ceramic and Silica Sand Workers of America.

The Federation won recognition in LOF plants with little display of force. The first test of strength came in 1936 when the Federation struck the Pittsburgh Plate plants and, soon after, LOF's. The union demanded of both companies an increase of 8 cents per hour, a settlement of inter-company inequities, a formal system of joint bargaining with the two companies, and the closed shop. The union won its wage demands;

agreement on the issue of joint negotiations; agreement that a joint commission would study wage differentials between the two companies as a basis for future joint negotiations of basic wages; but was forced to drop its union-security demand.

The lid blew off in the glass industry after the end of the war. In 1945, a thirteen-week industry-wide strike was touched off by a series of incidents in LOF's Ottawa plant. As in other mass-production industries, there was marked improvement in labor-management relations when the men returned to work. Since 1945, the seriousness of strikes has been in the back of the minds of every union leader and company executive. They feel that the strike may have helped to impress all concerned with their responsibilities, and thus, indirectly, the strike may be partially responsible for the present relationship.

Even so, it has taken years for the present relationship and attitudes to develop. Union and company people never speak of a turning point in their relationship, but in the history of bargaining these factors should be borne in mind:

1. "Big Glass" recognized mass-production unions three years earlier than the major steel, automobile, rubber, and electrical manufacturers. The start of collective bargaining in glass was gradual and relatively peaceful in contrast to strife over initial recognition in other mass-production industries. Neither party was bitter toward the other.

2. By 1936, the Glass Workers had what amounted to industry-wide bargaining and was pressing for the union shop. The union-security issue, now fairly well settled in glass, is still a thorny issue between other large employers and large unions.

3. The company and the workers at LOF have enjoyed a considerable measure of economic progress since collective bargaining began. The company's net worth grew from about $35 million in 1936 to $45 million in 1945. The company is continuing to grow. It has made a profit in every year since 1933. It has consistently held its own with its principal competitor, Pittsburgh Plate Glass, both in technology and customers. On the union side, in the last ten years, workers' basic wage rates have almost doubled, and take-home pay has been further increased by substantial bonus earnings.

Agreement Making Through Industry-Wide Bargaining

"Big Glass" did not merely capitulate to union demands when the two companies agreed to bargain jointly. Rather the companies sought stability in the movement of base wages and looked upon joint bargaining as a means of protection from the union's whipsawing tactics. Neither company would let itself be used against the other; nor would the locals work against each.

Joint negotiations, at least theoretically, result in the same base wage rates for comparable jobs in both companies and determine their movement upward or downward. In practice, however, joint bargaining has not standardized wages or labor costs between the two companies because they have different piece-rate and bonus systems and some differences in production processes and operations. Although inequities between the two companies were settled as of 1940 on the basis of the report of a Joint Commission on Wage Rates established in 1937, the average earnings of employees in comparable classifications show wide variations. The joint negotiations affect the smaller manufacturers, comprising "Little Glass," since their contracts negotiated with the union closely follow the pattern set by "Big Glass."

"Big Glass": Pattern Follower

With the key plants of Pittsburgh Plate located in the Pittsburgh area, wages and working conditions of glass workers are directly influenced by negotiations in the steel industry; with LOF's major plants located in the Detroit area, negotiations are vitally affected by automobile patterns.

The union and the companies arranged their negotiations in 1946, 1947, and 1948 so that they might bargain after other key national wage patterns had been determined. To eliminate internal wage whipsawing, they strike a balance between the external whipsawing between autos and steel. A cardinal objective of the Glass Workers has been to win economic benefits at least equal to those won by potential rival unions. Even within the CIO, the Glass Workers is open to raiding by other larger unions. It must be able to deliver at least as much, if not more, to glass workers than adjacent unions obtain for their members. In addition, the union must keep up with the patterns of the AFL-affiliated craft unions. So far, the Glass Workers has held its own.

Joint Negotiations with the Glass Workers

In the 1941 contract "Big Glass" agreed "to continue the present practice of cooperating with the union to the best interests of both parties." This was defined during off-the-record talks to mean that employees would have to join the union and pay dues.

This measure of union security was finally granted because the companies had recognized that they were better off dealing with a union run by glass workers than one which might be dominated by steel or automobile workers. By giving the Federation a measure of security, the companies probably figured that they would be spared some of the headaches of interunion rivalries and jurisdictional disputes. A large majority of the workers in most of the plants were already members and several plant managers had been cooperating in getting all eligible workers into the union as a means of avoiding strife between members and nonmembers.

The informal cooperative arrangement was formalized and made uniform for all plants in 1946. Under this agreement, if the union had not secured voluntary membership of an employee during the first thirty days of employment, the company would immediately try to do so. If, within thirty days after that notice, the employee had not paid his initiation fee and regular dues from the date of employment, he would be terminated. The union seems to be satisfied with this provision, although it differs from some union-shop provisions in the sense that the companies are under no obligation to discharge a worker who is not a union member in good standing, but only if he fails to join and make specified financial contributions to the union. Since it is technically a union-shop clause under the Taft-Hartley Act, its continuance would seem to require an election, but LOF has assured the union that it will "publicly and privately" recommend to its employees that they vote to retain the present provision.

The procedure of joint contract negotiation appears on balance to be satisfactory to the parties concerned. The companies and the union generally feel that the joint negotiation process provides an orderly means of moving together and keeping in step with the economic pattern of the steel and automobile industries. Some company officials and local union presidents, however, believe that LOF would be better off bargaining by itself. But no one is seriously proposing individual contract bargaining, largely because both groups realize that cutthroat wage competition would never be permitted by the companies or union; and more important, because both sides have found that the contract establishes only the framework for settlement of crucial issues in individual plant bargaining.

LOF's Collective Bargaining under the Agreement

A fairly consistent and logical pattern is apparent in the collective bargaining process at Libbey-Owens-Ford. The company knows what it wants; its labor policy, though not written out in formal terms, is positive and clear-cut. The union has definite objectives. Both parties have been remarkably successful in defining the areas of common and conflicting interests and in working out reasonably satisfactory compromises on points where their aims are in conflict. Mutual trust is based primarily on the fact that each side can predict, with reasonable certainty, the actions and reactions of the other.

Wages and Production

Since production of a large volume of glass at low cost is the company's aim, full utilization of its plant facilities in which there is a large investment is important. About 40 per cent of the cost of making glass goes for wages. Thus positive cooperation of the workers can be a tremendous asset in getting maximum production.

Over 70 per cent of LOF's production employees are compensated on an incentive wage system. For 76 per cent of the men this standard is set for a group which varies in size from 3 to 300 men. The base rates for jobs are set in joint negotiations, but production standards used for determining bonus earnings are established at the local level. Such standards are an important wage-setting element, since the bonus usually comprises at least 30 per cent of total earnings of affected workers.

The mechanics of the rate-setting process for hourly-paid employees is rather simple. If a job is created which is new to a plant, the local union and plant management check with their main offices to see if the job exists elsewhere in the company. If so, the base rate already in effect is automatically assigned. If not, or if there is a disagreement between the company and union as to whether it is new or old, descriptions of similar jobs are sent to the plant's union and management, who then try to agree on a base rate. If agreed to, the rate goes into effect when approved by the company's director of industrial relations and the union's first vice-president. In case of disagreement, the company's proposed rate goes into effect and, if disputed, is handled as a regular grievance. (Pertinent sections of the 1946–47 LOF Agreement are given in an appendix to *Case Study No. 2.*)

In the case of bonus rates, the local union and management—through time study and negotiation—next determine how many units an average worker must produce in order to realize his full bonus possibility. They have agreed that an average worker, at normal incentive rate of production, should earn his base rate plus 35 per cent of base rate as bonus. About 86 per cent of bonus workers are on a 50-50 constant-sharing system, which means that the company splits 50-50 with the employee on all units produced above the production standard. In case of disagreement on the production standard, the company's proposed rate goes into effect, and if disputed by the union, the matter is settled as a grievance.

By 1947, LOF and the Glass Workers had apparently reached a working agreement on this fundamental matter of incentives. The LOF executives felt that their company's productive efficiency was exceptionally good and that it was improving constantly. They had no complaints about men refusing to do a fair day's work for fair pay. On the other side, the earnings of production workers were at an all-time high, and their take-home pay, according to union estimates, was at least 20 cents per hour more than that received by comparable workers in Pittsburgh Plate and at least 23 cents per hour above the average for workers in the nearby automobile plants. Furthermore, the union and men were not worried about the tempo of the work. "Nobody is killing himself," one leader explained. "The boys are just turning out the glass because they know that the union will protect their rates."

The parties believe there are certain factors which are basic to their successful administration of the incentive system:

1. The emphasis on a 50-50 sharing system is psychologically important in gaining worker acceptance of the incentive principle. Negotiation is more flexible because the determination of the production standard is less critical to management since it shares equally on *all* units produced above the production standard. It is easy for union leaders to sell the 50-50 principle, and it illustrates to members the extent of the union's job control.

2. Bonus rates on a job cannot be changed by the company unless there is a change in method or process. The union has a guarantee that management will not reduce rates as worker output increases on existing jobs. When management decides it needs more production and if the union agrees, the union can (and has many times) persuade the workers down the line "to raise it up a little."

3. Each side avoids making an issue over *authority* and *right* to set or approve rates. The company is required under the contract to confer with the union on all new rates, but it has the *right* to establish such a rate if it is unable to come to an agreement with the union. As a practical matter, the company negotiates the rate with the union before it is put in, because the union has an ultimate right of protest and the union's prior approval clearly outweighs other considerations.

4. The company is under pressure to install the rate as quickly as possible because the agreement provides that it must pay a worker his average bonus until the rate on the job goes into effect; a worker with this

guarantee has no practical reason for expending any more effort than he would under a day rate.

5. The incentive to produce under the bonus system is buttressed by continuous management effort to show workers that job security is dependent on high efficiency. The fear of workers that their jobs will be eliminated by new processes and new machines which can produce more efficiently is a further incentive.

Reactions to Rate Setting

A secure union is perhaps as interested as management in a rational rate structure, because it minimizes strife. One out-of-line rate can create hundreds of inequities. The union leader has an interest in time study or any other approach which tries to relate job values, so long as he has some control over it. Often union officials at LOF time the jobs jointly with a representative of the industrial engineering department, but in all cases accept time study only as a guide in final rate determination. Basically, union negotiators judge a rate primarily on how they think the workers will make out.

The present LOF operating people also seem to feel that rates cannot be set by time study alone. They want to know "what the boys *will* turn out on the rate, not what they *can* turn out." If the rates are never considered O.K. by the union and informal groups in the shop, as well as by the individual, the rate never will be given a chance to prove its validity. The company will negotiate a rate higher than the one scientifically determined if that is the price for getting the employees to work all-out under it. The price is considered small if, in addition, management can persuade the men to go along with such changes as the introduction of new machinery.

Some of the executives and industrial engineers call this kind of rate setting "appeasement." They feel that it creates inequities and, if continued, will result in a rate structure out of line with that prevailing in the community or the industry, and one which will put the company in the squeeze when prices drop and the men cut back their production to spread the jobs around. But top operating people at LOF take this view with a grain of salt. They fully realize that the wage structure is loose but do not believe that the men will ever cut production back to prewar levels. In this belief they are supported to a degree by the opinion of many union officials.

The union and the men understand that the bonus system and the present rate-setting process are, in effect, a profit-sharing system. They know that they have to keep production up and many of them also realistically recognize that, at some time in the future, out-of-line rates will have to be adjusted as they come up for restudy with changes in production processes and methods. Leland Beard, frequently referred to as the LOF man in the international, has said: "LOF has always treated us right for those months of the year when they needed the glass. The only difference is that now they need it badly all twelve months. Nothing in the history of our relationship indicates that this present era will continue. We certainly hope it will and you can be sure that we'll do everything to help, but too much optimism would be unwarranted and unhealthy."

If production per man is kept near the 40 per cent bonus level and if other costs and prices either cancel themselves out or change little, top company officials see little danger in the present rate policy. They ask, "What would be the result of a tight policy pursued at this time in anticipation of poor market conditions and large cutbacks in production by individual workers?" They answer their own question this way: "Labor trouble today, and no hope of labor peace in the case of a downswing later."

Both sides are primarily concerned with today's problems. At the same time, they do not believe they are jeopardizing their chances for a sound solution to future wage or other union-management problems. A settlement of today's problems may be outmoded by any one of several possible changes in, for instance, market or raw material situations, but the *manner* of settling those problems can be applied to these other situations when they arise. Their real achievement has not been their contract or their wages, they say, but rather their way of working together.

Security and Seniority

The main objectives of the Glass Workers, like other mass-production unions, are seniority and security. More money is important, according to union officials, but the ability to get it depends on the extent of union control over jobs. As one official puts it: "This union was organized on the seniority issue—and seniority today is the thing which the workers still hold most important."

Layoffs and rehiring are based almost exclusively on straight seniority. The senior employee is promoted, in practice, if he can handle the job, and the burden of proof rests upon management to show that he is not able to perform the work. Management officials recall their dire predictions in 1936 of what was going to happen when departmental seniority went into effect. They were amazed to find that after two weeks production was back up to its normal level.

Top LOF officials indicate that seniority has not been a problem in most of the plants; that it has not unduly restricted the selection of qualified workers for promotion; and that it has not impaired over-all efficiency to a noticeable degree. The reasons seem to be that the union, along with management, is interested in increasing output under the bonus system. Since an incompetent worker can be a liability to his whole group, the union does not demand that the senior employee be given preference unless he is qualified. And in the few cases where preference is not demanded by the union, employees are more likely to accept the decision than if management had made it. The union can take such a reasonable and responsible position in seniority cases because it is secure and it knows that management is not only cooperating to build membership but that it is not trying to break down the seniority system.

Managerial Rights

Both parties have learned to avoid managerial rights as an issue in bargaining. The LOF policy is to exercise its functions, but not to define them specifically or defend them as such. This is apparent in LOF's habit of getting union acceptance before bonus rates are put into effect; of invariably consulting the union in advance of exercising management's right to schedule operations, introduce new machinery, and speed up processes, and usually before taking any disciplinary action. Managerial decisions are implemented by making them acceptable to employees.

The company, apparently, has learned to operate this way as a result of some tough going with the union in the past. The 1945 strike is a case in point. It grew out of LOF's decision to open in its Ottawa plant a line which had been idle during the war. Although the bonus rate was subject to an unsettled grievance when the line was shut down, and union officials warned that the men would not go back to work on it until the bonus was changed, management gave the order for resumption of operations. At the time, all local and international union officers and company executives were trying to negotiate a new agreement. The union officers after some discussion agreed that technically the company had the right to start the line, but by then the Ottawa local had shut down the plant and the local and international officers were unable to get the men back to work. Meanwhile, LOF and Pittsburgh Plate served notice that as a matter of principle they would not negotiate further on the new contract while the men were on strike. The issue, the companies said, was union responsibility. The union countered by calling an authorized strike in all plants of both companies. The economic power appears to have been equal. Since that time the company has become convinced that it is useless to ask union leaders to do things which are "politically" impossible. Both sides seem to feel that talking about principles rather than practical problems can be dangerous.

To LOF executives, union responsibility is not something which is secured by contract clause or federal law. To them, a union is responsible if it tries to sell the men in the shop on something which may be unpopular but desirable in the interest of all; and if it reports the straight story on union-management meetings.

DAY-TO-DAY BARGAINING IN THE PLANTS

The Glass Workers and LOF have a broad concept of day-to-day bargaining. To both, it is a means of continuous communication on an ever-increasing number of mutual problems: production, seniority, scheduling, discipline, absenteeism, safety, and so on. As the spokesman of workers, the union wants to be "in the know" and to "put out the word." The company wants the union's help in getting the workers' slant on managerial problems and in explaining important managerial decisions to the men in the shop.

Grievances

Grievance handling is flexible and informal, keyed to settling problems, not making rules. The formal grievance machinery in the contract is typical of that commonly found in the mass-production industries—a grievance ascends by steps from employee-foreman level to top management and international officers where, if no agreement is reached, it is submitted to arbitration.

The pressure is on plant managers to "keep grievances away from the Nicholas building"—the company's main office—even though this means less company-wide uniformity in rate standards and procedures. At the same time, the union feels that most of its day-to-day problems are best settled at the plants. The local unions, being anxious to preserve their independence, want to show that they can get things settled quickly right on the home lot. In general, the union likes the local-autonomy tradition and is hesitant to jeopardize it no matter how strong the desire to win a concession obtained at another plant.

In 1947, an estimated 98 per cent of the formal grievances were resolved at the plant level, and there were no arbitration cases. Most of the plant-level grievances are settled by the foremen and union's grievance men. The supervisory force is acclimated to the union-management relationship because LOF has trained and promoted its own workers to supervisory positions; many of them have been union members or officers. The international union and the company's main office play a role similar to the contract—in the background, but constant counselors and sources of strength.

Both parties want issues settled promptly, so the grievance procedure is frequently short cut, especially in the plants. A case that is not settled with the foreman may go to the plant superintendent or to top plant management in a matter of hours. Unlike the old days recalled by some union officers, plant managers are now readily available to union officers and will discuss any mutual problems, both because their superiors want it that way and because they can see that as a practical matter it pays off in square feet of glass.

Although most grievances are settled by informal conference, regular monthly meetings of the union's industrial relations committee and plant management are being continued. At these, both management and the union can submit grievances, although recently the matters discussed have been general in nature. These regular meetings are considered important because, in addition to discussions of general problems, they afford an opportunity to educate new management representatives and union committeemen in the workings of the relationship.

Information Sharing

The endless hours which LOF management spends discussing problems with the union representatives have a practical purpose. Management has a case to sell, and through frequent contact with union officers it has a better chance to put the company's story across and to find out what is in the workers' minds. At LOF, the executives seek out the union to discuss matters which many other management officials are fighting *not* to discuss with unions.

The union is given information on all bonus earnings so that individual employee complaints can be checked immediately. Departmental production schedules tell union officials how much glass is being turned out. The union is always informed of changes in production schedules, and so can immediately allay possible rumors. The company discusses with the union proposed changes in processes and introduction of new machinery. If it could not introduce new processes and machinery, shift work from less efficient to more efficient plants, and make more products with less manpower, LOF's very survival would be in jeopardy. There is clear evidence that union-management consultation, which usually precedes such technological change, has helped to implement management decisions.

The company continually keeps before the union the problem of competition: competition between plants, between LOF and other glass manufacturers, and between existing production processes and possible laborsaving changes. (This does not include competition between departments or individuals within different plants.) The campaign to produce glass cheaply is also carried on by union officials, who explain the issue to the men in this way: "So long as the company is making money off men, they aren't going to tie up money in a machine. Buying a machine is taking a big risk for the company; they've got to use it for years to get their money back. But they'll either make money off you, or they'll buy a machine that they know they can make money on." Since, with the bonus system, increased output accrues to the worker's immediate advantage, technological changes to meet competition are somewhat more palatable to the workers. There is no doubt that the talk of competition and the importance of costs have been imprinted on the workers' minds.

Even when management reserves the right to make a decision, if it directly affects the men and the union, the company officials find out the union's reaction and will make their decision in light of that reaction. In most plants, for example, management lets the men determine their own daily starting times and even allows groups to have different times if their work is independent. In scheduling operations the union is consulted, and when possible given a choice of alternatives and allowed to take the question to the members. As L. G. Bryan, vice-president in charge of production, stated: "We simply try to put ourselves in the other fellow's place and think the thing through from that angle. Then we try to reach a fair solution based on as good an understanding of all sides of the question as we can get."

ATTITUDES OF THE COMPANY AND THE UNION

Management does not compete with the union for the allegiance of LOF workers. It feels, apparently, that an individual who is an ardent member of a strong union also can be a loyal member of the company's team. The company is careful, however, not to endorse publicly any individual union leader; it stays out of the union's internal affairs, although it is aware of the importance of management decisions to the future of individual union leaders. Because of LOF's attitude, the union can itself express allegiance to the company through its actions in the plant, and can even do so on paper in joint union-management statements to the men. For example, such statements were issued after the 1945–46 strike, the 1947 negotiations, and the 1947 wage reopening conference. (Excerpts from these statements appear in *Case Study No. 2.*)

The union and the company have good reputations in their communities and take active parts in local civic affairs. The company in recent years has bolstered the reputation of the union wherever possible, apparently recognizing that a union which is well integrated in the community will not strike to gain entirely unreasonable objectives. On its side, the union leadership knows full well that when major demands are made to the employer and a strike is in the offing, it will need the sympathy and support of the community.

The Union's View

Local union officers who deal with LOF appear to have a great deal of respect for the company. The company's preference for dealing with strong local unions is to these officers an indication of its intelligence and smartness, rather than of any idealistic belief in labor organizations. Basically, the union respects the company for following a labor policy which is good business as far as management is concerned.

The international union officers are more skeptical. They say they prefer dealing with LOF executives to those in certain other companies because the LOF people know what the problems are, what company policy is for settling them, what the company wants, and so they get decisions more quickly and easily. But the international officers have doubts about LOF's avowed acceptance of unionism. They point to the company's attitude toward the locals of the white-collar workers in the Glass Workers. LOF has opposed these locals because it says that office workers and production workers should not belong to the same international union. To this contention a union officer snapped, "The real reason is that they haven't figured out yet how the office workers can help them get out the glass."

The union also worries somewhat about the competition among LOF plants. It does not think that interplant competition has yet resulted in wage competition, but it is making studies to be certain that this has not and will not happen. Only a few jobs in competing plants are directly comparable, so base rates—theoretically the same—and production standards vary considerably. But the international emphasizes, "We will never let our locals be pitted against each other."

Admitting that the present LOF executives have an intelligent labor policy, these union officials are still afraid of executives who might some day take their places. And, finally, this point was raised: "LOF is really playing ball for the moment. But, if 'Big Steel' and 'Big Auto' start to bust unions under the Taft-Hartley Law, they'll pull LOF along with them. We must always keep on guard."

The union has not won all its objectives. It would like an ironclad understanding that the company would take disciplinary action only after consultation with and approval by the union. It would like more control over decisions to introduce new processes and machinery; and probably more control over jobs if production and employment should be curtailed in the glass plants.

Management's View

LOF officials think they have seen a change come over the leadership of the Glass Workers during the past few years. They think these leaders have found that their prestige is increased and their standing in the union better assured by their being responsible. They say the union leadership is showing more courage in saying no to the troublesome few who would like to boost themselves at the expense of the other members. And management likes the personal character of the present union leaders. Various union officials have often been characterized publicly by management in such terms as "tireless workers," or "a dedicated man who is in the union only to do what he can for the glass workers," or "the most honest man I've ever known." There are no charges that union leaders are conniving politicians or racketeers.

But management is not completely satisfied. It does not want the union to secure greater control over jobs. It recognizes that the union directly or indirectly can prevent the company from achieving its goals. Although it regards unions as "political" organizations, management would probably prefer that they be more like business organizations. The company has no absolute guarantee that the contract will be honored; it has no assurance that the union will continue to cooperate in increasing output. It cannot prevent irresponsible union leadership from rising to power. Finally, there is always apprehension that the union might seriously interfere with legitimate managerial functions.

Management's only real security, it feels, lies in the *hope* that it can help to create intelligent and realistic human relations which will continue to result in stronger and more responsible unions in its plants and in the kind of constructive relationship which has existed in the past few years.

Favorable economic conditions have affected the development of the present constructive relationship. In the event of a depression, the company and the union would have to cope with different and more serious problems. It is futile to predict how this kind of relationship might stand up under adverse economic conditions. But the experience gained in the process of union-management consultation and cooperation in the past years will help both sides to face new problems with greater realism and keener insight. The development of a sound labor-management relationship where each side has confidence in and respect for the other is a tangible asset, making it possible for both company and union to work more effectively under any condition—whether favorable or adverse.

A Postscript

Little change has taken place at Libbey-Owens-Ford since October 1948 when the study was published. The central personalities, both in LOF and the union, are still there and are still convinced of the value of their ways of operating. Management continues to use the grievance machinery, broadly defined, as a means of communication with the union officers regarding proposed new rates, production schedules, and all other matters affecting employees. Rates for new jobs and changed operations, in effect, are negotiated rates. Decentralization of labor relations responsibility to plant managers is even more strongly insisted upon by the top company officials in Toledo. And they stress the importance of understanding the "political" situation faced by union leaders. The basic wage structure follows steel and auto patterns. Union security is, if anything, tighter, not in formal terms, but terms of management attitudes. The union considers the LOF arrangement a strong union shop. Bonus earnings at LOF continue to boost take-home pay above take-home pay in other manufacturing plants in the company's environs. There have been no strikes or arbitrations. All outward evidence indicates the continuing validity of the most significant elements of the original study.

CHAPTER 9

The Dewey and Almy
Chemical Company

and the Chemical Workers (AFL)

DOUGLAS McGREGOR, *Professor of Management, School of Industrial Management, Massachusetts Institute of Technology*, and JOSEPH N. SCANLON, *Industrial Relations Section, Massachusetts Institute of Technology, are authors of* NPA Case Study No. 3. *Their full report, condensed in this chapter, was published in December 1948.*

This is the story of a peaceful and healthy union-management relationship. It is not a spectacular story, but one which demonstrates that warfare and strife between a union and management are not inevitable. It supports the conclusion that peace and health are natural, if a few fundamental but inherently simple requirements are met.

The Dewey and Almy Chemical Company, founded in 1919, employs slightly under 1500 people in its administrative offices, research laboratories, and plants throughout the world. The total employment in two Cambridge, Massachusetts, plants—the major plants with which this study deals—is about 1100. Of these, approximately 550 are hourly-rated factory employees, 200 of them women. (Statistics on the number of hourly-rated employees from 1934–47, on their seniority distribution in 1939 and 1947, and on age distribution in 1940 and 1947, are given in Tables 1, 2, and 3 of *Case Study No. 3.*)

The company could be classified in the chemical industry, as its name implies, or, being a manufacturer in eight different fields, it could be classified, for example, as a part of the shoe industry, the textile industry, or rubber industry. Most of its output is sold to other manufacturers rather than directly to distributors or consumers.

Dewey and Almy, which in many of its lines faces stiff competition, is a reasonably successful enterprise. Its growth has been steady, but not spectacular. Its fixed assets (at cost) grew from $188,000 in 1924 to $8,132,000 in 1947; dividends in 1924 were $9000 and in 1947 were $430,000; net earnings in 1924 were $20,000, and in 1947 were $671,000; sales in 1924 were $418,000, and in 1947 were $14,260,000. (In *Case Study No. 3,* Table 4 gives figures for intervening years, and Appendix A reproduces the Dewey and Almy Annual Report for 1947.) Since 1941, net earnings have not risen proportionately with sales, because of a variety of cost and price factors, but neither worker productivity nor wages has been unduly important among these. With some of the company's products, labor productivity and spoilage are major factors in economic success; in other lines, product quality and readiness to meet unpredictable customer needs are critical.

Whereas the diversification of products has provided relatively stable employment, it has created problems in collective bargaining, particularly with respect to demands that the company conform to industry practice. The company pays wages and salaries and provides benefits for its employees above the average of all the industries to which it belongs, and above the average of the community generally. This would not have been economically possible if Dewey and Almy had operated exclusively in certain of the industries to which it belongs.

All in all, the company has not bought labor peace at the expense of financial stability. That stockholders believe in Dewey and Almy's financial stability is attested by the current public evaluation of its stock at 22 as against a book value of 13.

This relationship began in 1939 when the Cambridge plants of the company were unionized as a Federal Charter Union (a union combining all crafts and skills) of the American Federation of Labor. In 1945, the local shifted to the International Chemical Workers Union (AFL). There is a union-shop provision and automatic check-off of dues. The bargaining unit includes all production, maintenance, and machine shop workers, except firemen and oilers, whose contract with the International Brotherhood of Firemen and Oilers (AFL) has been substantially the same as that of the production workers. (A brief description of the other unions with which the company deals appears in Appendix B, *Case Study No. 3.*) In general, the company's major personnel policies and employee benefits are identical in all its American plants and there are no important differences in contract provisions from one plant to the other. However, in the day-to-day administration of labor relations, local plant management is autonomous.

There has been one work stoppage in the history of the relationship between the company and the Chemical Workers in Cambridge. This, in 1943, involved a dozen employees in one small department, who struck over a wage rate. When settled after two days, all except one of the affected employees returned to work without incident and without change in rates. Since the union was recognized, two issues with the production workers and one with the firemen and oilers have gone to arbitration. On one occasion, a federal conciliator was called in briefly during negotiations.

It has been argued that union-management relations tend to develop through three stages: a militant stage; an administrative stage, after the union has been accepted, when both parties must develop new policies and procedures; and one in which the parties work together to improve the competitive position of the industrial enterprise for mutual gains of the union and of members of the company's organization, its stockholders, and its customers. Dewey and Almy and the Chemical Workers, like some other companies and unions, skipped the first stage almost completely. Even so, there were many problems, and there was one period of acute conflict before the parties achieved their peaceful and healthy relationship.

THE "CLIMATE" OF THE RELATIONSHIP

The history of the relationship between Dewey and Almy and the Chemical Workers may be roughly divided into three periods, although there was no definite beginning or end to them.

1. Well-meaning paternalism when the company's president negotiated the contract and the union took both minor and major grievances to the president.

2. Open antagonism to top management and the union by the company's middle and lower management.

3. Shift to new attitudes and skills in human relations on the part of both management and the union.

Organization of the Union

The organizational campaign at Dewey and Almy was started by the AFL in the winter of 1939 at the request of certain employees. After a mass meeting at which many employees signed membership cards in the union, the company was requested to recognize a Federal Charter Local, and to negotiate an agreement.

Management believes that pressure for union organization came chiefly from outside the company. The union officials believe there were only two important outside influences—the general nation-wide trend toward unionization and the successful organization of another plant in the vicinity. One other happening seems to have been important. A year or so earlier, Dewey and Almy's president had hired a personnel director, and many workers felt that if the president felt it necessary to bring in a man to deal with them, they needed a union to act as intermediary.

The situation prior to the organization of the union was neither good nor bad. The wage level was above the community average, but probably below the community average of unionized companies. There was a somewhat haphazard system of individual rather than job rates. There were few fringe benefits, but these were not then common in the community. Employment had been increasing since early in 1936, so there was no immediate threat to job security. Apart from wages, perhaps the chief source of employee dissatisfaction was the behavior of some of the men among the lower levels of management. Many workers felt there was favoritism and discrimination in work assignments, promotions, and pay rates.

When the organization drive took place, some company officials favored fighting unionization with a generous wage increase and an appeal to employee loyalty; others favored more militant, if indirect, antiunion tactics; some felt that unionization was inevitable sooner or later and that it would be a mistake to fight it. Under the regulations of the National Labor Relations Board, management could either agree voluntarily to a membership-card check, or it could demand that an election be held by the NLRB to determine whether the employees wished to be represented, and if so by what union. Unions generally considered that a company's refusal to submit the recognition issue to a voluntary card check indicated a policy of resistance.

Through several days of intense discussion Dewey and Almy's president listened to any and all opinions on the problem, including those of the regional director of the AFL. Although he was somewhat surprised—and perhaps a little hurt—at the success of the union, he recognized some of the reasons for unionization. He was not unaware of the weakness of his management organization, although he failed to see then how his own paternalism had helped to perpetuate this weakness. In the end, the president decided to recognize the union on the basis of a membership-card check.

Following the union's certification by the NLRB, the president made a determined effort to clear up uncertainty about unionism felt by many of the employees who had not joined. Because he adopted this attitude, all but a handful became and remained members. This early decision to afford the union some degree of acceptance significantly affected the stability and peace now in evidence.

The initial negotiations, carried on chiefly between the company's president and a regional AFL representative, were amicable in every way. The company, in return for the union's acceptance of certain principles which management regarded as essential, was reasonably generous with respect to union demands. Before the relationship could become healthy in the day-to-day sense, many problems had to be solved. Nevertheless, the faith of the company's president in the possibility of a sound union-management relationship was perhaps the most significant single determinant of the relationship that ultimately developed.

Contract Negotiations

During the first three or four years the Dewey and Almy relationship was complicated by the different structures of the two organizations. Management was accustomed to a certain kind of bargaining with its customers and suppliers, whose agreements made during discussions were binding. But the union officers and members of the negotiating committee, elected by the rank and file, were not given authority to bind the union, only to make certain demands. Negotiations would proceed for several days until a satisfactory set of terms had been worked out. Then the union's committee would go back to the membership and ask for ratification or rejection of each item in the agreed-upon list. The union members usually accepted the favorable terms and rejected the unfavorable ones. Considerable annoyance was generated in management when the union committee returned expecting to start further negotiations from the base of the earlier management concessions.

Eventually, management came to understand the nature of this problem and union officials to recognize why it made a farce of bargaining. They agreed to carry on negotiations in the conference room as though they were final. The resulting agreement, containing various compromises, could only be accepted or rejected as a whole by the union body. If rejected, the union could send the negotiating committee back to start over again, or elect a new committee. Except for one sad experience, during which the help of a U.S. conciliator was required to resolve the conflict without a strike, the union has never found it necessary to reject the agreement negotiated by its committee.

The president's paternalism created a second problem in negotiations, which were conducted with the union committee by three or four people in top management. The president was not in a position to see how well provisions of the previous contract had worked out on a day-to-day basis; nor could he adequately foresee the problems of middle and lower management in administering the new clauses of the contract. So long as he negotiated without consulting foremen or plant superintendents, the agreement was almost certain to contain unworkable clauses. Moreover, the spirit of the terms agreed upon was unknown to any but the negotiators themselves, so that later actions of other members of management did not necessarily conform to the intentions of the negotiators.

On their side, union negotiators reacted childishly to this paternalistic attitude. They would bring in a long list of demands, some patently unreasonable, without supporting evidence. Their attitude was "there is no harm in trying," and they frequently won concessions which they did not expect. Middle and lower management were in a difficult position because top management always gave in, and the tensions generated by these factors were greatly intensified during the war. Gradually, the president began to recognize that such bargaining was all give and no take. It became apparent that leniency and benevolence led merely to larger demands from the union and not necessarily to higher morale or more productivity.

More and more members of management were brought into the actual negotiations until representatives from every level of operating management were present. Management now enters negotiations with a list of demands, carefully thought out and evaluated beforehand. This has tended to change the whole character of the negotiations. Furthermore, management representatives at the negotiations are charged with the responsibility of keeping their associates fully informed as to what is going on. By the time the contract is finally completed, all members of the management organization are fully informed and have contributed to it.

The union, too, has changed its way of negotiating. There remains little of the "do it because it will make us happy" which flavored the old relationship. Union negotiators enter the conferences with complete readiness to discuss facts, examine evidence, consider the merits of the case. The members of the union's executive board seem to have a genuine respect for management's skill in collective bargaining. A few union representatives say that the company has become progressively tougher to deal with, but there is no evidence that this change has alienated the union or made the relationship worse. Members of the executive board are unanimous in stating that they are dealing with a fair and reasonable management organization, while they regard themselves as competent adversaries in the game of collective bargaining.

Paternalism had one important positive value in promoting the long-run health of the relationship. The company president gave the union needed support during its formative period, and convinced union officials of top management's fairness and sincere desire to establish healthy relations. There probably would have been a considerable period of acute conflict if the president and a few of his associates had not assumed personal responsibility for negotiation and administration of the agreement, since most of management lacked the vision and skill at that time to take on these responsibilities.

One other important factor in negotiations is the complete absence of a legalistic atmosphere. With few exceptions, the emphasis has been upon the spirit of the agreement rather than upon legal technicalities. The company president has always insisted, and demonstrated, that his word is as good as his bond. A violation of the union contract by either party is taken seriously by both, even if the violation is clearly inadvertent.

On the whole, it can be said today that the parties have learned how to negotiate successfully. Both are satisfied that their agreement is a good one. (Appendix C in *Case Study No. 3* presents excerpts from the 1947 agreement which seem most pertinent to this study.)

Administration of the Agreement

Day-to-day relations were plagued by the same problems as contract negotiations during the first years of the relationship. Top management, particularly the president, assumed almost exclusive responsibility for dealings with the union. This was perhaps inevitable since most of the men in lower and middle management were not sympathetic with the union, had not been trained in human relations, and were not adequately informed about the provisions or meaning of the labor agreement. A further cause of early discord grew out of the president's conception of the personnel department as a substitute for line management in labor relations. Union members tended to carry all problems to the president or the personnel director and to regard middle and lower management as unimportant and incompetent. By-passed by both workers and top management, the foremen and superintendents were frustrated and felt that their side of the story was neither heard nor understood.

Matters were brought to a head when the company's president accepted a war assignment in Washington early in 1943. The responsibility and most of the authority for personnel administration were delegated to a consultant who was given the title of director of industrial relations. This director formulated policies, settled grievances, became an official weeping post for union officials. The vice-president, the general manager, and the new director of industrial relations adopted the policy that it was necessary to avoid a strike at all costs, since the company was engaged almost entirely in filling contracts for the armed services and for lend lease. The rest of the line management viewed operation of this policy in terms of excessive leniency toward the union, a complete breakdown of effective discipline, union disregard of management prerogatives, and a general reduction of efficiency. They began to feel they could not operate the plants. Their antagonism toward the union and, even more, toward the personnel director—whom they regarded as champion of the union cause—became acute. Friction mounted, grievances arose over the tiniest details, arguments over literal and legalistic interpretations of work rules and policy became interminable.

Early in 1944, top management recognized the necessity for a major change. The vice-president and general manager agreed to assume full responsibility for labor relations, and the personnel function was redefined as a staff function, a purely advisory service to management. Middle and lower management were given full responsibility for administering the labor agreement. There was an immediate change for the better. The personnel department was able to assume an important and more natural role. Within six months most members of the line organization were relying heavily upon the personnel director for advice and counsel.

About this time a regular series of foremen conferences was started. Through them the foremen began to develop leadership skills and the foremen's responsibilities and authority were redefined. This, with the replacement of several individuals when it became clear that they could not learn how to manage people effectively, began a genuine strengthening of the line organization at all levels.

Today, line officers, including middle and lower management, have an understanding of collective bargaining, accept the union, and have reasonably adequate skill in administration.

Attitudes Toward Each Other

Attitudes of the union and management toward each other are genuinely friendly. All the way through the management organization, the "political" nature of the union organization and its consequences for collective bargaining are understood and accepted. Management often adjusts to these "political" necessities and protects the position of union officials, even if a concession which might not otherwise be reasonable is involved.

Union members in general openly express genuine confidence in top management and their belief that whatever happens they can count on the best break possible. Naturally, they feel that some members of management are better to deal with than others, and from time to time they become aroused over what they consider to be an unreasonable attitude on the part of an individual. These difficulties, however, tend to work themselves out. The member of management who cannot command the respect of the union is certain to receive the careful scrutiny of his superiors.

As in any such relationship, a few members on each side remain relatively hostile. Such individuals have not, however, interfered with the growth of a healthy and friendly relationship. The parties, by and large, discount the troublemakers, saying they cannot make bad relations unless other factors are present which undermine confidence.

Neither the management nor the union feels that there are any acute problems in their relationship today. Some management people point to a problem of worker-productivity, but they say a solution to this is largely management's responsibility, rather than the union's fault. Other company officials point to the need for demonstrating that union members enjoy a high degree of security, and further, for finding ways to increase it, but this can hardly be termed a problem. One or two of the top management representatives are concerned about the possible consequences of the trend toward industry-wide bargaining. The president, for example, fears a leveling effect on a good relationship if unions continue what he believes to be their present tendency to force all locals to conform even in minor details to master contracts, the terms of which are established by the international. This, however, is not a present problem at the main plants of the company. Management, on the whole, shows no tendency to regard the situation as perfect, but rather a confident attitude that management and the union together can solve such problems as do exist.

Most of the union representatives emphasize the problem of seniority and point out that the agreement permits management to make certain exceptions to strict seniority in layoffs. They seem to feel that a major need is for the company to accept straight seniority, but at the same time indicate that this problem was materially improved in the last contract, and is about as good as they can expect. Union spokesmen feel the pension plan is somewhat inadequate, but the burden of the discussion is that not enough benefits can be obtained under the present arrangement where the company is sole contributor to the pension fund. However, they concede that many employees would not be interested enough to join the plan anyway. A problem, not important at the moment, may develop with regard to incentive rates applied on jobs now filled by women. There are complaints that the work standards are constantly being changed and apparently there is little knowledge on the part of the workers of the factors involved. Certainly there is an educational job for the union on this whole question.

Considerable probing revealed no problems of greater significance. If the long-predicted recession occurs, there is some fear that high levels of wages and salaries cannot be continued. The company has attempted to improve productive efficiency in order to be better able to meet competition. Technological change and a constant improvement in manufacturing techniques have made this aspect of the situation somewhat dynamic. Departments have been moved from Cambridge to plants owned by the company in other localities. Work loads have been lightened and in many situations jobs have been eliminated. This has placed a strain on the collective bargaining relationship. However, joint participation in facing this type of problem has worked out successfully in the past and there is every reason to believe that if these problems continue, the parties will be able to devise ways and means of meeting the situation satisfactorily.

MANAGEMENT'S STIMULUS TO HEALTHY RELATIONS

Most policies, procedures, and practices which help to create a healthy relationship at Dewey and Almy have grown out of the immediate needs of the situation as well as the underlying philosophy of the management organization.

Two-Way Communications

Effective communications to and from workers, achieved by a number of methods at Dewey and Almy, are stressed by management.

Weekly management policy meetings have the active participation of the company's vice-president and general manager, the general superintendent and chief engineer, and their subordinates down to the foremen. Agendas, distributed for advance study, cover a wide variety of subjects, ranging from a difficult or unusual grievance to major company policy. The judgment of the whole group usually determines action finally taken. Immediately following such meetings, each superintendent calls in his foremen to discuss what has happened. Minutes are kept and distributed afterward, and important policy decisions are distributed to all management and union officials.

Weekly management-union meetings, in addition to grievance and negotiation sessions, afford an opportunity for the union's executive board to explore problems with the personnel director and to suggest issues to be taken up at the next management policy meeting or to be referred to appropriate members of management for further discussion with the union.

A loose-leaf manual containing all policy and contract interpretations, working rules, procedures, etc., is edited and distributed by the personnel department to union officials and management, and policy statements of general interest are posted on bulletin boards. Issued after full discussion by everyone concerned, they are not regarded by the union as matters of management fiat, but as summaries of accepted procedure or policy. (An illustration of the policy papers is found in Appendix F of *Case Study No. 3*.) Other published materials include an employee booklet, a company newspaper, and each new union agreement.

Some members of management feared that the extent of joint discussion would encourage the union to insist on bargaining over matters which lie largely within the area of management prerogatives. The union expects to be consulted before major policy decisions are reached or procedures are changed. However, it respects management's rights in these matters and there is rarely any difficulty even when the final decision is contrary to the union's suggestions.

Special Committees

Any complex administrative or policy problem may be referred to a management or union or joint committee at Dewey and Almy. For example, all matters affecting job rates—changes in job content, new jobs, requests by workers or management for re-evaluation of job, etc.—are referred to a special union-management committee.

The history of this committee illustrates the sincerity of the philosophy of bilateral rather than unilateral management action. When the union was organized, rates at Dewey and Almy were man rates rather than job rates, and there were many charges of unfairness in administration of wages. Shortly thereafter a management committee, set up to explore the possibilities of job evaluation, settled on a general plan and started to get job descriptions. The union, asked if it wished to participate in this management effort, set up a union committee. It studied the principles of job evaluation, management's particular plan, and then evaluated a sample group of representative jobs. Its evaluations were compared with those of the management committee and the differences jointly ironed out. Following careful explanations to the union body and allowance of time for any worker to have a hearing if he thought his job was incorrectly rated, the entire plan was submitted for acceptance or rejection at a union meeting attended by approximately 90 per cent of the members. The vote to accept the plan was unanimous, and the joint committee was set up to administer it.

Another example of joint participation grew out of the union's agitation in 1943 for revision of the promotion policy. It was argued that seniority was not given enough weight, and that there was considerable discrimination in promotions. A joint committee spent six months studying various promotion policies in effect elsewhere and eventually recommended a policy which was adopted. It provided for plant-wide bidding for openings and gave heavy weight to seniority. A permanent union committee was set up to investigate each promotion and to work with management in the administration of the policy.

The policy worked fairly well during the acute manpower shortage, but by 1945 management began to feel that it was interfering with efficient operation. Moreover, it felt that the union committee could not assume enough responsibility, because of pressures from the members to make seniority the sole determinant of promotion. In the 1945 negotiations, management proposed a new policy, maintaining the bidding system, but giving the union committee considerably less responsibility, and making skill, competence, and productivity the determining factors in promotion. Under this policy, the union committee is given the data on all proposed promotions before they are finally announced. If it finds a potential unfairness, the whole matter can be discussed with management before a final decision.

Several factors made it possible for the union to accept management's proposal on promotions. Probably the most important was the change that had taken place in worker-foreman relations; second was a better understanding of the problems related to promotion and of everyone's stake in having the best man on the job; and, finally, management was willing to make concessions for its acceptance, although this probably would have carried little weight alone.

A committee is also responsible for assuring that the rule regarding absences both before and after paid holidays does not work hardships. A committee of superintendents meets after each holiday to consider cases in which the foremen recommend payment or the workers request payment as an exception to the literal statement of the rule. The type of joint activity typified by Union-Management Production Drive committees during the war has never developed far, even though the present management organization could probably make it work effectively. There was an attempt in one department in 1943, but it was at a time when the relationship was strained and was dropped.

Interim Negotiations

Informal negotiations are undertaken when changing conditions or unforeseen experience make a new contract provision unworkable. Management believes that such provisions should be re-examined and re-negotiated during the life of the agreement, so long as they do not give one of the parties an unfair advantage.

Grievances and Complaints

Management's attitude toward grievances was considered in some detail in 1942 at a series of company meetings. (An outline discussed at the meetings is presented in Appendix D, *Case Study No. 3*.) The resulting policy was embodied in a handbook given to all new employees. This made clear that management did not want "grousing for the sake of grousing," but welcomed discussion with any employee who presented a complaint in good faith. It pointed out that violations of the union agreement would be handled under regular grievance procedures, and that other complaints concerning management actions, if not satisfactorily cleared up by discussion with the foremen, could be referred to higher levels.

Although management accepted this policy in principle, it did not become part of everyday practice for several years. In 1944 at the height of wartime tension, management felt that too many unnecessary grievances were brought up and carried too far up the grievance ladder. A meeting was held with union officials where management presented its point of view. (Management's points are given in Appendix E, *Case Study No. 3*.) Subsequently there were fewer grievances, but it was not until after the foreman training program had been under way for several months in 1945 that the problem began to resolve itself.

Recorded grievances have been constantly decreasing for the past several years. Of 78 grievances during the period March 1944 to July 1947, 45 were in 1944. (Tables 5, 6, and 7 in *Case Study No. 3* present data for this period on the number of grievances, their nature, and disposition.) The development of a screening process by the union undoubtedly eliminated many of the grievances that might otherwise have gone to the top steps of the grievance procedure.

Union officials became concerned because too often they had to argue a questionable grievance to the last step in the procedure. They were wasting valuable time and usually lost the case. On their own initiative they developed a new procedure. Now, before a grievance is carried beyond the superintendent, it is subject to review by the executive board of the union. In no instance in the past two years has a grievance gone to the company president's office (the last step before arbitration) without first having been thus reviewed. The executive board permits the aggrieved person or group to come before it and state the case. If it feels that the grievance has merit, processing continues under the grievance procedure. If not, or if the board feels there is no reasonable expectation of winning, approval is withheld and the grievance is dropped. The aggrieved worker or group can appeal the board's decision to a regular membership meeting. If a majority of the local membership upholds the appeal, the grievance is processed on through to arbitration if necessary.

The small number of grievances does not mean that the union has not functioned properly. Rather, the relationship has developed to a point where many complaints which would constitute grievances in other plants are quickly and informally settled.

The Welfare of Workers

The company's history and the actions of individuals in management provide evidence that the welfare of workers has been a major concern. Management representatives who have not demonstrated humanitarian interest in employees, or who have been unfair or discriminatory, have been transferred outside the line organization, or in some instances forced to resign.

Technological changes involving displacement of workers have been handled with genuine concern for the workers as individuals. Many steps have been taken to protect workers against the possibility of arbitrary action. For example, in 1942, a joint union-management committee arrived at a mutually satisfactory set of disciplinary rules. The committee established fixed penalties for only two types of infraction, drinking on the job and smoking in violation of the rule. All other disciplinary penalties were to be determined on the basis of the circumstances of the case. The agreement states management's intention to give a clear warning— with copies to the union—in advance of disciplinary action when the offense is repetitive (tardiness, unsatisfactory performance of duties, etc.), and provides for a five-day cooling-off period in cases involving penalty layoff or discharge. Thus the union can discuss the case with management before a final penalty is enforced.

While arbitration under the agreement is limited to cases involving interpretation or alleged violation of the agreement, the company's president has flatly stated that any case involving alleged discrimination against an employee will be permitted to go to arbitration if not settled prior to that stage. One such case has been arbitrated. Neither of two cases which have gone to arbitration during eight years of the relationship of Dewey and Almy and the Chemical Workers involved discharge. This, however, does not mean that management has failed to maintain reasonable standards of performance. During the twelve months prior to July 1, 1947, 23 members were discharged, and not one of these cases resulted in a grievance which went beyond the second stage of the procedure. (The breakdown on these discharges is given in Table 8, *Case Study No. 3.*) Penalties against two workers during that period were modified from discharge to a penalty layoff as a result of grievances.

UNION STRENGTH AND STABILITY

The new Federal Charter Union in 1939, unlike Dewey and Almy which was an established institution, had to develop an organizational structure and a set of objectives and policies. Members, untrained for these tasks, had to learn largely by trial and error. As a Federal Charter Union, there was more freedom to develop in self-chosen directions than might have been possible otherwise. While the union adopted a general pattern similar to most AFL locals, it received little direct coaching from headquarters unless it called in AFL representatives.

The elected officials took their responsibilities seriously. They were determined to keep the organization extremely democratic. They struggled with the problems of negotiation and administration of the agreement. By trying this and that, with the aid and support of a friendly company president, they solved their early problems in one way or another.

A Self-Confident Local

The fact that union leaders have not had to match wits with legal experts or fight to get a sympathetic hearing and the range of problems solved jointly with management have been helpful in the union's growth. The local has demonstrated in two real tests of strength, however, that it can successfully meet crises. The first test came in 1943–44 when the union and its members had to withstand the active resentment of lower and middle management; the second came in 1944–45 when responsibility for industrial relations was shifted to line management, with a less paternalistic attitude. The trend since 1939 has been one of increasing strength and competence—symptoms of a healthy organization.

The current agreement was successfully negotiated without the presence of an international representative. The only time the local has required and accepted any considerable amount of outside aid was during the period of strained relations in 1943–44. The AFL representatives provided that aid, and strengthened the union's self-confidence at a critical time. Among problems which the union has met reasonably well are those connected with wages, protection against discriminatory management action, promotion, layoff, day-to-day relations with lower and middle management. It has acquired a union-shop contract.

The union has brought the general wage level from a point at or below the community average to near the top. The average hourly rate of union members in 1939 was 60 cents, in 1947 was $1.14. But in addition to increased wages, the union has consistently bargained for and won other monetary increments—benefits in the form of vacations, paid holidays, life and sickness insurance, and a retirement annuity plan.

Although management can be credited for some of the gains, they were all acquired after the union was organized, and union officials and members argue that they would not have achieved their present benefits without unionization. Management agrees with these contentions.

Union Responsibility

This strong and self-confident union has accepted its full share of responsibility for the maintenance of a sound internal wage structure. Although some members of management say the union is committed to a policy of straight seniority, promotions of candidates other than senior ones are frequently made with full knowledge of union representatives, and grievances seldom result. Management members acknowledge that the union has in some instances accepted responsibility for withdrawing demands when the welfare or competitive position of the company was shown to be affected. The simple device of screening grievances through the executive board is a clear indication of the ingeniousness and resourcefulness of the local union.

One other factor contributing to the general stability of the union and the relationship today is the tendency to re-elect officials whom they believe are doing an adequate job. The office of union president is usually sought earnestly and there is always a good deal of electioneering for this office. The annual election has tended for the past two or three years to result in the re-election of most of the other officers, and most of the members of the executive board. This is not a matter of dictators perpetuating themselves in office. What it does reflect is confidence in the union officials and an absence of the attitude which sometimes results in the election of a new group of belligerent and antagonistic officers who have promised to "show management where it gets off."

The union's internal communication problem has been solved less effectively than that in Dewey and Almy's management organization. By and large, the union officials have not been outstandingly successful in communicating to the shop stewards and the rank and file the knowledge and understanding which they have acquired in working with management. From time to time, the union has attempted various methods to overcome this, but none has been carried through successfully. Most of the important knowledge which workers should have filters out to them informally. The company is still small enough so that the absence of more formal procedures does not seem to cause an acute problem. However, this lack of effective communication could cause trouble if critical collective bargaining problems should arise in the future.

As is characteristic of many unions, attendance at this union's meetings is small unless important company-wide issues are at stake. Union officials have expressed concern over this problem, and have tried the usual devices for encouraging attendance, without marked success. However, this may not be too important. If a really serious issue affects their lives or threatens their union's existence, the members probably will participate more actively.

This union has achieved most of the goals for which any union organization strives. The provisions which appear at first glance to give the company greater leeway than is usual have been written into the agreement only after extensive joint study and as a result of genuine bargaining in which the company had to give in order to get. Furthermore, the union has been treated as a partner on all important matters. This type of consultative management and union participation does not happen in company-dominated relationships. The union has never hesitated to stand up for what it considers to be its rights. On occasion there have been strike threats and other displays of union strength. Only if one assumed that the alternative to open warfare was a company union would the conclusion of company domination of this relationship be tenable.

THE COMPANY'S COMPETITIVE POSITION

No matter how peaceful and happy the collective bargaining relationship may be, it cannot be regarded as healthy if it interferes with the fundamental economic purpose of the business enterprise—the production and sale of goods or services at a profit.

Union Attitude

Members of management at Dewey and Almy point with some pride to the union's attitude toward the welfare of the enterprise. Union officials or negotiating committee members may argue heatedly over the question of the effect of a given action or policy upon the economic position of the company. However, if management offers a convincing argument that the company's competitive position would be adversely affected, union members are willing to adjust or modify their demands. The union has demonstrated this attitude on many occasions—in connection with promotion policy, seniority matters, introduction of technological changes, and various wage and other monetary demands. If management motives were suspect, there would be cynical suspicion when "the welfare of the company" was under discussion.

Worker Effort and Productivity

Opinions differ on the complex question of worker effort,[1] and convincing data are not available at Dewey and Almy. Management does not believe there is a deliberate restriction of output or unwillingness to give a fair day's work on the part of the workers in general. Most management officials accept without question that, with a few isolated exceptions, the workers believe they are doing a good job. Moreover, they generally agree that worker effort is at least average for unmeasured industrial jobs paid on a daywork basis. However, quite a few middle and top management representatives feel that worker effort is certainly no higher, and possibly slightly lower, today than it was before the war.

On the other hand, the union officials and representatives and a number of workers who were interviewed feel that worker effort is higher today than it was before the war. While the workers are quite ready to agree that the measurable change in productivity (or direct labor cost) undoubtedly has resulted to a considerable extent from improvements in

[1] The term "worker effort" is used to maintain the distinction between the worker's contribution to productivity and management's contribution through technological change and improvements in method and equipment. There is no question that over-all productivity per worker has increased markedly since 1939, but management feels that worker effort has not increased.

method and equipment, their reasoned opinion is that they, too, have contributed to the end result.

The Dewey and Almy foremen on the whole tend to support the union's opinion that worker effort has increased. They were decidedly unhappy during the war when standards were lowered and discipline relaxed because of the scarcity of labor. They feel that the situation has now been remedied and that the workers are doing a good day's work.

There appear to be no important factors in this situation which *should* cause high worker productivity. Good will toward a kindly management cannot in itself be expected to produce unusually high standards of performance. There is no formal participation by the union in production problems (cost reduction, methods improvements, quality control) which might provide greater understanding, and hence greater motivation to do a better job. Moreover, except for women in one of the plants who are on an incentive plan, there is no clear-cut relationship between the rewards received for work and the effort which the worker must put forth. Most of the rewards from employment are obtained by maintaining a level of productivity which is accepted by the foremen as satisfactory (and which is not measured, but merely judged). Benefits other than wages are not related to the amount of effort above the minimum accepted as satisfactory. A profit-sharing plan which was in effect from 1940 to 1942 was not effective in creating such a relationship, possibly because of the absence of participation by workers. Incentive wages, where they have been applied, have appeared to help this situation somewhat, but there is no clear-cut agreement that they would make a major difference even if applied on other types of work.

Under present conditions, the chief basis for high worker effort is good management leadership. Most members of the management group recognize this. They do not blame the workers or the union for what they consider to be inadequate worker motivation, but believe management has to solve it. The situation with respect to worker effort is not ideal, but there is no evidence whatever of slowdowns, restriction of output, or other such unhealthy practices.

Management does feel, however, that constant vigilance is required to prevent the development of what amounts to featherbedding. And it has taken a firm stand with respect to such matters. There is evidence that such practices have been fostered by two or three union representatives who feel rather strongly about the protective functions of the union. It is hard for workers and the union to take the long-run view that such inefficient practices tend to undermine job security by weakening the competitive position of the company. However, this does not seem to be an insurmountable obstacle, but rather a perennial difficulty which can be overcome only by constant education and sound leadership on both sides.

The Outlook

For the future, the relationship cannot remain healthy unless it continues to grow and mature. It has successfully progressed through the second—administrative—stage. It seems to the investigators that it must soon move into the third—cooperative—stage, if it is to remain healthy. Management and the union have worked together successfully in solving many industrial relations problems. They have not really begun to cooperate on the problems of efficient production. There is no active or persistent interference by the union with the achievement of the economic purpose of the enterprise, but there does remain a somewhat passive lip service to the importance of this purpose rather than an active, enthusiastic attempt to achieve it.

The situation is hopeful with respect to these problems. If present trends continue without severe setbacks, the next decade should see the gradual development of high-level participation and cooperation as a new phase of this fundamentally sound and stable relationship. It is up to both management and the union to capitalize on the investment they have made in good union-management relations.

A Postscript

Since this study was published in 1948, Dewey and Almy has grown considerably. Its sales volume has doubled and its plant facilities have expanded accordingly. Much of the expansion has taken the form of new types of products, particularly plastic film, battery separators, and organic chemicals. In 1948, the Cambridge plant was the largest in the company. Two plants located in the Midwest now have more factory employees. Total employment in the Cambridge plant has decreased considerably, partly because of discontinuing some of the products made there and partly because of the geographic decentralization of the company.

The relationship between management and the union has continued healthy, despite the difficulties that have accompanied the process of rapid growth. Perhaps the primary difficulty has been the necessity for top levels of management to spend much less time on the problems of the Cambridge plant. This shift of emphasis has undoubtedly had its effects, but they have been largely compensated for by a continuing effort to develop the ability of middle and lower levels of management to maintain healthy employee relations.

The picture is not completely white, however. Even though most of the indicators of industrial peace have been much on the favorable side, it is also true that during negotiation of a new union agreement the union staged a strike in December 1952. The differences were confined almost completely to economic issues at a time when the company's financial position was relatively unfavorable and prospects were dim for improving the profit position of some phases of its Cambridge operations. The strike, which seems to have left no noticeable scars, lasted for one week.

On the whole, the original description of the relationship is still accurate and pertinent in all important respects.

CHAPTER 10

Hickey-Freeman Company

and the Amalgamated (CIO)

DONALD B. STRAUS, *now with Health Insurance Plan of Greater New York, is author of* NPA Case Study No. 4. *His full report, condensed in this chapter, was published in January 1949.*

Since April 1919, when Hickey-Freeman Company recognized the Amalgamated Clothing Workers of America as the representative of its employees in collective bargaining, the habit of mutual respect and compatibility has become a part of the daily life of plant executives and union leaders. The president of the company has publicly expressed his opinion that the union is an asset to his business; the head of the union is quick to praise the company's policies.

Hickey-Freeman is the second largest manufacturer of men's clothing in Rochester, New York. In that center for top-quality clothing, it is generally conceded that the company's quality standards are the highest in the area. It employs about 1500 workers, and has a capital investment per worker of about $1400. The business was started in 1899 by its president, Jeremiah G. Hickey, and Jacob L. Freeman, who died in 1924. It was merged with Beeckel Baum in 1908, and Morton J. Baum—son of the original Baum—is now the executive vice-president. The company's stock is closely held, the majority in the hands of the active management. Both Mr. Hickey and Mr. Baum have sons who can provide continuity to the owner-management arrangement.

Hickey-Freeman has not bought labor peace in the form of unduly high wages and other expensive working conditions. The company's profits in some years have been higher and in some years lower than the average for men's and boys' clothing manufacturers. Like its industry as a whole, it has shown a profit in every year from 1929 to 1947 except in

1931, 1932, and 1938. (Table 1, *Case Study No. 4,* shows comparative figures for these years on net profit on sales after taxes and surplus adjustments.)

The relationship between the Amalgamated Clothing Workers of America (CIO) and Hickey-Freeman is affected by collective bargaining which takes place on three levels: national or industry-wide bargaining periodically fixes general wage levels and continues or modifies the basic contract provisions; the region (in this case embracing all except one of the six leading men's clothing factories) settles matters peculiar to the area; and plant bargaining, within definite restrictions, governs those few items which differentiate Hickey-Freeman from other Rochester firms.

Amalgamated's membership in the Rochester area is divided into twelve main locals, two locals covering subsidiary plants outside of Rochester, and seven affiliated locals which cover workers outside the normal jurisdiction of the Amalgamated. (A list of the locals appears in Table 2, *Case Study No. 4.*) A Joint Board, consisting of elected delegates from each of the locals, negotiates for all of the various locals and to Rochester employers it represents the only union entity.

Unionization in the men's clothing industry dates back to 1862. The Amalgamated Clothing Workers, however, did not get started until 1914 when a minority group split away from the United Garment Workers of America (AFL). Sidney Hillman was president of Amalgamated until his death in 1946, and his name continues to dominate the labor relations story in the men's clothing industry. Management executives as well as union officials are unanimous in the opinion that, more than anyone else, he was responsible for evolving the present teamwork.

One of the issues which caused the union split in 1914 was industrial unionism. Mr. Hillman and his followers wanted to include in the union all workers connected with the industry, regardless of their skill or occupation. But just as important in the development of the union were four basic principles which Sidney Hillman stressed throughout his career. These are:

1. Use of an impartial chairman familiar with the industry for settling disputes arising under the contract.

2. Rejection of the inevitability of perpetual conflict between employers and unions in favor of the belief that both parties have many objectives in common.

3. Cooperation with employers under contract with Amalgamated to permit advantageous competition with nonunion firms.

4. Organization and action on an industry-wide basis.

In 1913, the United Garment Workers had directed a series of unsuccessful strikes. By 1915, the Amalgamated began to lay the groundwork for bringing Rochester into its rapidly expanding orbit. Intense opposition was encountered from the employers and from the Rochester Clothiers' Exchange (the employer association of the manufacturers), and organizing progress was slow, although determined.

In July 1918, there was a small strike in one unit of one of the companies for increased wages. The situation was tense and could have become general throughout Rochester. The postwar boom had piled up orders and a shutdown was to be avoided at all costs. But instead of a further demonstration of strength, Sidney Hillman gambled on the peaceful route. He persuaded William Z. Ripley of Harvard and Louis Kirstein, president of Filene's in Boston and former administrator of the Board of Control and Labor Standards, to act as negotiators.

These two men persuaded the business leaders to meet with Sidney Hillman for a discussion. Mr. Hillman's personality was so unlike that which the companies' presidents expected, and they were so favorably impressed with a union philosophy which denied the need for struggle between labor and management, that when he suggested submission of the controversy to arbitration, they agreed. Mr. Kirstein and Mr. Ripley were chosen as the arbitrators. When the decision was announced, it covered not only the struck shop but the whole market, and it provided for a wage increase of 10 to 20 per cent, time and one-half for overtime, and a 48-hour week. Both sides accepted the award and collective bargaining in Rochester was off to a peaceful start.

DEVELOPMENT OF COLLECTIVE BARGAINING

The 1918 wage arbitration indicated a wary acceptance of the union by the employers. But no agreement, signed or verbal, was reached as to the nature of this acceptance.

Meanwhile, Amalgamated in other parts of the country was successfully concluding contracts that lowered the work week to 44 hours. A thirteen-week strike in New York over this issue was won by the union on January 22, 1919. One day later, the Rochester Clothiers' Exchange announced—without discussion with or mention of the union—that it would put the 44-hour week into effect on May 1. On February 6, the Amalgamated Joint Council in Rochester demanded that the 44-hour week be made effective at once. This led to negotiations which were concluded a week later with the signing of the first Rochester contract, to become effective on April 1. (That contract is reproduced in Appendix A, *Case Study No. 4.*)

The first agreement was brief—partly because Sidney Hillman was wise enough to avoid needless controversy. The more important clauses were:

1. The union concedes and recognizes the right of the manufacturers to operate their plants on the so-called "open shop" principle.

2. The employers recognize the right of their employees to bargain collectively.

3. Individuals or groups of workers have the right to present their complaints direct to the firm's labor manager. The aggrieved workers shall have the right to call in as their spokesman a third party.

4. Both parties agree to arbitration as a method of settling disputes. There shall be no stoppages of work because of disputes or dissatisfaction. The award of the arbitrator shall be final and binding on both parties.

The brevity of the contract did not result from any unusual trust between the parties, but rather from their decision to rely on what amounted to negotiation by arbitration.

Negotiation by Arbitration

The method of arbitration established in Rochester was a valuable aid in surmounting the initial obstacles to the collective bargaining experience. William Leiserson (now a member of the NPA Committee and director of the Labor Organization Study of Johns Hopkins University), the first impartial chairman, not only handed down fair and equitable decisions, but took pains to explain them, thereby creating a code of industrial ethics which guided both union and management representatives. Whenever possible, Dr. Leiserson referred the case back to parties for further discussion by a joint committee which he appointed. Even in cases where he failed to bring about agreement through mediation and was forced to hand down a decision, Dr. Leiserson sought guidance from the disputants. Usually he cleared his decision first with a small committee of union and management representatives in order to avoid implications which he might not see in making the award but which might become troublemakers as a precedent.

Dr. Leiserson not only wrote full opinions, but after each decision he attended management conferences and union meetings to discuss their contents and hammer out general acceptance of the principles which he helped to form. In March 1922, the Clothiers' Exchange issued a document called "Understandings to the Agreement" which distilled the arbitrator's decisions into a series of rules. These were divided into chapters which provided a useful point of departure for management and union negotiations. The number of cases going to arbitration slowed down.

However, once the basic principles were established, both management and union representatives were quick to use the growing "body of law" as a technique for winning cases on minor interpretations, and the downward trend in the number of cases brought to the chairman came to a halt. The impartial chairman, to remedy this, handed down straight awards without any further comment. From then on the use of his offices diminished to nothing. There has been no arbitration case in the Rochester area for eighteen years, and Hickey-Freeman has had only one since 1929. The machinery for settling disputes—an important feature of the initial agreement—is now more of a symbol than a practical necessity.

Growth of the Closed Shop

Union security was recognized by Sidney Hillman as an emotional shoal which could wreck the initial negotiations, so he steered clear of it. By 1922, the union was sufficiently accepted so that the 1919 open-shop clause was dropped. No union-security provision took its place, but there was a delicate introduction to the subject: "The power to hire shall remain with the employers, but in time of unemployment, it is understood that consideration shall first be given to persons who have been employed in local shops doing work for members of the Clothiers' Exchange." This was merely phrasing an established practice—but this is typical of the development of the Rochester contract.

In 1925, the union asked for a preferential-shop clause, but when this met with strong employer resistance the demand was dropped. Shortly thereafter, the Joint Board set up an efficient employment exchange, and within six months 98 per cent of the jobs in the Rochester market were filled through the exchange. For all practical purposes, the closed shop was in effect, but it was not until several years later that it was formally recognized in the contract. When the union requested an automatic check-off, it was welcomed by the company. When most of the labor world was in a turmoil over the effect of the impending Taft-Hartley legislation, the clothing industry extended its contract with the Amalgamated to 1952, thus insuring continuation of the smoothly running pattern of relationships over a period that seemed headed for conflict elsewhere.

The present director of the company's labor department feels that the closed shop and check-off are essential to the kind of management-union relationship that has developed. It greatly fortifies the union's strength both financially and "politically." Over the years, the ability of the union to act independently of short-run considerations often has produced decisions favorable to the employers. The union has demonstrated its concern with the economic realities of the company in bad times and in good times. During the depression years of 1933–35, the union negotiated three successive wage cuts of 15 per cent each, and the union loaned money to several Rochester factories when commercial banks refused to extend credit. Even in prosperous times, its requests for wage increases have been moderate, based upon sound reasoning and reliable statistics. In 1947, a year of extravagant union claims, one Hickey-Freeman official said, "The Amalgamated has never made a wild demand." Such moderation in the union movement can be practiced only by officials who are secure in their jobs and who have a strong organization free from factional divisions.

Constructive Unionization

Amalgamated's constructive behavior could not have survived without an enlightened management attitude. Several years of bitter union-management struggle preceded the 1919 settlement and great credit is due those management leaders who recognized the change in the union's philosophy. Management completely revised many of its fundamental methods of personnel administration in order to take advantage of this change. The strong personality of the company's president, Jeremiah G. Hickey, played an important role in the development of industrial peace at Hickey-Freeman.

It is clear, both from outside evidence and from Mr. Hickey's own conversation, that he and Sidney Hillman took to one another from the start. If it was Mr. Hillman who first brought the concept of industrial democracy to the Hickey-Freeman plant, it was Mr. Hickey who translated the concept into management practice and who saw that the fundamental principles of this new method of operation became ingrained into the daily habits of everyone in a supervisory capacity. Today, Mr. Hickey sets the tone for the labor policies of his company, but he rarely takes an active part in the administration of these policies.

Sharing-the-Work

The union has urged and management has accepted the general rule that whatever work is to be done shall be divided equally among all of the employees. As a result, production and employment bear curiously little relationship to each other. During the years 1933 through 1947, employment remained remarkably steady, dropping only in the war years, 1943–45, because of the shortage of labor rather than lack of work. Production, on the other hand, fluctuated sharply in keeping with business conditions. (Statistics on employment, productivity, and earnings are given in Tables 3, 3-A, 3-B, 3-C, and Exhibit 1 of *Case Study No. 4.*)

The industry-wide principle of sharing-the-work is scrupulously observed by Hickey-Freeman, despite the fact that strict adherence imposes a severe burden on management planning. Hickey-Freeman is convinced that the advantages of sharing-the-work far outweigh the disadvantages. Direct labor costs are not dependent upon the number of people employed, since work is paid for by the piece. Furthermore, because skilled employees are so important in a factory making high-quality clothing, it is important to keep the trained working team together even in slack times. In order to even out seasonal production, Hickey-Freeman undertakes long-range scheduling of work and plans its merchandising in order to sell approximately equivalent amounts of clothing in all seasons.

Cyclical variation requires putting the principle of share-the-work into practice on a large scale. As production moves downward, hours of employment are gradually reduced to the point where work may be closed down for a full workday each week. If the decline goes still farther, each shop may be shut down for a period varying from several weeks to several months and during this time laid-off workers can either go on unemployment relief or else look for work somewhere else.

Sharing-the-work also presents day-to-day difficulties. In rush periods, management is reluctant to allow overtime to pile up, whereas the union resists putting on more workers, since when the work gets back to normal employees may not have enough work to earn a full day's wage. When business is slack, the fast workers get a smaller percentage of the work under the principle of sharing than they otherwise would. However, ceilings placed on earnings are calculated so that the faster workers can earn more than the others, but not so much as if they worked the full factory hours.

A Piece-rate Industry

Workers in men's clothing usually are paid on a piece-rate basis. Although unions have been traditionally antagonistic to this method of payment—linking it to the speed-up—the spread and stabilization of the piece-rate system since the early thirties have had the active cooperation of the Amalgamated. Sidney Hillman, who felt strongly that unionized employers must not be placed in an unfavorable competitive position, recognized the necessity of controlling labor expense by keeping productivity up. This led to a transformation of the principle of "equal pay for equal work" to one of "equal labor cost to manufacturers for comparable work produced."

Even so, in its early history, Amalgamated shared the traditional union antagonism to piece rates. When depression hit the Rochester clothing industry in 1921, most of the workers were on a weekly wage; only 45 per cent were on piecework. The Clothiers' Exchange asked for a 25 per cent wage reduction which the union turned down. The matter then went to arbitration. The employers presented irrefutable arguments that labor costs had to be reduced if the industry were to survive. The union proved that wages were already at rock bottom—low in terms of living costs and in comparison with competing markets. Dr. Leiserson found that the wages of week workers averaged from 20 to 25 per cent less than those of pieceworkers, but that the production of week workers was lower still. Because this pointed the way to both increased wages and reduced labor costs, he decreed that employers could require employees "to work on a basis of measured production which fixes the unit cost per piece in line with the existing piece rates in the market." Making the point that there was "little possibility of getting any worth-while amount of cost reduction by cuts in wages," he went on:

In industries where labor relations are chaotic and unregulated except by strikes and lockouts or dictatorship by one side or the other there may be some cause for forcing wages down just as arbitrarily as they were forced up. But neither justice nor sound industrial policy can justify holding wages to reasonable levels by arbitration machinery in the interest of industrial stability on a rising market and then when the market falls not using the same machinery to safeguard the workers' standards of living.

Since this decision, Hickey-Freeman has shifted to piecework in most jobs. During the first few years of conversion, almost every rate went to arbitration. The arbitrator's decisions fell into a pattern, however, which indicated that the gains in production brought about by piecework should be shared equally by management and labor. As both parties recognized this pattern, more and more rates were settled by negotiation.

In the early days, when a job was to be converted to piecework, management would often make a preliminary time study. Workers, aware of this, would deliberately slow down. Then management usually made a rule-of-thumb computation based on the theory that piecework would increase production by roughly 50 per cent. A note giving the date and rate on the changed job would go to the employees involved and to the union, which quite frequently would result in the whole section walking out. Then the union had to get them back to work—usually with the promise that if earnings did not increase, the rate would be taken up as a grievance.

Today, new rates are set by a more orderly procedure. A union and management negotiator discuss the situation frankly and off the record, to reach an agreement before a new rate is announced. Hickey-Freeman has two guiding principles on rates: Once you set a rate, even if it is too high, it can never be adjusted downward except along with others in a general wage reduction or unless there is a change in method or specification for that operation. But whenever a rate that is too low is noticed, it must be adjusted upward as soon as possible by agreement with the union. These are not the rules of a spendthrift management; they have been developed after years of hard experience as actual measures of economy.

Industry-wide Wage Stabilization

During the depression years of the thirties, the impartial umpire system was powerless to control the downward pressure on wage rates. With production dropping off, continued employment was labor's main objective, and managers of the various joint boards recognized that to achieve this the employers' costs would have to be cut to the bone. Wage cuts were easily negotiated as union and management teamed together in a life-and-death competition with manufacturers in other areas. A state of chaos was developing which Amalgamated sought to control by stabilizing labor costs throughout the industry. It found ready cooperation from the employers.

In the clothing industry it is almost impossible accurately to compare jobs in different shops because there are so many ways to manufacture a suit, to divide up operations, and so much difference in styles and quality. The union did not attempt to set up uniform piece rates, but established a uniform minimum labor cost for the entire garment. The garments were classified into a number of distinct and identifiable grades, with each grade assigned a minimum payment for the labor that goes into it. So long as this minimum was paid in wages for each garment, the manufacturer could divide up the work among as many employees and in any way he chose. In practice, it was discovered that competition between localities appeared in the form of exceptions agreed to by employers and local union officials. In 1939, therefore, the Amalgamated created a stabilization department which has to approve all rates, and has seven full-time investigators policing the industry's rate structure.

All Hickey-Freeman's clothing is above the top grade in the classification, but nevertheless the garments are given a labor price in relationship to the basic grades. These labor prices and the piece rates that go into them are negotiated by representatives of the firm and the Rochester Joint Board. Since there are some 250 separate job categories of clothing and since each category has its own piecework structure, this rate-setting job even in the local firms is difficult. Both management and union officials feel satisfied that the day-to-day negotiations on the rates have maintained an equitable interplant relationship.

The Contract—A "Scrap of Paper"

The written contract is much in the background in the Hickey-Freeman relationship. Not a single copy is available in the union headquarters, although other records are currently and efficiently maintained. There has been no need to refer to the contract for so many years that the one copy is kept in a safe deposit box. At the plant the same story is heard. Only one or two copies are typed and they are seldom referred to. Disregard for the written word, and a corresponding concern with the intention of the agreement, is evident throughout the relationship. Personal conversations or telephone calls settle most matters, and experience has taught that misunderstandings can better be ironed out by further discussion than by harking back to a recorded statement. In many cases the contract remains unaltered long after practices are changed by mutual and unwritten understanding.

THE RELATIONSHIP'S EFFECT ON MANAGEMENT

The top management group has averaged well over twenty years of service at Hickey-Freeman. Among the foremen, the average length of service is seventeen years and the average seniority for the workers is sixteen years. (Table 4 in *Case Study No. 4* gives the details on the seniority distribution of workers.) Fifty-five per cent of the workers are women. The low turnover rate throughout the organization has contributed greatly to informality in the plant. The flow of work seems to follow well-worn channels efficiently but without haste.

Creation of a Labor Department

When the company first began to deal with the union, Mr. Freeman was in charge of manufacturing. He decided that he was emotionally too close to the experience of fighting unionization to handle personally the complex problems that collective bargaining would bring. During the war he had got to know and respect a young economist, N. I. Stone, whose job with the federal government was to help settle labor disputes that arose in factories handling government orders for uniforms. Offering the job of heading a new labor department at Hickey-Freeman to Dr. Stone, he said, "We want to hire a man who is 51 per cent prolabor, because we are antilabor enough ourselves to keep the balance."

Dr. Stone took the job and remained with the company until 1925. During that time he established the labor department and helped build the foundation for the successful and creative labor relations which have developed. As a friend of Sidney Hillman, with a definite prolabor reputation, Dr. Stone was enthusiastically received by the work force. He was quickly overwhelmed with demands for wage increases. Individually, each one seemed small enough and most appeared to be justified. Actually, he granted a great many within a short time, which mounted up somewhat more rapidly than he had anticipated. As he learned more about profit margins and the effects of rate changes, he became a cautious bargainer. At the same time the union was still new and rambunctious in its role of cooperator. Although friction had developed between union leaders and the company's labor manager by the time he left, his successors say he left his imprint on both the philosophy of top management and many of the labor techniques that are still in successful operation.

Changed Role of Foremen

The foreman was dictator in his shop when the union was organized. He hired, fired, set rates, settled complaints by arbitrary decision, or shifted the workers around as he saw fit. He was able to vent personal dislikes and play favorites, and many sold their favors for a cut from a worker's pay check. Management had suspected these excesses and would have preferred to eliminate them, but the foreman was accountable for keeping costs down and quality up. How he accomplished this was of no consequence as long as employees failed to complain.

The union in its concern for rates and working conditions ran into direct conflict with these shop autocrats. In order to obey the spirit of the contract, severe restrictions were placed on the power of the foremen, and the labor department was given the responsibility for the personnel functions which had been part of the foreman's job. Fitting the foremen into their more restricted role caused the new labor department its major problems. Relatively few of the foremen who were with the company in

1919 seemed able to make the transition and many either left or were fired within two years.

Management believes that it is more efficient and economical to have an expert labor manager perform personnel functions, either directly or by giving counsel, than to try to train every foreman to be an expert in labor relations as well as in the making of suits. To further emphasize this division of responsibility, a new type of foreman has been added in the shops. Called production supervisors, they handle the routing and flow of work. The regular foreman has been left with one concern only: quality.

There is no issue of foreman unionization in the Rochester clothing industry, and the Amalgamated's constitution bars foremen from membership. An active foreman's club is primarily social. Most foremen today command high salaries and their relationship to both management and the Amalgamated seems entirely satisfactory. The company has experienced some difficulties in adjusting the salaries of the junior and assistant foremen to maintain the desired differential between their pay and that of pieceworkers during periods of high production or slack times. This has been solved mainly by awarding generous salary increases on the basis of merit.

The Labor Department—A Line Job

No organization chart has ever been drawn up by the company, and official titles or designations are usually lacking, so that those used by the author in describing the company's operations do not necessarily have their counterpart in company terminology. However, a study of the plant's operations shows clearly how the company's requirements for quality, cost, and production are coordinated. (A chart drawn up by the author appears in *Case Study No. 4.*)

Responsibility for quality and design, which means responsibility to a large extent for maintaining the very reputation of the company, is placed in one division and that for all matters pertaining to productive efficiency and costs is in another division. The head designer, Hugo Gemignani, works with the quality foremen on the technical problems of making the clothing that he has designed, but he confers with and works through Harold Rauber, head of the cost and production division, when it comes to putting these designs into production.

Under Mr. Rauber's division are two departments—a technical and engineering department and a labor department. Unlike most production men, Mr. Rauber's training and background were in the field of industrial relations, and both of his assistants also had their initial training in that field. Lester Bartlett has charge of the physical aspects of the building, the flow of work to the shops, and all the technical aspects of production. Paul Brescia has all the usual labor department activities of hiring, recruiting, rate setting, discipline, and negotiating with the union, but is also responsible for those aspects of production and costs which are closely associated with the productivity of workers, quality (cooperating with Mr. Gemignani and the quality foremen in the proper training of workers, checking upon their methods of sewing and cutting, etc.), and the coordination of all policy decisions before they are applied to the human aspects of manufacturing. He reports directly to Mr. Rauber as coequal of Mr. Bartlett, but shoulders more direct line authority.

As a line official, the labor manager has authority to make decisions. He participates in the formation of top policy and is responsible for seeing that these policies hit no labor snags. When he negotiates with the union, the union representatives recognize that a final decision can be reached without checking back to top management. The company feels that this has greatly facilitated its dealings with the union.

The Union—Partner to Decisions

Both management and union people are fond of talking about the spirit of partnership that exists in their joint recognition of the main objective: to make clothes well and at a profit. Time spent in spotting and eliminating a cause for a potential grievance is never wasted, according to Hickey-Freeman's management. A large percentage of the labor manager's time goes to the discovery and handling of unborn grievances, which takes him into the very origins of company policy.

The development of production methods for a new style provides a good example. When the new style is chosen, the designer's plans and patterns are taken to the labor department for analysis. The labor manager calls in the union's shop chairman and the foreman concerned for discussion on production changes required by the new style. Each affected job is examined as to quality, piece rates, and equal division of work. Objections to the plans may be raised and the designer consulted about eliminating them. If a change in piece rates is involved, these are negotiated separately by the labor manager and the union's plant chairman. By the time the plan is ready for introduction to the shop, it has become a jointly endorsed plan. The plant chairman and the labor manager then try out the new style on a test group in a selected shop, partly to discover flaws but mainly to establish a nucleus of workers who can sell the changes to their co-workers.

Rate setting is a constant process because even a slight change in production usually upsets the piece rate that applied to the former operation. Whenever the job is changed too much for the worker to reach his accustomed earnings at once, he is put on week work. As in the case of piece rates, week-work pay is determined jointly by union and company and is set individually in each case. The aim is to set the week-work rate low enough to provide an incentive for the worker to build up speed, and yet high enough so that he will not feel the new job is a penalty. In this task, the union usually sees eye to eye with management, since a slow worker deprives other workers of enough work to build up their piecework take-home pay.

The fact that piece rates and week-work rates are set within very narrow limitations, involves heavy responsibility for the union and management. No one rate out of the 250-odd that are established will make much difference to anyone other than the individual workers affected; but the effect each rate has on the interrelationship of all the others is important. The labor manager has absolute authority to negotiate these rates for the company and to make the final decision. This again emphasizes his role as a line officer of the firm. On the other side, the union negotiator—often the shop chairman—also comes with the authority to reach an agreement.

The extent of union-management cooperation at Hickey-Freeman is illustrated by the company's expansion program immediately after the war when the demand for men's clothing mounted rapidly. The labor supply around Rochester was inadequate to fill all the new positions, especially in the sewing jobs. The company therefore decided to explore the possibility of setting up shops in small country towns, where needlework would be done on various clothing parts sent from the main plant.

Before going ahead, the company consulted the union, which readily agreed to cooperate. Shops were set up where the labor supply seemed most promising, and the union gave the company complete freedom to employ whomever it wished, although technically the closed-shop contract covered all such workers. This was necessary in order to recruit workers, most of whom were new to industrial work and had inherited an emotional resistance to unions. Also, the Amalgamated was not anxious to sign up members who were to work in an experimental factory which might close down at a moment's notice.

After several months, the company told the union that it planned to make these workshops permanent. Shortly thereafter, the union's business agent and the labor manager visited the country shops and told the workers about the good relationship between the union and the company, explained about the closed shop and why all workers who wished to remain with the company had to join the union. At the same time, a wage increase was announced which more than covered union dues.

The word "seniority" is not mentioned in the contract, and is seldom heard at the Hickey-Freeman plant, but the observance of seniority is routine. Layoffs have been virtually eliminated by the share-the-work plan. Piecework payments automatically reward the best workers in any given category of work, and since most trades can be learned only by long training, there is little transferring from one type of work to another. Promotions from the more routine jobs to a trade are usually made on a seniority basis provided the individual's record is satisfactory. If it is not, the question is invariably discussed with the shop chairman and an agreement reached with him before any action is taken.

No more than one or two employees are discharged a year. Not since 1930 has the union seen fit to challenge a case of firing all the way through the grievance machinery and it rarely questions management's decision on this matter. Several factors account for this. The scarcity of skilled workers in recent years has made management reluctant to get rid of anyone with experience. But even when labor was plentiful, the labor manager never acted on a discharge until he had unquestionable proof as to the worker's incompetence, dishonesty, or other qualities that made him unfit for the job. With such proof, the labor manager first calls the union employment office to go over the details of the case and, when it is possible or desirable, a transfer is worked out. There are no severance pay provisions which in other industries often make the technical difference between a quit and a discharge a matter of great monetary importance.

The phrase "management prerogatives" at Hickey-Freeman has little meaning and no warlike connotations. Perhaps one reason for this is that both union and company leaders have, over the years, recognized each other's sphere of activity and have respected the boundaries as a satisfactory division. But, oddly enough, at Hickey-Freeman this mutual respect has produced in daily practice some of the most complete intermingling of management and union activity to be found in American industry.

This intermingling is especially marked in the office, provided by the company, of the union's elected plant chairman. John Turiano, the plant chairman, is a first baster, one of the most skilled occupations in the men's clothing factory. Mr. Turiano, who started work in the clothing industry when he was fourteen, has been with Hickey-Freeman since

1927, and has been the plant chairman for five years. When he is not earning his wages at the bench, the union pays him at his average hourly rate. Giving Mr. Turiano an office of his own was no act of altruism on the part of the company; it would also like to pay him for this time, but the union does not allow this.

The plant chairman is considered invaluable by management. Both union members and supervisors bring their problems to Mr. Turiano. During a typical day he may have to go over payroll vouchers with workers who have grievances on the amount. If an error is found, Mr. Turiano makes a note on the payroll slip and tells the worker it will be corrected the following week. Or, importantly, if the amount is large, Mr. Turiano makes a special notation so that it can be paid immediately. All such corrections must be approved later by the labor manager, but in practice Mr. Turiano's decisions are never overruled. An experienced employee may need to shift to part-time work, but the foreman would rather have her stay on full time. Mr. Turiano goes into the case carefully and if he feels the request is justified, arranges it. Or a foreman may be distressed over continuing poor workmanship of an employee in his shop. Mr. Turiano thoroughly discusses the situation with the production supervisor and the worker involved and arranges a mutually satisfactory shift of the worker to a better-suited job.

THE RELATIONSHIP'S EFFECT ON UNION AFFAIRS

The nerve center of the Amalgamated in Rochester is the Joint Board. Its headquarters includes a large auditorium with a well-equipped stage, several other meeting rooms, the Rochester branch of the Amalgamated Bank, and offices.

Abraham Chatman is manager of the Joint Board. In 1919, he was a top collar baster at Hickey-Freeman, and as one of the first and most active members of the union, his qualities of leadership soon asserted themselves. Within a few years he was elected to the union's top position of manager, which he still occupies. Over the years Mr. Chatman has completely absorbed Hillman's philosophy of union-management cooperation and is largely responsible for implementing it in the Rochester market. Management representatives with whom he deals have complete faith in Mr. Chatman's integrity.

Membership Participation

Mr. Chatman has built a strong organization, and his position as manager is unchallenged although, as stipulated in the union's constitution, elections are held biennially. As far as could be determined from interviews with workers, union members, and company executives, Mr. Chatman has retained his position through genuine popularity. Almost all the workers interviewed asserted that no one, not even Abraham Chatman, could hold his office without rank-and-file approval.

The man who appears to worry most about the democratic functioning of the union is Mr. Chatman himself. Since the war there has been a large influx of ex-GI's into the industry. In a general way they thank the union for good working conditions and satisfactory wages, but feel that the battle has been won. A low attendance at meetings indicates that the newer employees have found little to interest them in union business or politics. This worries Mr. Chatman, who points out: "These men and women are the ones who will one day have to run the Amalgamated. Right now, times are prosperous and there is little to make them realize what the union has accomplished. Unfortunately, lectures cannot teach union fundamentals as well as picket lines."

But lectures and other classroom work are, in the manager's opinion, of value and he has recently secured the full-time services of an educational director whose job it is to revitalize rank-and-file interest in Amalgamated. This program has been given a high priority on the union's agenda and there is even some thought being given to making attendance at some of the lectures compulsory for new members—a drastic policy for a union.

One of Amalgamated's principal contributions to constructive collective bargaining has been its ability, when the economic going got tough, to make decisions which benefited the industry but which were, at the time, unpopular to its members. It has been able to do this because of rank-and-file trust in the union leadership, a trust which was based on past union victories that were won within the active memory of the members. Whether or not the union can maintain this kind of loyalty under a mature and undramatic atmosphere remains to be seen. This question is of paramount concern not only to Amalgamated but the employers with which it deals.

Discussion of a union problem can originate either in a local meeting or by direction of the manager. He and the Joint Board are served by the facilities of an elaborate research organization attached to the Amalgamated's national office in New York. From there are disseminated statistics and factual data which the Joint Board in turn passes on to the membership at the local meetings.

The formation of demands for annual negotiations often starts in the locals. The executive board of the local may request from the research department the latest available data on the cost of living, sales of men's clothing, and other economic factors of the industry, or perhaps information concerning other fringe items. After full discussion, instructions are given by the local's delegates to the Joint Board for discussion. The Rochester members of the Amalgamated General Executive Board (including Mr. Chatman) then present the Rochester viewpoint at the top union level, where the union policy and plan of action—which are binding for all practical purposes on the regional and local groups—are established. Mr. Chatman explains to the Rochester group any differences that may exist between the national policy of the union and the policy formulated locally. Here again, there is evidence that a reasoned course can be taken without destroying effective unity because over the years the workers have genuinely accepted the philosophy that what is good for the industry is good for the workers in it.

In operation, the Amalgamated is a smoothly functioning organization with few internal battles and "political" maneuverings that beset the path of some unions. Its widespread banking operations, the administration of insurance plans, of wage stabilization programs, and of research activities, are all controlled with the kind of efficiency that one would expect in a business corporation rather than a "political" organization, which a union must be. Amalgamated has gone through its periods of internal strife. It has had its trouble with communist minorities, but a strong policy against this group was zealously followed with complete effectiveness.

The workers have fared well in this relationship, from the point of view of both economic and fringe benefits. (Gains for 1940 through 1947 are shown in Table 5, *Case Study No. 4.*) Amalgamated, a pioneer in the field, has negotiated fringe benefits which represent one of the most complete insurance coverages for unemployment, accident, sickness, and death so far developed by any union.

A Postscript

There has been no basic change in the excellent relationship between union and management at Hickey-Freeman that existed at the time *Case Study No. 4* was issued in January 1949.

CHAPTER 11

Sharon Steel Corporation

and the Steelworkers (CIO)

J. WADE MILLER, Jr., *now Director of Personnel Administration, Dewey and Almy Chemical Company, is author of* NPA Case Study No. 5. *His full report, condensed in this chapter, was published in April 1949.*

All parties concerned—employees, management, stockholders, and customers of Sharon Steel Corporation—have gained from the improvement in the company's economic position which has coincided with and partly grown out of its collective bargaining relationship. In addition, both management and employees have realized important noneconomic benefits during the years since 1937 when their constructive relationship began.

The company's competitive position in the basic steel industry has improved significantly during the course of the relationship. With only one strike—and that the industry-wide steel strike of 1946—during the relationship, the company has maintained a virtually uninterrupted flow of production. It has acquired new plants and expanded existing facilities with the union's assistance. Man-hour productivity has increased steadily. Sharon's profits and dividends have increased at a faster rate than for the industry as a whole. The company's capital investment per ton of rated ingot capacity is the lowest in the industry. A less tangible, but important benefit, is that management's job has been made easier as a result of the comparative freedom from union opposition to managerial policies and methods.

The employees have gained average hourly earnings which compared favorably with community and industry averages—and in a few years exceeded that of the industry. They have a higher degree of long-run job security as a result of Sharon's improved competitive position. They have achieved important satisfactions through membership in an effective, responsible, and strong union.

Customers and the public have benefited by the increased quality of the company's products and by the uninterrupted flow of production which have marked this record of industrial peace.

There are certain external causes of peace in this situation over which the company and employees have little control. These factors have helped to achieve peace, but have not assured it. They are: the sustained high demand for steel since 1939; pattern bargaining in the steel industry, which has eliminated for Sharon much of the haggling, exhausting debate, and emotional frustration which frequently characterize contract negotiations; the absence of any serious threat of rival unionism; and absence of a strong left-wing element within the union.

The more important internal causes, which are within the direct control of Sharon's management and the union, have grown out of the mutual confidence and regard of the union and management. Despite the fact that truly healthy relations thus far have been more the exception than the rule in the basic steel industry, Sharon has been able to achieve its relationship while subject to substantially the same industrial environment and collective bargaining agreement as those which have applied to the large majority of its competitors.

The constructive nature of Sharon's industrial relations was underscored by the changes which took place when it assumed control of a plant which previously had been operated by another large basic steel producer. Although strikes and arbitration cases had been common in this plant under its previous owner, no instance of either has occurred since Sharon took control. Furthermore, the plant's wartime production records, which had been considered unsurpassable, were exceeded in many departments within a short time after Sharon became owner.

The Company

The Sharon Steel Hoop Company, incorporated in Pennsylvania in 1900, originally owned no furnaces or other basic steel-producing facilities. By the time it became the Sharon Steel Corporation in 1936 it had acquired some facilities of that type; and now owns a number of steel plants, several coal and coke properties, and leases a by-product coke plant from the federal government. The biggest single step in the company's expansion program was taken in December 1945, when it acquired from one of the large steel producers the Farrell, Pennsylvania, plant. Its most important other plants are located at Sharon, Pennsylvania, and Lowellville, Niles, and Warren in Ohio. All told, total plant investment has increased steadily from about $18 million in 1938 to $21.5 million in 1944 to $35 million in 1947.

This report deals with only three of the company's plants, which are covered by a single agreement between the company and the United Steelworkers of America (CIO). They are the plants at Sharon and Farrell, which are on adjacent properties and combined for operating purposes, and at Lowellville. These plants are geographically concentrated and produce by far the largest amount of Sharon's total output. The other units and subsidiaries of the Corporation are covered by separate union agreements. The production of steel ingots is confined to the Farrell and Lowellville plants. Sharon's varied products are sold to manufacturers of automobiles, electrical equipment, household appliances, aircraft, oil industry equipment, agricultural machinery, and many others.

The Corporation's annual rated ingot capacity in 1947 was 1,672,000 net tons. In rated ingot capacity, Sharon is ninth among the basic steel producers of the United States; and it ranks thirteenth in net sales volume. Net sales for the company have increased every year since 1938 with the exception of a small decrease in 1944. Its consolidated net sales for 1947 amounted to almost $94 million. Net income increased steadily from a loss in 1938 to a profit of almost $7 million in 1947, and dividends paid to holders of common stock have more than quadrupled since 1939. The Corporation earned $10.89 per common share in 1947, which placed it fifth in the industry in that respect.

The company's competitive position appears to be good and is clearly much stronger than before World War II. What Sharon's position may be if and when the demand for steel products begins to decline from present high levels is exceedingly difficult to forecast, since there is little agreement as to what a normal demand for steel may be in our postwar economy.

Management's Approach to Bargaining

The management of the Sharon Steel Corporation is closely identified with the personality of its president, Henry Arthur Roemer. This results both from Mr. Roemer's talent for leadership and from the fact that he has brought into the company most of the present key management personnel.

Henry Roemer, the son of a blast-furnace worker, took his first job as a waterboy in a steel mill, and by the time he was twenty-one was a mill superintendent. During subsequent years of steady advancement, he became widely known for his ability to put run-down steel companies back on a profitable basis of operation. In 1931, Mr. Roemer came to the Sharon Steel Hoop Company as its president, although many steel men believed the company had no hope of ever again showing a profit. Henry Roemer's experience as a mill hand has had great influence upon his attitude toward his employees and the union—"I always remember that I might have been on the other side of the bargaining table myself." And it had an equal influence on the union and its members—"At the age of 17, the old man was a sheet mill 'rougher' in the old Struthers works of the Corporation. *He* knows what a union means! I understand he was a member of the Amalgamated [Amalgamated Association of Iron, Steel and Tin Workers of North America] at that time."

Throughout most of his managerial career, Mr. Roemer has stressed the importance of complete understanding between labor and management. This attitude has been clear in the company's approach to labor relations from the time the union was accepted. An incident which occurred in the Farrell plant shortly after it had been acquired by Sharon makes clear the three characteristics which have formed the cornerstone of Sharon's approach to the union. Local union officials told Mr. Roemer that seniority was their biggest headache at the Farrell plant, that after almost eight years of collective bargaining, the union and the plant's previous management had not been able to agree upon even the units to which a seniority plan was to be applied. The union officers were amazed when Mr. Roemer replied: "What kind of seniority do you want? If you work up a plan that suits you and if it seems fairly reasonable to us, we'll adopt it." The startled union officials proceeded to develop a seniority plan which was later accepted by the company.

This incident illustrates, first, management's sincere, straight-from-the-shoulder manner. Shortly after the union had been certified, at a discussion with Clinton S. Golden, then regional director of the Steel Workers Organizing Committee (SWOC), Mr. Roemer made clear that the company faced serious economic problems, but said management would lay its cards on the table and pitch in to make the relationship work, and that it fully expected the union to do likewise.

The second characteristic is management's open-mindedness and flexibility. The seniority issue, for example, was not prejudged and no dogmatic take-it-or-leave-it proposals were put forward by the company. Instead, there was a willingness to give full consideration to the union's suggestions. The flexibility on management's side is also indicated by the fact that in every possible way company officials have kept lawyers and legalisms out of the relationship; and they have sometimes relinquished certain of the company's contractual rights when it appeared that the relationship would be improved. Sharon's president and other management officials have confidence in their own bargaining ability and in the sincerity and reliability of the union.

Firmness is the third characteristic of management's over-all approach demonstrated by the seniority incident. Unwillingness to settle for peace at any price is evident throughout the company's relations with the union. This is recognized by union members, one of whom had this to say about the bargaining qualifications of an official in one of the plants: "He's a hell of a good steelmaker and knows his business. He's tougher than hell, and you can't put anything over on him. He pulls no punches, but he's a square shooter." The Sharon management is determined to prevent its industrial relations policies from causing any unjustified interference with the proper execution of managerial responsibilities toward either the owners or the customers of the Corporation. (Mr. Roemer has held a large block of stock in the company ever since he first assumed the presidency of Sharon Steel.)

The Coordination of Policy and Practice

Uniformity in understanding and application of this approach at all levels of management have been achieved at Sharon in varied and more or less informal ways. The first attempt was made after the NLRB election which preceded recognition of the union. Mr. Roemer invited key management and union officials to a banquet. During the evening, Mr. Roemer carefully outlined his policy for dealing with the union, and told top union officials: "We are partners by virtue of this contract—we're in bed together whether we like it or not." Several high-ranking members of management who failed to make the recommended adjustment have since been dismissed or transferred.

The coordination of policy and practice is not primarily a matter of after-dinner speeches, however. Its basic features consist of the customary techniques of memoranda, conference, direct personal contact, and example. Informal methods have seemed to be satisfactory for several reasons: the strong and active day-to-day part which Henry Roemer, with his office in the Sharon plant, has played; the small size of the company compared with some of its competitors; the fact that line management in the typical steel company ordinarily involves few levels.

Top management does not hesitate to delegate authority to subordinates. With such delegation, accelerated as the company has expanded, more decisions can be made in the plants, but it also increases the need for effective coordination. There is still the difficulty of thoroughly disseminating policies among lower plant supervision, which may necessitate the use of more formal procedures. The prospects for long-run stability depend to some extent upon Mr. Roemer's success in securing continuation of his approach. However, the prospects seem bright. One executive, originally skeptical of Mr. Roemer's ideas on the union, says he now is firmly convinced that those ideas are not only practical, but form the only basis for a sound approach to industrial relations.

Line-Staff Relationships

There is a significant change from the days when the sole responsibility for industrial relations was vested in a line official, such as the works manager. At the Sharon and Farrell plants primary responsibility falls on a plant superintendent of industrial relations. Similar responsibility at the Lowellville plant until recently seems to have been borne by the official who serves as general industrial relations executive for the entire Corporation—who is known as the director of personnel.

The director of personnel is responsible for all labor-management issues classified as matters of company policy. He exercises the equivalent of line authority, especially in connection with grievances and complaints. Perhaps as a direct result of this intermingling of line and staff authority, there exists at Sharon a relatively high degree of mutual assistance and support between line officials and staff personnel. The industrial relations personnel inform management officials about the status of collective bargaining problems, and do not seek increased influence with employees or union at the expense of other management personnel.

Except for the exercise of line authority, the industrial relations organization at Sharon is not unlike that found in most steel companies of comparable size. Therefore the industrial relations department at Sharon has not been a major cause of industrial peace, although it has certainly made a contribution.

The Employees

The three plants had over 6000 hourly-rated employees on June 30, 1947—2645 at Sharon, 2223 at Farrell, and 1301 at Lowellville. Approximately one-quarter are classified as skilled workers, one-half as semiskilled, and the remaining as unskilled. The age distribution is not unusual for the steel industry, the largest age group being 20–24 years old. Sharon, however, has a low rate of turnover and an unusual number of long-service employees. In September 1947, in all the Corporation's plants and subsidiaries, there were 112 employees who had been with the company for more than 40 years, and 922 for more than 25. Since the end of the war, turnover has averaged approximately 2.8 per cent for the Sharon and Farrell plants and 3.5 per cent for Lowellville, where until a recent expansion program was started there was uncertainty as to whether the plant would remain in operation.

A constructive discipline policy has contributed to the low turnover rate and to industrial peace. The largest number of employee discharges in any one year at the Sharon plant, for example, was 30 in 1942, and the figure has been as low as 5 in 1938 and 7 in 1944. This cannot be explained by the wartime shortage of labor or by the fact that the agreement provides for joint review of all cases involving discharge or suspension of more than 4 days' duration. Rather it lies in management's attitude and the way it handles infractions which in many plants would bring immediate discharge. Nor does it mean that inefficiency or incompetence is tolerated. Deficiencies of that type earn a quick and irrevocable discharge.

The excellent relationship at Sharon cannot be attributed to community influences or the ethnic make-up of its workers. Steel plants owned by other companies operate in the same area and with the same labor supply, but frequently with very different bargaining results. There is considerable industrial unrest in the communities in which Sharon's plants are located.

The Union

An employee representation plan of the type common in industry during the 1920's and early thirties was in existence at Sharon prior to any attempt by the SWOC to organize the company's employees. The company's Plan probably was intended as a means of preventing organization by an outside union, but apparently its function as an antiunion device was not pushed to an extreme. One month after an announcement calling attention to benefits to be derived under the Plan had been issued by management, it issued a "Memorandum of Agreement," dated May 20, 1937, in regard to the SWOC. This pointed out that (1) SWOC had presented a contract to the company under which it would become bargaining agent for the company's employees who were members of SWOC; (2) the company had advised SWOC to have an election held in the plants under NLRB supervision to determine whether the employees wanted SWOC as their representative; (3) if a majority voted for SWOC, the company would negotiate and sign an exclusive bargaining agreement with SWOC, with the contract substantially in the form already admitted; (4) all eligible employees at the Sharon and Lowellville plants would constitute the bargaining unit.

Recognition of the Union

Judging from the memorandum, management had accepted the view that if the employees really wanted to be represented by the SWOC, then that was the way it should be. Whereas the union's proposed contract provided that it was to represent the *members* of SWOC, the company provided that *all eligible employees* would constitute the collective bargaining unit. This stand was taken despite the fact that "Big Steel" had recognized the union as collective bargaining agent on a members-only basis, and that "Little Steel" opposed recognition on any basis whatever.

The NLRB election was held, with no unpleasantness, five days after the "Memorandum of Agreement" was issued. There was a clear union victory. The first contract was negotiated promptly and easily as a result of the company's prior acceptance as to form and the union's failure to press for such concessions as the union shop or check-off.

The long-run success of Sharon's collective bargaining relationship and the maintenance of a high order of industrial peace resulted in large measure from the nature of the initial period of organization and recognition. In the words of one company official, "1937 still pays off." Within a 20-mile radius of the Sharon and Lowellville plants, the SWOC was fighting for its life against the powerful resistance offered by "Little Steel" employers. Lockouts and strikes were widespread, violence and bloodshed were the order of the day, and many employees were ultimately to be fired for union activity when the employers won a temporary victory later in 1937. There were many economic pressures from many sources which might have led Sharon to join "Little Steel" in opposing unionism. When top management made the decision to consent to the NLRB election, Sharon was in a precarious position from both a productive and a competitive standpoint. This fact was not lost upon union or employees, and increased the company's prestige in their eyes.

A Strong and Responsible Union

Union leaders from the international and district offices of the United Steelworkers of America (formerly the SWOC) have played a significant role in this relationship from the start, and more recently the local leadership is becoming equally important. An important element in the success of this relationship has been the union's scrupulous regard for its commitments, informal as well as contractual, and legitimate obligations. Officials and members have not gone back on their word or resorted to legalistic quibbles in order to escape some binding obligation. And the union leadership has usually been willing to match management's flexible attitude toward the agreement when it appeared that both parties could gain by adopting some change in procedure or interpretation.

The membership in each of the three local unions is now well over 90 per cent of all eligible employees in the Sharon, Farrell, and Lowellville plants. A maintenance-of-membership clause became a part of the collective bargaining agreement during World War II. The leadership in one local customarily is centered in not more than one individual at a time; the second is led by three individuals who usually operate as a team; the leadership in the third is split between two more or less competing groups. Membership participation in the union's day-to-day affairs has been rather slight in the latter two locals, but the other has not had a particularly outstanding record on this score. However, all three have been typified by an active interest on the part of the various committeemen, especially those serving on the negotiating and grievance committees.

The company has directly encouraged a high degree of union responsibility. It calls upon union representatives for constructive proposals rather than mere complaints, as illustrated by the seniority incident at Farrell. Most officers of the Farrell local were able to adjust to this new type of management approach and to meet its challenge. One or two, who were unable to do more than talk tough and pound the table, quickly faded into the background. One of the chief lessons to be drawn from this study is management's demonstration that the way to develop effective leadership in a union local is to give a reasonable amount of responsibility to the union. Even in the early days, when the union's position was relatively weak, management never took advantage of it but actively encouraged membership in the union. Such assistance played a considerable part in strengthening the locals and did much to influence the union's attitude toward collective bargaining in general and toward the company in particular.

The Sharon district office of the Steelworkers union deals with both the Sharon and Farrell locals, and the Youngstown district office deals with the Lowellville local. Each office has its own officials and staff under the leadership of a district director, elected every four years by members of the local unions within the district. Theoretically, the district officials are not directly active in the relationships at a particular plant, except with regard to such matters as negotiating a new agreement, handling third or fourth steps in grievances, and other matters of major importance. In the relationships with Sharon Steel, however, the directors have been more active at the plants.

The fact that its two largest plants are located within the Sharon district has made the quality of leadership there particularly important to the company. John W. Grajciar has been director of that district since 1941. Employed in the basic steel industry since he was eleven years old, he first joined the union in 1913 and has been a union officer since 1918 (first in the old Amalgamated union). Mr. Grajciar and Mr. Roemer have been closely acquainted for a number of years and their personal amity has influenced the relationship between Sharon and the union.

John Grajciar and his predecessors as well as James Griffen and his predecessors in the Youngstown district have evidenced a marked talent for constructive collective bargaining. The effect of such leadership has loomed large in the development of industrial peace. Their unusually active participation, however, may not have been wholly beneficial in its effect upon the type of leadership developed in the locals. Union officials recognized this problem after it became apparent that union members were regularly by-passing local officers and bringing their problems direct to district officials. Consequently, an active effort was begun to increase the authority and responsibility of local officials. The basic problem was to train local officers so that they could fulfill their responsibilities, and then to see that they got an opportunity to utilize what they had learned. In pursuing this purpose, higher levels of authority were able to pass on to local officers their own effective methods and attitudes.

The union has made continuing efforts to avoid factionalism within or among the locals. This became increasingly difficult after the acquisition of the Farrell plant, and also was harder because two of the locals are in one union district and the third in a neighboring district. Even so, all three have managed to work together effectively.

The international union has also played an important part in putting this relationship on a firm basis. One of the main reasons for the comparatively peaceful transition from nonunion to union status was the mutual confidence shared by Henry Roemer and Clinton S. Golden which enabled them to deal effectively and constructively with each other. Other international union representatives also assisted in launching unionism at Sharon without the strife and violence which were then so common.

KEY FEATURES OF THE RELATIONSHIP

The outstanding feature of the union-management picture at Sharon Steel is that from the start both parties devoted their energies to making the relationship work for their mutual benefit. No time was wasted attempting to undermine or betray it. The company did not welcome the union with open arms. However, management felt that since there was no way of heading off unionism, the next best thing was to have a responsible union which was truly representative of all eligible employees. Therefore the company officials have always refrained from mixing in the "political" affairs of the union, or from publicizing the escape period under the maintenance-of-membership clause. And it has been known to encourage nonmembers to join the union. The union is just as determined to make the relationship work. There is little table pounding and bluffing. Private talks with many union leaders have indicated a minimum of bias against management. There are no indications of any active radical element at the Sharon Steel plants, nor of any thought of using the relationship as a means for gradually undermining the position of management or ownership.

Out of this mutual acceptance has grown the responsibility and cooperation which characterize the present situation. One illustration of these characteristics is the approach used to solve a postwar scrap shortage which threatened temporary curtailment of certain operations at the Lowellville plant. Mr. Roemer invited John Grajciar to go to Washington with him to help make the necessary contacts in an effort to alleviate the shortage and to give the union a better understanding of the steps which were being taken to correct the situation. Another such incident occurred during the industry-wide strike in 1946. Mr. Roemer provided space so that pickets could remain in a company building instead of outside in the cold. They received his assurance—and accepted it—that no one would take advantage of the situation in order to enter the plant while the picket line was thus adjourned.

A final indication of management's acceptance of the relationship is provided in a letter written by Mr. Roemer, which was quoted in the September 1947 issue of *Sharonsteel Record,* for the information of employees:

In my humble opinion the provisions of the Taft-Hartley Act, however interpreted, should make little or no difference in the relationship between the men and management of this company. If we approach the question from the human angle rather than from the legal standpoint . . . if we

work harmoniously together in the solution of our problems of production
. . . and if we continue to do a good job for Sharon Steel . . . neither men
nor management need have any fear of either the provisions or the penalties
embodied in this Act. . . . Do we play ball with each other or do we invoke
the law? I very much prefer the first measure and that is the way we intend
to operate.

Grievance Procedures

It is difficult to state accurately the total number of grievances or their
nature, because until the last few years a majority were not recorded, and
were settled informally without ever entering the formal grievance procedure prescribed by the contract. However, from 1937 through 1947,
576 grievances were formally recorded at the Sharon Plant. Of these, 29
per cent dealt with working conditions, 25 per cent with wages, and 14
per cent with safety. The remainder were divided among eight additional
categories. After the war there was a sharp decline in the number of
grievances dealing with wage matters, and a sizable increase in those
concerned with problems of safety. The number of grievances per year
has varied widely. There has been no resort to arbitration.

The informal method of handling grievances seems to have been in-
spired primarily by management, but it remained satisfactory to the
union for a long time. Management's willingness to settle grievances on
such an informal basis seems to stem primarily from the importance
placed upon achieving prompt settlement. The stress on promptness is
evident in a statement of the industrial relations director of the Corporation: "I am out here at the plant by 8 o'clock in the morning. I want
to be here so that if any grievances or problems occur in the night shift,
they can be taken up with me, if necessary, before the people involved
leave the mill. I find that this stops a minor incident from mushrooming
into undue proportions and causing us trouble."

The written grievance procedure also emphasizes prompt settlement
by placing time limits upon the submission of each grievance to a higher
level of the procedure. Moreover, direct short-circuiting of the lower steps
is prescribed for grievances involving an issue which is beyond the authority of the management officials who participate in the lower steps of the
grievance procedure.

A large number of grievances have been settled without resort to the
formal procedure. In the first place, since the grievance procedures formerly did not make the allowances for expediting settlement, the informality had firm roots in the past. Secondly, by-passing of virtually any

procedure could usually be justified or rationalized by the need for promptness. And, finally, the personal relationship between high-level union and company officials further encouraged informal settlement of grievances. But even when the formal procedure nominally has been followed, it has been marked by a considerable degree of flexibility.

As a factor in the development of industrial peace, the prompt settlement of grievances has undoubtedly been of great importance. The same informality, however, in some ways may have retarded the development of a healthy relationship. Lower management officials, by-passed in the procedure, have been denied valuable experience and training in dealing constructively with the union, and their prestige has almost certainly been reduced in the eyes of the employees and the union. On the union side, by-passing of the lower steps of the grievance procedure has meant that most local union officers have had little opportunity to represent their membership on major grievances. As part of the steps being taken to increase the responsibility of the local union officers, the union is now in favor of reducing the informal handling of grievances.

Sharon nevertheless has managed to settle effectively most of the grievances brought by the union. Sharon has not simply bowed to the union's demands. Actually, the percentage of grievances which have been granted by the company has averaged about one-third of the total number of recorded grievances. A large percentage have been compromised, and more than one-fifth have either been withdrawn by the union or refused by management. The net effect of informality has been favorable.

Wage Policies and Job Classifications

Total expenditure for wages and salaries at Sharon, including Social Security taxes, increased from $3.9 million in 1938 to $28.5 million in 1947, both figures approximating one-third of net sales for the respective years. In the same period, average hourly earnings rose from 80.7 cents to $1.47, an increase of 82 per cent. Both the trend in hourly earnings and the relationship between total payroll and net sales were fairly representative of the basic industry as a whole. And the average hourly earnings at Sharon for that period also compared favorably with the general average for steel producers in the Sharon-Youngstown area. The small size of the differentials makes it questionable that these wage advantages have operated as a strong motivating force toward industrial peace. On the other hand, the fact that Sharon has been able to maintain at least an approximate equality with the wages paid by its competitors has removed a potential obstacle to harmonious relations.

The general methods of wage payment at Sharon have not differed greatly from those used elsewhere in the steel industry. In addition to straight hourly rates, there are tonnage rates, piece rates, and other forms of individual and group incentives. Approximately 50 per cent of the wage earners at Sharon are covered to some extent by some form of incentive payment, but there is no profit-sharing plan or other type of plant-wide or company-wide incentive.

The really important favorable impact of wages upon the development of industrial peace at Sharon seems to have been the simplicity and flexibility of wage policy. Management has refused to adopt changes which introduced complexities into the wage structure or which made it impossible for a worker to figure out his approximate earnings without the help of a slide rule or a complicated set of graphs. It has been cautious with regard to industrial engineering activities. Employees engaged in those activities have been carefully selected and trained, with as much stress placed on the human aspects of their work as the technical phases. Sharon's industrial relations director also fills the position of chief industrial engineer, thus enabling him to maintain a high degree of coordination between industrial engineering and the over-all personnel policies and practices. Even when it is technically defensible to support a refusal for an increase, decisions are made on the basis of the effect on good industrial relations. This attitude may at times have cost additional dollars in the company's total wage bill, but it has more than paid for itself in long-run harmony.

Some companies in the steel industry introduced various modifications in wage-payment methods during World War II, but Sharon did not follow their lead. To a great extent, this accounts for the fact that Sharon did not bring a single case before the War Labor Board. In contrast, wage disputes involving most of the steel companies which attempted to introduce changes in wage-payment methods crowded the dockets of the regional boards. By adhering to existing methods of wage payment until the necessary changes were explained and justified to the employees, Sharon has avoided much strife and misunderstanding.

With respect to the relationship between rates paid for different jobs within the company, Sharon's record has not been much better than that of most employers in the basic steel industry. This problem in the industry had become so serious over the years that the War Labor Board in 1944 directed 86 steel producers, including Sharon, to correct existing inequities within a specified time. The companies were ordered further to establish a rational system of job classification which would avoid the recurrence of new inequities, and to carry on job evaluation and classification jointly with the union. The program was carried out effectively at Sharon, although with considerable antagonism among employees, particularly those workers who stood to benefit least by anticipated changes in wage rates. This hostility was directed against both management and the union, since the program was a joint one. Whereas it would have been virtually impossible to remove all opposition to so basic a change, had management and the union taken adequate steps to inform the rank and file, opposition might have been reduced.

By 1947, most production and maintenance jobs in the company had been evaluated and placed in one of 30 job classes. The rates assigned to those classifications ranged, in consecutive 4-cent increments, from $1.09 to $2.25. With few exceptions, the jobs were classified in the same labor grade and paid the same hourly rate prevailing at most of Sharon's competitors. In some instances, the new rate assigned to a particular job was sufficiently high to include the old standard rate and most of the possible premium payments under the original incentive system. This largely nullified the incentive system as a motivation for greater production. Although this aspect of the program caused management much concern, thus far no major upward adjustment of the incentive rates has been made.

Communications and Joint Consultation

Sharon's management considers good communications as an important factor in the development of a healthy collective bargaining relationship. It accepts the view that the employees have a right to expect adequate information regarding policies which affect them, especially if the union and its members are expected to have a high degree of responsibility and to cooperate in making necessary adjustments. For example, management held a series of conferences with union representatives well in advance of the contemplated purchase of the Farrell plant in 1945. Similarly, conferences were held regarding a proposal to increase the blast-furnace facilities at Farrell by 20 to 25 per cent. Typical of the stress put on communications, is the fact that an industrial relations official once spent the better part of three days explaining a specific phase of the incentive system to a local union representative. Once the representative grasped the problem, he was of great assistance to management in helping to explain the problem to other employees.

Highly formalized procedures of communication are the exception at Sharon. There have been occasional memoranda addressed to the employees as a group, and a few such extraordinary procedures as the banquet which followed the NLRB election in 1937. But the function of maintaining a satisfactory flow of information from management to union and in the reverse direction is largely by informal and personalized methods—conferences between one or more management and union officials, a letter, or a telephone call. Communications within management also are informal. For example, Sharon has never operated a full-fledged foreman-training program. In one way or another, however, top management has succeeded in communicating its policies to lower levels promptly and effectively. Communication up the line is another question. Apparently nothing approaching consultative supervision or multiple management has been given any serious consideration at Sharon.

In like manner, the union's internal communications system has relied to a great extent on informal contacts and personal relationships. The recent emphasis upon increased responsibilities of the local union officials has stimulated the communication of much information from the district office to local officials, and on from them to members. In addition, union publications of various types have played a part in keeping members generally informed on the union's problems and policies.

The attempts to maintain a free flow of information between management and the union at Sharon do not indicate a desire on the part of management for joint consultation or participation by the union in the actual decisions of company officials. When management conferred with the union on the contemplated purchase of the Farrell plant, it was not asking the union to participate in the decision to make the purchase—but merely to advise the employees of the impending purchase and to seek their cooperation in meeting whatever difficulties might result. There has been no attempt to undertake a formal union-management cooperation program similar to those which have been developed in various other companies in the steel industry. With the exception of joint safety committees, the only instance of true joint participation at Sharon was the job evaluation specifically ordered by the War Labor Board.

The Sharon management, however, has not clung tenaciously to its decision-making prerogatives and resisted every attempt by the union to give advice and counsel. There is a pronounced lack of emphasis upon the "management prerogatives" clause of the contract. In the course of developing and maintaining mutual assistance, both management and the union have learned and acknowledged that effective communications within and between the parties are mandatory if the union and its members are to play their proper roles in strengthening the company and helping to assure its future progress and development.

The flow of information between the parties apparently has been adequate, and it is difficult to see how that fact could have failed to make a positive contribution to industrial peace. Communications within the respective organizations have perhaps been less notable, but not so much so that they should be termed unsatisfactory. Whether the contribution made by these factors might have been greater had more formal procedures been followed is a matter of conjecture, but the communications and consultation as practiced at Sharon have made a definite contribution to industrial peace.

Problems Affecting the Relationship

Complex problems still exist in this healthy relationship. One of these involves safety regulations and practices. Sharon's accident record has not been particularly bad in comparison with other firms in the steel industry. Nevertheless, a large percentage of the employees seem to be convinced that management has not made working conditions as safe as possible. Joint safety committees have been in operation for several years, but their authority and scope of activity have usually been insufficient to permit real accomplishment. Whether the employees' belief is right or wrong, the fact that they feel management's attitude on safety matters is deficient constitutes a weak spot in the existing relationship.

. A second problem is the existence of a certain amount of interplant rivalry among the employees. Many workers in the Sharon and Lowellville plants are convinced that eventual slackening of the demand for steel may lead to the transfer of some operations from their plants to the Farrell plant, with consequent layoffs. For this reason, these workers have suggested a form of company-wide seniority. This dispute could conceivably cause a serious split within the union which would not augur well for the future stability of the relationship.

A third problem is the complaint heard from both sides that the relationship in some respects is too flexible and informal. Some intermediate levels of management clearly resent being by-passed by top management decisions, even though actual overruling of lower management decisions has been infrequent. On the union side, John Grajciar is now definitely opposed to the high degree of flexibility that has developed in the relationship, because the informality tends to encourage by-passing local union officials. It is difficult to evaluate this question. The fact that officials on both the management and the union sides have mentioned it, however, gives credence to the claim that there is too much flexibility.

The over-all pattern of the relationship shows the inevitable two sides of the coin. On the one side, there is a high degree of responsibility and cooperation which has grown out of the full acceptance of the relationship by all parties concerned. On the other side, some sizable problems show up. The encouraging thing is that the parties to the Sharon relationship have developed a talent for jointly tackling such problems and finding mutually beneficial solutions.

A POSTSCRIPT

There have been no significant changes in the relationship at Sharon's three plants since early in 1949. Management and the union have continued to discuss their problems freely and frankly and seem to find amicable settlements without serious difficulty.

As always, there have been certain unavoidable frictions, the most important of which have resulted from problems that were industry-wide rather than confined to Sharon Steel itself. Unions in the three plants went along with the industry-wide strike of April 1952, and two of the plants had a brief strike, involving only a few workers. However, if the *Case Study* were being written today, it would not be necessary to make significant changes with respect to the status of the relationship or the apparent reasons for industrial peace in this company.

CHAPTER 12

Lockheed Aircraft Corporation
and the Machinists (AFL)

CLARK KERR, *now Chancellor, University of California at Berkeley, and*
GEORGE HALVERSON, *Institute of Industrial Relations, University of
California at Berkeley, are authors of* NPA Case Study No. 6. *Their full re-
port, condensed in this chapter, was published in November 1949.*

The preservation of peace between the Lockheed Aircraft Corporation
and the International Association of Machinists (independent when the
study was made, now AFL) has been a substantial achievement. Their
experience demonstrates how a collective bargaining relationship can be
faced by enormously difficult and complicated problems and emerge,
though by a narrow margin, without resort to force. Throughout this
changing relationship, there have been no official strikes, in contrast to
long and bitter strikes which have occurred at the other unionized West
Coast airframe companies over substantially the same types of problems
settled more amicably at Lockheed. The record of Lockheed and IAM,
however, is by no means perfect. It has been marked by thousands of
grievances and considerable intervention—especially during World War
II—of third parties.

The Lockheed-IAM relationship developed from 1937 to 1949 through
five clearly delineated periods:

1. The "sweetheart period," 1937–41: A small company and a small
union met in harmony.

2. The war at home, 1942–45: The company expanded enormously.
The union undertook aggressive day-to-day bargaining to sell itself to the
ever growing and changing group of employees; the company became
protective about managerial rights.

3. An era of good feeling, 1945–46: Lockheed consulted with the

157

union about reconversion problems, increased wages, and maintained higher comparative levels of employment than other airframe producers.

4. The time of troubles, 1947–48: Business prospects on which the good feeling was partly founded deteriorated gravely. The company became defensive, the union became belligerent.

5. The new harmony, 1949: The company's profits and prospects had improved; the union had regained almost complete membership support.

THE PARTIES AND THEIR PROBLEMS

The Lockheed Aircraft Corporation is one of the largest and best known of this country's airframe manufacturers, which assemble planes from parts and materials usually manufactured by separate companies. The airframe industry on the Pacific Coast includes one major producer, Boeing Aircraft Company, at Seattle, and six major companies in Southern California: Consolidated Aircraft Corporation and Ryan Aeronautical Company in San Diego; and Douglas Aircraft Company, North American Aviation, Inc., Northrup Aircraft, Inc., and Lockheed in the Los Angeles area. Southern California's airframe industry grew from 12,000 employees in 1938 to 32,000 employees in January 1940, and reached a peak of 280,000 employees during World War II, about one-third of all employees in the United States airframe production. In peacetime, the ratio has been one-half or more.

Financial Insecurity of the Industry

The basic problem confronting all airframe companies has been financial insecurity. Their market has been highly unstable, consisting of civilian demand from a relatively small number of purchasers and the government's military demand. In peacetime, the immense overcapacity for airframe production has led to strenuous competition among producers of commercial and military planes. Problems faced by the industry are illustrated by the fact that the monthly production, in terms of airframe weight for both military and civilian use, rose from 2.4 million pounds in January 1940 to a peak of 103 million pounds early in 1944, and fell to 1 million in July 1946.

Lockheed was founded in 1912, when airframe manufacturing was a shoestring industry. An intermediate owner went bankrupt in 1930, and the company was subsequently purchased in 1932 (for $40,000) by seven men, four of whom were still company officials in 1949. Robert E. Gross, one of them, is still president. Lockheed grew during the war from a single small plant to seventeen plants. During the early part of the war, it was the largest airframe producer in the United States. Later, its employment level was exceeded by Douglas, Boeing, and North American. Shortly before the war, Lockheed's employment was at about 4,000; in 1944, it was at 94,000; and by 1949, it was down to 13,500 employees in two large plants which were operated in Burbank.

Lockheed's postwar program was severely affected by four unforeseen events: operational difficulties with its major plane, the Constellation, led to its temporary grounding; the major domestic buyer of Constellations curtailed purchases following a strike of airline pilots and other difficulties; the world-wide shortage of dollars caused foreign purchasers to reduce orders below anticipated levels; and a "feeder line" transport (the Saturn), after an investment of $7 million, which proved expensive to build and incapable of the desired performance, was abandoned. For a time, production was slowed down and planes in various stages of completion remained unsold. Such uncertainties have constituted a major short-run pressure on the company in the conduct of its industrial relations, particularly since labor is about 50 per cent of the cost element in the airframe industry.

Unfavorable Climate for Unionism

An industrial climate of aggressive resistance to unionism prevailed in the Los Angeles area and in the airframe industry throughout the 1930's. Lockheed was the first airframe company to agree to collective bargaining in Southern California, and its acceptance of the union was voluntary. This involved going against the predominant policy of the local business community, and a reorientation in the thinking of Lockheed management.

Rival Unionism

First recognized at Lockheed in 1937, Lodge 727 of the International Association of Machinists by 1949 represented nearly all of the hourly paid factory employees and most of the hourly paid office and technical employees. (A separate IAM local, Lodge 1638, represents the guards; the Engineers and Architects Association, a local organization with neither AFL or CIO affiliation, has largely covered salaried engineers and other professional technicians since it was accorded recognition in 1944; and AFL's International Brotherhood of Electrical Workers won bargaining rights in 1948 for a small number of maintenance electricians.)

The IAM, originally a craft union but later operating on an industrial basis, has a reputation for responsible conduct and reasonableness. It has a record of effective representation of its members, with a minimum disruption of production. The union is noted for its democratic administration, and for the integrity and constructive approach of its national as well as many of its local officers.

Rival unionism, perpetually faced by the IAM, has created a problem for the union which has had a major impact on its relations with Lockheed. The United Automobile Workers (CIO) started organizing in the Southern California aircraft industry in 1936; the IAM in 1937; and the two unions have divided representation of the area's airframe employees. The intense rivalry between IAM and UAW prior to World War II became an uneasy truce during the war, but competition resumed in the postwar period. In addition, IAM's jurisdiction has been threatened by some craft unions in the AFL. Even when conflicts over bargaining rights have not been going on within an individual company, gains by one of the contestants elsewhere have been used as a bargaining tool in the company. Conflicts over the terms of agreements and their administration, therefore, have not been only union-company controversies, but also union versus union.

Wartime and Postwar Strains

Wartime increases in the work force and faster turnover created joint problems for the company and union at Lockheed. At the start of the war, maintenance of a work force of 4000 meant that about 5000 different persons a year were employees of the company and potential union members; at the high point of the war, 76,000 new persons were hired in a single year. In addition to wartime engineering, procurement, and production difficulties, the company was swamped with problems of hiring, training, assigning, and paying. Top executives could devote less time to relations with the union.

The union had to create an organizational structure which could accommodate the vastly increased membership. Shop stewards, at one time numbering more than the total of prewar employees, had to be selected and trained. The union could not relax constant organizational efforts to gain and hold as members thousands of people new to manufacturing employment who had never belonged to unions. Federal limitations on wage increases and other contractual gains forced the union to rely on aggressive administration of the contract to prove its value. The new membership produced rival leaders; and the contest for leading union positions added further pressure. The processing of grievances became a mass-production enterprise.

Prewar production was on a handicraft basis, but wartime production was of the assembly-line type. The increasing division of labor brought a transition from the journeyman worker to the specialist; a new wage structure had to be created to match the new job structure. There was a general sense of dissatisfaction with poor housing, transportation, and eating facilities. Under these unfavorable circumstances, the company and union were faced with new problems requiring joint action, or at least joint discussion.

When the war was over and employment dropped drastically, mass layoffs created many questions of seniority, and work assignments were less highly specialized. Employees had to be transferred and retrained and thousands of workers were down-graded. Each lateral and downward movement was the source of a potential grievance. The rate structure had to be reworked to adjust to the changed technical nature of production. Lockheed's rates often had been higher than those in the rest of the Southern California industry, and competition encouraged the company to attempt to get them back into line. These changes to shorter hours and lower pay came, furthermore, at a time when the cost of living was rising and workers outside the airframe industry generally were getting wage increases, increasing the internal frictions for the Lockheed and IAM relationship.

Strife Without Strikes

Peace was encouraged in this relationship, however, by certain fundamental conditions in the physical and economic environment. The prewar aircraft worker performed many tasks and had creative opportunities. His product had romantic connotations; and the development of each new plane was followed by individual employees with personal interest. Although the war changed this substantially, employees still identified themselves with the company's products and the frequent reports on uses of Lockheed planes on war fronts lent some glamour even to menial tasks. After the war the nature of the work partially resumed its prewar characteristics.

Aircraft work has one of the lowest accident rates of any industry, and the plants are pleasant places in which to work. Buildings are usually spacious; the air and floors are clean; the temperature is not artificially raised by production processes, and there are no offensive odors, although there is constant noise.

Other favorable conditions in the Lockheed situation were the fact that when collective bargaining was started, the single plant was small enough

(1000 employees) to permit personal contact of many employees with top management, which eased the initial relationship, and peacetime competition with other companies has tended to identify the employees with Lockheed. The occasional but obvious financial difficulties of the company have dampened the desire of employees for precipitous action. The company has several times been close enough to the margin of survival so that unwise moves by the union could have placed the jobs of its members in jeopardy. The government, single purchaser of the product during wartime, would not permit the employer and union to fight, and before and after the war, the parties could ill afford it.

Despite their problems, no single authorized strike or lockout has occurred during the twelve years of bargaining between IAM and Lockheed. A dissident group of welders stopped work in 1941, but this was quickly handled by the prompt action of union and management leadership. The union membership voted to strike three times: in 1945, to stimulate prompt action by the company and War Labor Board, and in 1947 and 1949 to speed up negotiations on new contracts which were approaching stalemates. However, neither vote led to a cessation of work.

There have been thousands of grievances, particularly during the war and postwar years. The parties have shown a sincere desire to settle these grievances themselves. In twelve years of the relationship, only 25 issues, of a total of over 30,000 formal grievances, were submitted to arbitration.

The company and union have stressed expeditious investigation and disposition of grievances at the lowest possible step in the formal grievance procedure. Most of the formal grievances, including the vast majority of those caused by wartime conversion of the rate structure, were settled by an on-the-spot investigation by a union and a company representative. Of all formal grievances filed in 1946, only about one in twenty reached the top union-management committee for consideration, and most of these were policy issues which could not have been settled at lower levels. Furthermore, both union and company officials considered this ratio to be unduly high, and primarily the result of the tangled seniority problems caused by layoffs. The parties have adopted a nonlegalistic approach to grievance processing, and cases have not been settled on the basis of precedents as such.

Government conciliators have participated in six contract negotiations; two dispute cases have been filed with the War Labor Board; some charges were presented to the National Labor Relations Board by the union or by individuals; and the NLRB has held various elections to establish jurisdictional rights. The War Labor Board played a decisive wartime role in wage setting in the Southern California airframe industry. It determined the general amounts of wage advances, approved and supervised the introduction of an industry-wide job-evaluation system, and set up the West Coast Aircraft Committee to adjudicate controversies over the program.

The temper of negotiations by Lockheed and IAM has been generally good, but not universally so. The wartime tensions left an imprint on the personal attitudes of representatives of both parties. Even so, there has been preserved a mutual respect and understanding, moderation in expression, avoidance of acrimonious denunciation, and a desire to continue the basic harmony of the relationship. Positions have been vigorously upheld, but take-it-or-leave-it proposals and refusals to hear out the other side are avoided. And joint discussions have covered a wide variety of subjects, although the company has drawn a line between subjects for joint determination and those reserved for managerial discretion.

MANAGEMENT, EMPLOYEES, THE UNION

Company personnel practices have had an important, although largely indirect, impact on collective bargaining. Lockheed has been well known for the liberality of its personnel policies. While management has believed it should take the initiative in formulating programs designed to promote the general welfare of the working force, it has not used them to throw the union off balance. Lodge 727 of the IAM has been democratic and largely autonomous. Consequently, the attitudes of its members (the employees) toward company employment practices have been a primary determinant of union policies. The union has actively encouraged introduction of the personnel programs and participated in planning and administering a number of them.

There is a general feeling that the company is interested in treating its employees right. This is particularly important where the contributions of employees to the final product are so marked—where labor costs are half of airframe costs, inspection of output rigid for reasons of safety, and complete assembly-line methods impossible. Lockheed's president, Robert E. Gross, set the tone of management's approach to the employees. Older employees and union officials attest to his personal magnetism, friendliness, informality, and sincerity, and to his ability as a compelling and inspiring speaker.

Lockheed was the first company in the Southern California airframe industry to put into effect six holidays with pay, liberal overtime payments, paid vacations, and sick leave; and it has generally set the pace in wage advances. It continues to rank among the most liberal in contractual agreements, and has taken a leading position in establishing employee recreational and other facilities outside of formal collective bargaining.

The Line Organization

Line officials bear primary responsibility for industrial and personnel relations at Lockheed. The industrial relations director, D. H. Cameron, is responsible to Courtlandt Gross, the general manager, who is one of the four top officials in the policy group. His department's essential functions are: (1) to develop and recommend policy to top management, (2) to issue policy and procedural directions to line management, (3) to advise and assist line supervisors in applying policy and handling specific problems, (4) to administer certain aspects of the personnel program, (5) to serve as the main point of contact between the union and the company, and (6) to prepare for and participate in contract negotiations.

Lockheed's continuing interest in personnel policies and procedures is indicated by the extent of experimentation with different methods and by the work of an expert industrial relations research staff, created during the war to conduct research and make recommendations on such subjects as absenteeism, turnover, upgrading, employee rating, testing, swing-shift problems, morale, employee attitudes, layoff problems, employee services, hours for women, fatigue and accidents, transportation facilities, and rest periods.

The supervisory problem at Lockheed has been a major one for the industrial relations office and for top management. Some union officials believe the industrial relations director has too little authority to obtain line supervisors' compliance with company policy, but say this is less true of Lockheed than some other companies. During the war, the problem of compliance was particularly difficult. But the strong support by top management of the industrial relations director gave him more actual authority than organizationally appeared to be the case. In an effort to reduce controversies between the staff and the line, personnel units, each headed by a representative acting for the industrial relations office, were located throughout the plants. This influenced supervisors to take more constructive approaches to human relations problems and encouraged more consistent application of policies and contractual provisions.

Before the war, when foremen were carefully selected long-service employees, their relations with higher levels of supervision were informal. During the rapid wartime expansion, however, large numbers of hourly-rated employees were promoted into supervisory positions without careful screening and many did not perform well. As compensation, the industrial relations office undertook more careful training and advice. Even so, various factors made supervisors feel less like managerial representatives than in the earlier days. Personal contact with top management was reduced and authority to make decisions was decreased for the sake of uniformity. Many were accustomed to union representation, and as the end of the war approached, in the absence of seniority rules, they feared discriminatory treatment in layoffs and discharges, or expected to return to the ranks of hourly-paid employees within the coverage of the IAM bargaining unit.

Some group and section supervisors became interested in unionization and the IAM supported their move, establishing in 1945 a separate lodge for supervisory employees and soliciting memberships. The IAM in 1946 requested recognition as the bargaining agent for section and group supervisors. The company refused emphatically, arguing that supervisors were properly part of management and could not effectively serve management if under obligation to follow union policies. Throughout 1945 and until an NLRB election held in 1946 the company tried to dissuade foremen from supporting the union, and at the same time, it undertook a management development program to improve the status and conditions of employment for supervisory personnel.

The IAM lost the election, but a new approach to the treatment of foremen resulted. The company emphasized the informality of relations between top management and supervisors, and added the position of supervisory personnel representative to the industrial relations office. Security has been provided for supervisors, and they have been carefully selected from within the ranks of the company, with successively higher positions filled as far as possible from the lower levels of supervision. Foremen have been consulted to a moderate degree on the formulation of company policy, and a planned program for the two-way flow of information has been gradually introduced. The foremen have been encouraged, and given the necessary authority, to settle grievances except when policy questions are raised. And a special effort has been made to explain to foremen the role of the union in modern industry and to train them in leadership techniques.

Selection and Orientation of Employees

Tests for selection of a labor force were developed and used extensively at Lockheed before the war, but during the war attention was turned to attracting applicants, with less regard for qualifications. Since the war, more careful selection has been resumed, but with less reliance on testing than on interest in the work and stability shown by the applicant. The company has employed Negroes and Mexicans without discrimination. The collective agreement has provided, further, that there should be no maximum age limit in the hiring of new employees.

New employees are oriented to their jobs and the plant through interviews; the presence of the union is explained and a copy of the contract is given them; supervisors check frequently to see how new employees are getting along. On-the-job training, necessitated on a large scale during the war, was undertaken in consultation with the union; and the union and company cooperated in instituting the first joint apprenticeship training program in the Southern California aircraft industry. Following a temporary postwar decline in training, Lockheed has revived its active interest in training programs and promotional systems.

Under the auspices of a joint management-union safety committee, Lockheed plants won top honors for two years in the aircraft section in the nation-wide campaign of the National Safety Council. Health programs are pursued vigorously. Complete physical examinations are given all new employees; regular re-examinations are provided for workers in hazardous occupations; a special health program is administered for the large number of physically handicapped workers; an industrial hygienist tests and checks for such things as dust, fumes, noise. To the extent possible with the great fluctuations in production and under existing seniority rules, management has attempted to take into account personality traits in developing congenial work groups.

The company and union have joined in a number of social, recreational, and welfare activities which have helped to meet the personal needs of employees. The Lockheed Employees' Recreational Club, before and after the war a social and athletic organization only, operated wartime feeding facilities, tool and merchandise stores, repair shops, service centers for handling money orders and utility bills, and so on. Another group activity, the Buck-of-the-Month Club, collects receipts from a voluntary payroll check-off from employees and spends them for a variety of charitable purposes, through outside organizations as well as for emergency welfare needs of individual employees. Union officials helped plan a number of services for employees which Lockheed provided during the war—among others, facilities for obtaining automobile licenses and ration books, for renting and buying homes; provision of visiting nurses; transportation arrangements.

Attempts to Offer Security

Insecurity of job tenure has been a constant unsettling influence for employees in the airframe industry. Within the limits imposed by its financial resources and market conditions, the company has sought to reduce the violence of employment fluctuations. For example, it began planning early in World War II for the postwar period, and, expecting continued peacetime demand for some of its products, it reduced its working force more slowly after V-J Day than most airframe companies. However well intentioned this action, Lockheed had a flood of grievances during the slower adjustment period, while the companies which slashed employment and made readjustments almost overnight progressed to a postwar basis more quickly, cheaply, and with less controversy. Mr. Gross has strongly advocated a government procurement program which would eliminate the wild fluctuations of the past, and the IAM has supported this program.

The company pioneered in the industry with insurance plans, beginning in 1935. Its present plan, worked out in cooperation with a union social security committee, is as liberal as any in the airframe industry. A voluntary retirement plan, one of two in the Southern California airplane industry, covers about one-half of the employees.

The principle of acknowledging seniority rights in layoffs, transfers, rehiring, and promotions, has further helped afford a sense of security. Seniority privileges were incorporated in the first comprehensive contract, but their specific application has been a continuing problem. It has been necessary to harmonize the flexibility requirements of an unstable production schedule with the rigidities imposed by seniority. The union has recognized that the company has needed some freedom of movement to obtain efficiency.

Until 1941, recognition of seniority was conditioned upon "all things being equal"; later upon substantially equal "ability, skill, and efficiency." Seniority was at first company-wide. As the division of tasks progressed, it became increasingly difficult to move people among distinctly different jobs, and seniority was made occupation-wide. Contracts in 1945 and 1947, however, allowed certain exceptions for treatment of employees of longer seniority; and in 1949, the parties agreed that employees with eight years or more of seniority, in the case of layoffs, must be placed on other jobs, regardless of occupational experience, and employees with five years or more of seniority must be considered for placement within the company, regardless of occupational experience.

Keeping Employees Informed

A free flow of information to employees about company prospects and policies has been attempted as part of Lockheed's program to achieve cooperative working relations. In prewar days this was an informal, personal exchange. Top officials, particularly the company president, were constantly in the plant talking with the workers, and Robert Gross also spoke to employees *en masse* from time to time. As the company grew and personal contact diminished the need for keeping employees apprised of constantly changing methods and schedules remained.

Some methods have been: publication of news on future prospects and current developments in the *Lockheed Star;* use of bulletin boards for announcements of working conditions, and plant rules and regulations; issuance to new employees of an employee handbook, containing information about the company and its products. Increasing attention has been given to more use of the supervisors for both upward and downward communication. A *Management Memo,* letters to supervisors on important specific points, and conferences have been used; and the representatives of the industrial relations office stationed in the plant have formed an important link. During the war, the union and line channels were used on an emergency basis to persuade employees to step up production when it was critically needed, with simultaneous explanations from shop stewards and supervisors. Discussion of a wide range of subjects takes place at meetings of the Joint Senior Labor Relations Committee, and the union's suggestions often have been accepted.

IDEOLOGIES, RIGHTS, AND SECURITY

A redistribution of management's rights and powers normally comes with the introduction of a union into a plant, and questions of management prerogatives and union power arise. Basically, the philosophy of neither Lockheed nor IAM has menaced the other, but the unsettled and changing production environment on occasion has brought the two parties to the brink of "political" incompatibility.

Managerial Philosophy

Lockheed accepted IAM without reservation from the start, but this attitude was not based upon fear or resentment. Apparently no conflict over loyalty of the employees was envisaged, even though the company earlier had operated in the tradition of a happy family. Management has viewed the union as a natural and, on occasion, helpful development. The union has made possible more effective consultation with workers about policies, more adequate information about what the employees think, and a new mechanism for self-discipline. The union, too, has assisted management, by policing the contract, in obtaining uniform application of policy by supervisory personnel.

Top officials of the company have shown a growing appreciation of the essentially "political" nature of the union and the internal and external pressures on union leaders. They have not prevented the union from taking full credit for gains to the employees, and at times have undertaken liberal grievance settlements to save a respected union business agent from "political" embarrassment. Lockheed has not generally taken as strict a view of its prerogatives as have other West Coast airframe companies. It has been willing to negotiate about matters not normally in the collective bargaining area, such as safety, and to discuss with the union a wide range of problems.

The company's philosophy resulted from several factors. The officials of Lockheed were young and liberal. The company, under its present management, began its development during the days of NRA and the passage and determination of the constitutionality of the National Labor Relations Act. Unionism in 1937, when the IAM was recognized, must have appeared inevitable. Furthermore, the alternative to the IAM was the UAW, which had recently been defeated following a widely publicized sitdown strike at Douglas.

The Union's Philosophy

The employees who became IAM members in 1937 felt considerable loyalty toward the company and toward President Gross personally. They had reacted unfavorably to the UAW sitdown strike at Douglas. When the UAW tried to organize at Lockheed, the employees rejected the organizers, but interest in self-organization to combat the UAW developed. If there were to be a union, they preferred one which could get along with management.

The IAM fully accepts the philosophy of private ownership and operation of industry. With this orientation, it has established an outstanding record of constructive effort in promoting the mutual interests of employers and workers without collusive actions against consumers.

From the beginning, the contract has been signed by IAM's Grand Lodge and District Lodge 727. In earlier days, the good relations between the local union and the company made it unnecessary for Grand Lodge representatives to maintain intimate contact with the situation. Since early 1946, however, a Grand Lodge representative has been assigned full time to serve in an advisory capacity to the District Lodge, and other Grand Lodge officials have also participated at times in bargaining at Lockheed. The national officers of the IAM enjoy a reputation for ability and statesmanship, and have been able to contribute experience and a point of view undisturbed by local pressures. Local leadership generally has followed the approach of the national IAM.

Proper training of shop chairmen, because of their key roles as connecting link between management and their fellow workmen, has assumed a prominent place in the union's activities. This has taken the form of regular meetings of chairmen to discuss problems, policies, and procedures, and preparation of comprehensive manuals to guide the chairmen. Treading the line discreetly between promoting the immediate interests of the employees and adjusting demands with consideration for the financial and operational problems of management has required the union leaders to exercise a fine sense of balance.

Certain union practices have made the relationship more satisfactory. The IAM has not pursued make-work policies for industrial workers. It has attempted to settle controversies without resort to strikes. (No strike may be started without sanction of the Grand Lodge, and then only after three-fourths of the local members have voted for it in a secret ballot election.)

The union is democratically managed, and considerable autonomy is retained by the district and local lodges which compose it. Provision is made for the referendum and initiative. All local officers are directly elected by the membership, and at Lockheed both union and nonunion employees are eligible to vote for shop chairmen. Provision has been made for trial of members before expulsion, and fees and dues are moderate. A considerable turnover of officers has had some drawbacks. It has reduced the general level of experience of the officials, made them less able to speak authoritatively for the members and exercise effective leadership, and impaired continuity of policy. The union has tried to counteract this by suggesting a change in the term of office, from one year to two years, but the membership has been unwilling.

Managerial Rights

The most serious controversy between the parties at Lockheed has been definition of the boundary between management and union rights. Neither the union nor management has had a static conception of where the line should be drawn. During prewar years, it was taken for granted that the area of collective bargaining was properly limited to wages, hours, and general conditions of employment. The 1937 contract included a clause pointing out the company's right "to manage the plant and direct the labor forces, including the right to hire, to suspend or discharge for just cause, to promote, demote and transfer its employees." The further statement that any claim that the company had exercised this right contrary to provisions of the agreement could be taken up as a grievance was added in 1941.

Despite the absence of more detailed specifications of management rights in the contract, the company has been concerned with the preservation of its rights. It has considered managerial rights to be all-inclusive and has worked them out on a case-by-case basis with the union instead of on an over-all basis of fundamental principle. As cases have arisen, the principle of management's right to proceed unilaterally, except as limited by the contract, sometimes has been the main point in dispute.

The company and union have worked out some arrangements harmoniously. This is illustrated by the union's no-strike clause and the company's no-lockout clause offered at the start of the war; and the clause in the 1947 contract expressing the union's willingness to work toward the objective of "achieving the highest level of employee performance and efficiency consistent with safety, good health, and sustained effort." It is also demonstrated by the expansion of joint activities beyond the customary limits to such matters as: job evaluation, a safety program, apprentice training, the wartime "Victory Committee," and the company's intermittent policy of consultation with the union.

The basic conflict over management's rights first arose when the union sought to change consultation into negotiations; to make what was until then a privilege into a contractual right, with joint powers to determine. The company viewed collective bargaining as periodic. It regarded the contract arrived at by such bargaining as one which the parties should follow whether they liked it or not. Either party voluntarily could go beyond the requirements of the contract, but could not be compelled to do so. The union during the war period began pressing for a different concept—continuous bargaining. The 1941 contract continued into 1945, and the union did not want to be prevented by an old contract from meeting new situations. As new problems arose or old problems appeared in a new light, the union thought they should be opened for settlement; the contract should be subject to constant review and renegotiation. This demand for constant negotiations has not been a historical request of the union. It was urged mainly during the war and early postwar period when the union had to meet the extraordinary demands created by the tremendous expansion and contraction in the numbers and kind of its membership and potential membership.

The first specific controversy started in 1941. The union wished to participate, through its shop chairmen, in the periodic review of employees for wage increases, which took place initially every six months, and subsequently every sixteen weeks. The company objected, but finally agreed to let the chairmen talk to personnel representatives before final action was taken, although the supervisors still had the right to make the decisions. An uneasy truce has prevailed on this issue.

A more serious conflict developed over the contract's provision for "special reviews" for any employee "in the event of a change of work or other condition which may warrant such review." There were an enormous number of these during the years of rapid expansion. The company claimed that the union could not represent employees in these since participation was provided for only in periodic reviews, and because union participation in special reviews would entail such continuous discussion between the shop chairman and the department foreman that neither could do his regular work. The union contended that the contract intended its participation in both types of review; that supervisors were claiming full credit for the wage advances; and that, as bargaining agent, the union could take part in all wage discussions whether they related to one employee or the entire bargaining unit. The dispute was finally settled in favor of the company in 1945 by the War Labor Board.

In 1944, two other disputes arose over what the company considered to be management rights. Some employees claimed that supervisors had written false or misleading statements on their records which prejudiced their periodic reviews. The union claimed that it had the right of access to these records and needed to see them to represent the employees properly. A private arbitrator ruled in favor of the union. The union submitted a charge to the NLRB when the company rearranged the time of the lunch period for all employees and the time and number of rest periods of women on the graveyard shift, accusing the company of refusing to bargain on "conditions incident to employment." The NLRB made no final disposition of the case, and the dispute finally ceased to be an active one.

Issues over the degree to which the union could participate in decisions came to a head in the negotiations to replace the 1941 contract, and a tentative agreement was reached in the summer of 1944, but the membership repudiated the agreement. The company broke off negotiations. A new dispute arose about this time, when the union urged negotiation on a new upgrading plan and the company refused on the grounds that the 1941 contract should be followed. Two other union requests which the company felt invaded management rights were for union representation of employees before management on any question involving interpretation or application of the agreement, and for negotiation and determination of any matters subject to bargaining under the National Labor Relations Act, even if they were not covered by the contract.

When a contract was negotiated and signed in June 1945, ten issues were unresolved and submitted to the War Labor Board. Half of these involved continuous bargaining. The Board rejected the general position of the union, and after the war, continuous bargaining did not remain an active issue. The union's position became more secure and the company began to inform the union more freely on postwar difficulties.

Management did not show the same disposition to draw a line between continuous and periodic bargaining over layoffs. Both parties recognized the complexity of the problem and the necessity for arriving at a workable solution. The internal wage structure also has been subject to discussion outside of contract reopening periods, as have problems arising out of mass transfers and downgrading.

Union Security

The security of the union was never menaced by efforts on the part of Lockheed to destroy or weaken it, but it has been sorely threatened by the possibility of members withdrawing their support, rival unionism, and insecurity of union officers. It was when these threats were at their peak that relations between the IAM and Lockheed were at their worst. Had union membership been compulsory, or had the National Labor Relations Act not facilitated transfers of bargaining rights from one union to another, or had the union been dictatorially managed, or had the war not taken place, the union and its leaders would not have been so insecure, and the relations between the parties so strained from 1943 through 1945.

Compulsory union membership has been opposed by the company as an unwarranted infringement on individual freedom of choice. Prior to the war the IAM requested a union shop but did not push the demand to the extent of a strike, and no form of union security aside from recognition was adopted. (The voluntary check-off of dues was first included in the 1937 contract.) During the war, the union became more insistent. Compulsory membership would have greatly reduced the effort and expense involved in its constant, mammoth organizing drive, and would have given the union a disciplinary weapon. Management rejected a request for the union shop in 1941, but agreed to furnish each new employee with a copy of the contract, including an application card and a form authorizing voluntary check-off, and a letter from the vice-president encouraging consideration of membership. Further, whenever the company opened a new plant, the jurisdiction of the IAM was automatically extended to cover it, so no organizing drives and elections were necessary.

The union's request for the union shop in 1943 was rejected during the negotiations which extended over the following two years. The union referred the issue to the War Labor Board reluctantly, because it knew the Board would grant a maintenance-of-membership clause, which might cause some employees to hesitate to join. On the other hand, it was even more concerned about withdrawals of existing members under conditions of government control which limited the gains the union could make. The Board granted maintenance-of-membership in 1945 over company protests, but the provision was strengthened in the 1947 contract, and in 1949 the clause which permitted members to "escape" during a specified period each year was removed.

The company has acceded to certain demands related to union security. It has notified the union of each new employee; furnished upon request information on the number of employees in each department, with rates of pay, hiring rates, job classifications, and shift assignments; supplied information on layoffs and seniority rosters; permitted organizing on company property during the free time of employees; and allowed time off and leaves of absence for union business. In addition, union representatives have been viewed as the authorized spokesmen of the employees. Shop chairmen have been given time off, at company expense, to handle grievances, and unusual freedom has been provided union officials in access to the plant and to company officials. While not always followed, orders have been given that supervisors treat union officials with respect and not favor nonunion employees.

The jurisdictional struggle between IAM and UAW at Lockheed, which IAM won easily, was largely limited to 1937–38, but IAM and the UAW have been rivals in NLRB elections in every major airframe company in the region except Lockheed. This interunion competition has had two effects on IAM-Lockheed relations. First, the union has needed to do as well or better at Lockheed than the UAW at other major companies to keep UAW from becoming active there again. Second, the Lockheed contract has been an instrument of attack as well as of defense. Contractual gains at Lockheed have been used in organizational conflicts elsewhere as evidence of the IAM's ability to secure improvements for its members.

The craft unions have been a recurrent source of concern to IAM. In 1941, the welders, who tend to be a separate group and who were in great demand early in the war, sought separate representation at Lockheed. The company would not accept them and the NLRB refused to designate the National Union of Aircraft Welders (Ind.) as bargaining agent. When some welders walked off the job in a dispute over wages in 1942, the company fired them, but rehired them later at IAM insistence. The welders' union was never again an active force at Lockheed, partly because an award by the WCAC under the industry-wide wage stabilization plan granted them wage rates generally conceded to be above what the plan permitted.

Other craft unions have sought bargaining rights, but petitions for elections filed by these unions, with two exceptions, were withdrawn or dismissed by the NLRB. An election was held for truck drivers in 1948, but IAM won. A petition filed by the Electrical Workers in 1948 resulted in a transfer of bargaining rights away from the IAM. The pressure from the craft unions has been reduced in two ways. First, the IAM has agreed to permit craft workers to hold two cards—one for IAM and the other for their craft unions. This has given the workers greater job security and allowed them to keep their allegiance to the craft union to which they earlier had belonged. The craft unions can count them as members and collect their dues; IAM bargains for them and preserves its jurisdiction. Second, the job-evaluation plan has helped to set at least an apparent ceiling on rates for craft workers, and it did not seem that even the craft unions could get rates comparable to those they had won in the construction industry under it; and further, craft rates have been raised to the highest practical levels under the plan.

The Taft-Hartley Act increased the possibility of craft fragmentation of the bargaining unit, and the independent status of IAM (at that time outside the AFL) made it even more vulnerable. The company and IAM have counted on the history of industrial unionism at Lockheed to lead to NLRB rejection of craft units, but this is no longer as forceful an argument as it was prior to the passage of the 1947 Act. More important has become the long record of unbroken relationships between Lockheed and the IAM and the favorable treatment accorded the craft groups. A further deterrent to craft split-offs is the 1949 contract provision for limited transferability of seniority for craft workers who might seek representation through their own craft bargaining units.

The union had to contend during the war, not only with organizing a huge and constantly changing work force, but also with almost insurmountable obstacles to maintaining the support of members. Few of the new employees had belonged to unions before, and some were antiunion. Wartime controls prevented an across-the-board wage increase, the 1941 contract's continuation until 1945 prevented the negotiation of nonwage gains. There was not much the union could offer employees in one lump sum as a reason for its existence. As the proportion of union members went down, the trend became cumulative—members wondered why they should bear the cost of union operation for the benefit of so many nonunion members. While union membership rose from less than 1000 in 1937 to nearly 40,000 in 1943, the ratio of union members to total eligible employees kept falling. At 80–90 per cent in prewar years, it dropped to 50 per cent in January 1942 and 40 per cent in January 1943, before it started up again to 65 per cent in January 1945, 80 per cent in January 1948, and 90 per cent in August 1949.

Union participation in periodic wage reviews was a decided organizing asset, but the main answer was the successful processing of individual grievances. In 1942, 1000 written grievances were filed; in 1943, 6000; in 1944, 5000; and in 1945, 6000; and many informal grievances were processed. Approximately 70 per cent of the 1943–5 grievances were over rates of pay, advancements, and reclassifications. Grievances dropped to 3000 in 1946, but increased again to 6000 in 1947, before dropping back to about 1500 between January 1948 and June 1949. In 1946, over half of the grievances involved layoffs and terminations, but again in 1947 rate cases led, largely because of the problems attendant upon the conversion to a new job and wage structure plan, and they also led in 1948 and 1949.

Union officers not only had to stand for office once a year, but had to run for office all the time under the wartime conditions. The lack of security of the established leaders offered an opportunity to the many in the new group of employees who aspired to leadership. A shop chairman got time off from work and might come to the attention of management as a prospective supervisor. The competition for elective offices was keen, especially since district lodge officers were placed on a full-time paid basis early in the war. An organized left-wing group developed within the organization in opposition to the moderates who were in power. Grievances became a weapon in this conflict. The winning of a grievance meant the winning of votes.

The pressure on the established leadership to get major gains from the company resulted in part in the two War Labor Board cases, the emphasis on continuous bargaining, and the protracted bargaining from 1943 to 1945. In the second half of 1944, the left-wingers, who had increased their control, led the attack on the tentative agreement negotiated by the officials of the union in mid-1944, which resulted in its rejection by the membership and the breaking off of negotiations by the company. The moderates maintained essential control, however. In addition to their own efforts, this was partly because it was difficult for the left-wingers to get most of the employees really to distrust the company. At the end of the war the left-wingers lost out completely. Many of them and their supporters were short-service employees and were terminated or laid off. With the end of wartime controls, also, the established officials again could make substantial gains for the members.

INCOME REQUIREMENTS OF THE PARTIES

The pressures on union leaders from rivals within and without their own union and the financial insecurity of the airframe industry have influenced actions of both the company and the union on wages. In addition, the federal government, as major customer, has not been neutral about prices, costs, or labor policies. The complete and simultaneous satisfaction of the union and company needs has not always been possible, but in every case, a sufficiently acceptable wage settlement has been developed so that peace has been preserved.

Union Needs

Members of a union expect the union to obtain wage rates and other economic provisions at least roughly equivalent to those prevailing in the area and in their industry and to meet changes in the cost of living. This requirement has been intensified for IAM since union membership at Lockheed is voluntary and the workers relatively mobile. Although, during the war, the rates in the airframe industry in Southern California were lower than in the shipyards, this was partly offset by the less convenient locations of shipyards and the more disagreeable work in them. Average hourly earnings apparently have been at about the same level as for durable goods manufacturing in Los Angeles, but this is hard to evaluate since the job structures vary considerably from one industry to another.

Comparisons with skilled craft rates are even more difficult. An examination of rates paid machinists, tool and die makers, electricians, carpenters, plumbers, painters, heavy duty truck drivers, and welders in other industries in Southern California over the period 1941–47 shows that

Lockheed rates were generally at or above the levels for similar craftsmen in other industries, with three exceptions. These were: prior to 1943, rates for welders in the shipyards were substantially higher than at Lockheed; craft rates for new construction were substantially higher; and craft rates were also somewhat higher in job shops. (Lockheed craft rates have also been much lower than in the motion picture industry, but this has exercised little pull.)

In the past decade, Lockheed wages have been at a higher level than in the rest of the airframe industry, and across-the-board increases have, on important occasions, come earlier. Lockheed and IAM also normally have led the Southern California airframe industry in fringe provisions. In February 1937, Lockheed's minimum hiring rate was 2 cents per hour above its largest competitor; the first Lockheed-IAM contract increased wages 6 cents to lead the Southern California airframe industry. As the labor market tightened, hiring rates were standardized among the several airframe plants, but jobs at higher levels were on no uniform basis.

The uniform job classification plan—known as the SCAI plan—ordered by the War Labor Board in March 1943 left each company considerable latitude, although it established ten labor grades with uniform minimum and maximum rates for each Southern California airframe company. Lockheed apparently administered the plan less strictly than did the other companies, for it generally was top or second from the top in average straight-time hourly rates during the period when all the companies were operating under the same plan.

In 1945, Lockheed was the first company in the airframe industry to accede to an across-the-board wage increase; and one of the first in any industry. This first round increase of 15 per cent boosted IAM's prestige and was subsequently adopted by the other airframe companies in Southern California. The second round increase in 1947 was less advantageous to IAM. Whereas IAM accepted an increase, limited to employees already on the payroll, of only 3 cents an hour to be paid immediately with an additional 2 cents in three months, UAW shortly won a 5-cent increase for all job rates at North American and criticized IAM for the Lockheed "wooden nickel" and for setting such a low pattern for the industry. The third round in 1948 was equally embarrassing to IAM, with acceptance of 5 cents across the board only to have other companies follow with 10-cent increases or their equivalent. Lockheed's average for the industry was maintained only because its continued easier administration of the wage structure generally raised rates by another 5 cents.

Protracted and at times heated negotiations at Lockheed in 1949 were caused in part by the unfavorable wage developments in 1947 and 1948. The union leaders had been severely criticized, particularly in 1948, by members, rival leaders within IAM, and leaders of UAW. The IAM-Lockheed settlement in 1949, however, was the first and largest wage increase in the industry. Average hourly earnings at Lockheed again gained their historical position of about 5 cents above the rest of the industry.

Company Needs

Lockheed's profits have fluctuated enormously, with a net income of $500,000 in 1938 and $8 million in 1942, and an operating deficit of $11 million in 1946. The relation of profits to wages before the war is obscure. During the war, the labor market was tight and the company operated under cost-plus-fixed-fee contracts, which normally might have pushed wages up rapidly. The purchaser, the federal government, did not permit this. The installation of the industry-wide wage stabilization plan did result in an average wage increase of 6 to 7 cents, however, in 1943. Also, since the labor-grade system permitted some flexibility, straight-time hourly wages at Lockheed rose by 32.9 cents during a period when no across-the-board wage increases were permitted.

In 1945 when the company was making profits, and expected large sales, it wanted to keep its skilled labor force intact, so Lockheed and IAM led off with the 15 per cent wage increase. In 1947, the company was losing money and markets had collapsed. The company very much objected to a wage increase, and agreed to it only after a strike vote. The union has given some attention to company ability to pay both during the war when it pressed constantly for higher rates and in the postwar period. It accepted the 5-cent increase in 1947, even though the cost of living had risen substantially, other manufacturing industries were granting pattern increases of 15 cents, and the UAW was bargaining with North American with the likelihood of getting a more favorable arrangement.

The company's overpaid rates, which at one time were being received by roughly 50 per cent of the employees, were costly and the object of bitter protests. They not only increased the company's wage bill but, because persons doing the same work were getting quite different rates of pay, caused unrest and grievances and negated efforts to obtain an ordered rate structure. The IAM agreed to methods of eliminating overpaid rates and by June 1949, only 10 per cent of employees were getting them.

The company's profits have depended less upon wages than upon volume; and volume has depended on total demand for the products of the industry and on Lockheed's share in that total demand. The industry has been highly competitive, but its products clearly differentiated from each other. Competition has been keen, but related more to quality and suitability than to price. The indirect labor costs for such technicians as draftsmen and engineers are enormous and are about as great for one plane of a given model as for ten. Further, volume production permits specialization of tasks with greater efficiency and a lower level of skill and pay. Lockheed could survive as a moderately high-wage firm indefinitely if it had volume market for its planes, and being a high-wage firm might have definite advantages, since higher wages can in part pay for themselves through lower turnover, a more skilled work force, and in other ways.

This does not mean that an airframe company can be unconcerned with labor costs, since wages are 50 per cent of airframe costs. Once price and volume have been set, profits depend on keeping down costs. Lockheed was caught in the short-run predicament in 1947 and early 1948 of having its volume and prices set, with leeway only on costs. It has had to be more concerned with costs in the short run than in the longer run when prices could be negotiated again. But wages are set in the short run and so cost-price-profit relationships for the shorter periods have been an important consideration.

Needs of the Primary Purchaser

The federal government's needs and actions as primary purchaser have had and will continue to have a direct effect on the economic compatibility of Lockheed and the IAM.

Lockheed and IAM began joint work on job description and job evaluation in 1941, and had held exploratory discussions over the prior two years. In 1941, the Southern California Aircraft Industry Committee was formed by the six major airframe companies, and unilateral work was begun on job description and job evaluation, since several of the companies—two of them unorganized—considered job description a prerogative of management. On March 3, 1943, the War Labor Board ordered the SCAI Committee's plan into effect and rejected the Lockheed-IAM plan. But the IAM never fully accepted the SCAI plan and preferred to deal separately with Lockheed. When the IAM withdrew from industry-wide discussions in the spring of 1945 followed by Lockheed's separate agreement to the 15 per cent wage increase, industry-wide stabilization ended. Lockheed and IAM began work on a new plan in 1945, introduced it in February 1947, and further revised it after the 1949 agreement.

The government-ordered SCAI wage-standardization plan, however, served both parties in essential ways. Standardization was essential to prevent excessive migration of workers from plant to plant. It was necessary to have some reasonable method of slotting the many new jobs. To a degree, the employees received assurance that their rates were in internal balance, and at the same time, the plan was flexible enough to permit adjustments to labor market pressures. Although the union criticized the SCAI plan, it used the plan to show members it was making gains for them. A further advantage was that failure to achieve promised benefits could be blamed on a ready scapegoat, the War Labor Board. The plan helped the union in explaining rates to individual employees, and permitted the union to tell members that a means existed for correcting inequities. The plan also reduced the potential competition between the IAM and UAW by assuring a certain degree of equality of treatment.

The President's Air Policy Commission, in its 1948 report,[1] pointed out that "a strong aircraft industry is an essential element in the nation's air power" and envisaged sustained federal purchases of airplanes to maintain the industry at a minimum level of effective capacity. It stressed that in carrying out this program "every effort must be made by the procurement agencies to see that the most effective use is made" of the taxpayers' money. In wartime the government controlled wages, even if rather ineffectively in the airframe industry, and settled controversies. In a tight labor market, competition for workers among the airframe companies could bid up wages indefinitely. In a loose labor market, but with the government paying the bill, wages could be bid up by organizational competition between the IAM and UAW. In either event, if it resumed purchases on a large scale, the federal government, directly or indirectly might wish to exercise some influence on wages and labor relations in order to moderate costs.

A Postscript

Of all the collective bargaining situations studied in this series, the Lockheed-IAM case probably evidenced the narrowest margin within which a peaceful bargaining relationship had developed. The original study in 1949 stressed the real and strong barriers to peace as well as the favorable factors. While making quite clear that the Lockheed-IAM

[1] President's Air Policy Commission, *Survival in the Air Age,* U.S. Government Printing Office, 1948.

record was by no means a perfect one, it pointed also to the fact that there had been no official strike recorded throughout the evolution of the lively and changing collective bargaining relationship. Subsequent to the preparation of the Lockheed-IAM study, the narrow margin of peace was squeezed significantly enough on one occasion—the fall of 1952—to vitiate at the least, this no-strike record. A three-week long strike, accompanied by considerable bitterness on both sides, occurred.

The strike resulted when IAM demands for higher wages and a union shop were adamantly resisted by a Lockheed management decision not to exceed the wage awards recently granted the UAW at Long Beach and North American and to resist the improved union-security demand. Even after government intervention had ended the strike and a new agreement had been executed, the wounds were slow to heal in the ensuing backwash of mutual recrimination and management insistence on such punitive measures as reinsertion of escape clauses in maintenance of membership, reduction of superseniority for stewards, and the requirement that union officials obtain special permission to visit the plant.

Thus, in the context of the tenuous Lockheed-IAM peace, on this one occasion, sufficient differences in viewing critical enough issues resulted in resort to war. Whether the experience of war has permanently set relations back a step or whether it has made the parties that much more reluctant to engage in war in the future is difficult to appraise. Certainly, the successful resolution of the current peace moves between the two rival unions will remove the most significant factor in the backdrop of the 1952 warfare. In any case, it should also be recalled that lack of strikes "is not the only criterion of good industrial relations, nor is their occasional occurrence a proof that relations are bad." The experience at Lockheed subsequent to the completion of the early study serves only to re-emphasize the conclusion of that study and the prefatory caveats it contained.

CHAPTER 13 _____

The Nashua Corporation
and Seven AFL Unions

CHARLES A. MYERS *and* GEORGE P. SHULTZ, *both of the Industrial Relations Section, Massachusetts Institute of Technology, are authors of NPA Case Study No. 7. Their full report, condensed in this chapter, was published in February 1950.*

The relationship between The Nashua Corporation of Nashua, New Hampshire, and seven AFL unions is strong evidence that constructive labor-management relations are a consequence of the "political" and economic compatibility of the parties. Yet the record is not all one of sweetness and light; problems have required many discussions and extended bargaining. Industrial peace has been won by good will and hard work by both management and the union leadership, local and international. The relationship meets the test of five basic criteria of good relations.

First, there has been a substantial degree of industrial peace. The company and the unions have settled differences without resort to strikes or lockouts; in fact, economic force is viewed as a last-resort weapon. No threat of a strike and no intervention of a third party were required by any of the unions to gain recognition. Only two cases have been taken to arbitration by the unions; once the unions and company jointly appealed to the War Labor Board for approval of a general wage increase. Neither state nor federal conciliators have ever been called in.

Second, there is a recognition and acceptance by the unions and by management of the needs of the other as going institutions. Top management officials are acutely conscious of the "political" problems of the union leadership; they accept the realities of unionism instead of denouncing unions. There is no feeling that the unions have driven a wedge between management and the employees, or that management must compete with the unions for the loyalty of the employees. The unions understand the needs of the company for continued profitable operation. There is a general feeling that the company has a good management. Both sides try to solve problems rather than insist upon unilateral rights.

Third, the relationship is regarded as equitable by both parties. The atmosphere of bargaining is not one of trying to outsmart the other fellow. On the contrary, open and full discussion of all proposals is directed toward reaching agreements which are mutually acceptable. International and local union officials say management is a fair but well-informed and good bargainer. Management, too, feels that the relationship is fair. The union and the company officials treat each other as equals.

Fourth, employees have security, dignity, and recognition as individuals. The Nashua Corporation has been able to make adequate profits and maintain a sound financial structure, and at the same time provide employees with a considerable measure of job security, as well as economic gains. Unionization, responsible for many of these gains, has brought other benefits to workers. Management, working with the unions, handles grievances and personnel problems in such a way as to increase individual job satisfactions. A sense of personal worth is further enhanced by the employees' participation in democratically run unions.

Fifth, the net effect of the relationship has not been detrimental to consumers and to the public interest. Whereas prices of the company's standard products have increased since the unions came in, the increases were in line with a national trend during a period of rising national income. The quality of the product has not suffered under unionization; in fact, it may be better because of the constant emphasis on quality. Management reports that output per man-hour has always been good. Customers have not been inconvenienced by failure to get prompt deliveries because of strikes. Although some of the same unions have organized the company's competitors, there is no evidence of collusion on price or output in the industry as a consequence of this fact.

Layoffs affecting most of Nashua's divisions began in March 1949 and totaled 8 per cent of employment by August, but there was no indication that relationship had deteriorated. Negotiations for new contracts were again under way in August, with no noticeable hardening of previous friendly attitudes. Both sides are confident that they can continue to settle problems by full discussion and patient negotiations. None of the union officials thinks the company will use a period of low business activity to tighten up on the unions; and no management official gives any reason to believe that the company will act differently. On the contrary, the management is thoroughly convinced that the unions play an important part in the successful operation of the business.

The beginnings of the relationship laid the groundwork for the present mutual trust and respect. The seven unions, of which the three largest include 96 per cent of the total union membership, are listed in the order of their size:

Local No. 270, International Brotherhood of Pulp, Sulphite and Paper Mill Workers—first contract, June 1937

Local No. 33, International Brotherhood of Bookbinders—first contract, October 1935

Local No. 359, International Printing Pressmen and Assistants' Union of North America—first contract, December 1934

The Stereotypers Union of Nashua, New Hampshire, a subsidiary of the International Stereotypers' and Electrotypers' Union of North America—first contract, August 1935

Local No. 3, International Photo-Engravers' Union of North America—first contract, January 1936

Local No. 352, International Union of Operating Engineers—first contract, November 1939

Local No. 14, International Brotherhood of Firemen and Oilers—first contract, June 1937

The Pressmen's Union, the first to organize any of the company's employees, approached management for bargaining rights in 1934, prior to the passage of the Wagner Act. Management apparently agreed to an informal election among the pressroom employees to determine whether the union represented a majority. As one of the top company officers now describes it, "We were surprised to see such an overwhelming vote for the union. We didn't think our employees wanted unions, and it was quite a shock to us."

Negotiations for a contract began in this atmosphere of management shock and some resentment. The chief negotiator for the Pressmen's Union, who was then an international representative from the Boston regional office, made certain demands in a manner which stirred up the two top management negotiators. The union negotiator made the usual demands—a wage increase, shorter hours and overtime, fixed complement of men on the presses, seniority clause, closed shop, and so on. Management considered the demands exorbitant, and "didn't know then that they always asked for more than they expected to get." Since negotiations went so poorly, the international representative was replaced by another representative from the Boston office. He asked management, "What have we got to do to reach an agreement?" Management liked this attitude, and a contract was signed. The first international representative, however, continued to service the local, and he and management got to know each other and get along well. He now is vice-president of the international union, in charge of the New England region, and his relations with the same two men in management are excellent. He says of the early days: "They found I wasn't so bad after all. Furthermore, we were fortunate in the excellence and responsibility of our first local union president. The company saw that we weren't trying to take them over, and that the union wasn't out to destroy it."

Management decided after the first contract that it would not fight unions, and if it were going to have them, it wanted to help develop as responsible unions as possible. It recognized that "unions could bring many things to light that needed attention, and which we would ordinarily not consider." Management made its attitude explicit very early. Yet the company was not ready to accept unionism as wholeheartedly as it does today. In August 1934, management pointed out to employees in one department the fact that if they were eligible to join the Pressmen's Union, each was "at perfect liberty to do so without prejudice to his job or standing with this Company." On the other hand, "We do not propose to operate a closed shop. The union man and the nonunion man will have equal standing with us."

The Company's Environment

The company's tradition of paper converting in Nashua, New Hampshire, dates back to 1849, and it is still known locally as the "Card Shop." In 1904 it was incorporated as the Nashua Card, Gummed and Coated Paper Company, and it has been in control of the Carter family since then. In 1916, the name was changed to Nashua Gummed and Coated Paper Company, which it was called while this study was being made. Top management has not been confined to members of the family. Vasco E. Nunez, who succeeded Winthrop L. Carter as president in 1944, joined the company in 1917; the vice-president and manager of manufacturing, Robert A. Brown, came with the company in 1919. These two men were the original negotiators with the unions, and their approach toward labor relations has set the tone for the whole management organization without interruption. A top executive points to the flexibility of this closely knit management organization. Prompt action on policy, he says, can be taken because all the board of directors except one are active executives with offices in the Nashua building. At the superintendent level, management is described as "alert and hard driving."

The Company's Products and Employment

The company does not manufacture any pulp or paper, but produces a diversified line of products which are normally classified in the converted paper products industry. Many of these are printed. It has been marked by a slow and steady growth. Between 1920 and 1935, the company expanded through acquisition of other firms and through development of its operations in both the United States and Canada. During World War II, it supplied paper products required by the Armed Forces and set up four new divisions for the manufacture of wartime products entirely foreign to its regular converted paper line.

Employment has risen generally at Nashua. (The trend in employment of hourly employees, exclusive of war departments, from 1929 through 1948 is shown in Table 1, *Case Study No. 7.*) Until layoffs in 1949, there were around 1100 employees, of whom one-third were salaried and not represented by the unions. By May 1949, total employment had dropped to 982, of whom 706 were hourly-rated workers. Monotonous jobs are few at this company, even though in 1949, 52 per cent of the hourly-rated jobs were classed as unskilled (18 per cent were skilled and 30 per cent semiskilled). With no large group of assembly-line workers, there is no accompanying problem of speed-up and slowdown.

Two facts about company employment stand out. First, there was no drastic decline in numbers employed during the 1931–32 depression or during the 1938 recession. Second, there is no pronounced seasonality of employment, even though it fluctuates mildly from month to month. Both facts are explained by the nature of the company's products and their deliberate diversification. The steadiness of employment, both seasonally and cyclically, has been an asset in employee relations. Furthermore, management has provided competent direction and good equipment to the work force in an effort to secure low costs. Thus employees have not been asked to compensate with lower wages or with unusual efforts for an inadequate management, but have been part of an effective work team. There are many applicants anxious to get jobs with the company, and the rate of voluntary separations and total separations are lower for the company than its industry as a whole. (Comparisons are shown by months from January 1947 through May 1949 in Table 2, *Case Study No. 7.*)

Competition in the Industry

The company's market is not protected, except for a few of its products which constitute only a small part of its total volume of business. On the contrary, the various branches of the converted paper products industry are highly competitive, and Nashua's products are sold (through branch offices in eight principal cities) in a national market. In the waxed paper branch of the industry, for example, the company has 37 competitors, most of them outside of New England. Many of these are integrated mills which produce their own paper and then convert it. Buyers of bread and candy wrappers are generally large firms themselves, with many sources of supply. Accounts are made on a short-term basis, and shifted if there is a significant price differential between firms. In economic terms, therefore, demand for the firm's products is highly elastic. The company is not a member of either of the two trade associations in the industry, although it cooperates in the exchange of wage-rate information.

Without the Nashua Package Sealing Company, Inc., a sales subsidiary of the company through which gummed tape and dispensing machines are distributed, the company's gummed paper division would be in tough shape. There are 23 principal competitors in this branch of the industry. The coated paper division, which has just been reorganized, was losing money before the war and survived during the war only because coated paper products were in great demand. Competition finally forced the company, early in 1949, to drop its regular line of coated products and to introduce some new products in that division. There is some product differentiation on specialty paper products—napkins, doilies, and other novelties—but even in these lines there are a number of competitors.

The Company's Financial Position

Consolidated net income data for the company and its subsidiaries were first reported in 1929. These show that in every succeeding year, through 1948, earnings were in the black and common stock dividends were paid. Some years were better than others, but the company did not experience the fluctuation in earnings characteristic of many industries.

Between 1929 and 1948, the net worth of the company and its subsidiaries increased 2.4 times, in terms of dollars. This is in part an indication of the extent to which earnings were plowed back into the business. Net worth declined somewhat during the depression, but between 1935 (the first full year following the entrance of the first union) and 1948, it increased 2.7 times. Net dollar sales increased 3.2 times during the same period.

The favorable financial position unquestionably has been helpful to the company's labor relations. A vice-president says on this subject: "Good labor relations presuppose the need for company profits. If you can afford to pay top wages in the community and in the industry, this is of prime importance. Other things are important too, but this is most important in our opinion."

Five principal reasons for good profits during most years in this competitive industry are given by management. First, there has been deliberate diversification of products, to avoid too great a dependence on any one product or any one type of customer. Second, there is a vigorous effort to develop and introduce new products. Third, unprofitable plants and product lines have been dropped rather than allowed to drain company resources. Fourth, continual and intensive efforts are made to reduce costs through methods study and waste reduction. Finally, and perhaps most important, employee productivity is high and it has been maintained at a high level for a number of years. There was no wartime or postwar decline in man-hour output, according to management, when labor shortages might have created it. One member of management said, "We feel we get pretty darn good production and this is one reason we've been able to keep our position in the industry." Some of this may be attributed to the incentive system, which covers three-fourths of the hourly workers. There is also comparatively little employee resistance to technological and process changes, because of the way in which the company and the unions approach these changes.

The importance of labor costs is not so great in this firm as in other types of industry. During the first four months of 1949, the wage bill for hourly workers was 13.7 per cent of net sales, while raw materials, supplies, and outside services represented 68 per cent. The company's ability to absorb the cost of wage increases is greater than if labor costs were a substantially higher percentage, but the company does not enjoy any advantage in this respect over its competitors. Profits in this type of industry also depend heavily on ability to maintain a high volume of production and sales, since the margin is small on the large staple items, such as bread wrappers. Thus, any interruption of production, such as a strike, would be extremely costly. Undoubtedly, this is one reason why management values industrial peace so highly.

The Company's Position in the Community

In its community, the company enjoys an outstanding reputation, and management officials are active in community affairs. The third largest firm in a fairly diversified industrial city, it employs about 6 per cent of the community's total labor force. In interviews with workers in Nashua, the Card Shop is mentioned more frequently than any other single firm as the best place to work in the city. Reasons are steady employment and the highest wages in the city for comparable work. These are not the only qualities of a good job, however. Some workers said, "They don't keep after you all of the time there if you mind your own business." Or, "They have a good union and the place is run by good management. My friends say if you stay there, there are chances to get ahead." These job characteristics, as viewed by applicants for work, give the Card Shop "the cream of the labor market," in the words of the company's employment manager. Even during the war, when there were opportunities for high wages elsewhere, the company did not have the usual difficulties in recruiting new workers.

THE LOCAL UNIONS AND THE INTERNATIONALS

The seven local unions and their internationals have gotten along remarkably well. There have been few jurisdictional difficulties, even though many of the jobs do not fall into a clearly defined craft. In fact, the existence of so many union groups may have given the individual worker representation which is intimately acquainted with his problem and directly oriented to his needs. While the international representatives keep in touch, the locals function democratically and have a high degree of autonomy.

There were good reasons for the drive toward unionization in the company, and management now recognizes this. Among those mentioned are: wages too low for the pressmen's craft; dissatisfaction with the modified Bedeaux incentive system; grievances over layoffs and failure to follow seniority; favoritism and discrimination by the foremen—a frequent comment; strict supervision, but no chance of a hearing; "everyone was joining unions"; and so on. A reason, which the union leaders say appealed to management, was the increasing need in the middle thirties for the union label on bread wrappers and other products purchased by union members in a growing American labor movement.

Membership and Jurisdiction

The hourly-rated employees, in June 1949, were represented by the seven unions as follows: Sulphite Union (or Pulp Workers, as it is called in some other localities), 257 members; Bookbinders' Union, 225; Pressmen's Union, 145; Stereotypers' Union, 15; Photo-Engravers' Union, 7;

Engineers' Union, 4; and Firemen's Union, 4. The jurisdictions of all but the two largest unions followed normal craft lines from the beginning, with the exception that the Engineers, without recrimination, split off from the Firemen (with whom its members were first affiliated) to form a separate local. The Bookbinders and Sulphite Union both admit men and women, while the others have strictly male memberships.

Even though there is no actual bookbinding in the strict sense of the word in the company, the Bookbinders' Union, which was the third to be organized, took the same jurisdiction it had in other converted paper plants. These jobs are spread through both the waxing and gumming divisions of the company, whereas the other printing trades' unions are concentrated largely in the waxing division. Apparently, the Bookbinders' Union could have taken jurisdiction over all the other workers in the plant when the local was first organized in 1935. But according to the international representative, it "didn't want to start any jurisdictional troubles" and was quite willing to see the Sulphite Union come in later and take over the remaining workers in June 1937. In turn, the Sulphite Union reports that there have been no real jurisdictional troubles among the locals. The Sulphite Union is to get any new jobs which do not fall within existing craft jurisdictions.

Wartime expansion of employment into new products complicated jurisdictions, but the local unions reached a satisfactory agreement. The Sulphite Union took jurisdiction over all new employees (mostly women) hired on the wartime jobs. Regular employees who were transferred to wartime jobs retained membership in their original local unions, even though the work they were doing was normally under the jurisdiction of the Sulphite Union.

Adding to the complexity of the local-union picture is the fact that certain of the unions are composed largely or exclusively of skilled workers— the Stereotypers, Photo-Engravers, Engineers, 100 per cent; Firemen, 75 per cent; Pressmen, 64.6 per cent—while others are predominantly semi-skilled and unskilled—Sulphite, 51 per cent semiskilled, 25.3 per cent unskilled; Bookbinders, 55.4 semiskilled, 11.3 unskilled. Yet the rivalries which might be expected between these groups seem to be kept at a minimum.

There is also a combination of nationalities in the different unions, as is true in most New England industrial cities. Fifty per cent of the wage earners are of French-Canadian extraction. This is about the same proportion as in the factory labor force in the city of Nashua. Other nationalities—distributed mainly throughout the three largest unions—are Irish,

Polish, Lithuanian, Greek, Finnish, Italian, Syrian, Swedish, and Russian.

Operations of the Locals

The local unions' affairs are conducted by their respective officials and grievance committeemen, all of whom work in the plant. The officials are extremely sensitive to membership wishes, expressed either in regular meetings or in casual conversations. All the locals have annual elections of officers, except the Pressmen, who changed to biennial elections, to "take advantage of the experience gained in office." However, the records show that presidents of the locals frequently have been re-elected over fairly long periods. Other local officers and grievance committeemen are changed more frequently. In one local, for example, there is a regular rotation of grievance committeemen so that more of the membership may get experience in union affairs.

About 30 to 50 per cent attendance at meetings for election of officers is considered good, but attendance is higher when issues affect members more directly, such as the contract. The three largest unions hold their meetings in rented halls, but the four smaller ones generally handle their affairs informally in the plant; the Photo-Engravers "just go in the dark-room and take a vote." A clear demonstration of membership interest in vital union affairs was the overwhelming turnout and affirmative vote for the union shop during 1948.

Membership participation in the contract negotiation process is fairly uniform in all the locals. There is a meeting to get the members' views; then formal contract demands are drawn up, frequently with the assistance of an international representative. Another membership meeting is held to give the local negotiating committee specific instructions on what it can accept, and another for final approval of a proposed contract. If negotiations are protracted, there may be several interim membership meetings at which the negotiating committee reports back and gets new instructions. All the local and international union representatives interviewed said that the membership approval is important—that it is no rubber stamp. In fact, on several occasions, settlements tentatively accepted by union negotiators were rejected by the membership meeting, and the negotiators were instructed to go back for more.

While each local retains its sovereignty, there is an attempt to coordinate contract proposals and present a united front on other factory problems through a Shop Council. Originally, the Council had nothing to do with contract negotiations, but was set up to form a credit union for employees. Subsequently other plant-wide questions, such as the condition of washrooms, were taken up; and in recent years, the Council, which meets monthly in the company's conference room, has discussed contract proposals. But the Council does not negotiate with the management on behalf of the constituent unions; each union handles its negotiations in separate meetings with management.

In past years, one of two different locals has set the pattern for the other locals by reaching agreement with management first. Thus the pattern-setting process does operate within the plant although the seven different unions reach agreements independently.

The pattern setters have been the Pressmen's Union and the Sulphite Union. Both settled at the same time in 1941; since then the Pressmen four times settled first and the Sulphite Union three times. The Bookbinders' Union used to be next, but in recent years it has tended to hold back until other agreements have been reached. Since 1947, the Stereotypers' contract has expired later than those of the other unions. The remaining three unions tend to accept the patterns established by the leaders.

Attitudes toward the pattern-setting process vary among union officials. There has been pressure to maintain a united front through the Shop Council; whether this will succeed remains to be seen. The Stereotypers withdrew from the Shop Council several years ago, with the frank explanation that a small, highly skilled group, dealing separately from the other unions can come out on top. A former officer of another skilled local explained that "the unskilled labor is in a majority in the shop as a whole, and they are trying to use the Shop Council to get as much as the skilled unions."

The Unions' Economic Needs

The level of wages in the Card Shop apparently was one of the most important reasons for union organization, especially where the union's jurisdiction included a high proportion of skilled workers whose wages could be compared directly with those received by members of the trade employed by publishing companies. Despite the company's argument that wage comparisons should be made with its industrial competitors, craft earnings in publishing concerns have become a sort of economic par in much of the bargaining in this company, although, excepting the local newspaper, there are no significant firms in or near Nashua which use the printing skills. Other possible pressures from outside the company which could have influenced the economic needs of the unions have been reduced for three reasons: First, average hourly earnings are good compared with other major firms in Nashua—$1.44 in 1948 compared with average hourly earnings ranging from 91 cents to $1.32 in other firms. Second, wages compare favorably with industrial competitors which use printing skills. (A wage survey made by the Waxed Paper Institute in June 1949, covering 32 production jobs common to 7 firms and 14 plants in the East and Middle West showed that Nashua's rank was first on 10 jobs, second on another 10, with various lower ranks on the remaining 12.) And third, there are no rival unions trying to organize the company's workers.

However, the pressure for craft rates comparable to those in publishing concerns has been supplemented by two sorts of pressures originating within the company. These are the claim of each of the unions to comparable treatment and the variation in the interests of the skilled, semiskilled, and unskilled workers. As a result of pattern setting in the plant, when the most skilled groups move toward the Boston rates for their craft, unions representing the less skilled groups feel that they must get the same increase. This carries the economic par of commercial printing wages throughout the entire plant. To avoid this, highly paid groups have insisted that their increases be made on a percentage basis, thereby raising their cents-per-hour gains considerably as compared with the unskilled workers.

Before World War II, negotiations were primarily concerned with the rates paid on particular jobs, so the histories of rates on particular jobs show considerable divergence as to the amount of change on each one. Beginning in 1941, however, general wage requests became the focus of attention, and especially since the end of the war, increases have been large. (Table 3, *Case Study No. 7,* summarizes the increases, showing also settlement dates and amounts for each of the unions.) Gains in wage rates, while they have not brought craft rates up to those paid in the publishing field, have apparently been sufficient to satisfy the economic needs of the unions at least reasonably well. The local and international officials point with pride to the record of wage increases won by the unions.

While the fringe benefits gained by the unions are not unusual, they also compare well with industry generally, with the company's competitors, and with other firms in Nashua. On these fringe benefits, the unions also tend to make comparisons with the publishing industry. This presents a problem and pressure during negotiations, since one union may concentrate on paid holidays, another on improved vacation benefits, and so on. As on the wage question, though, the unions have not been compelled to follow any set pattern, and the concessions have been substantial enough to be reasonably satisfactory.

Local Autonomy

The international unions have deliberately encouraged the locals to handle their own affairs without much help. The role of the international representative in contract negotiations is similar in all the locals except the Engineers and the Firemen. Because they have so few members, they are attached to nearby locals in Lowell, Massachusetts, and the business agents of the Lowell locals come to Nashua each year to conduct negotiations. In the other locals, the international representatives come into the negotiating sessions only if the bargaining reaches an impasse. Clearance of initial contract proposals with the international representative is to get his suggestions and advice, rather than his approval as a necessary step before proceeding further. After agreement has been reached locally with management, it is a requirement of all the internationals that the contract be signed by the international president (or his representative) as well as by the local committee. But there has never been an occasion when the local union voted to accept an agreement and the international later rejected it. On the contrary, there have been a few instances in which the international representatives cautioned the locals against going too far or advised them to accept an offer which the local people felt was not good enough. But even then, according to a former local officer, there was never any dictation.

The Unions and the Community

The outstanding reputation of the company in the community rests in substantial part on the quality of its labor-management relations. The unions share in the credit for this accomplishment. The local unions in the Card Shop were among the first to be organized in Nashua, and they enjoy the prestige that a long record of accomplishment has given them. Today Nashua is a strongly unionized industrial city. The Textile Workers Union of America (CIO) has the largest membership, totaling 3000 workers employed in five different plants, not all textiles. Yet when that union first organized the largest mill in 1941, its leaders sought the advice and assistance of the well-established locals in The Nashua Corporation. Apparently there was no AFL-CIO friction at that time, and there is none today.

Day-to-Day Relations

The course of collective bargaining has been shaped by the way day-to-day problems have been handled by the unions and management. There is no sharp distinction between contract administration and contract making. The unions' approach has been oriented toward the local situation. Management's approach is flexible and practical, but the unions do not take advantage of this to rewrite the contract continually. Both parties are satisfied that their daily relationships are good; neither side feels that the other has "pulled a fast one."

Three management characteristics which have influenced the attitudes of the locals were mentioned consistently by union people: "You can always get to them without any trouble. There is no stalling. . . . They are willing to discuss any problem. There is nothing arbitrary about the company's attitude in negotiations or in day-to-day relationships. . . . Management has always called the union people in to tell them about what's going on, rather than hitting them cold with a decision."

Present top management attitudes, which have affected relations from the start, are also revealed in interviews: "We try not to set down on paper any general policy on management rights or prerogatives. We don't sit down ahead and say what we will do or won't do, but we wait and see what the peculiarities of the case are. We like to stay away from making decisions on the basis of precedents. . . . We like our contracts to be as simple and as short as possible. . . . We like to feel that our relationship is such that if any problems come up which are not covered in the contract, we can discuss them with the union and settle them. . . . We consult with the union representatives before taking action on a wage rate for a new job, a discipline case, or any other problem which will directly affect union members. . . . We try to encourage the expression of grievances. . . . When union people want to see you, they like to be received as soon as possible or have some definite time set. I always try to see them as soon as possible if they have a problem. I usually can put off what I'm doing."

It took time for the executives' attitudes to spread through the management group. Several of the superintendents and a foreman explained their change in approach: "We resented the unions coming in, because it put us on the spot. There have been things that have made me sore, but older top men calmed me down and leaned over backward. . . . Only two superintendents had trouble at first with the unions. One was retired on age. The other has changed completely. I have found that if you treat the union people right, they will do the same for you. But it took me a while to learn this lesson. . . . One of the most important things making for good relations here is the realization that top management is fair, wants everybody to be fair, and by gosh there will be difficulties if everybody down the line isn't fair."

Responsibility for Labor Relations

Line management is responsible for labor relations, and top management considers it an important responsibility. The industrial relations manager has considerable prestige and importance in the management organization, but is largely in a staff role. Before the unions came in, the company had only an employment department which performed some welfare functions, in addition to the usual services of a central employment office. With unionization, management hired a personnel manager from outside the company, but apparently he did not get along well with the company or unions. When he resigned, the company did not replace him immediately, but top management officials handled many of the labor relations problems. Then in 1945, the company promoted the superintendent of the largest division, who had twenty years of experience with the company, to the job of industrial relations manager. His promotion to the top executive level indicated to the rest of management and to the unions the significance that the company attached to industrial relations. The approach of the present industrial relations manager is the same as that of top management, and it explains a large part of the current good relations between the company and the unions. Union officials speak highly of his accessibility, fairness, knowledge of workers' problems, and willingness to discuss any question fully.

The industrial relations manager clarifies the line-staff relationship like this: "I never give an order to any of the superintendents. I have no authority to do that. I can make recommendations, and I use persuasion. This is a selling job. But if there is a fundamental disagreement, I go to the vice-president in charge of manufacturing (to whom he reports). If he believes I'm right, then he issues an order in his own name." The comments of superintendents bear this out. They go along with his recommendations on routine matters, but if they cannot agree, the superintendent refers the matter to his own superior. The fact that the unions view the industrial relations office as a place where they can get results if they are turned down by foremen and superintendents, suggests that perhaps the purely staff role is departed from on occasion. However, since none of the superintendents or the foremen expressed any feeling of resentment toward the industrial relations function, it is reasonable to conclude that the essential characteristics of the staff role have been maintained.

The Grievance Procedure

Steps in the grievance procedure are not spelled out in any of the union contracts. There is only a no-strike, no-lockout clause with provision for conciliation and arbitration of unsettled "differences arising under the agreement." The result is that the procedure is more or less informal and may vary somewhat between divisions. This informality seems to facilitate the disposition of day-to-day problems.

Grievances are supposed to be discussed, but sometimes are not, in this order: Step 1, the employee with the grievance, the shop committeeman, and the foreman; step 2, the employee and his committeeman and the division superintendent or his assistant in some divisions; step 3, the local union officers, with the committeeman and employee, and the industrial relations manager. A possible fourth step is to go to top management, but apparently no cases have reached this step. With the exception of one grievance which was taken to arbitration, all have been settled by the end of the third step since the industrial relations manager was appointed in 1945.

Some superintendents insist that all grievances be taken up with the union committeeman and the foreman first, but apparently others are willing, or prefer, to let grievances come directly to them. The latter feel that they have all the data at their fingertips and would rather make sure that all shifts get the same treatment. A foreman in one division feels that having all grievances go through foremen is a vast improvement. "It used to be that the help would come down from the personnel office and tell the foremen what they got. It was murder before the change." A few union representatives chafe under this new requirement. They "believe all grievances ought to be settled right away in the industrial relations office." Others feel that top management should give the foremen more discretion.

In any case, a large proportion of grievances are now settled before they reach the industrial relations manager. Superintendents of two of the three largest divisions made rough estimates, since no records were kept, of step-1 and step-2 grievances. Between 40 and 50 per cent of all grievances are settled by the foremen, and 40 per cent or more by the superintendent. The remainder, probably not more than two or three cases a year, go to the third step. By contrast, in the third division, few grievances are settled by the foremen alone, most of them going directly to the superintendent.

The Foremen and Labor Relations

Before the unions came in, the foreman was the ruler of his crew, could snap the whip. The general loss of prestige with unionization and by-passing in the grievance procedure apparently led to some talk of forming a foremen's union several years ago.[1] Top management got wind of this, and discussions with the foremen led to the establishment of a Foremen's Association. The agreement to require all grievances to be heard first by the foremen grew out of these talks. The Association meets four times a year, and the industrial relations manager now uses one of these meetings to discuss the new union contracts with the foremen. However, this is the only information they get on contract negotiations. Summaries of negotiation meetings and counterproposals to the unions are routed only to the superintendents.

There is no formal foreman training or conference program. Management arranged for a series of industrial lectures for the members of the Foremen's Association, but these lasted only one year. Nor is there a foremen's manual, employee manual, or other collected written policies to guide foremen in handling labor relations problems. This is because of the company's dislike for "putting any more in writing than is necessary." Copies of some new policy statements are sent to foremen, but this is a recent development. Some superintendents apparently try to bring foremen in on discussion of policy questions and divisional problems, but not all are able or willing to do this. Furthermore, certain information still reaches the foremen after the local union officials have been informed.

Communication within the management group, to the foreman level, still is not so effective as it is on the union side. One management official admitted that in a few divisions the foremen "are glorified office boys" because the superintendents "don't delegate proper authority to them," and several union representatives also mentioned this apparent lack of recognition for foremen. Perhaps it is a sign of progress that management recognizes the new kinds of skills needed in superintendents and foremen. "We look for superintendents now who can handle people; never mind

[1] There are approximately 37 foremen in the company, or an average of one to every 18 employees. Foremen get a substantial pay differential over the men working under them, and they also get overtime pay. In the photo-engraving and stereotyping departments, the foremen are also members of the rank-and-file unions. The superintendent in charge of the division stated that this union membership had created no difficulties for effective management.

the technical problems. But on foremen we have stressed the technical side pretty heavily, and this may be partly responsible for our problem."

General Personnel Practices

Flexibility, considered so important by management and unions, has contributed to the fact that the company has no well-defined and conscious personnel program. However, some general practices which are important to the relationship can be identified. Although there may yet be a slight carry-over of paternalism from preunion days in some aspects of these activities, the unions do not appear to resent this, and on the whole, the assistance of the unions has been welcomed and encouraged.

New applicants are interviewed in the industrial relations department, but actual hiring is conditional upon the foreman's approval, although he "must have a good reason before he can turn a man down." New employees are trained by old hands until the foreman feels they are qualified. Each foreman rates his new employees twice during the first year, and annually thereafter. Each rating is discussed with the employee. If a rating is poor in two successive periods, the foreman talks with the man, and if the superintendent participates in the discussion the union committeeman is brought in also.

The company's policy is to promote hourly-rated workers and foremen from within the organization. Although there is no seniority clause in the union contracts, the worker with greatest departmental seniority usually has the first chance to take a better job, unless a junior is outstandingly superior. The senior man has six months in which to make good on the new job or go back to his old job. Seniority also is generally followed in transfers, down-grading, and layoffs, but not always.

The informal disciplinary procedure is for the foreman, and possibly the superintendent, to talk with a worker on the first offense; and then to give him a "letter of censure" for the second—a copy of which goes to the local involved. On the third offense, the case goes to the industrial relations manager, who must approve all discharges, and the union representatives sit in on this final session.

General wage changes are arrived at through negotiations with the unions. Nevertheless, the company has a policy of paying equal to or above community rates on comparable jobs. Internal wage administration is based in part on a job-evaluation plan introduced several years ago. Some rates have been brought up but none has been reduced as a result of the plan. Union officials do not participate in the plan although its details have been explained to them. The company does not insist on following the plan literally; there is still bargaining over actual job rates. The unions have some suspicion of the plan but no outright hostility to it.

Approximately three-fourths of the rated hourly jobs are on incentives —mostly individual incentives. Prior to unionization, the incentive system was a modified Bedeaux type, but as a result of union objections, only 15 per cent of the incentive jobs are still on the original point-hour plan; the rest are on a class system. Rates on new incentive jobs are set by time study. There has been no real attempt to explain time-study methods to union representatives or the men, though they have been shown how to figure the point hour on which earnings are based. Even so, rates on new jobs are also negotiated with the union. "Sometimes you have to compromise to get a rate accepted," explained the industrial relations manager who assists the superintendents in rate negotiations, after the industrial engineering department has made the studies and proposed a rate.

An accident prevention and safety program was started in 1932 because the accident frequency rate was high—142 per million man-hours worked in 1931 and 122 in 1932. By 1941, the rate had dropped to 4.1, but it increased again during the war and postwar years. A new safety program was established. A foreman's committee makes recommendations on safety hazards, which are acted upon by a general committee, composed of union and management representatives. Although accident frequency has dropped below 10 from a postwar high of 21 in 1947, "a general lack of enthusiasm for safety work," especially the committees, is reported. Top management, however, has been and is greatly concerned with safety problems.

The usual type of suggestion system was established by the company about 1936, but since 1942, the evaluation committee has included two union representatives. The award system is unusual in that each accepted suggestion, initially awarded $5.00, is considered at the end of the year for a supplementary award. There are comparatively few supplementary awards, but they have been as high as $150. During the postwar years, there has been a steady increase in the number of suggestions, but some management officials feel that there is "a tremendous field of untapped improvements" in the plant if they could get at them. The company has not done more than a great many others to tap employee ideas. There have been no joint production committees of any sort, and apparently management is not yet ready for this type of joint activity.

Among employee activities and services, usually paid for by the company but with some union participation, are: An annual shop party handled by a shop activities committee on which there are union representatives, superintendents, and office employees; soft-ball and bowling leagues, run by the shop activities committee; a cafeteria for plant employees, office people, and management officials; and an employee magazine, principally full of "personals" from employee correspondents to each department.

Management proposed a pension plan combining retirement income with life insurance in 1944, after advance discussion with the unions and superintendents and foremen. The plan provides for joint contributions and compulsory retirement at 65, with annual pensions equal to 40 per cent of the participant's total contributions. A 1947 amendment provided additional benefits for employees with 25 years of service. An insurance plan provides sickness and hospital benefits. Employees pay half the cost, but the unions have asked for the company to assume full cost. The company maintains a small dispensary with a full-time nurse. A credit union, started some years ago by the local union presidents through the Shop Council, is run by employees with the help of the company controller.

THE BARGAINING PROCESS

Four themes seem to be apparent in the day-to-day settlement of problems, as well as in negotiations: informality and flexibility; settlement of cases on their individual merit rather than on the basis of precedent or rules; emphasis on understanding of each other's needs and demands; taking as much time as necessary to work out difficulties. Three cases illustrate the way in which management and the unions have been able to work out troublesome problems. If the matters involved had been deferred or confined to the formal period for contract negotiation, the tensions built up in the meantime might easily have disrupted the relationship.

Case 1: Variations in Incentives

One of the strongest employee objections to the original Bedeaux-type incentive system was eliminated by a jointly-negotiated modification. In 1934, the union's principal objection was the week-to-week variation in incentive earnings that resulted from causes, such as mechanical breakdowns and interruptions in the flow of work, which were beyond the control of the individual worker. Management finally agreed to accept a 13-week moving average as the basis for computing a man's weekly pay. "We hadn't appreciated that this fluctuation that the men didn't understand discredited the whole system," explained one company official. A class system was established at the same time, so that if a worker's 13-week moving average point hour were above a set figure, he would automatically get the flat rate of pay established for Class I. Four lower classes were established, but soon nearly all workers (about 97 per cent today) were at the maximum rate of pay for their jobs. Although this appears to be a flat hourly-rate system instead of an incentive system, management feels that production would fall off substantially if it were abolished, and at least one union president agrees. Some complaints about the system are unsettled; one is the fact that earnings suffer when machines are not in top condition.

Case 2: Reorganization of the Coating Division

Early in 1949, the company decided to reorganize the coating division, which had been losing money before the war and again showed a heavy loss in 1948. The company had developed a new product which could be made by this division, and which would take up part of the slack left by dropping existing products. Because quality on this new product had to be practically perfect, productivity high, and overhead reduced, management wanted the best men on the job. The vice-president explained these reasons and the chances for the program's success to representatives of the Sulphite Union, whose members were affected, in February 1949. The company asked the union to agree to breaking the seniority line in a few cases, so that the most highly efficient workers could be retained. There was no question that some men whom the company planned to displace could do the job, but only that they could not do it as well as those chosen to stay—a judgment based on years of employee ratings. At a subsequent meeting, the union rejected the company's proposals, which also included individual wage increases on about half of the jobs affected.

During further negotiations, the company adjusted its proposal to some extent, but the union continued to argue for strict seniority. The company stressed that "this is not a slack-time layoff, but a reorganization," which necessitated special treatment. An arbitrator, proposed by the union, after one hearing in May 1949, upheld the company's contention. The industrial relations manager promptly wrote to the other local unions, quoting the original explanation of the reorganization needs and stressing that this special case did not imply any change in management's past seniority policy and practices. Management's explanation apparently did not satisfy the unions, for they were determined to seek a definite seniority clause in their 1949 contract negotiations. But there was no bitterness, and the loss of the arbitration was accepted with good grace by the local and international union representatives.

Case 3: Job Changes in Specialty Printing

In the specialty printing division there are three different types of printing processes. If there were work on one type of press but not on another, the senior man would work on it. This required quite a bit of shifting, which management said was costly because it required training each man to run each type of press. At a meeting with the Pressmen's Union in 1949, management proposed that each type of press have its own crews. Present employees would choose the type of press they wanted to work on, and their seniority would be based on their total seniority in the division. This was a major change for the men and the union. After five meetings, in which the union's international representative participated, an agreement was reached. "We gave on some points and the union gave on some points," explained the division's superintendent. The union representatives then explained the changes to members in several meetings; despite the fact that forty-two men were affected, only one grievance resulted the month after the plan started. A superintendent explained management's approach this way: "Of course, we could have said, it's not written in the contract, so we won't recognize it; but the men wouldn't have seen it that way. What good's a prerogative of management if you don't get the full cooperation of your people?"

The Nature of the Contracts

The contracts are short and simple, but supplements are frequent and they are changed if they prove unworkable. These supplements may be attached to the contracts, or may be letters to the locals. The formal contracts with each union are almost identical and have few changes from their original form. The main difference in the separate contracts is the clause providing special wage classifications and job rates, and this clause is quite detailed.

In addition to the wage-classification and wage-rate clause, the principal clauses common to all agreements include: (1) a union-shop clause, with dues check-off authorized individually and irrevocable during the term of the contract; (2) a no-strike, no-lockout clause, combined with provision in case of differences arising under the agreement for a five-man arbitration board, composed of two company representatives, two union representatives, and a mutually agreed-upon chairman who has the deciding vote; (3) an equal-division-of-work clause; (4) a clause permitting union members to refuse to work on struck work from other plants organized by the union; (5) time-and-a-half pay over eight hours daily and forty hours per week, and for four specified unpaid holidays if worked; (6) six paid holidays, except if any fall on Saturday, with double time-and-a-half pay for any work performed on these holidays; (7) paid vacations—one week for one year's continuous service, and a graduated scale up to two weeks for five years' service; (8) a clause providing that "the complement of men on present machines will remain unchanged while present standards and methods are in effect," but that any new machines "shall be subject to a mutual agreement between the two parties as to complement of men and rates"; and (9) a provision for re-employment of employees after military service.

Conduct of Negotiations

Contract negotiations, on the company side, are handled by the industrial relations manager, with authority delegated by top management. Since there are several separate sessions with each union, management keeps a brief record of the discussions. These are filed for later reference and form the basis of a detailed letter from the industrial relations manager to the local union secretary outlining the reasons for each management proposal. The union representatives thus have a clear statement which can be used in oral reports at union meetings. Dangers of misunderstanding and possible distortion of the company's position are further minimized by sending copies of these letters to top company executives and superintendents. Neither party has ever used attorneys to conduct bargaining or permitted them to sit in on bargaining sessions.

Separate bargaining with each of seven unions, understandably, sometimes results in lengthy negotiations, with new contract settlements occurring long after the expiration dates of the old contracts. However, no union representative looks upon the extended negotiations as an evidence of poor relationships. This is not a case of peace through the domination of one party by another, but one where bargaining strength is evenly balanced.

The course of bargaining is shown by the record of the 1948 negotiations, which were the first conducted under declining business conditions. Negotiations began with the Pressmen in June and there were six meetings before an agreement was reached on October 18. In the meantime, bargaining meetings were held with the other unions. Altogether, the industrial relations manager conducted twenty-four separate sessions with the seven unions during a six-month period before negotiations concluded in December.

The Pressmen, for example, originally presented 26 demands, ranging from a 30 per cent wage increase, 10 paid holidays, and liberalized sickness insurance to individual wage-rate grievances and a suggested improvement in operating methods. The initial meeting explored, one by one, the union demands. In the next meeting, the industrial relations manager stated the company's position, stressing the favorable wage structure as compared to those of competing firms and as related to the cost of living. Management's view of general business prospects and specific comments on the outlook for the company's products, as recorded in notes on the sessions, indicated balanced pessimism. Apparently, this statement did not satisfy union representatives.

In the next meeting, the company offered to increase wages by 5 per cent, but continued to resist most of the other demands. After a membership meeting, the union came back with a 15 per cent proposal; at which point negotiations seemed to have reached an impasse. The union's international representative was present at the fifth meeting. After preliminary jockeying, he proposed a 10 per cent increase, explaining that there seemed to be no prospects for stabilized living costs, which had gone up almost 10 per cent since the previous year. The company negotiator said he had "held fast at 5 per cent because we were too far apart for any compromise," but that he could now go to 7.5 per cent, not as a "jockeying figure, but as what we can do and think is right." The union still insisted that 10 per cent was justified.

About two weeks later, another session was held. In the meantime, the wage question had been thoroughly aired in a union meeting and in conversations with the members. At first, the union negotiators stuck to their 10 per cent demand, but then dropped to 9 per cent. The company would not budge, but indicated some concessions might be made on other issues. The union committee retired for a private meeting, then offered to settle for 8 per cent, subject to union ratification, saying, "This is as low as we can go." The company negotiator suggested a luncheon recess, held a hurry-up meeting with his president and vice-president, and returned to agree to an 8 per cent general increase, along with a package including four other rate adjustments and two fringe concessions. This proposal was tentatively accepted by the union committee and later approved at a membership meeting.

What were the principal pressures during these bargaining sessions? First, there was pressure for peace. No one wanted or thought of a strike;

there was confidence that differences could be settled through patient bargaining. A company policy of making changed wages retroactive to the date of contract termination helped to make this patience possible. Second, the product market, through its influence on prices and profit margins, put pressure on the company to proceed with caution in raising the level of labor costs. The unions know that wage settlements with the various work groups must be reasonably consistent, so they tend to think in terms of total labor cost rather than simply the wage costs of the immediate group involved. Third, the rank and file did not expect their leaders to settle until the membership was convinced that a given offer was good. In this sense, the long negotiations, punctuated by membership meetings, served an important communications function. Finally, settlements made by the Pressmen in other localities, even though the firms involved were not all comparable to Nashua, provided a point of reference at least for local thinking and argument.

Management Rights and Union Security

The thorny issues of management rights and union security have never troubled the relationship at Nashua. Management's confidence in its efficiency and feeling that flexibility is needed in its operations have meant that no effort has been made to draw a sharp line "between mine and thine." Almost from the start, the problem of union security was resolved in negotiations and day-to-day relations. Management refused the union shop because it did not want to force workers into a union, and did not like to put into writing what it was willing to give to the unions in actual practice. On the union side, one international representative pointed out that his union had asked for a closed shop the first year, and renewed the demand each year. However, the issue was never forced since the union felt that security could be worked out in other ways. Instead of pressing for the union-shop clause, the union showed management that it was willing to operate on a sound constructive basis.

However, in 1948, union-shop elections were held by the NLRB under the Taft-Hartley Act and under the state's Willey Act.[2] Clauses became a formal part of each contract since the vote was overwhelming in favor of the union shop. Of 701 eligible voters in the seven separate elections,

---

[2] This act, passed in 1947 as a result of the Taft-Hartley provision enabling states to prohibit any or all union-security clauses, required a two-thirds vote of all employees eligible to vote, before a union-shop clause could be legal. The votes were so overwhelmingly in favor of union shops and the expense of conducting the elections were said to be so great that the state legislature repealed the law in 1949.

80 per cent voted, and of these, only three members of the Sulphite Union and one in the Bookbinders voted no.

In 1949, the company was facing a market situation in which the large wage increases of the previous postwar years probably would not be matched. Management was aware of the possible repercussions of this on the union membership, and the "political" difficulties thereby created for the union leaders. There was, however, no feeling that the shoe is now on the other foot and it would be a good time for management to cut the unions down to size. And none of the unions thought that the company would take advantage of the less favorable business conditions to weaken the unions.

A Postscript

Since completion of this *Case Study* in 1949, there has been no basic change in the nature of the relationship between the company and the seven AFL unions. Four times the collective bargaining agreements have been renegotiated and settlements have been reached after intensive and lengthy bargaining. As was the pattern in the previous years, the parties have made responsible collective bargaining the means of settling their differences—without the need for a resort to strikes or lockouts.

The adjustments in direct money items were generally as follows: 1950, 5 cents per hour increase; 1951, 10 cents per hour increase; 1952, no general increase but additional company payments on the existing hospital-surgical-medical insurance plan; 1953, 5 per cent increase in wage rates plus one additional paid holiday. The best summary comment is doubtless that of one of the key people in the situation. His final sentence in answer to a request for supplementary information was: "The relationship between the unions and management continues to be excellent."

CHAPTER 14

Marathon Corporation

and Seven Labor Unions

R. W. FLEMING, *Institute of Labor and Industrial Relations, University of Chicago,* and EDWIN E. WITTE, *Department of Economics, University of Wisconsin,* are authors of NPA Case Study No. 8. *Their full report, condensed in this chapter, was published in September 1950.*

There has never been a strike or a lockout at the Marathon Corporation. Arbitration has never been employed; neither the company nor any of the seven unions with which it deals has resorted to the courts, only twice has conciliation been used. Governmental agencies have been called in only twice when the law required it, and in both cases, the parties ended by settling their own problems. This record has not been achieved at the expense of the company, the employees, or the consuming public. The employees have been well paid, profits have been satisfactory, the company has grown steadily, and there has been no collusion against the consumer through arbitrarily high prices.

This report, in a sense, is a companion to two earlier *Case Studies,* that on Crown Zellerbach and that on The Nashua Corporation. The three studies in the same industry were made in order to see how unions which have peaceful relations with one company fared with companies in other parts of the country and under differing bargaining conditions, and to explore the effects that size of the bargaining unit and the presence of multiunion bargaining had on specific relationships. There are similarities in these studies, but there also are significant points of difference. For example, the Pacific Coast study stressed the importance of multiple bargaining; Marathon, like the other Wisconsin paper companies, bargains individually; Nashua also bargains individually, but is considerably smaller than Marathon. The Pacific Coast study involved only the two paper unions; Marathon has contracts with seven AFL unions (one of

209

which was independent at the time of the study), including both the paper unions; Nashua has contracts with seven AFL unions, but only one of the paper unions. More important to industrial peace in all three cases than environmental factors or location have been the attitudes of the parties and the ways they approach their problems.

THE COMPANY

The paper industry is important to the Wisconsin economy. In June 1949, it had more than twice as many employees as the dairy products industry, for which the state is famous. Furthermore, in the eighteen principal paper-making counties, 42 per cent of the gainfully employed industrial workers in 1940 were on the payrolls of pulp and paper companies. And Marathon Corporation is the second largest employer in Wisconsin's paper industry.

History and Growth

The 40-year-old Marathon Corporation is well and favorably known within its industry and its state. Perhaps the most outstanding fact in its history is the enterprise and imagination with which management met problems in a way which led to continued expansion and growth. The company grew out of a plan, which fell through, to develop water power for public utility purposes. Its first paper plant was founded in Rothschild, Wisconsin, in 1909. In 1927, it began specializing in the manufacture of food packages and food-wrapping materials; and since 1946, Marathon has been a wholly integrated operation from the cutting of pulp wood to the final printing of the completed package. It has consistently given special attention to development of new products, not only in the food-wrapping field but also in utilization of chemical waste.

An indication of its growth is found in the annual reports of the company for the years 1929 through 1949. For example: In 1929, the average number of employees was 1718; in 1949, 6144. In 1929, products and services sold amounted to about $10 million; in 1949, to $60 million. Net profits in 1929 were $756,000; in 1949, $4.5 million. In 1929, preferred stock dividends of $96,000 and common stock of $440,000 were paid; in 1949 the respective figures were $242,000 and $1.8 million. Land, buildings, and machinery (gross) amounted in 1929 to $7.6 million; in 1949, to $47.8 million. Net worth in 1929 was $6.6 million; in 1949, $43 million. (Figures for the intervening years are given in Table 1, *Case Study No. 8.*) Today there are 1.3 million shares of common stock outstanding of which, in April 1949, the directors controlled directly only 6.2 per cent. This figure is a bit deceptive because of indirect family holdings, but there is little doubt that such holdings constitute far less than the majority of the voting stock.

The Employees and Plant Locations

Marathon employs approximately 3000 production and maintenance workers in four Wisconsin plants and one in Michigan, and about 2400 additional workers in its Canadian operations. None of the individual plants would be classified as large:

Menasha, the biggest with about 1500 production employees, consists of a paper mill, a machine shop, a wax refinery, an ink-manufacturing plant, and complete plants for printing, waxing, coating, and laminating paper and paperboard.

Rothschild, with 630 employees, is a sulphite pulp mill and paper mill which supplies the other plants.

Menominee, in Michigan, with 350 employees, is a paper mill and the Waxtex household roll manufacturing plant.

Wausau, with 370 employees, consists of two manufacturing plants for paperboard packages.

Ashland, with about 125 employees, produces lightweight papers suitable for making napkins, in its paper mill and converting plant.

The Canadian part of the system consists of about 5000 square miles of timber lands and a bleached sulphate pulp mill in Ontario which supplies the needs of the other plants and sells the balance of its products on the outside market.

In each of the cities—where population ranges from 2000 to 30,000—Marathon is an important employer, its wages equal the best in the area, and its employment is, as a general rule, more stable than the local average. Nearly all of industry is unionized in these cities. However, Marathon has been able to be quite selective in choosing its employees in some towns but has had to compete for employees in others.

The production jobs at Marathon are mainly for men. In March 1949, there were only 170 women in the United States operations, and their jobs were almost all in the semiskilled category. The work runs the gamut from highly skilled to common labor. An idea of the job spread in the U.S. operations is gained from wage figures as of January 1, 1949. With the base rate of $1.07 for women and $1.20 for men and an effective range up to $2.00, the average employee made $1.42 per hour.

Stability of Employment

National cyclical fluctuations have not affected Marathon more than the other two paper companies. The number of employees at Marathon changed almost imperceptibly during the early thirties. This was accomplished by sharing the work and by the employees' acceptance between April 1931 and July 1933 of a wage cut which approximated 25 per cent. Despite the across-the-board cut (applicable from top executives down), employee earnings held up reasonably well.

Seasonal employment, which constituted an early problem, particularly in the Wausau and Menasha plants, has been fairly well ironed out through planning and product diversification. Aside from a general upward trend in employment, now leveling off with the completion of the company's building program, employment figures during 1947 and 1948 showed little monthly change. Another evidence of stability is found in the seniority record for production employees; in 1948, for example, 60 per cent of Marathon's male workers had been with the company over 5 years and 20 per cent over 20 years. (For total number of hourly paid employees in each U.S. plant by months in 1947 and 1948 and the seniority distribution of male workers during 1948, see Tables 2 and 3, *Case Study No. 8.*)

The Company's Personnel Policies

Continuity of management leadership has been provided at Marathon by D. C. Everest, who was made general manager of the new paper mill in 1909. Mr. Everest, when the study was made, combined the posts of general manager and president,[1] and no one denies that he has been the principal architect of the company's record of industrial peace. But for the last several years he has withdrawn from the labor relations scene, and there is no evidence that company policy will undergo a marked change under foreseeable leadership.

In the early days, Marathon had no formal personnel department. Nevertheless, management showed keen awareness of the importance of the company's relations with its employees. The plant was small enough for the management to know practically all the employees and deal with them personally. Almost from the start, the company used periodic letters to explain company attitudes and policies. This practice, formalized

---

[1] Shortly after the report was written, Mr. Everest retired as president and became chairman of the board of directors. About a year later, he resumed the presidency for a while, until John Stevens, Jr., one of the company's vice-presidents, was elevated to the presidency. Mr. Everest remains as chairman of the board.

since 1938 in an annual letter, has given Mr. Everest a chance to put across his basic belief that the interests of the employees and the stockholders are, in the long run, identical; and that only through cooperation can either the company or its employees be successful. This basic belief continued after unionization, as indicated in his 1948 letter: "The cooperation between the several unions and the management has been a great source of satisfaction to me, as I hope it has been to you."

In Marathon's early relations with its employees, there were some features which have often been associated with paternalism. Many of these measures, however, simply fitted in with the Marathon philosophy that it is good business to be interested in the welfare of one's employees. The investment per employee in a paper mill is heavy. One of the problems of the successful mill manager is to retain his work force, and papermakers, shortly after the turn of the century, were a skilled but foot-loose group.

Mr. Everest was something of a "father confessor" to many of the employees. At the Rothschild plant, Marathon had company-owned houses, stores, and a company hotel for single workers; but the company got out of the store business as soon as possible, and over the years sold the houses to employees. Marathon was one of the first employers to encourage the Wisconsin Industrial Commission in its safety campaign, and it published one of the first regularly issued safety bulletins. Marathon employees were brought under a group life insurance policy in 1919— one of the earliest of its kind, issued by the Aetna Life Insurance Company. The same year, it employed a nurse for the plant and families of employees. The following year, Marathon added a group policy providing a weekly indemnity for sickness and nonoccupational injuries. There were other touches along the way—a library for employees, a recreational program, a house organ (*The Marathon Runner*), and a continuous service bonus, though the bonus was discontinued after a few years.

The company attitude on such activities is summed up in a letter from Mr. Everest to all employees published in *The Marathon Runner* in December 1920: "When I made the announcement regarding the Continuous Service Bonus some men made the remark that it was only a scheme of the 'Old Man's' to get the men to stick here. . . . What, under the heavens, did they think I was trying to do? . . . (The 'Old Man') is scheming to get you to stick to Marathon and to make this the best place to work in this part of the country."

In providing services to its employees, the company has not sought control over the lives of its employees or tried to keep them out of unions. In

1931, before Marathon was even "threatened" with union organization, Mr. Everest was widely hailed by labor groups for his suggestion that current economic difficulties be remedied by the temporary establishment of a five-day week for all industry with the same weekly wage then being paid. And when unionism was in the air the company accepted it without either opposition or deep-seated resentment.

In 1934, Marathon established a personnel department, but for some time, there was no coordinated personnel policy among the plants, unless matters reached the top level. There is now a central personnel division in Menasha, headed by a director, who is responsible to the executive vice-president in charge of U.S. operations, who in turn is responsible to the president. Four departments, under the personnel director, are headed by managers of wage and salary administration, placement, training, and employee services. The director and his departmental managers are staff officers who exercise authority through the line officers of the other divisions. In addition to the headquarters staff, there is a personnel supervisor in each plant who reports to his plant manager, but has functional responsibility to the personnel director. The personnel division's functions conform to established and well-known patterns. The line officials generally rely upon personnel representatives for help. This keeps the personnel people close to daily operations and makes their advice fully effective.

THE UNIONS AT MARATHON

All production and maintenance employees at Marathon are unionized. The greatest number belong to the AFL paper unions—the International Brotherhood of Pulp, Sulphite and Paper Mill Workers, and the International Brotherhood of Paper Makers. But in addition there are: the International Association of Machinists (independent at the time of the study, now AFL); the International Photo-Engravers' Union (AFL); the International Stereotypers' and Electrotypers' Union (AFL); the International Typographical Union (AFL); and the International Printing Pressmen and Assistants' Union (AFL). All these unions are noted for their mature acceptance of the American economic and political system.

Forerunner to Unionization

First efforts at unionization in Wisconsin's paper industry immediately after World War I were unsuccessful. Most of the state's mills were then unorganized, and the Paper Makers and Pulp Workers staged a statewide organizing campaign, which met stiff resistance from the companies.

For one reason or another, no serious effort was made to organize Marathon. Some employees joined the union, but the group fell apart. Some persons on the company's board looked unfavorably on unions; Marathon joined with the other companies in aiding at least one company which was struck. The incentive and bonus plan was instituted at that time, which may have had some effect in discouraging union organization. Even so, there was never any real or open conflict between Marathon and the unions.

From the time the paper unions faded away early in the twenties until the summer of 1933, the only employee representation at Marathon was through occasional informal groups picked by management to serve special purposes. Employee representation increased, however, after the National Recovery Administration started operations in June 1933. Mr. Everest was called to Washington to work on the NRA paper code. There he renewed contacts made during World War I with the presidents of the paper unions—John P. Burke of the Pulp Workers and Matthew Burns of the Paper Makers—and learned to know and respect them.

Marathon threw its full support behind the NRA. Even before the paper industry's code of fair competition became effective, the company switched to an eight-hour day for shift workers and a 40-hour week for others, and raised hourly rates so that the weekly wage would approximate that of July 1, 1933. This increased Marathon's employment substantially. Marathon's support of the NRA was not lacking in self-interest. Free and unrestricted competition was a perpetual problem to the paper industry and the code offered an opportunity for some stabilization.

The NRA encouraged formation of mill councils on which elected employee representatives served. Marathon encouraged its employees to join with the company in establishing councils; and councils operated in the Rothschild and Menasha plants, but the employees of the Wausau plant voted against it. Opinions differ on the part which the mill councils played in the development of employee relations. Top company officials say they worked well and served a genuine purpose, pointing to the close parallel between subjects discussed then and contemporary discussions. Union officials say elections were never taken seriously because employees realized the impotence of any organization which had no outside support, and some members of management who were in the employee ranks at that time agree. The fact that the employees were suggesting, rather than bargaining, seems to be shown by minutes of some of the meetings, but minutes also indicate that some gains were registered in council discussions. Moreover, the councils gave both the company and the employees some experience in collective dealings prior to the coming of the unions. The fact that the councils existed but were not deemed adequate by many employees may have hastened the coming of the unions. Significantly, quite a few of the men who were active in the mill councils later were active in the unions.

Recognition of the Paper Unions

The paper unions had been organizing for some time, and when the Wagner Act in 1935 gave them new life, they began to press Marathon for recognition. Passage of the Act also convinced Mr. Everest that unionization of practically all industry was inevitable. This being so, he thought the company would be better off to anticipate action which might result in any disruption of its labor relations. Even without top management opposition, organization at Marathon was not simple. Employees' enthusiasm for unionism was somewhat retarded by the fact that Marathon had always been a leader in wages and working conditions. The lower echelons of management, who were in closest contact with the employees, looked on the coming of unions with considerably less enthusiasm than top management. Even so, the two unions' efforts—they employed a single organizer—were successful.

By October 1935, a meeting was arranged between the company's board of directors and the presidents of the Rothschild locals of the Paper Makers and the Pulp Workers. Recognition of both unions followed shortly thereafter, and the first real contract, covering members of both unions in the Rothschild plant, was signed in July 1936. A union-shop demand was withdrawn temporarily because of a request from management that the employees be given time to adjust to the new relationship. In 1937, the company signed a new contract with the paper unions covering all its plants.

Recognition of Other Unions

The printing unions had entered the picture at Marathon by the spring of 1937. The first two to seek recognition were the Pressmen and the Electrotypers. The Electrotypers signed a contract covering the Menasha plant in 1937 and now has about 37 members. The Pressmen's Menasha local signed a joint contract in 1937 with the two paper unions, but subsequently negotiated separate contracts. Lack of organizational diligence in 1937 permitted the pressmen in the Wausau plant to join the Pulp Workers, where they remained until the pressure of the Wage Stabilization Act gave them an added incentive to break away in May 1945 to form their own local. The 270 members of the Printing Pressmen at Wausau and Menasha are covered by a joint contract.

Marathon's two or three compositors were originally members of the Pulp Workers, but seceded in August 1937 to join the International Typographical Union. There are five members of this union at Marathon. The company was not averse to this action because it permitted establishment of an Allied Printing Trades Council and use of its label, which has become increasingly important over the years.

Until late 1943, all of Marathon's photoengraving was done outside, most of it by the Appleton Engraving Company. Marathon purchased the Appleton company in 1943 and inherited a contract with the Photo-Engravers, which it has continued for the 26 members who compose this group.

Since the printing unions have relatively few members employed at Marathon, their locals which deal with Marathon include members employed at other plants and in other geographical areas. Marathon's employees account for varying percentages of the total membership of these locals. Marathon does not follow the pattern of the printing unions established with other local employers, however, because in most cases it employs more skilled printing tradesmen than do the other employers. For bargaining purposes, the unions use commercial job-shop rates, but the company believes such rates are inapplicable because they do not reflect competitive rates in the food-packaging industry.

The small number of members in the printing unions, coupled with their important position in Marathon's connecting operations, suggests that the company could afford to comply with almost any demands of these unions, no matter how unreasonable, simply to avoid a stoppage of work. In practice, however, each of the unions watches the other negotiations carefully, and the company attempts to grant concessions which are relatively uniform.

The International Association of Machinists became involved after Marathon acquired the Whitmore Machine and Foundry Company in Menasha in 1941. The Whitmore employees were unorganized, and this was unacceptable to the other Marathon employees, all of whom belonged to one union or another. Marathon had maintenance machinists in the Pulp Workers Union, but the new machine shop was not a maintenance unit. For the Pulp Workers to assume jurisdiction might cause trouble with the Machinists, which had many similar plants organized in the Fox River Valley. On the other hand, there was some thought that if the Machinists came into the Whitmore unit, that might lead to raiding of the Pulp Workers' maintenance machinists. Despite these difficulties, none of which ever assumed serious proportions, the IAM was recognized and a contract signed in 1946. It has 55 members, who account for about two-thirds of the membership of the IAM local covering the Neenah-Menasha area.

Impact of Jurisdictional Problems on Strikes

The impact of labor troubles would be serious for both the company and the unions because of the peril of permanently lost customers, and the resulting loss of jobs.

Raiding by both the CIO and the AFL craft unions has been a possibility at Marathon. Like their brethren on the Pacific Coast (see *Case Study No. 1*), the Wisconsin paper unions have to give some consideration to keeping their rates for skilled men close to those craftsmen are getting elsewhere, but apparently their battle has not been so difficult. So far as the CIO is concerned, the incumbent unions keep a sharp eye out for signs of activity, but no real threat has ever developed.

Potentially, the more serious problem is the danger of jurisdictional struggles among the seven unions. The possibilities inherent in the Whitmore unit have already been mentioned; the break-off of the Wausau pressmen from the Pulp Workers left some ill feeling; and jurisdiction over certain other jobs is, and has been, disputed. So far, imagination, flexibility, and good faith have led to amicable solutions.

Strike action by any one of the seven unions would be serious. Although strikes of the different unions would not be equal in intensity, a really serious issue would probably, though not inevitably, result in concerted action. Action by the Paper Makers and Pulp Workers probably would be concerted and would shut down the whole system quickly. A like result would obtain if the Printing Pressmen went out, because they are an integral part of the total operation. If the compositors stopped work, the company might be able to keep going indefinitely by getting the work done elsewhere, but the same probably would not be true of either the photoengravers or the electrotypers. Cessation of work by the Machinists would probably be the least serious because the machine shop is a relatively independent unit.

THE DEVELOPMENT OF COLLECTIVE BARGAINING

Multiple bargaining was considered during the paper unions' organizing campaign in Wisconsin, since it was already established on the Pacific Coast. In 1937, Wisconsin companies with union agreements coming up sent representatives to a meeting to discuss this question. The group endorsed individual bargaining, but took the initial step in setting up what later became the Lakes States Pulp and Paper Association "to co-ordinate the study of wage rates in the cooperating mills." The Association, covering Wisconsin, Minnesota, and Michigan, gathers, coordinates, and disseminates statistical information on wages, hours, and working conditions in member plants. Even so, there are wide variations in wage increases among the participating companies, and in base rates, arrangements for the work week, shift premiums, vacation and insurance plans, and so on.

The two paper unions also have an organization in which their representatives in Wisconsin, Minnesota, and the upper peninsula of Michigan participate—the Tri-State District Council. The Council meets twice a year, before and after annual negotiations, to exchange information and compare bargaining requests and results, and, most important, to give delegates an opportunity to discuss day-to-day problems and their solutions. The member unions submit relatively uniform demands to all companies in the area, but do not seriously attempt to arrive at identical agreements.

There is still an occasional stirring of interest in multiple bargaining. However, both sides seem to feel that, because of the wide diversity of products among the plants and the fact that many of their operations are not comparable, certain of the plants could not survive if required to maintain the standard of the more profitable companies.

System-wide Bargaining at Marathon

Although the company would have preferred a single contract covering all the unions, it now has a master contract with both paper unions in the Wausau, Rothschild, Menasha, Ashland, and Menominee plants; with the IAM, the ITU, Electrotypers, and Photo-Engravers, it has separate bargaining sessions and contracts for the Menasha plant, the only plant where these unions are involved; and has a single contract for the Pressmen at Menasha and Wausau.

The annual bargaining session with the Paper Makers and Pulp Workers takes on the same aspect of the goldfish bowl as in the Pacific Coast pulp and paper industry. The sessions, rotated among the different plants, are usually attended by about 70 people. The vice-president in charge of manufacturing, the personnel director and his manager of wage and salary administration, all plant managers and some of their superintendents, and all plant personnel supervisors, attend for the company.

The union contingent, headed by several international representatives, includes local presidents and their bargaining committees. Neither side calls in lawyers or outside consultants.

The personnel director makes the opening presentation for the company and the international representatives lead off for the unions. As discussion gets down to basic points, other representatives on both sides participate. Experience shows that the achievement of a meeting of minds takes one to three days. Both groups come armed with the authority to make a decision, though the action of union representatives is subject to ratification by the locals.

No transcript of the record is kept, but company representatives keep notes from which minutes are compiled for distribution to company and union people. Despite the fact that both the company and the unions have shown a real interest in and consciousness of the contents of their contract, they have not been loath to insert a clause in the contract which can be negated by an agreement shown in the minutes. The minutes, therefore, have been an invaluable tool in interpreting the contract. Both parties believe this to be in line with a common-sense approach to contract administration.

Management Rights and Union Security

Article I of the paper unions' contract, the content of which originated with the unions, may have avoided overemphasis on management rights in this relationship. This clearly calls for cooperation of the company and the employees in advancing the economic welfare of both, the safety and health of the employees, the quality and quantity of output, economy of operation and reduction of waste, and cleanliness of plant and protection of property. Since employees had not previously questioned the company's ultimate responsibility to manage, even without this Article, management had little need to worry about protecting its prerogatives. The minutes of grievance and bargaining sessions over the years bear out this confidence. Occasionally, though not often, one of the unions has raised a point which management feels is peculiarly within its province and it says so. Neither side seems to get excited when this happens.

The first system-wide contract with the two big paper unions granted labor's demand for a union shop, thus removing union security from contention. This may have required some soul searching on the part of the company, for in 1934 it had emphasized the company's insistence upon an open shop in all its plants "to protect (the) inherent desire of every individual to be free to seek employment wherever he chooses." However, after the unions dropped their demand for a union shop during the 1936 negotiations, the company's representatives saw the friction which developed between union and nonunion employees. This influenced their conclusion that relations would be more satisfactory if all employees belonged to the union. And management may have been influenced also by the fact that some of their competitors had already made such a concession.

For a while, some persons in management resisted the union shop as did certain long-service employees. However, these attitudes changed as it became clear that management was sincere in its belief that all employees should join. The company has never been asked to discharge an employee as the result of the union-shop clause except for failure to pay dues, and few of these cases have actually resulted in dismissal. The unions have never asked for a check-off, preferring that dues be collected in person.

Living Together in the Early Years

Despite the ease with which the unions arrived on the scene, a harmonious relationship was by no means assured. There was some genuine "grass roots" opposition to the unions; the lower echelons in union and management were inexperienced in cooperating in the plant; and even at the top level, the union and company still had to feel each other out. Invaluable experience was gained when, in 1937, the parties worked together on the installation of a job-evaluation plan.

The company's rate structure was thrown out of line by the juggling of the NRA days and other factors. Naturally the matter of wages came up at the first meeting with the paper unions. The company suggested a joint job-evaluation program, and with some reluctance the unions agreed to participate and go along with the plan. The fact that this cooperative effort was undertaken at a time when it was not the fashion among other companies to work with the unions on job evaluation served to develop mutual confidence.

The same policy in relation to job evaluation applies today. It does not affect, and never has, some of the craft operations, but it covers about 2400 of the approximately 3000 production employees in the U.S. operations. In practice, the union representing the particular employees is asked to name four men to serve on a job-evaluation committee, with the president of the local sitting as a fifth, and ex officio, member. "Consultants" (men working on the particular jobs under discussion) may also be drawn in by the union. Meetings are held on company time with reimbursement for time lost. Both the foreman and the union representative know in advance that the job analyst will visit their department, and one or the other introduces him to the man whose job is to be studied. Before preparation of the job description, employees on the job, the foreman, and other supervisors are asked to agree on the nature of the job. Based on this information, classification is made by a joint committee of management and union representatives. Either side may ask for review of a rate which it believes to be unsatisfactory. In accordance with the usual practice, an incumbent's rate is never reduced, but a new employee working beside him will carry the newly established rate.

The first job-evaluation program was completed prior to World War II. Across-the-board increases just prior to wage stabilization upset the balance between skilled and unskilled rates, with the result that following the war the whole thing had to be done over.

ADMINISTERING THE CONTRACTS

A major reason why there has never been a serious conflict in this relationship is the manner in which the parties administer their contracts. Both sides have shown respect for the contract, while exhibiting sufficient confidence in each other to make changes where daily events have seemed to make this advisable. The company early established with its employees, and with the unions when they arrived, a reputation for absolute integrity and a willingness to sit down and talk about any subject. And the unions consistently have demonstrated their responsibility. Mr. Everest's guiding hand can be seen in the day-to-day administration of the contract as well as in other actions important to this good relationship. He has stressed the practice of treating the unions as bona fide representatives of the company's employees, rather than as outside agencies, subject to suspicion; and he has insisted that the company never take advantage of short-term deals in the continuing relationship with the unions.

The Handling of Grievances

The grievance procedure set forth in each of the Marathon contracts follows a common pattern of progression. In practice, however, the parties do not always follow it strictly. While it is difficult to say just how many grievances are settled at any given point, in recent years not a single grievance has reached the last stage of arbitration involving the president of the company and the presidents of the international unions. Immediately below this level, the vice-president in charge of manufacturing estimates that he has not had more than 1 per cent of the grievances. Of formalized grievances—and these are a minority—most are settled at the level of the plant manager. The managers probably spend more time in grievance sessions than is usual, but this avoids the possibility of having union officials hash over grievances with subordinate officials who may not have the authority to settle the issue. Furthermore, the handling of grievances keeps the plant managers close to the problems of employees and gives them an opportunity to explain some of the company's problems to employees.

The Problem of Seniority

Management and the unions hold different views on seniority. The company is committed to promoting on a seniority basis with qualifications. Where it finds that it cannot follow seniority, the question is subject to discussion with the union. Occasionally, the company reluctantly will go along with a trial promotion, but only in cases where it is unable to make a clear and rational case for one man rather than another. When the company finds that a trial appointee does not work out, it discusses the case with the union. And, according to the company, the union goes along with removal of such appointees.

Views on trial promotions vary. A top executive thinks it works out all right, since the company will not agree to it except in a close case and the promoted man, who knows that he is on trial, makes a special effort. A plant personnel supervisor, formerly on the union's grievance committee, says that the company sacrifices some efficiency by the practice, but that these losses are more than made up by time saved from haggling and in good will.

Discipline and Discharge

The company's work rules, which are appended to contracts and incorporated by reference, contain a clause at the outset which reads: "Noncompliance with the following rules shall be considered good cause for disciplinary action or discharge and will be administered by the Company according to the seriousness of the violation."

In practice, when work rules are broken the company notifies the union. Shortly thereafter, as soon as each has had a chance to gather the facts, and if it is deemed necessary by either side, a joint meeting of company and union representatives is held, before which the employee who has violated the rule ordinarily is asked to appear. The work rules do not require the company to do this. It could take unilateral action and permit the union to vent any dissatisfaction through the grievance procedure. Instead it prefers to avoid a grievance and have the employee representatives in from the start.

Frequently during the union and management discussions of cases subject to discipline or discharge, the penalties are modified as a result of either union or company suggestion. The minutes of some of the sessions reveal how the procedure works, and also that considerable weight is given to the union's opinions on penalties. (The minutes of three cases— one dealing with reporting to work under the influence of liquor, grounds for immediate dismissal; one with causing a disturbance on company property, a fight in this case; and one with a shift worker who left his job before he was relieved by his partner or released by his foreman—are given in *Case Study No. 8.*)

This system, according to the company, does not undermine effective discipline. One of the top manufacturing people says that over the years the company has found that the people it has to discipline are those with whom the union is also having trouble. He thinks the penalties which are invoked usually fit the case, with the advantage of better employee acceptance and understanding. A company personnel supervisor makes two further points. Investigation by the union sometimes turns up information which the company has overlooked, saving the company from making a move which the union could have shown to be based on a false premise. Discipline and discharge cases have never caused any serious dispute in the relationship, whereas the procedure provides the company with an opportunity to discuss basic problems with the union.

Routine Intercommunication

Conferences between company and union officials are by no means confined to formal occasions. They cover a wide variety of routine matters. A joint discussion may involve a particular employee and his personal problems but not necessarily constitute a grievance or matter subject to bargaining under the contract. Or the company may plan a picnic; it asks the president of the local to suggest the names of employees who would be interested in helping the company make the plans. The safety program is not a joint program in the literal sense, but there is an employee committee selected in consultation with the local union president.

Another subject of company and union discussions is pensions. The unions suggested in the 1947 negotiations that the company do something about improving its informal pension plan. The company said it had the matter under consideration and by the 1949 negotiations the company was ready to discuss pensions. Certain problems remain before the plan which it is proposing can be made effective, but those are expected to be solved at a reasonably early date. No one thought to ask whether this was a subject which had to be taken up with the union, perhaps because the unions have proved their responsibility and reasonableness to the company.

A Look at the Records

Statistical records prove that industrial peace has not been achieved at the expense of the company's ability to make a profit or the employees' ability to make a satisfactory wage. Marathon not only has made a profit in each of the last twenty years, with the exception of 1932, but its profits compare favorably with other firms in the industry. (Table 4 of *Case Study No. 8* shows profits both as a percentage of sales and of net worth as compared with listed corporations in the paper and allied products category for the years 1936 through 1947.) In general, Marathon's profits run just below the paper and allied products group on the basis of sales, and just above on the basis of net worth. Whatever may be the deeper meanings of this, on the surface it is apparent that Marathon's profits have been satisfactory.

Statistics on wages for each of the unions involved in this report would be unduly burdensome, and it is sometimes difficult to find a fair measure for comparison.

The printing unions customarily ask Marathon to meet commercial job-shop rates in Milwaukee, Chicago, and New York. The company, however, does not admit the validity of this argument, claiming that the cost of living, local area rates, and competitive rates must all be considered. Bargaining usually results in rates which the company and unions concede to be above local levels and comparable with competitive rates within the industry, but somewhat below metropolitan standards.

Negotiations with the IAM have a short history, but rates in the Marathon machine shop are as high as comparable rates in the Fox River Valley. These are still slightly below those of maintenance machinists, however, who are members of the Pulp Workers. This is the goal toward which the IAM shoots.

The paper unions classify Marathon, along with three or four other companies, as the wage leaders in Wisconsin. As compared with the paper and allied products group generally, both nationally and in Wisconsin, Marathon is slightly ahead. (See Table 5, *Case Study No. 8*, for a comparison of average weekly earnings in the three categories for the years 1939 through 1948.) Marathon's average straight-time hourly rate doubled in the period between 1940 and 1949, and weekly earnings, including overtime, went up about two and one-third times. Both outdistanced the rise in the cost of living.

Various fringe adjustments account for a sizable amount in Marathon's over-all wage bill. Marathon figures that it puts roughly 15.88 cents per hour into pay for unworked holidays, vacations, group insurance, night-shift premiums, and the differential between 36-hour and 40-hour workers. The company's insurance program is noncontributory and is rated by the unions as the best they enjoy. (Table 6 in *Case Study No. 8* shows coverage for employees and dependents for life, accidental disability and death, weekly health and accident, daily hospital benefits, miscellaneous hospital charges, and surgical benefits.)

Labor turnover, as a measure of job satisfaction, is probably most meaningful in times of full employment, so for comparative purposes 1947 is a good year. During each month in that year, Marathon's turnover rate was considerably below that of the paper and allied products group generally (as shown in Table 7, *Case Study No. 8*).

Investment per employee in a paper mill is heavy—in excess of $14,000 for every Marathon employee in the United States, according to the 1947 annual letter to employees. And the company knows that labor as a cost of manufacturing has gone up over the years because of changes in operations. But it is difficult to present meaningful data on labor productivity. It is perhaps sufficient to say that the subject has not been a bone of contention between the parties.

Prospects for the Future?

A rosy past offers no complete assurance that the future at Marathon will be as good. If Mr. Everest has been so important to the relationship, can it survive him? In essence, the almost equally uniform answer from company and union representatives was: "There will probably never be another guy quite like him, but our relationship ought to go on just about the same. After all, you must remember that he hasn't taken any part in the negotiations or the labor relations picture for several years now, and everything has gone on all right. By this time, his philosophy is so well soaked in all the way up and down the managerial structure that most of the others share his views."

But some of the problems of the future may be tougher than anything the parties have had to face in the past. It does not take much effort to conjure up a few:

1. The years since 1937 have been almost all good years, in which it has been possible for the company to give something each time the annual

bargaining sessions rolled around. What will happen during the lean years?

2. For 25 years, the company has had its sights set on complete integration from forests to food wrappings. This has meant steady expansion and ever-increasing employment. Now the goal has been reached. What will happen if the company remains static and technological changes are proposed which will displace workers? What about seniority? So far, seniority has related almost entirely to promotions. Now layoffs may come into the picture.

3. The fact that the company has grown so fast in recent years has left it with a major managerial problem of reorganizing to meet vastly larger problems. Can it do this successfully?

4. Not only the company but the international paper unions face the fact that the leadership which has been so long in the saddle may change before long. How will this affect the relationship?

5. Most of Marathon's plants, while still small, have grown considerably. The personal contact of the past will not be so easy to attain in the future.

6. The practice of writing one thing in the contract and modifying or negating it in the minutes may rise to plague the parties, because the contract has much wider circulation than the minutes, and the individuals who made the original agreements may gradually pass from the scene.

7. A number of potential points of friction between the incumbent unions might spell trouble if any should break into the open.

None of these possibilities, however, represents a matter so serious that it cannot be overcome by the same brand of integrity, good faith, and willingness to bargain which the parties have shown in the past. Furthermore, they have managed to build up a tremendous reservoir of good will which can withstand hard knocks.

A POSTSCRIPT

The relationship at Marathon continues to be much the same as it was at the time this study was completed in 1950. There have been no strikes or lockouts, and employment-wise the company is growing. New plants have been added in Oswego, New York, Sunnyside, Washington, and at the Northern Paper Mills in Green Bay. Employment has also risen in the chain itself as described at the time of the study. The company's position in general continues to compare favorably in the paper and allied products industry, and its labor-management relations continue peaceful and stable.

CHAPTER 15

Minnequa Plant of Colorado
Fuel and Iron Corporation

and Two Locals
of the Steelworkers (CIO)

GEORGE W. ZINKE, *Professor of Economics, University of Colorado, is author of* NPA Case Study No. 9. *His full report, condensed in this chapter, was published in October 1951.*

Steady progress in the development of mutually advantageous collective bargaining marks the nine-year relationship between management of the Minnequa Plant of the Colorado Fuel and Iron Corporation and two locals of the United Steelworkers of America (CIO). There has been a continuous and conscientious effort to improve the techniques of scientific and objective bargaining. As more and more areas of employment relations have been jointly explored and solved, the company, the union, the workers, and the general public have gained.

Despite the fact that industrial relations in the West have certain peculiarities not found in the East, a comparison of the situations at the Minnequa Plant in Colorado and at Sharon Steel's Pennsylvania and Ohio plants reveals striking similarities in the underlying causes of peace. The high demand for steel and pattern setting in the steel industry—factors beyond the control of both companies—have contributed to their good relationships. But more important in both situations have been the internal factors which the parties to the relationships themselves controlled.

THE ENVIRONMENT

The Minnequa Plant grew out of a purely western plan for the concurrent building of a railway to serve the area and development of the

West's potentials for manufacturing and mining facilities. Construction of the plant was begun in 1880 by Colorado Fuel and Iron Corporation and, in April 1882, the first steel left the Minnequa Plant, rolled for the rails of the new Denver and Rio Grande Railway.

In one of the struggles of rival industrial empires which characterized the turn of the century, the Rockefeller interests gained control of C. F. & I., and in 1903, John D. Rockefeller, Jr., newly elected president, undertook a huge expansion program. The company thereafter experienced steady growth until 1933. At that time, the corporation, faced with a top-heavy capital structure and losses incurred during the depression, went into receivership. A subsequent reorganization featured no essential break in the administration of C. F. & I., and the Rockefellers' financial control continued.

The Company Today

The Minnequa Plant in Pueblo, Colorado, is only one of C. F. & I.'s manufacturing properties. The company now includes steel industrial operations in seven other plants: in Oakland and South San Francisco, California; Clinton, Palmer, and Worcester, Massachusetts; Buffalo, New York; and Mt. Wolf, Pennsylvania. The present coast-to-coast corporation was completed as a financial structure after John D. Rockefeller, Jr., sold his 52 per cent majority control in 1944. These interests were purchased by a Wall Street syndicate headed by Charles Allen, Jr., broker and chairman of the board of the Wickwire Spencer Company, one of the oldest steel products manufacturers in the United States. With the assistance of Floyd B. Odlum's Atlas Corporation, the Allen syndicate, which already controlled the Wickwire Spencer Company, arranged a merger in August 1945, of the eight plants which now comprise C. F. & I.

The largest producer of steel west of the Mississippi, the Minnequa Plant is keyed to the West today as it was in the past. Its varied products are bought by a variety of industries, including farming and construction. Rails and related products for the transportation industry constitute some 50 per cent of the Pueblo production. By-products from the coke plant are supplied to the chemical industry. During World War II, a large percentage of the plant's production was converted to shell forgings.

Properties owned by C. F. & I. supply Minnequa's raw materials: ore from Wyoming and Utah and coal, fluorspar, limestone, dolomite, and timber from Colorado. In addition, C. F. & I. owns a subsidiary, the Colorado and Wyoming Railway Company, which transports raw materials and finished products in and out of the Pueblo steel plant, and serves properties in southern Colorado and Wyoming, as well as other industries to a minor extent.

With a rated capacity of 1,272,000 tons of ingots, for several years preceding the outbreak of the Korean War the Minnequa Plant could produce 1.3 per cent of the entire normal steel output of the United States. The plant's 1950 capacity for steel rails was 23.3 per cent of the total national capacity. According to 1950 statistics of the American Railway Engineering Association, Minnequa is a leader quality-wise: no other rail producer features a lower record of failures per track mile. The Minnequa Plant has been running recently at nearly 100 per cent of rated capacity in all its operations. As part of C. F. & I., the plant is part of the tenth largest steel company in the nation. In 1950, 7700 persons were employed at Minnequa.

Because of the plant's slow, measured growth, there has been extreme variation in the age and condition of equipment. Despite this, Minnequa is reputedly the safest and cleanest mill in the United States. A steam generating plant and a battery of coke ovens, built on the plant's property during World War II by the U.S. Defense Plant Corporation and subsequently purchased by Minnequa, augmented capacity by 20 per cent. A new Morgan rod mill was completed and placed in operation at Pueblo in 1949. This mill, which increased C. F. & I.'s wire production capacity by 33 per cent, is said to be the most modern rod mill in the world. Other recent installations include modern soaking pits, new fence fabricating machines, new diesel switching locomotives, facilities for making new type products, as well as extensive repairs and improvements.

Since 1944, C. F. & I.'s industrial and financial records have been impressive. In the years between the end of World War II and the outbreak of the war in Korea, the corporation normally employed in all of its operations about 15,000 persons, of whom approximately one-half were at Pueblo. Actual ingot production increased during pre-Korean years at a rate faster than that of the steel industry as a whole. Net income increased to $10 million in the fiscal year ending June 30, 1949, from $6 million in the fiscal year ending June 30, 1948. During the same period, net worth rose from $58 million to $66 million. Dividend records made since 1949 have been impressive, but the value of these records as a guide to C. F. & I.'s normal growth is diminished because they reflect mobilization activities. A better indication of the normal development of the investment to serve the peacetime West is the fact that, in the five years following World War II, C. F. & I. spent over $18 million to modernize its Western Division. In 1949, the invested capital per employee for the corporation as a whole was registered at $5220; for the Minnequa Plant alone, invested capital per employee amounted to $8750.

The Management Organization

Management men who had come up in the steel industry replaced coal executives and financiers after the 1944 reorganization. The presidency in 1946 passed to Carl Meyers, who entered the steel industry at an early age as a roll hand; and J. J. Martin, who became vice-president of national operations and works manager of the Minnequa Plant, has spent his life with the steel industry. A. F. Franz, who was works manager at the Buffalo plant of the Wickwire Spencer Steel Company, later came to Pueblo, and in 1949, he was elected executive vice-president of C. F. & I.[1]

Mutual confidence between men and management is one of the most important factors in the production of steel, and nothing wins the workers' confidence more surely than the knowledge that management officials have come up through the industry. Conversely, old-timers in the industry have a unique insight into the value which steelworkers place on behavior of management. The C. F. & I.'s officials know, too, that unless respect is combined with a sense of active participation, many a worker will look upon himself as a man working for a day's pay rather than as a *steelworker*.

One of the chief reasons for the successful industrial relations at Minnequa is C. F. & I.'s flexible, decentralized management design, which keeps the corporation close to local plant managements, and local plant management close to the employees. Howard J. Jones functions as manager of industrial relations for the whole company, with offices at Buffalo. Acting under his general direction, George E. Diggory is superintendent of industrial relations at the Minnequa Plant. Mr. Diggory has had long service as a management official at Minnequa. Although final discretion in corporation policy is reserved by C. F. & I's top personnel, all lines of authority are designed to integrate decision making at all levels, down to the foreman who deals with the individual worker and the union's shop steward (usually called "griever" at Minnequa).

The corporation's conception of vertically integrated but liberally delegated authority is substituted for the theory of top-down command. The autonomy at all levels of supervision results in widely diversified policies regarding firing, suspension, and even promotions. However, the collective bargaining relationship is strengthened rather than weakened by this

---

[1] Mr. Franz was elected president of the national operations in February 1952, and Carl Meyers became vice-chairman of C. F. & I.'s board of directors.

diversity. The individual worker and griever dealing with lower management know that they are not confronted by persons with no authority. If a case goes to higher steps of the grievance procedure, a good record is available from the earlier discussion. As long as supervisors know that they can really deal with cases before passing them up the line, there is no strong temptation to assert extra authority by making individual deals.

One reason why such a flexible policy is successful is that the superintendent of industrial relations acts as a line official as well as a staff adviser. Mr. Diggory, working closely with the highest line official, works manager J. J. Martin, automatically closes the gap between line and staff. Without line authority, Mr. Diggory would hardly be able to review action of lower echelons of line management. The fact that he makes final decisions on appeals eliminates the tendency of lower levels to buck staff suggestions offered only as advice.

Mr. Diggory interprets a major part of his function to be that of review and processing of appeals rather than handling every detail along the line. He reserves action in many matters until he is asked to intervene, then exercises his final discretion in conformance with general principles and policies, and carefully explains to workers or grievance men the reasons for his decisions. Mr. Diggory feels that not enough progress with educational programs has been made. Although there are regular and frequent meetings of supervisors, there is a relative dearth of gatherings where foremen can discuss problems and policies in a broad educational way. A better approach to foremen on every plane of information might eliminate a number of appeals cases.

The Labor Force

Minnequa's work force is composed mainly of a mixture of English and Central European stock, but it includes Latin Americans and Negroes in numbers roughly proportionate to their representation in the community. The company has no set policy on employment of minority groups, insisting only that prospective employees meet minimum qualifications; but a few shops within the plant have not yet freely accepted all groups. Women comprise about 4.5 per cent of the work force.

The company's labor force is highly stable, especially the skilled workers, because there is no market for any of their steel-specialized skills elsewhere in the state. Despite wartime and postwar disruptions, nearly a quarter of the employees have been with the company for twenty or more years. Some have been there well over fifty years. Since the end of World War II, absenteeism has declined to an insignificant figure, and labor turnover fell from 4.5 per cent in 1948 to 2 per cent in 1950, about one-third below the estimated national average.

The Union

The two locals of the United Steelworkers of America (CIO) represent all production, office, clerical, and technical employees at Minnequa. Locals 2102 and 3267, like other Steelworkers locals, function under a rather centralized form of administration. But that organizational structure matches in substance, if not form, the manner in which economic power is concentrated on the side of employers with whom it deals. The steel industry's practice of following the leader in determining wages and other employment conditions means that policies have been applied virtually on an industry-wide basis.

Despite the Steelworkers' centralized structure, the locals at Minnequa enjoy wide freedom, which is encouraged by the international office. Their constitutions take into account their area's special traditions and circumstances, and give the individual union member an opportunity to participate in the conduct of union affairs. Initiation fees and dues are low; provision is made for direct popular election of officers (with proxy voting ruled out), for rank-and-file ratification of proposed agreements with the employer, and for examination of the union's books by an audit committee. Elections for union offices at Pueblo have so far been closely contested, and incumbents are always scrutinized for any possible oligarchic tendencies. The presidents of the two locals, William White and Jack Thomas, express their belief that hard-fighting, two-party opposition is the only sure guarantee of union democracy. The situation at Minnequa indicates healthy rivalry rather than factionalism based on political ideologies.

Both locals keep the agenda for union meetings sufficiently open so that routine union business will not crowd out matters of real concern to individuals. This does not mean, however, that the locals favor injection into union affairs of personal political ideologies. The CIO's Political Action Committee exists for threshing our political differences and stimulating legislation; and ideological arguments are usually handled by it, even at the local-union level—which relieves the collective bargaining process of masked political grievances. The locals at Minnequa face the problem of attracting rank-and-file members to union meetings. The old-fashioned free rider accepted union benefits without belonging to the union; the new free rider, who has not made sacrifices for the union, merely holds a card and refuses responsibility for the conduct of union affairs. Among its efforts to activate such persons, the union features strong appeals for participation in *Steel News,* the locals' weekly newspaper, and union meetings are timed to accommodate all shifts.

Liaison between the union's international organization and the two locals is maintained by two men: Charles J. Smith, director of the United Steelworkers' District 38, which includes ten states; and the field representative for the area, Michael J. Soldren, who is also a member of the Steelworkers Executive Board. Mr. Soldren, with headquarters in downtown Pueblo, is most intimately in contact with the Minnequa locals, although he also represents the union in other parts of the Rocky Mountain area. Mr. Soldren not only has a background of work in steel mills, but helped to set up the Steel Workers Organizing Committee (SWOC), the predecessor to the United Steelworkers of America. When Mr. Soldren participates in the grievance procedure and in arbitration with management, he gives the local members a sense of direct personal contact with the parent body and the benefit of facts bearing on bargaining throughout the nation. In cooperation with the local unions, he attempts to bring to the community an awareness of the union's philosophy of mutuality in industrial relations. In addressing service clubs and other civic organizations, and urging local union members to participate in civic and charitable affairs, he attempts to demonstrate that unionism, far from being antagonistic to local institutions, can enrich the community's life.

The Colorado locals conduct annual educational conferences for workers with the assistance of the University of Colorado at Boulder. These provide a broad background of information on the union's place in the community, on labor law and legislation, on general economic trends, and other topics of general community interest. Leading employers under contract with the Steelworkers in Colorado are invited to these conferences. As a supplement to local educational work carried on regularly at Pueblo, the conferences are designed to encourage participation in local union and community affairs throughout the year.

The Minnequa locals realize that theirs is a task of education and stabilization. The members who were active in the early days of organization entertain high hopes for mutual industrial living through collective bargaining based on facts. Their emphasis on reason is paralleled by management, as indicated by Mr. Franz' statement that: "The company attributes its success in collective bargaining to its policy of taking positions only in the light of the facts and objective moral values, so that only honest differences of opinion can emerge during collective bargaining, these to be resolved through the regular steps established by the contract."

FORERUNNERS TO THE PRESENT RELATIONSHIP

Four distinct periods preceded the present system of mutuality through free collective bargaining by management and the two locals at the Minnequa Plant. The first was a casual and occasionally heavy-fisted type of relationship. Second was a pattern of paternalism and a company union. Next came a period of confusion during which neither the workers, their representatives, nor management was sure who should bargain with whom. The fourth came after the Steelworkers became bargaining agent in 1942, an era of tripartite labor relations during which the government's wartime regulations exercised a strong influence on developments at Minnequa. ,

The transition from company unionism to mutuality in collective bargaining shows the changed climate of public opinion after 1930. The company was prepared to accommodate new desires for greater mutuality, and when in doubt, was ready to accede to the test of law rather than calling for a test of force. The union, in its turn, exhibited patience and responsibility in its relations with management and individual workers. Fair dealing during the transitional period, unmarred by extraneous issues raised in the heat of industrial warfare, contributed greatly to the present successful relationship and its promise for the future.

The Antiunion Period

Management's usual approach to labor relations in the early part of the century was distinguished largely for its lack of system. Violent industrial conflict in 1913 had threatened to halt industrial progress in the Rocky Mountain region, and it was particularly intense in the Rockefeller mining properties in southern Colorado. This industrial warfare, costly in lives and dollars, dramatized the need for some consciously ordered scheme of labor relations. In an attempt to find a solution, C. F. & I. in 1915 launched a systematically organized employee representation plan for its miners, and for its steelworkers at Minnequa in 1916. The plan, commonly called the Rockefeller Plan, attracted nationwide attention. It covered many more employees than any other plan then in existence, and seemed to depart from the firm opposition of financiers and industrialists in steel to any form of labor organization. It did not, however, mean that the steel industry was more receptive to the overtures of unionism from groups affiliated with a national body such as the American Federation of Labor. In fact, as employee representation plans gained management acceptance during the 1920's and part of the thirties, they often were introduced as a means of forestalling unionization rather than for their intrinsic merits.

Company Union in Operation

The Employee Representation Plan which was in effect at Minnequa from 1916 to 1937 was admittedly the company's organization for its employees rather than the employees' own organization. At elections called by the president of the company, who also handled appeals about the validity of election results, the individual worker voted for employees who subsequently represented him in dealing with management. This had the effect of establishing collective rather than individual contacts between workers and management, a practical means by which workers might communicate with management at all levels. At the same time, management gained a new medium of communication down the line. The ERP, however, was never intended to be collective bargaining in the sense contemplated by the Wagner Act. Employee representation imposed upon management no requirement to compromise on matters of policy, whereas collective bargaining does require compromise. The workers had no independently organized pressure to alter management's policy beyond the general state of demand and supply in products and labor.

Under ERP the employees were divided into carefully mapped out divisions and subdivisions of the plant, which served as election units. Business was transacted by four joint committees composed of six employer and six employee representatives. The committees dealt with safety and accidents; sanitation, health, and housing; recreation and education; and cooperation, conciliation, and wages. The president's industrial representative customarily acted as chairman and a company secretary recorded the minutes. Expenses of employee representatives for the time lost from work were carried by the company. The ERP committees met regularly; the company supported them, regardless of the state of the labor market.

Discussions in the committees went far beyond those of usual employee representation groups. For example, at Minnequa, the committee not only discussed the customary individual wage grievances, but on several occasions general wage demands were pressed successfully. In 1918 C. F. & I. was the first steel plant to adopt the eight-hour day and to pay time and a half for more than eight hours' work. Its customary memorandum of agreement on wages always continued a general proviso that the company would pay substantially the same wages as competing steel mills, including those located in the East. To implement this, the company several times sent committees of employee representatives to the East, at its expense, so that they might study competitive wage rates. Although the tendency in handling grievances, the principal function of most employee representation plans, was to steer clear of anything but individual grievances, ERP at Minnequa between 1933 and 1937 handled 40 grievances of small groups or departments out of a total of 460 grievances. However, tie votes on grievance cases were automatically resolved in favor of management.

Confusion on the Employees' Representative

Since the lack of an obligatory arbitration terminal for unsettled grievances had tended to discourage the bringing of grievances before the ERP committee, in 1934 the employee representatives suggested a provision for such arbitration. While discussions of this matter were going on, the Wagner Act was passed, which raised questions of the status of employee representation plans. Company and employee representation officials felt that ERP could qualify under the law so long as the employer had nothing to do with the election of employee representatives. In 1936, ERP was revised so that procedures governing the conduct of elections were to be determined solely by employee representatives. At the same time, other changes were made, including provision for a board of arbitration with final and binding decision in the event of grievance deadlocks, and election of a chairman and secretary for joint committees.

In 1937, however, a Supreme Court decision made it clear that unions organized and supported by companies could not qualify as collective bargaining units. A revision committee of employee representatives undertook establishment of an independent labor organization, without the company's actual support but in consultation with it. The resulting Employees' Representatives' Organization (ERO) carried over certain forms and practices of the old ERP, although employees took over payment of administrative costs on the basis of monthly dues. The company recognized ERO, entered into negotiations with its officials, and subsequently agreed to various beneficial terms and conditions of employment before a vote of all employees was taken to provide the formal mandate for ERO to act as the employees' bargaining agent.

Direct polling of all eligible employees took place in February 1938, but the ballot listed no alternative organization, and the question was put in such a way that the maintenance of benefits achieved by ERO was linked with the organization's continued existence. The arrangements already made by ERO officials were endorsed by 98 per cent of eligible employees.

Confusion over who should bargain for the workers mounted during the following years. The Steel Workers Organizing Committee had been active in Pueblo for some time, and public records show that it had a nucleus of SWOC membership among C. F. & I.'s employees in 1937. About a month after the ERO election at the Minnequa Plant, the SWOC alleged to the National Labor Relations Board that C. F. & I., through its relationship with ERO and other unfair labor practices, was interfering with its employees' right to self-organization. The NLRB held a hearing in Pueblo and another in Washington, and on March 29, 1940, ordered C. F. & I. to withdraw recognition of ERO and to completely disestablish it, on the grounds that there had not been a break in the continuity of operations under the old ERP, and the election offered employees no free choice. The order was upheld when the company petitioned for review by the Tenth Circuit Court of Appeals.

During the three years while ERO's status was being tested at law, it continued to function at C. F. & I. In the meantime, SWOC had continued to organize, but failed to receive a majority in an NLRB election held in March 1941. After the Court decree ordering disestablishment of ERO in June 1941, the vice-president of the company told ERO officials that the organization was no longer the bargaining representative for employees at Pueblo. Apparently some ERO officials still felt the ERO could be salvaged. In addition, a group of employees executed articles of incorporation for a new employees' representatives' organization, to be known as ERO, Inc. The SWOC stepped up its organizing activities. Management permitted all three groups—ERO, ERO, Inc., and SWOC —to solicit membership in their respective organizations during working hours in the plant.

In July 1941, ERO was officially dissolved and some of its officers joined forces with ERO, Inc. The company recognized ERO, Inc., when it produced 4000 signed membership cards, verified by an independent certified public accountant. (SWOC had refused to furnish proof of majority status except through the offices of the NLRB and also refused to share a ballot with ERO, Inc.) But in a judgment dated June 8, 1942, the Tenth Circuit Court of Appeals found that there had not been a sufficient break of continuity between ERO and ERO, Inc. The court recognized that the company had acted in good faith by permitting the company to comply by withdrawing recognition from ERO, Inc., and keeping notices posted for thirty days announcing this action.

Meanwhile, the NLRB held another election to determine whether SWOC had majority status at the Minnequa Plant, and in July 1942, SWOC received a slim majority of 58 per cent of valid votes.

Tripartite Labor Relations

The early relationship between the Steelworkers and Minnequa's management, when difficulties were increased because the parties involved were just becoming accustomed to each other, was complicated by wartime conditions and the intervention of the National War Labor Board. The Minnequa Plant came under the jurisdiction of the Ninth Regional War Labor Board, except in so far as it was subject to settlements made for the steel industry as a whole.

In addition to the usual labor-management problems, wartime conditions created frictions and other problems with the influx of new and inexperienced personnel, heavy turnover owing to the draft, added duties and long hours, and congested housing conditions for workers. Under this combination of circumstances, it was useful for both management and the union at C. F. & I. to have the Regional War Labor Board close at hand. They not only went before the Board when in opposition, but in a number of cases submitted joint applications for specific wage increases.

The proximity of the Regional Board had some less desirable effects also. When the collective bargaining process tended to stall, it was natural for one side or the other to threaten to take the case to the Board. Perhaps some defeatism also crept into private negotiations because of the belief that certain matters would have to go to the Board in any case. There were charges and countercharges that one side or the other was trying to use the Board, which not only were time-consuming but introduced artificial issues into collective bargaining and fostered mutual distrust.

The grievances which were submitted to the Regional Board from the Minnequa Plant were sufficiently diversified and numerous to warrant official establishment of a special Board of Reference to handle C. F. & I. cases. Some of these grievances clearly expressed wartime circumstances, but others had a normal peacetime tenor. For example, one case involved the steel industry's unwarranted internal wage differentials. This was ameliorated only by industry-wide action.

In prolonged hearings of a steel panel set up in late 1943 to advise the War Labor Board in Washington, voluminous testimony was offered by the steel companies and the United Steelworkers of America bearing on the Steelworkers' demand for a general wage increase for all its member locals. Although the union's testimony was not found convincing as to the equity of granting such a general wage increase in 1944, the WLB did not allow matters to rest there. The evidence showed that there was a great deal of labor unrest in steel mills because of a pronounced lack of internal balance of wage rates paid for particular jobs within plants. Although the WLB was practically bound to prevent general wage increases, the stabilization regulations allowed room for granting limited sums to permit removal of intraplant inequities. The WLB established a steel commission to examine the entire wage structure and to guide the parties in the task of planning and simplifying revisions. From the outset, this new wage equity program contributed to stability in steel labor relations. It was especially helpful at the Minnequa Plant, where there was an inherited problem of wage inequities. With the demise of the WLB in 1945, the wage equity program was continued on a purely voluntary basis at many steel plants, including Minnequa.

THE SPIRIT AND LETTER OF THE CONTRACT

That a contract can become a legalistic strait jacket for labor relations if either party tampers with its spirit is well understood at the Minnequa Plant. The written contract between C. F. & I. and the Steelworkers has become a *living* employment bill of industrial rights and duties for five plants of the company's structure.[2] Its letter is clear, concise, and free of cold legalisms or restrictive clauses. It is generally understood that any rule of special treatment for individuals would make the contract merely a point of departure for workers seeking a maximum of individual advantage outside of the collective agreement. The union recognizes that this would reduce its role to that of a mere job broker; management knows that such a rule would easily expose it to charges of unfair labor practices.

The individual worker at Minnequa is represented in collective bargaining at two distinct levels. There are the company-wide negotiations by C. F. & I. and all the locals at five plants, usually held in Buffalo, where Minnequa's workers are represented by local delegates and the subdistrict's international representative. At the second level, there is the purely local bargaining which specifically applies general benefits obtained in the company-wide bargaining, and also arrives at supplemental

[2] The two California plants and the Mt. Wolf, Pennsylvania, plant are not included in the C. F. & I. contract with the United Steelworkers.

agreements to cover peculiarly local conditions. A special local committee handles negotiations on applications of the national agreement, but the general grievance committee at the Minnequa Plant also participates in negotiation of special supplementary agreements.

The Economics of Steel Labor

National bargaining also affects the individual workers at Minnequa. The pattern of wage-rate adjustments in steel has been similar throughout the industry for many years, and the pattern is set by negotiations between the Steelworkers and some leader in the industry, usually the U.S. Steel Corporation. Relative price stabilization in the industry has encouraged wage stabilization. The individual companies make strong efforts to win customers from each other on the basis of rapid and correct deliveries of high-quality, specialized steels, rather than through competitive cutting of prices.

Minnequa had a wage differential of 2.5 cents per hour less than eastern plants until 1947, but the pattern of wage-rate adjustments was maintained. In the last 25 years, the following industry-wide adjustments have been made: Two 10 per cent increases in 1923; a 10 per cent and a 15 per cent decrease in 1931 and 1932, respectively; a 15 per cent increase in 1933; 10 per cent increases in 1934, 1936, 1937, and 1941; an increase of 5.5 cents per hour in 1942; and increases of 18.5 cents in 1946, 12.5 cents in 1947, and 9.5 cents in 1948; a pension setup in 1949; and a wage-plus-benefit increase estimated at a value of 16 cents per hour in 1950.

From the outset, the Steelworkers has faced the facts of pattern setting realistically. The union has a national wage-policy committee which draws up uniform demands, on the basis of all its locals' recommendations. The national wage-policy committee is composed of approximately 180 regional representatives and national officers and has the services of the national office's research staff. It evaluates the locals' recommendations in the light of general economic conditions, national economic policies, and other over-all considerations. It then attempts to reconcile particular geographic and economic interests within the union. The resulting recommendations go back to the locals for discussion before demands are put in final form. The intermediary between the national committee and the locals is a regional wage-policy committee which communicates special regional aspects of proposed policy and shapes the adaptation of general concessions to the particular area's circumstances. Thus the main demands presented management on the occasion of company-wide bargaining are made in the light of prior determination of wage policy at the union's national level, and the offers and counter-proposals of management are significantly influenced by what happens throughout the industry.

The existence of the national wage-policy committee does not alter the basic fact that workers already know something about general economic conditions, wage movements in their own region and other parts of the country, and the financial status of their company and industry, and that they will press for any remedial action which they feel is justified. Rather, the national committee seems only to open a new channel of communication on issues that concern the workers. This need was recognized by Minnequa's management before the advent of the union, as evidenced by the early policy of sending groups of employees to the East to observe comparative conditions for themselves.

Members of the locals at Minnequa, interviewed about their reactions to national involvement in bargaining, had reactions similar to investors in corporate mergers that offer increased financial strength and security at the same time that they open broader fields of enterprise than those normally accessible to small concerns. This seemed particularly true in the recent issue over private pensions for steelworkers, the outcome of which was adoption of a uniform system of private pensions in the steel industry. Mr. Soldren takes the position that negotiations for pensions conducted on an employer-by-employer basis would have yielded a multitude of differing plans, their variations reflecting the degree of union bargaining strength in each plant. With that, a series of complicated inequities would have arisen to plague both management and the union, since workers would have been induced to shift to those plants featuring the most attractive pension plans. For the union to have sought pensions on a piecemeal basis might well have been to invite defeat, whereas success was made possible by a uniform and simultaneous demand which left relative competitive positions in the industry unaltered. It still meant to the industry either a reduction in profits or a general price rise, and the latter is what actually happened.

The C. F. & I.'s management appears to recognize the union's need for involvement on the national industry level, since this is where ruling decisions in the steel industry are made. During the 1949 national strike over pensions, for example, the plant management made no effort to open the plant or start a local back-to-work movement. The union in its turn strictly patrolled the picket line to prevent injection of political animosities and any violence or abusive behavior. C. F. & I.'s management was the first company to accept President Truman's request for a 60-day truce during which the Fact-Finding Board could make an investigation and report. The follow-the-leader type of bargaining (discussed at somewhat more length in *Case Study No. 9*) poses some problems for the collective bargaining relationship at Minnequa. However, there is ample scope for vigorous bargaining on company-wide and local levels in the application of generally agreed upon policies peculiar to the company and its locality. The parties at the Minnequa Plant are making the most of these broad opportunities.

Objective Job Classification

The system of job classifications is one of the most important features of the contract at C. F. & I. The industry's job classes provide only an objective framework; the system's actual application is left to bargaining by plant management and the unions.

The contract in 1947 provided for a joint committee to complete a specific program "for the ultimate elimination of all wage-rate inequities including the tasks of developing the principles for determining a fair day's work and the guideposts for assigning trade or craft journeymen to the respective starting, intermediate, or standard rates." The committee, representing management and the unions at all five plants covered by the agreement, has been able to draw on information available from management's contacts with wage experts throughout the steel industry, and also data from the wage experts in the union's national office.

The internal needs of management and the unions at Minnequa are met by the job-classification system, on new jobs as well as old ones affected by technological or organizational changes. To management, this has meant that costs could be calculated better. It has been an invaluable aid to the union in defining the individual worker's status as a right, and educating the worker to see it that way. Union meetings where wage matters are discussed can be conducted without bickering because the system exists as an impersonal frame of reference. The union can screen out many personal complaints and better assume its responsibility for assisting management in the maintenance of discipline under the contract.

The way the parties jointly work out difficult job classifications is indicated by experience with the new Morgan rod mill. Unpredictable kinks were still being straightened out eight months after workers had shifted to the new mill. The mill not only ran at partial capacity for some time, but job classifications had to be tentative until there was time for the jobs to "jell." The company's tentative classifications, accepted by the union, involved no demotions, but take-home pay was diminished in cases where incentive earnings, temporarily held in abeyance, would have exceeded hourly rates. This was partly offset by adoption of 10-hour shifts, since the contract provided for overtime premiums for work in excess of eight hours.

In approaching the task, the initial step of management and the union was to reach agreement on job descriptions, on the basis of which the company's tentative classifications were re-examined in the light of labor grades established by the national committee studying wage inequities and of the local situation. Although the contract provides that in cases of disagreement the company may proceed unilaterally, subject to appeals through the grievance procedure, every effort was made to reach agreement on the proper labor grades. Of 23 job classifications discussed in 1950, 10 were accepted by the union without dispute, the company made concessions on 7, and the union provisionally withdrew objections to the rest. Many workers were upgraded because some reclassified jobs affected relatively large concentrations of workers. In all this processing the union retained its contractual right for reconsideration in the light of further information or experience. Both union and management handle the difficult job of dealing with ever-changing job content on a strictly factual level.

Incentive Payments

Incentive payments established by the Minnequa contract usually affect groups of workers, since steel production involves teamwork. Under joint union-management formulation and supervision, the system of incentive payments permits workers to share the fruits of increased productivity to which they contribute. The way new incentives are established, when warranted by new or changed machinery or process, was illustrated at the new Morgan rod mill. No new incentives were established pending the final shaking down of the new operation to a standard routine. The cost of this trial run, however, was to be shared equitably, in that incentives when finally established would be paid retroactively on the basis of records of actual production.

Permanently established teams of workers are required to man the delicate and expensive equipment used in the high-speed operations of a steel mill. Therefore the importance of having a stable and efficient organization has grown, while the importance of obtaining cheap labor has declined. When Minnequa's management passed into the hands of men who had won their names in the steel industry for efficiency of operations it was possible for them to eliminate a 2.5-cent wage differential with the East, even though with regard to resources Minnequa is in some respects a marginal plant, and though it was hardly the favored child of the basing point system. The present management's ingenuity, combined with new cooperative attitudes among the workers, makes it possible for the Minnequa plant to compete successfully in quality of products and speed of delivery.

Agreement on Seniority

Industrial peace was not attained at Minnequa until substantial mutual understandings about seniority had been reached. The first recorded grievance under the initial contract of 1942 involved seniority. Two years later, a departmental work stoppage dramatized a seniority question that had become entangled with problems of race and employment of women to do the work normally done by men. During succeeding years, management and the union differed considerably over the meaning of the contractual seniority clause. A list of grievances submitted to management after an unauthorized two-day strike, which ended in April 1945, included the issue of seniority in all major departments of the plant.

The parties agreed to submit the seniority issue as a whole to the War Labor Board. The biggest bone of contention was seniority in case of promotions. The company argued that once a person was promoted ahead of another having greater seniority, the promoted person would thenceforth have greater seniority in every respect. The union held that an individual so advanced should retain his normal seniority in layoffs, transfers, and so on. The Board, in July 1945, substantially upheld the union's position. But this seemed to have been merely a paper understanding. In September 1945, when a plant-wide work stoppage occurred, seniority was one of the precipitating causes. The War Labor Board was on the verge of issuing an order to the company to show cause for noncompliance, when the Regional Board offered to mediate. The parties then decided to resolve the issue by collective bargaining.

From the end of 1945, the parties began registering the fact that seniority is a complex problem with many facets. The 1942 contract had briefly listed technical requirements through which workers might qualify under a limited seniority system—but management was listed as the judge of ability. While the 1945 contractual seniority clause was not generally expanded, it differentiated, in accordance with the War Labor Board ruling, between promotional seniority and other seniority. A multiple approach to seniority problems was further evidenced by provision for a joint committee to establish an apprenticeship program in line with the standards of the U.S. Department of Labor.

The 1947 contract created a new joint seniority study committee. Emphasizing the distinction between promotional seniority and seniority for other purposes, it explicitly recognized the union's need for assuring members that long-continued service would be rewarded and management's responsibility for efficient operation of the works. For the first time, there was no specific statement that management should be the sole judge of ability. Subdivisions on seniority problems included several matters of mutual concern not previously detailed. One of these new provisions applied to interplant or interdepartmental transfers. Section E of the 1947 contract's seniority provision pioneered in facing the human facts of technological change in a new way, by specifying that transfers caused by such changes "are matters for which adjustment shall be sought between local plant management and local grievance committees."

This provision applied when the new Morgan rod mill was brought into operation. Workers were given the alternative of accepting severance pay and applying for re-employment, or of accepting suitable transfers to the new mill. Acting in democratic caucus at a union meeting, the affected workers chose transfer rather than to risk not being re-employed by accepting severance pay—a substantial amount in some cases. On receipt of this decision, management staffed the new mill, so far as practicable, with workers who had worked in the old rod mill.

This recent event at the Minnequa Plant demonstrates that seniority, historically a negatively oriented protective device, can contribute positively to mutual interest in production. In general, the C. F. & I. contract reveals that the contest between union rights and management prerogatives may be transformed into forward-looking cooperation. An article in the 1947 contract records management's exclusive right to direct the working forces, but at the same time acknowledges the union by stating that "the company, in the exercise of its rights, shall observe the provisions of this agreement." This article is immediately followed by a much more extensive one, entitled "Responsibilities of the Parties." A contract that asserts responsibility as much as rights warrants public confidence.

LIVING UNDER THE CONTRACT

Continuous day-by-day bargaining, geared to a joint solution of problems, is undertaken at Minnequa in a spirit of full mutual recognition and association. Neither management nor the individual worker looks upon the union as a formal agency to be consulted only when there is friction. Whereas there is no coddling of workers, the union and management sincerely try to provide the workers with a sense of participation and individual dignity.

The Handling of Grievances

Grievances at Minnequa can be settled at any one of five stages. First, the aggrieved worker, the foreman, and union representative attempt settlement. A great deal of preventive conciliation is accomplished during this step, and it also is a filing point for grievances which involve contract interpretation at higher levels. Step two, in practice tending to be the first formal step, involves the superintendent of the department or his representative and union representatives. Step three is handled by the plant grievance committee—sometimes the international representative also—and the plant superintendent or his representative. Fourth is the top echelon meeting of company and union representative, with the international union representative participating. Next comes arbitration. Minutes are taken at steps three and four, and time limits are given for steps two and three.

There is considerable variation in the amount of time consumed in settling disputes, but a check of typical grievances showed no startling delays, nor any tendency to hurry grievances unduly. Figures show that the number of grievances handled at Minnequa has declined substantially since 1942. There were 92 second-step grievances in 1943 and 10 in 1949; 50 in 1943 in the third step and 9 in 1949; and arbitrations dwindled from 14 in 1943 to none in 1949, although some important arbitrations took place in 1950. The decline resulted from the successful culling of requests and complaints which could be handled informally, leaving the higher steps for formal contract interpretation. This decline was accomplished in several ways.

George E. Diggory, in 1944, blocked out areas in which grievances occurred most frequently, and thereafter he and other supervisory personnel concentrated on root causes of industrial unrest.

A sharp drop in 1946 grievances reflects the advent of management leaders who had a more direct interest in and acquaintance with problems faced by the workers. It was rarely necessary for workers or union officials to start the formal grievance procedures. Also at about this time, step one was changed from a more or less routine filing stage for grievances to a kind of joint, informal clearinghouse in which the problem was to sort out genuine matters of contract interpretation. The parties realized that if such a clearing system were highly developed, without any loss of worker equities, little time would be wasted at higher levels in discovering that an alleged grievance was not a genuine contractual grievance. The settlement of differences at step one also was facilitated by on-the-spot investigations of alleged grievances by union officials and representatives of the industrial relations superintendent.

The union organization is well suited for high-quality handling of grievances at the lowest possible level. In daily relations with management, the locals continuously represent the individual worker, rather than debate how the plant should be run. Management, acknowledging the important role of the unions, invites newly elected officers for an informal get-acquainted discussion immediately following their election. The union encourages the individual worker to feel that filing grievances, making requests, expressing complaints, and communicating ideas about improved employment relations are matters of right under the fundamental recognition clause of the contract. At the same time, it stresses the importance of separating matters that lie within the contract from such things as matters of purely personal concern, and mutual problems which, however pressing, have not been discussed or agreed upon in union-management negotiations. The same ease of communication characterizes the relation of officers of the local and of the international union.

The union and management both make allowances for the other's shortcomings in organizational respects. Management officials may complain that the turnover of grievance men resulting from the union's "political" nature necessitates a great deal of repetition in educating the new personnel; and union officials sometimes claim that foremen take advantage of green grievance men, and may not be sufficiently disciplined for not sticking to the contract. However, each side goes out of its way to compensate for these shortcomings. The danger that the kind of mutual accommodation practiced at Minnequa may cause grievances to go directly to high levels, with resulting disrespect of workers for union and management officials down the line, is recognized. Each party is hopeful that when more time, energy, and money can be allowed for the important work of educating foremen and grievers, greater contract responsibility can be developed and assumed by the rank and file in both union and management.

A clear separation of the employee's and employer's interest in grievances has also encouraged the settling of grievances strictly on their merits by permitting the union's griever to do an increasingly factual job.

Being cut off from any management affiliation, the griever can freely cite the facts. At the same time, his union advancement depends upon getting cases settled in the spirit of the contract without favoritism for any special group of workers. Under the present setup, ten chief grievers and a reasonable number of assistant department grievers are provided under the contract. If and when one of them is promoted to the rank of working foreman—by no means unusual—he ceases to act as a griever. His interests still are served by fairness in handling grievances and by giving accurate advice to higher levels. The parties have not overlooked the fundamental need for preventing each from meddling into the other's affairs. The 1947 provision entitled "Responsibilities of the Parties" bound each party to respect the other's organizational integrity, and specifically pointed out that it was the "exclusive right" of the union "to discipline its officers, representatives, and members," and of the company "to discipline its officers, representatives, and employees."

A grievance procedure serves one of its most useful functions in preventing explosions which occur when there is a sore spot, and when complaints are allowed to fester. A breakdown of the causes of 498 grievances at Minnequa from 1945 through 1948 (see Table 1, *Case Study No. 9*) shows that the procedure at Minnequa is serving this important industrial relations function. This record covers the years when seniority could have created difficulties in any relationship, and there were more grievances concerning seniority—30 per cent of the total—than for any other cause. This figure for the whole plant was checked against figures for the separate departments to see if the problems seemed to be concentrated in a limited section of the plant. The survey showed that seniority grievances were by far the most insistently contested and prolonged grievances in all departments. The Minnequa Plant's grievance procedure also registered accurately other known soft spots of relations in steel. The most usual grievances after those on seniority were wage-rate inequities (66 grievances filed), and these are now being attacked by the joint wage-rate equity program.

The Workers' Safety

The safety record at Minnequa is the pride of both management and the union. The Minnequa Plant was placed in the "Safety Hall of Fame" by the National Safety Council in October 1950 for having achieved the most outstanding safety record ever recorded for the steel industry, and the steel industry now ranks among the five safest industries in the United States. Between 1948 and 1949, the Minnequa accident-frequency rate (disabling injuries per million hours of workers' exposure to danger of accident) dropped from 3.94 to 2.47, compared with a decrease for C. F. & I. as a whole of 7.58 to 4.35. And C. F. & I.'s 1948 frequency rate had compared favorably with the entire industry's rate of 19.5. (Table 2, *Case Study No. 9*, shows the number of lost-time accidents, the frequency rate, and severity rate at the Minnequa Plant for the years 1942 through 1949.)

This record of dollars saved, more steel produced, and human misery avoided, can be credited largely to the collective bargaining relationship. Works manager J. J. Martin, known as one of the "toughest" safety men in the United States, receives a constant flow of information on which to base strategy of accident prevention, personally reviews every lost-time accident, permits no trifling in the matter of discharging careless workers, and assumes final responsibility in all safety matters. There are constant efforts to involve the individual worker in the plant in the safety program, directly and through the union.

With the union's entry in 1942, the former safety organization became a full department and the program was made bilateral. The plant was divided into four zones, each under the full-time responsibility of a trained assistant superintendent of safety. In addition, nearly all supervisory personnel have gone through a course in safety instruction provided on company time. A safety suggestion system introduced in 1943 is now used in nearly every part of the plant. Support of the system is illustrated by the fact that in one year in the wire mill, 633 suggestion cards were turned in, of which 592 suggestions were put into operation, three rejected, and 38 remained under consideration.

In 1947, the safety program was made contractual, with a joint safety committee made up of five labor and five management people meeting with an advisory group from the safety department. The committee meets once a month, but special meetings are called when necessary. It has the power to make recommendations to management on over-all safety provisions. The contract stipulates that the joint safety committee should under no circumstances handle grievances. Instead, the safety committee handles the factual evidence about safety problems from the viewpoint of prevention rather than equity, and thus reduces the number of grievances. By this device, the parties to collective bargaining have not only opened up a new area of mutuality, but have strengthened old areas. Safety matters account for only 5 per cent of the total number of grievances.

Training Young Workers

The apprenticeship training program, organized nearly half a century ago, has become another cohesive agency at Minnequa. Labor and management have a cooperative agreement on apprenticeship standards with the Vocational Division of the U.S. Office of Education, the Federal Committee on Apprenticeship, and the Division of Vocational Education of the local public schools. The agreement contains a highly articulated listing of apprenticeship standards, administered by a joint committee appointed by the Colorado State Board of Vocational Education, and composed of two company members, two from the union, and one public member recommended by the local school board.

In order to qualify for training, apprentices must be 18 to 25 years old (with special provisions for veterans) ; must have a high school education or the equivalent; must pass certain aptitude tests; and must be approved by the apprenticeship advisory committee. The ratio of apprentices to journeymen was established by collective bargaining, and is included in the contract. Although in times of expansion the program could conceivably be too restrictive to meet all the needs of the company, the quality of the trained men is undoubtedly high. Each of sixteen trades requires a minimum of 144 hours of related school instruction per year, which is paid for by the company if completed. In addition, work must be performed under competent supervision for a specified number of hours.

The apprenticeship advisory committee, rather than the employer alone, judges whether the apprentice is suited for the work he wants to do. Should any difference arise between the apprentice and his employer, the latter's word is not necessarily final; either may appeal to the committee for adjudication of the difference. The apprentice has become a junior, rather than a workboy as in the old days. For example, today's beginning apprentice at Minnequa receives the wage paid to persons classified in the lowest labor grade, and regular hourly wage increases of 4.5 cents are granted at six-month intervals. If he passes an appropriate examination, the apprentice can advance to the wage rate for labor grade 8 during his fourth year. At this point, he receives four-fifths of the wages of a rougher. Furthermore, today's apprentice is covered by the workmen's compensation laws just as is any other worker.

In general, the young apprentice's education is not confined to picking up the tricks of the trade. International Correspondence School materials are provided to give the apprentice a broad view of his industry. The contribution to industrial peace of this broad conception of apprenticeship was summarized by its technical administrator, W. A. Hinds, as follows: less favoritism; a high caliber of personnel; and a more settled type of worker. It is also evident that the young worker who comes up through this mutually sponsored apprenticeship program is unlikely to develop either an antiunion or an anti-company bias.

Effects of Increased Productivity

A steady increase in productivity has occurred during the bargaining relationship that started at Minnequa in 1942. This is so despite shortages of materials and manpower which characterized the early years of collective bargaining. Labor productivity of the nation's manufacturing industries as a whole (measured in production per man-hour) fluctuated appreciably during the period 1942 through 1949; no net gain of productivity was achieved over the entire period. The Minnequa Plant's labor productivity (measured by accumulated tons per man shift) also fluctuated from 1942 through 1949, but did so on a higher level of productivity throughout, and only partially in rhythm with over-all national fluctuations. And Minnequa showed a 6 per cent gain over the entire period. (A comparison of year-by-year figures for the 1942–49 period appears in Table 3, *Case Study No. 9.*)

Some of Minnequa's productivity gains undoubtedly were caused by modernization of equipment following 1942, but much can be credited to the spirit that prevails in the plant. In its *Annual Report* to the stockholders for fiscal 1949, the corporation, referring to the highest capacity operation in any peacetime year, stated: "These production achievements were made possible by the cooperative effort of both labor and management."

Workers in the steel industry welcome increasing labor productivity, if only because they realize that it augments the fund from which higher living standards may be realized. Yet increasing labor productivity, whether reflecting technological improvements or more effective human teamwork, also arouses the worker's natural fear of demotion or displacement. The steel industry has not yet solved this long-standing human problem. Nevertheless, both management and union leaders at Minnequa are making a sincere effort to minimize the adverse effects on workers of improved mechanical and human teamwork processes.

THE TRANSFER PRINCIPLE

The transfer of specialized functions which continuously grows out of the successful collective bargaining relationship is a creative process of social evolution which is as important as technological progress and growth. The findings at the Minnequa Plant may be summarized in terms of this principle of labor economics which the writer originally discovered in making a study of the history of labor relations for the country as a whole.[3] When we observe the evolution of scientific, objective labor relations at Minnequa, we are actually witnessing social progress which parallels technological progress made in the installation of electronic controls or other modern devices. Moreover, the two types of progress, social and technological, are interdependent; one advances the other.

As management increasingly shares personnel administration with the union, it gains more time and energy for the study of improved mechanical and business methods. The foreman who is relieved of some grievances can give more time to controlling the flow and quality of product; the office manager who deals only with union stewards rather than listening to everyone's complaints can devise better work-organization charts. Once collective bargaining is well established, top management increasingly relies on personnel management for representing the company to the union. This is an economical division of labor, since top management is usually composed of production men rather than persons trained as personnel administrators. Though these men command the respect of workers and may play a valuable role in labor relations, it undoubtedly aids production to have them spend most of their time in solving technical problems.

The same specialization of functions may be observed in the union when collective bargaining becomes firmly established. At this point, the union need not rely on slogans to achieve union solidarity, but may turn instead to a process of giving every member something to do, selecting for each function those best able to perform it. Each member then can feel that he has the opportunity to use and develop his individual talents in representing the union in some capacity, as a griever, a safety man, a member of a production committee or compensation or pensions committee, or in some other way.

With a progressive specialization of functions under collective bargaining, studied, measurable, and verifiable procedures are substituted for a random growth of industrial habits and practices, many of which may be undesirable. This is creative evolution. There is active and healthy competition on the side of management, as top management and person-

---

[3] George W. Zinke, *History and Theory of Labor-Management Relations in the United States,* mimeographed textbook, 1948.

nel officials define and redefine their proper spheres in the light of emerging production problems. Rivalry within the union constitutes healthy competition, since influence within the union depends upon competent performance of specialized functions rather than upon lung capacity or ability to pound the table.

This creative evolution takes place as many employment relations functions are transferred from the exclusive control of management to the arena of joint problem solving. The Minnequa Plant has demonstrated such transfers in the following functions: setting up job classifications; defining layoff and promotional status; control of safety and health conditions; determining the most efficient working hours; creation of job satisfaction for the individual worker; maintenance of plant discipline; provision of medical facilities and Red Cross training; heeding the problems of the young workers; administration of pension plans; and even considering the worker's problem of technological change.

The transfer principle operates continuously, because one thing leads to another—sometimes unexpectedly. Remedial grievance handling has led to preventive conciliation by way of a joint committee on wage inequities. A joint seniority study committee discovered that the solution of seniority problems brings a better approach to labor's problem of technological change. Pooled judgment in the establishment of job definitions and in job classification has led to a renewed mutual interest in methods of incentive payments. In these respects and others, the Minnequa Plant has illustrated a continuity in the transfer of functions that can be shared, a factor which has been noticed wherever collective bargaining works effectively, and particularly in the series of NPA studies.

The continuous transfer of functions from the sphere of exclusive management prerogative into the arena of mutuality not only involves functions that already exist, but frequently leads to discovery of new functions which may be shared. For example, under collective bargaining there arises a new demand for equal educational opportunities to help individual workers develop their talents with a view toward advancement. The union plays its role in negotiating for trial periods in cases of promotions, while management plays its role in making certain types of training available generally rather than selectively, as in the case of the Minnequa Plant's joint apprenticeship program. Progress is being made in affording workers equal employment opportunities regardless of race, creed, color, or sex, though this is a relatively new phenomenon.

This social evolution cannot operate unless public opinion favors union-management cooperation. Collective bargaining on the present large scale is doubtless an expression of the American genius for enriching community life by bringing potentially hostile natural and social forces into harmonious relationships. The Wagner Act was projected with characteristic fearlessness in a time of depression, and with typical reliance on facts at hand. Part of the Preamble to the Act states: "Experience has proven that protection by law of the right of employees to organize and bargain collectively safeguards commerce from injury, impairment or interruption, and promotes the flow of commerce by removing certain recognized sources of industrial strife and unrest, by encouraging practices fundamental to the friendly adjustment of industrial disputes arising out of differences as to wages, hours, or other working conditions and by restoring equality of bargaining power between employers and employees."

This popular insight into what was required in 1935 has been implemented by years of practice. Today, the following statement of fact might well be added to the preamble of the Act: "As a result of public policy encouraging collective bargaining, employers and employees have gained in the knowledge of each other's problems and thereby have increased joint participation in their solutions. With an increased knowledge and participation has come increased responsibility on the part of both employers and employees. It is the purpose of this Act to encourage this increased sharing of functions, thus promoting collective bargaining of wider scope and better faith which would be beneficial to the public interest."

The public interest in collective bargaining grows increasingly important. Our national economic life is steadily becoming more interrelated and complex, and we urgently need to know as much as possible about the way in which labor and management and the public may cooperate on higher levels. The collective bargaining relationship at the Minnequa Plant shows that there is ample scope for industrial self-government within the framework of a sympathetic national policy of labor relations. All concerned, labor, management, and the public, may claim their due share of credit.

A POSTSCRIPT

Since this study was issued in 1951, C. F. & I. has continued to grow, with the addition of six new plants in Delaware, New Jersey, and Pennsylvania. The Corporation now ranks as the ninth largest steel company in the United States; and the Minnequa Plant in 1953 produced 60 per cent of C. F. & I.'s total output of ingots. By 1953, between 8000 and

8500 persons were employed at Minnequa—about 40 per cent of C. F. & I.'s total employment.

The Corporation's expansion and modernization program, not including the purchase of four East Coast plants, involved during the year ended June 30, 1953 an outlay of $20 million. The latest and one of the most important additions to the Minnequa Plant is a seamless tube mill opened in 1953, the first of its type in the West, which is producing goods for the expanding oil and gas industry of the West and Southwest.

Measured in terms of a dollar of constant value, C. F. & I.'s sales doubled from about the time of the 1944 merger until 1952, and increased another 27 per cent between 1952 and 1953; income before federal taxes in constant dollars in 1953 was about five times that in 1944; net worth in constant dollars had increased by 20 per cent in 1952 compared with 1947, and by 50 per cent in 1953; and total assets in constant dollars doubled from 1947 to 1953.

These favorable showings, according to C. F. & I., resulted from increased productivity and lowered unit costs brought about by the Corporation's continuing modernization program plus the increased efficiency and cooperation of the employees. The Company describes its labor relations as excellent, and points out in the 1953 Annual Report: "Negotiations with the United Steelworkers of America-CIO in June 1953 were conducted in a cooperative manner. . . . Most of the Corporation's labor agreements expire on June 30, 1954. In addition, our Pension Plans and Social Insurance Programs will then be open for negotiation for the first time in approximately five years. The Corporation has agreed to participate with the United Steelworkers of America-CIO in a joint study of pensions and insurance in preparation for the forthcoming negotiations."

CHAPTER 16

The Lapointe
Machine Tool Company

and the Steelworkers (CIO)

GEORGE P. SHULTZ and ROBERT P. CRISARA, *both of the Industrial Relations Section, Massachusetts Institute of Technology, are authors of NPA Case Study No. 10. Their full report, condensed in this chapter, was published in November 1952.*

Words that describe the situation at The Lapointe Machine Tool Company in Hudson, Massachusetts, are criticism, discussion, problems, production. The goal of the company and Local 3536 of the United Steelworkers of America (CIO) is high output, with the dollar results shared fairly, and people try to keep their eye on the goal.

The relationship started in 1944; then there was a costly 11-week strike in 1946, which union and management remember well. The atmosphere in negotiations is now one of good faith and good will and there has been no strike in the last six years. The union has not forgotten the strike weapon, nor management the possibility of its use, but it would be used only after intense and sincere efforts first to negotiate an agreement.

Industrial peace is a by-product of the pursuit of their goals by management and the union. The emphasis is on the problem, not on personalities, not on justifying past practices, not on jockeying for position. Under these circumstances, members of the strong local union speak their minds on a wide range of topics; and so does management. Industrial peace is not the result of suppression of grievances but of giving them open and thorough airing.

Two aspects of this union-management relationship make it of special interest in contrast to the other *Case Studies* in the series. First, the peace that exists in this company has survived good times and bad. The highly volatile machine-tool business was way down in the period 1948–50, but has been way up since the outbreak of the Korean War. Thus the special problems that arose during periods of contraction as well as expansion can be examined. Second, to a much greater extent than in any of the other cases studied, the union and management at Lapointe have actively cooperated on production problems. This joint participation is vigorously addressed to the real problems of the business. The direct result is increased productivity, for which monthly bonuses are paid on the basis of an established ratio of payroll to the sales value of production. Indirectly, this approach has promoted the stability of the relationship, since it has increased understanding of individual and collective problems.

The quality of the peace is high, judged by the same tests used in the study of The Nashua Corporation. There has been a substantial degree of industrial peace. There is recognition and acceptance by the union and by management of the needs of the other as a going institution. The relationship is regarded as fair by both parties. Employees have security, dignity, and recognition as individuals. And the net effect of the relationship is not detrimental to the public interest.

The treatment given the authors bears witness to the nature of the relationship. Key management and union officials were willing to answer any question we asked and to provide any information that was available. We had introductions from the plant superintendent to the foremen, and from the union president to the stewards and men on various union committees. We were then put on our own to go anywhere we wanted to go and talk to anyone we wanted to talk to. This complete freedom was given while the parties were in the midst of contract negotiations and during a well-contested campaign for the office of union president. We talked altogether with about 80 people, including almost 50 production workers. We made a conscious effort to talk with new as well as long-service workers and with people on all three shifts. When we mentioned that we were impressed with the freedom given us, the reaction was, "We have nothing to hide."

THE COMPANY AND ITS ENVIRONMENT

Some fifty years ago, J. N. LaPointe, a machinist, was given the job of making square holes in metal. He first drilled a round hole and then laboriously filed out the corners. Then he had an idea: why not replace his handpower with a machine? Thus he built the first broaching machine. The size, the complexity, and the possible uses of this precision product have expanded and changed in the intervening years, but the basic idea remains the same.

Company Organization

Lapointe is organized to do a complete job in the production of broaches and broaching machines. It will do the necessary machine-design and engineering work, produce both cutting tools and machines to use them, and install and test these expensive precision instruments. To provide its rounded service, more or less unique in the industry, the company employs people for a variety of technical jobs, as well as for factory work. For example, Lapointe employs development engineers, who have a number of outstanding innovations to their credit, and maintains a metallurgical laboratory along with its expensive heat-treating equipment.

Just over 1000 people, 80 per cent of them factory workers, are employed at Lapointe. The management is conducted with a minimum of staff. A production control department works out schedules for the plant and its expediters follow work in process. But the line-management organization is otherwise completely on its own, solely responsible for the processing of grievances, discipline, contract negotiations, training, and so on. There is no line-staff problem because there is no staff. The personnel department is limited to an employment and record-keeping office. The foremen and supervisors are self-reliant, if for no other reason than that they have no choice. Dealings between the parties, therefore, are conducted directly and exclusively by the people who have authority to make decisions and the responsibility for carrying them out.

In part, the present organizational structure is a carry-over from a company of only 300 employees, probably too small to justify an extensive personnel staff. In the rapid expansion to meet demands of the Korean emergency, production was increased through added hours and shifts, with additions to management made where they were needed—at the foreman and shift-superintendent positions—and these were almost entirely drawn from the work force and had been union members. Management's policy has been to keep down the overhead expenses and select men for supervisory positions who can get out production by "knowing the jobs and knowing the people."

Jobs and the Work Force

The production processes at Lapointe call for a wide variety of metal-cutting and assembly operations. The use of broaches is particularly applicable to the type of job performed in the mass-production industries. In a single stroke, the broaching tool performs both the rough and finish machining operations on a standardized part and does it with great precision. As a consequence, production of the broach itself is almost on a job-lot basis. Each is fashioned to do a particular job, which means that the plant workers have wide variety in their precision work.

Not every worker has to be highly skilled in his occupation, since the fussiness required varies with the job. But virtually every worker must be able to read blueprints, use such craftsmen's tools as micrometers, set up and operate his machine, and most important, have the capacity to take responsibility and show individual judgment in his work. As a result, work at Lapointe tends to attract and develop an inquisitive and self-reliant type of individual. As a matter of fact, recruitment of workers is made easier for the company, since Lapointe is known as a "good place to learn your trade."

The factory work force is largely male, although there are a few female operators; and since the company's real growth has occurred since the 1930's, the work force is relatively young. There is a core of long-service employees who fall, generally, in the 45–55 age group. But three-fourths of the workers, including some with high seniority, are under 45 years of age; and the average employee is about 36 years old.

The Product Market

Lapointe sells in a competitive market. About five other U. S. firms make broaching machines, and at least twenty make broaches or cutting tools. In addition, potential competition is always threatening, particularly in the cutting-tool end, since entry into this phase of the machine-tool business does not require tremendous capital outlays, but can be on an alley shop basis. And there is also competition from the rest of the machine-tool industry which have other kinds of milling and grinding operations. Broaching, done by Lapointe, must be sold not as the *only* method but as the cheapest method in competition with these other types of machine-tool builders.

Competition is made more severe by the feast-and-famine nature of demand for machine tools. Demand is high in any war or investment boom, and the industry expands to take this lucrative business. These periods of high profit are likely also to be periods of price controls and high taxes. Once the demand for the end product levels off, even though at a high level, demand for machine tools falls sharply. Thus, when the rest of the economy may be experiencing a boom, excess capacity hangs over the machine-tool market, and cutthroat competition may occur.

The cooperative approach to production problems at Lapointe was developed to cope with the unstable pattern of employment caused by this boom-and-bust type of demand. The union has sought ways to achieve greater job security and higher take-home pay. The company has stabilized employment and profits by developing new applications of the broaching method, by providing a complete service job from engineering to installation, and by standing ready to produce cutting tools, which wear out, as well as machines which do not wear out.

The Labor Market

The labor market from which Lapointe draws its employees includes not only Hudson, Massachusetts (a small town with a population of about 8500), but also five or six surrounding towns and a labor force of slightly more than 20,000 workers. There are few other metal-working plants in the area; the other major firms are in the shoe, plastics, and textile industries. Without dominating the area, Lapointe is its largest company and pays the highest wages. The advantages derived from being in an area where there is little competition for labor from comparable plants and where it is surrounded by firms in relatively low-wage industries are partly counterbalanced for Lapointe because of the impossibility of hiring skilled workers when demand increases. For the most part, Lapointe must count on its older employees to train the inevitable green help.

The fact that both the company and its employees need each other gives to each a degree of bargaining power but also makes it important to both that union-management relations be as stable and constructive as possible.

THE UNION

Information about the union, its organization, growth, and government, provides an important part of the environmental backdrop for union-management relations. Such data on Local 3536 of the United Steelworkers of America (CIO) help in assessing its character, stability, and the way it meets the standards of a democratic society.

Organization of the Union

Union organization in the fall of 1944 was basically an inside job. Not that the district office did not help—Roy Stevens, director of the union's

Worcester office, and Dan Murray of his staff gave the Lapointe workers courage and personal aid at critical moments, in addition to membership cards, circulars, and advice. But the original impetus and sustained effort necessary to start the union came from the workers. The personal bitterness of one man, who later became the local's first president, was the energizing force, but others responded. Each man had his own reasons for joining the union, his own grievances and fears. The more usual ones seemed to relate to the quest for seniority in layoffs and increased wages, dissatisfaction with the piecework system and with the favoritism of foremen.

Whatever the reasons for its start, the union's organizing campaign was not bitter. The basic tone of union statements made during the campaign was constructive—not so much "hate management" as "get a better deal for yourself." During the campaign, international officials of the Steelworkers emphasized the democratic, responsible, and efficient nature of their organization and the importance to the union of a membership which would take an alert interest in the local's affairs. According to union officials, "The company didn't realize how much foundation work we had done. They didn't fight because they didn't think we could succeed." At any rate, the company's only overt action during the pre-election campaign was to call the employees together and explain the voting procedure and rights of the employees.

The election was held on December 19, 1944. There were 427 eligible voters and 416 valid ballots. The count was 236 for the union and 180 against it.

Growth of Local 3536

The workers at Lapointe have never been apathetic, as illustrated by the fact that almost all of the people who were eligible voted in the union certification election. From the point of view of increasing its membership and strength, the local's problem was one of winning the allegiance of active people rather than of stimulating the interest of a group that did not care what happened.

By 1950, when the union-shop clause in the contract was put into effect, this job had largely been accomplished. Only three people had not already joined the union voluntarily. Since 1950, many new men have been hired and have been required to join the union after 30 days of employment. Of 47 production workers we talked to, 17 had come to work at Lapointe after the union-shop clause had taken effect. None spoke resentfully of having to join the union; in fact their comments about the union and the union-management relationship were generally favorable. There are, no doubt, some new men who would prefer not to have to pay dues ($2.00 per month); but as the union president remarked, "Those are the guys we got the union-shop clause for."

The real story of the growth of the local union unfolded, then, in the years between 1945 and 1950, during which three general periods can be distinguished. The first period lasted about a year. The union acquired few additional members during this year of uncertainty and struggle, marked by formal grievances and heated disputes. Those who joined the union at this time apparently did so as a result of highly personal feelings. Toward the end of 1945 came a contract reopening on wages, and as was the case in the rest of the steel industry a strike. Although the union's membership constituted only about 60 per cent of the work force, the strike at Lapointe was completely effective. After a little over a month, "Big Steel" settled for 18.5 cents, but after nine weeks Local 3536 was still out. The company obtained an injunction in a state court forbidding, among other things, picketing by Lapointe workers. The Worcester office of the Steelworkers provided pickets from another local; but the company sent out letters stating that the strike was over and a few employees—not over 30, but the number is a matter of disagreement—crossed the picket lines and came back to work. Finally, after eleven weeks the strike was settled. Both parties were anxious to get back to work and both adopted a more constructive attitude toward their mutual problems.

During the next two years, no particular membership campaign was conducted; in fact, there was some hesitancy about taking into the union anyone who had not solidly supported the strike. Within the work force, there initially was considerable bitterness against those who had crossed the picket lines, but open expressions of antagonism gradually disappeared. The union by the end of 1947 had gradually acquired as members about 70 per cent of the work force, primarily because it had demonstrated that it could get management to listen to grievances and make corrections, and that it could really achieve the goals set forth in the organizing period.

In December 1947, after considerable investigation and discussion, the parties decided to try the so-called "Scanlon Plan" for union-management cooperation on production problems. The Plan (discussed in more detail later) had been proposed originally by the union, and the union officials took an active part in its operation. The workers credited much of the achievements under it to the union. In its membership drive conducted during the fall of 1948, the union emphasized the point: "If you want to have a voice in what's going on, join the union." Apparently, this appeal struck home, for almost everyone signed up. As one worker put it, "The union is important here. I joined because I wanted to have a say in union affairs." This feeling was reflected by the nonsupervisory employees in the engineering department who were included in the bargaining unit from the start and the office workers who asked the union to organize them toward the end of 1948.

Democratic Union Government

The active, self-reliant, and outspoken members of the local have a chance to express their views on all issues that come before the union. Contract demands, formulated by an elected negotiating committee acting in consultation with a representative from the union's Worcester office, are discussed in at least one meeting of the local and the membership has the final vote on the contract. The officers of the union are elected by secret ballot every two years, and anyone who has attended at least six of the last twelve regular union meetings can be nominated for office from the floor. There are spirited contests for the presidency; only one man has been elected for more than one term in office.

There was no evidence that the expression of minority views was discouraged; in fact, a number of workers who made critical comments about some particular union program added that they did so without fear of discrimination. The union leaders said, "We want people to say their piece in the union meeting. That's the place to disagree and settle our arguments. Then we can face management with a united front." There are, in addition, certain safeguards for individual rights written into the union constitution, but it is the spirit—respect for the individual, his opinions, and his right to express them—with which they are regarded that counts.

With three shifts and a 52-hour week, there are some problems connected with getting a large percentage of members to routine meetings, but attendance is good when an important issue is up for discussion, and the voting in union elections is heavy. For example, about 80 per cent of eligible members cast votes in the June 1952 elections. And in 1952, there were about 50 individuals serving, willingly and with enthusiasm, on committees of various sorts and in the different union offices.

Decisions on contract demands and settlements, on strikes and on grievances are, first and last, the local's business, as stressed by organizers in 1944. But members of the local union are also strong followers of the national union and its programs for the simple reason that it has helped them many times in the past and will undoubtedly do so many times in the future. Members realize that their contract settlement is not independent of that won in basic steel, and they are proud of the pension plan, won in collective bargaining with the aid of national union specialists and of precedent set elsewhere.

Development of the Relationship

The causes of industrial peace may be dug out by going back to the period of less satisfactory relations and by tracing the subsequent events that have led to the constructive and stable relations existing today. The critical years for the development of this relationship were 1945 through 1948.

1945: Probing and Unrest

The dissatisfactions that had led people to join the union were translated into the objectives of union bargaining strategy: security on the job, a chance to question piece rates, higher wages. The company, concerned with protecting its rights, adopted a legalistic approach to contract negotiations and interpretations; and there was personal antagonism between union officials and the company's spokesman, an attorney with whom the Steelworkers dealt elsewhere. In the shop were all the typical problems of adjustment by foremen, stewards, and union members to the changed situation created by the existence of a newly formed union.

Relations, however, were not unusually bad at first. Both parties made initial gestures of friendship, made possible, perhaps, by the fact that the organizing campaign was not vicious or bitter. A key figure on the union side recalls that the present owner, on the night of the election, congratulated him on the union victory. And the regional office of the Steelworkers put out a short handbill pointing out the union's intention to work for a decent, understanding, cooperative relationship that would benefit everybody. Despite subsequent events, these were not empty gestures, as indicated by later developments and the fact that the statements are still remembered.

Nevertheless, good intentions did not solve difficult initial problems. A chief cause of friction in the plant was the piecework system that covered the direct production workers. The parties still argue about how bad, but agree that it was bad. From management's point of view, piecework had drawbacks. Management couldn't schedule work or deliveries because operators "would pick the good jobs from the rack and hide them." Management had to constantly track work down to be sure it was being done. The job of setting rates and settling grievances went on constantly and piecework kept the foreman always on somebody's "list." Even so, management did not want to change to a basis of time payment. The individualized work on job-lot orders made it necessary, management felt, to have some kind of incentive: "You can't watch everybody; you've got to give them some reason for making an effort to put out the work."

Many of the comments of union members about piecework paralleled those of management. They resented the inequities created by the "tough" and "gravy" jobs; they felt that a man who had piled up good earnings in the beginning of a week would be given tough jobs at the end "since his average could stand it." Workers readily confirmed the practice of restricting output as an accepted device to prevent a cut in the rate. At the same time, the workers not on direct production jobs had complaints. Their earnings were lower; and, as one worker put it, "If they (the piece-workers) turned out more, I had to inspect more. He got paid for it, but I didn't. I was a second-class citizen around here."

Trouble with piecework was accompanied by many formal grievances. The men in the shop felt that "either the foreman couldn't settle or he wouldn't settle." One of these grievances resulted in a short walkout. Two went to arbitration, where one was settled in favor of the company and the other in favor of the union, but the settlements were not satisfactory to either side. The first contract between Local 3536 and Lapointe, signed on May 25, 1945, provided among other things for no strikes during its one-year term and for the possibility of reopening "due to a change in Government Wage Stabilization Policy." Along with other Steelworkers contracts, this one was reopened in the fall of 1945. The Lapointe workers chose to strike, and local negotiations awaited a national settlement. Along with the rest of the nation's steelworkers, those at Lapointe struck on January 19, 1946.

1946: The Strike

You cannot talk for long to an old-timer at Lapointe without having him tell in detail about the strike—how he felt; how his wife felt; how much it cost. This is as true of management people as of those in the union. The strike left a memory of cost, of serious intent, and of balanced power. There were negotiations at the end of the 11-week period and some feverish activity and excitement at the start, but, in between, there was "time on our hands," and food for thought.

A top management official put it this way: "During the strike we did a lot of real soul searching. . . . The more I thought, the more I was sure of one thing. We had to make some changes." And an international union official said: "During and after the strike, I found among the active members of the local union a greater appreciation of the problems of the company than at any other shop I am familiar with. They saw they had lost customers. They knew the company hadn't kept delivery dates for years. . . . Not that they cared about the company. . . . If that plant collapsed, the worker couldn't just pick up his tool box and go get another job."

The strike undoubtedly exhausted both parties. The union was not permanently weakened; it had apparently grown stronger. The members had gained confidence in their strength, but they were ready to rest a while. The company made no effort to conceal its desire to get back to operation: "We told them we needed production. We wanted to keep our customers. We said that we'd welcome any ideas from the union that would help with production and bring about a better relationship. I don't know whether or not they took that seriously at the time but, anyway, we were ready to listen."

The reflection during 1946 was made more penetrating and objective, in our opinion, by changes in a number of key people. All the changes did not come at once, but between 1944 and 1948, several new faces appeared in the top-management organization and a different set of officials assumed responsibility for day-to-day operations, and now there is no attorney sitting in on contract negotiations. In June 1946, the local elected a new president to serve for a two-year term. These people were not new to the situation, but were new to their responsibilities, and able to look at the past at least relatively free from the bias of personal involvement.

By the end of 1946, the stage was set for change. Strength was roughly balanced. Sources of grievances were recognized. No one knew quite what to do except that it was necessary to do better.

1947: Exploring a Cooperative Approach

The change in Lapointe's union-management relationship came as the parties jointly worked out a plan for cooperating on production problems. The story of this joint effort and others like it has been told elsewhere [1]

[1] *Fortune,* January 1950, described the Lapointe experience, as did Fred G. Lesieur, in "Local Union Experiences with a Cooperative Plan," *Proceedings of the Fourth Annual Meeting of the Industrial Relations Research Association,* December 1952, p. 174. See also, John Chamberlain, "Every Man a Capitalist," *Life,* December 23, 1946; Joseph N. Scanlon, "Profit Sharing Under Collective Bargaining: Three Case Studies," *Industrial and Labor Relations Review,* October 1948, pp. 58–75; and George P. Shultz, "Worker Participation on Production Problems: A Discussion of Experience with the Scanlon Plan," *Personnel,* November 1951, pp. 201–211.

but because of its importance to this relationship, it is summarized here. The local's new president, Jack Ali, was an hourly-rated worker and had impressed members of management as being "shrewd but responsible." One of the union members called Mr. Ali's attention to John Chamberlain's article in *Life* describing the results of union-management cooperation at a plant in Ohio, also organized by the United Steelworkers of America. Mr. Ali went to management with this idea: "A cooperative effort to work out production problems, combined with provisions for sharing the gains created by group effort on a share-and-share-alike basis." Skeptically, but jointly and with dead seriousness, the parties looked into this approach, visited plants where it was being used.

The two parties began adapting the cooperative approach to their own situation. This led union and management representatives through the intricacies of the rate structure, the past fluctuations in product-mix, the labor content on different kinds of jobs, problems of administering the plan, and other important aspects of the company's operation. After seven months of this, they were ready to start the formal operation. They had already learned a good deal about such operations, by the process of exploration. They had acquired a new measure of trust and confidence in each other, which grew because of their strength, not despite it.

Joseph N. Scanlon, a former official of the Steelworkers and then and now on the staff of the Massachusetts Institute of Technology's Industrial Relations Section, had helped the people at the Ohio plant get started, so the parties soon turned to him for guidance. The measure of his contribution is suggested by the fact that the parties automatically called their cooperative approach "The Scanlon Plan."

1948: Trial and Error

The big question was: "Will the Scanlon Plan work?" The attitude of a number of key people is summed up by a union member: "We didn't know for sure whether the other side would play ball or not. We knew this thing would work if everyone tried to make it work. And we were going to make damn sure that if it didn't work it wouldn't be our fault."

The first month under the Scanlon Plan was December 1947. The bonus, paid to every employee including supervision, was 25.54 per cent of the payroll, a rough measure of the productivity increase. Examples of informal and cooperative efforts to increase production abounded—300 employees made 266 recorded suggestions during thirteen months. The picture was rosy according to a letter written by the local's president on January 13, 1948 (see excerpts in *Case Study No. 10*). He pointed out that pieceworkers were now willing to do any job, good or bad, and since there was no favoritism in giving out jobs, the worker could give all his attention to the job at hand. The indirect worker, he said, now did everything to service the direct worker as fast as possible, because if production went up there would be something extra for him. Employees were working as a team, not harder, but more steadily, and the amount of spoilage had been reduced, which meant that work moved faster to the shipping room or "pay-off window."

In January 1948 and February there were bonuses, but by March production had dropped and there were no bonuses for March, April, or May. The cause for the dip in production was simple and well understood, though not excused, by everyone. Management had not anticipated the Plan's effect on production and what had looked like a big backlog of business was shortly dissipated. After considerable discussion of the reasons for the problem and the prospects for the months to follow, union and management agreed that the work force should be held together, even if this meant no bonus during the lean period. In the meantime, management concentrated on sales. The bulk of the job-lot type of business typical of Lapointe had to go through the engineering department before coming into the shop. The engineers proposed postponement of their summer vacations to process the work. With relatively little production, July and August figures looked bad, but by September production was rolling. The September and October bonuses were 25.5 and 19.3 per cent of the payroll. (Month-by-month financial results of the Plan for December 1947 through February 1949 are shown in Table 1, *Case Study No. 10.*)

Experience had shown that production could be increased significantly under the Plan, but the financial results left something to be desired from management's viewpoint. Bonuses were paid in good months, but management absorbed the deficits in bad months. After full discussion of this problem in union meetings as well as in the union-management screening committee for the whole plant, and despite the existence of a recently signed contract, the union agreed to set aside in a reserve half of the first 15 per cent of any monthly bonus. If money remained in the reserve at the end of the year it would be paid out as a bonus.

Then another crisis developed. There were indications that the year 1949 would be a bad one for the machine-tool industry. At the same time, the company was working hard on the development of broaches for use in the production of jet engines. This meant payroll expenditures, but until the development was perfected, no matching sales dollars. Should the union demand that this payroll be taken out of the calculations? The business they did have was largely a reflection of similar developments of the past. If this one paid off, it would help secure the future. The union decided to go along for a month, for two, and then three months. Then the development hit; production picked up; and in February 1949, the bonus was 18.45 per cent.

During 1948, the changed approach to production problems was tested and retested. Everyone knew the reasons in the months when they got a bonus; they had earned it. In the months when there was no bonus, they knew the reason too, and did their best to improve the situation. With this new emphasis on production, and the disappearance of piecework, grievances in the shop were fewer and more easily settled, informally and at the department level. Both parties had worked together on tough problems. Management had agreed not to lay people off; the union to the reserve. By the end of the year, their changed relationship—based on a balance of power, a common purpose, and a sense of fairness—was firmly established.

PROBLEM SOLVING

Contract negotiations and day-to-day handling of problems are as important in this as in any other union-management relationship. The contract is the law of the shop, and both parties abide by it. At the same time, they are flexible and constructive in their approach to day-to-day problems.

Contract Negotiations

The essentials of contract negotiations appear not so much in the negotiating sessions themselves as in the situation within which the negotiations take place. There are certain unchangeable factors in the environment, more or less beyond the control of either of the parties. Both union and management are well-informed and realistic about the economic problems facing the machine-tool industry, and they have learned how to work together on these problems. Both parties are tough-minded in the pursuit of their own interests, though experience has convinced them that economic force is appropriate only as a last resort. Within this framework, negotiating sessions are friendly but serious encounters between good bargainers.

The negotiating procedures are informal, not much different from those in many other companies described in this series. The average time for negotiations is about four or five sessions, each lasting from four to eight hours. Typically, the first session is devoted to a presentation of the union's demands which have been approved by the union membership, but occasionally management may also present its demands for contract changes. The second session is mainly devoted to management's point-by-point discussion of each demand. Some of the issues may be settled, but the items that cost money take longer.

Management is represented by the executive vice-president, Ed Dowd, who is spokesman in meetings, and by the comptroller, the plant manager, and the general superintendent. They consult with the company's owner and president before and during the negotiations. The role of the conciliator—who has been called in during the last three negotiations—seems limited. He is chairman of any meetings he attends and a symbol of the parties' serious intentions.

Union members are represented by the local president and a negotiating committee, elected every two years. All are full-time employees at Lapointe. For the more critical sessions, the local likes to have Roy Stevens of the union's Worcester office there as well. As in the case with all Steelworkers, the membership must approve the settlement before the contract can be signed.

Once the contract is signed it is regarded as law. When a man is hired, he is handed a copy of the collective bargaining agreement and the shop rules. In addition to clauses mentioned earlier, other important provisions warrant attention.

Since 1945, when the first contract was signed, the hiring rate for unskilled labor has increased about 90 per cent to $1.23 an hour, and the other base rates in the wage structure have gone up commensurately. There is no rotation of shifts. Second-shift workers receive 8 cents per hour wage differential, and third-shift workers 12 cents per hour. Lapointe not only pays considerably higher wages than any other firm in the Hudson labor market; but also average hourly earnings, including the current rate of productivity bonus, are above those paid by most New England firms and compare favorably with machine-tool builders throughout the country.

Six holidays are payable even if they fall on Saturday; and holidays worked are at the rate of time and one half with another day off at the regular rate of pay. Factory workers and engineers are entitled to one week's paid vacation after one year's continuous service and two weeks after five years. Office employees receive one week's paid vacation after six months' continuous service, and two weeks after one year. A typical hospital, sickness, and medical service plan is voluntary and contributory.

A noncontributory, funded pension plan provides retirement benefits for those over 65 years of age having 15 years of service with the company. Total disability benefits are also provided.

Seniority in layoffs was changed in 1950 from a departmental basis to a plant-wide basis because of the cyclical nature of the industry, the high training costs, and the desirability of maintaining a work force with multiple skills. There is no superseniority for union officers, although foremen promoted from the ranks do retain their seniority. The union feels that "every man has to take his chances on keeping his job." The agreement provides for 48-hour posting of job vacancies or new jobs. Any employee may file for the position provided his job classification is lower than the job for which he is bidding. (And also provided, since 1951 when the expansion of the work force created many openings, that the employee has worked for six months on his job.) The workers like this posting because it affords the opportunity to learn additional skills; and the company likes it because it develops a flexible work force by permitting employees to learn a trade from start to finish. Although seniority weighs heavily in selection, ability to do the work is of prime importance. In the event no one bids on the job, the company may select an employee for promotion or employ a new man.

Hiring, formerly a function of the foreman, has been informally reassigned to the personnel department because of the increased numbers being employed and their relative lack of skills. The foreman may refuse a man hired by personnel. In the event a skilled worker applies for a job, the foreman determines his skill and assigns him a commensurate wage. Automatic pay progressions are provided at intervals in the learning period. Although management originally did not readily agree to this provision, several company officials remarked that "this review system makes for better selection."

Discipline is initiated by a warning from the employee's foreman and records of warnings are kept by the personnel department. Repeated warnings or a gross violation of rules are reported to the union steward as well. The foreman actually imposes the discipline or orders discharge, but all discharge cases are subject to the approval of the plant superintendent or his assistant, and both discipline and discharge cases are subject to the grievance procedure.

Day-to-Day Problems

The way daily problems are met is more significant than contract provisions which are, in a sense, problems that have already been solved.

Four examples, each representing a different area of interest, illustrate the process of solving day-to-day problems.

The first example shows the way the parties found to train green help when the outbreak of war in Korea created the sudden demand which continued throughout 1951. Lapointe, operating in a labor market without a large quantity of skilled tool and die makers, expanded employment by 100 per cent from May 1950 to February 1951, while the machine-tool industry as a whole expanded 50 per cent; and since then Lapointe has again doubled its employment. Production has more than kept pace with employment. One top management official has estimated that new employees were made productive members of the work force in one-third the time it took at the start of World War II, before the union and the Scanlon Plan. The company's management officials, along with the new workers, give the old-timers in the work force a large share of credit for the remarkable training job. The heavy weight given to seniority in lay-offs and the importance of the whole group's achievements in production undoubtedly influenced the willingness of the experienced workers to show the new man the tricks of the trade, help him out when he was stuck, and lend him their personal tools. However, when the expansion became great and rapid, and the new men were put on the second or third shifts where there were relatively few experienced workers, the system bogged down. The new employees did not understand or feel the need for incentives since new people did not become eligible for bonuses until they had been employed for three months. The union sensed this problem and acted on it.

First, the union asked for and got a temporary adjustment in the bonus computations as compensation for the burden of large training costs. Then union officials asked that their president be allowed to get small groups of new workers together on company time to answer their questions and explain the bonus plan. Everyone agrees that this induction program was effective. As one of the new workers remarked, "I guess personnel said the same things as the union, but coming from a guy out there, it really meant something."

The wage inequity program provides another example of the give-and-take of workers, union, and management. Elimination of piecework and establishment of earned rates perpetuated a rather chaotic and inequitable wage structure. There were two phases in a program to correct this situation: initiation of a plan to develop job classifications with a proper relationship to each other and to establish rate ranges within the classifications; and an attempt to apply wage increases to base rates only.

In line with the 1948 agreement, the union negotiating committee, whose members represent all areas of the plant, met to formulate a job-classification system. Their plans, devised through consultation with numerous workers, amounted to simple and informal job evaluation. When this was completed, the committee and the local union president met with management. In consultation with the foremen, management considered the plan thoroughly and, by and large, adopted the union's proposal. The creation of rate ranges and the fitting of workers into these ranges remained. Substantially the same procedure of getting information and membership approval was followed. The resulting increases varied from 5 to 23 cents per hour. The established norm was not altered, instead the costs represented a transfer from one group of workers to another; and the company could incur additional wage costs only in the event that there were deficit months not adequately covered by the reserve. The basic wage structure now seems fair and equitable to the company, the union, and its members.

The second phase of the wage inequity program, directly concerned with the earned rates, was worked out in regular contract negotiations. The earned-rate workers themselves requested the union to apply any wage increase obtained in 1950 to the base rate only. This was done. There were 82 original earned rates which were an average of 26 per cent above base rates; today, through the effect of both phases of the wage inequity program, there are only 49 earned rates, averaging 11 per cent above base rates. Thus, mainly through the good will of those who had the earned rates, this large and difficult problem has been cut down to size.

The third example shows how a worker pursued an idea for saving time, with the result that the general level of productivity was increased and other Lapointe employees benefited along with the several men who worked out details of the idea. A cylindrical grinder had a job in which the regular process was to start the machine, grind off a little stock, press the stop button, wait for the machine to coast to a stop, then "mike" the broach and start all over again. Nobody had any complaint about productivity and output on this job, except the grinder himself, who thought there was too long a wait. He had a vague idea for applying some kind of electric brake on the machine to make it stop faster. His foreman liked the idea, but when the two suggested it to management they were told that it would cost $1200 to buy a speed control and scrapping of the present speed reducer would lose $450. The foreman and grinder in a chat with an electrician found the practical solution. The electrician suggested something which, when tested, worked. It cost about $15.25 plus a couple of hours for the maintenance man to install and now has been applied to seventeen other machines. And it saves one hour a day per machine.

The fourth example has to do with the way electricians took the initiative in meeting a problem when the plant expanded to a three-shift, seven-day operation in late 1950. When this happened, the electrical assembly department which had been working a five-day week had to increase its work. Rather than interfere with the electricians' week end off, management scheduled an extension of daily hours for the electricians. This schedule resulted in a backlog of machines requiring electrical installation and the smooth flow of work was interrupted. To better cover the shop while new men were trained, the electricians worked out a new arrangement whereby two groups would work, some longer hours during the week and others to work as long as needed on Saturdays. The new hours proved more satisfactory for production, but imposed hardships on the week-end workers. Furthermore, even more flexibility was needed because of the concentration of shipments in the last two weeks of the month.

The electricians initiated action again, but their new plan still did not work well. Finally, they decided to work from seven to five from Monday through Friday and a half day Saturday. And, "until new men were properly trained, we would work Saturday afternoon or even Sunday." This schedule worked out to the satisfaction of both management and the workers.

THE SCANLON PLAN

According to Joe Scanlon, it is a misnomer to call this cooperative approach a "plan." Rather, "it's just people who have identified a common objective, working together to achieve that objective." The Scanlon Plan is as simple and as difficult as that. Its heart is in the ideas on production and the criticisms of current practice contributed by people at all levels of an organization. Production workers are not given a "sense of participation"; they are asked to take part in the real thing.

Financial Results

Profit figures are not available, since Lapointe is a privately held corporation; however, the owner said he was well satisfied with the financial results of the cooperative approach. His statement was backed by the fact that he has recently applied the same approach to operations of his plant in England.

From the employees' point of view, the financial pay off is reflected primarily in the monthly bonus, which results from an improvement over the group's performance as it was before the Plan was adopted in December 1947. (The basis and method of payment of the bonus are set forth in the section of the Collective Bargaining Agreement printed in an Appendix to *Case Study No. 10.*) The bonus percentage is thus a rough index of productivity change.

During the 45-month period, January 1949 through September 1952, there were only nine months when there was no bonus, and the cause in these months was mainly a lack of business. In only one month, September 1950, was the size of the deficit large; this resulted from the sudden hiring of many green hands to meet the demands of the Korean emergency. (An adjustment was made, however, in February, March, and April 1951, to compensate for the effect of green help on production per dollar of payroll, since it did not seem fair for the employees to pay the training cost through reductions in the bonus.) While a 52 per cent achievement in June 1952 stands out, uniformly good results were attained in 1951 and 1952. (A monthly breakdown for the period January 1949–September 1952 is given in Table 2, *Case Study No. 10.*)

The period January 1949 through June 1950 is characterized by a relatively low level of demand. There were some good bonuses at its beginning, but as demand slackened in the middle of 1949, the emphasis shifted. The basic problem was to maintain employment, which dropped off sharply in the machine-tool industry generally. Lapointe's low point was 260 employees in October 1949, a level only slightly below the average of 281 for the year 1948. The accomplishment is remarkable in view of the fact that performance did not once drop below the norm from February 1949 through March 1950. Thus the cooperative approach paid off for the employees in this period partly in terms of bonuses, but more basically in terms of job security. For its part, the company was able to retain its skilled work force and to make its profit record a more stable one. Following the outbreak of the Korean War, the problem was to fill orders, not find them. The bonus figures from then on reflect the quality of the necessary training job.

The Extent of Participation

Increases in productivity have stemmed basically from participation in solving production problems by people throughout the company, although they may come in part from steadier work by some individuals than when they were under piece rates. The participation takes many forms. Within the work force, information sharing about the best ways to do various jobs is widespread. Coordination between departments is better: engineers, schedulers, and production workers consult with each other on new or difficult problems. Virtually every member of the work group helps to solve immediate or expected problems. The 47 production workers with whom we talked seemed generally to think that these informal efforts were "at least as important" to production as the more formal, recorded suggestions.

The recorded suggestions, nevertheless, are of vital importance. Informal efforts probably would be much less extensive in the absence of some way to take ideas to the top level in the company. Each department elects a production committeeman who collects suggestions and talks them over with the foremen at periodic intervals. If there is no agreement at the departmental level or if the idea involves more than one department or more money than the foreman is authorized to spend, it goes to a screening committee of union and management representatives where it is discussed further. The committee passes its recommendation to the top company representative, who makes the decision. This committee also goes over bonus figures and gets information about immediate and long-run business prospects. Every three months, all the production and screening committeemen meet for a general discussion of problems, prospects, and suggestions.

The recorded suggestions for the period December 1947 through September 1952 provide tangible evidence on the extent of participation. (The number of suggestions made, number of people making their first suggestion, and total number of employees for each quarter during this period are given in Table 3, *Case Study No. 10.*) In four and a half years, 1506 suggestions were made. Four out of every five have been accepted and put into operation; about 5 per cent are still under consideration, and the rest have been rejected for the time being.

More significant, perhaps, than the number of suggestions is the number of people who have made them and the extent to which this number grows. By the time the program had been in effect for a year, one-third of the employees had made a recorded suggestion. The success with which new employees are assimilated into the work group is indicated by these figures: Two years ago the company employment was 288 people, about half of whom had made at least one suggestion; now the number of people who have made a suggestion is 401. Well over 100 of the new people have already taken part in the more formal aspect of the union-management cooperation.

In addition to bonuses and job security, the employees seem to be getting on-the-job satisfactions. Constant reference is made by people throughout the organization to the "good bunch we have working" in "our shop." This does not mean that there are not some tensions within the work force. New workers tend to be most interested in the quantity of production, whereas long-service employees are more concerned for quality since they are thinking of the firm's reputation. A few workers feel that a man should get some individual compensation for a suggestion, though those who have made the most suggestions did not make this comment. But there is virtually complete agreement that union-management relations are good and that every individual has a chance to clear up his grievances and make his ideas known. As one worker put it, "If a man doesn't get a hearing around this place, it's his own fault."

Management's Attitudes and Problems

Most management men are not accustomed to accepting and welcoming critical comments and suggestions about production problems from employees. Lapointe's management people have shown that they are big enough to take criticism and accept worth-while ideas. If they were not able to, the cooperation they are now getting from the work force would soon change to resentment.

The working background and union experience of most of the management people have helped them understand the practical importance of having men work with rather than against them. They are convinced that the man at the machine has a significant contribution to make to production. At the start especially, the attitude of the owner was of great importance: "If a man isn't broad-minded enough to take constructive criticism, then he does not belong in management. . . . The people out there know a lot more about some things than I do or than the foreman does. Nobody has all the answers."

The executive vice-president presides at the quarterly meetings of all people on the production and screening committees. He reads off a suggestion. It gets bounced from one individual to another. An outsider has difficulty in distinguishing management from union members. In this environment, management people gradually drop their defensive attitude. But this relationship is not one-sided. Management can dish it out as well as take it: "We don't hesitate to tell them if we think they are wrong. This is no kid-glove proposition. The men on the machines want the foreman to do his job. They don't want a weakling. They want a man who knows his job and does it." From the point of view of getting things done, management is in a strong position. Its decision-making and coordinating functions are more willingly accepted by workers since these functions are more clearly understood. And, of great importance, management has far more reliable information upon which to base its decisions.

Information sharing flows in both directions. This is not so much a matter of conscious policy as it is a result of the cooperative efforts. Apparently, the question was once raised whether too much information was available. Figures supporting the bonus calculation—sales, payroll, inventory changes—were originally dittoed and widely distributed. Then it was pointed out that there was some danger that the information would get into the hands of competitors. When the subject was discussed at a screening committee meeting, the procedure was changed. The figures are read to screening committee members and a written copy given to the union president. This question has never arisen since, despite the fact that price and cost information, for example, is supplied whenever it is needed. The problem might be different if a competitor were across the street. Judging from the past, however, both union and management would shortly recognize the problem and learn how to use essential information without undue risks.

Cooperation and Union Functions

The union was formed at Lapointe, as elsewhere, to fight the battles of the man at the bench, its classic functions being to win more money and to protect job security. In a situation like that at Lapointe, does the union change its objectives? Do they merge with those of management so that no conflicts of interest remain? Local 3536's objectives have not changed, and they do not coincide with those of management, though a substantial area of common interest has been identified. Cooperation on production problems has provided an additional and effective means of getting for its members more money and greater job security. But the importance of the collective bargaining contract as the basic rule of the shop is not diminished.

There is no doubt, however, that the cooperative approach places temptations before both union officers and members. Suppose, for example, that an individual is loafing on the job, doing as little as he possibly can. What should other workers in the department do? Workers do, of course, ask a new man or a loafer to play ball with the rest of the group. The pace of work is not excessive; in fact, many workers observed that, "They don't expect you to kill yourself here." But if the man does not respond, the rule of the shop is, "It's management's job to do the disciplining." Thus the union is a jealous guardian of a man's rights under the contract. There are no conflicts of production and union objectives, because with both officials and members the union always comes first. Any union official who translated the word "cooperation" into personal discrimination against some individual or who took on disciplinary responsibilities would surely be chastised at the next meeting and defeated at the next election.

Furthermore, Lapointe's management has no disposition to hand the disciplinary job to the union. Among other reasons, it realizes that such a move would create a revolution in the union and destroy the cooperation from which both parties benefit. Thus there exists at Lapointe a keen sense of essential function. No one characterizes this situation as "one big happy family."

STABILITY OF THE RELATIONSHIP

Union-management relations at Lapointe may be peaceful and constructive now, but will they stay that way? This relationship is stable because it operates in the self-interests of the company, the union, and its members. That does not exclude the possibility of a short strike at some future time, though it seems remote today. We believe that the basic stability of this relationship is deep enough to withstand such a test. The cooperative approach has worked out so satisfactorily that the parties would, in all probability, return to it as soon as their collective bargaining differences were settled.

Naturally this relationship could be upset. If, for example, a new owner were to put into effect a strong antiunion policy, there can be little doubt of what would happen. Assuming that he was primarily interested in a good return on his money, however, he would probably try to perpetuate the relationship rather than to destroy it.

The good union-management relationship is not based on personal friendship and good will, though these now exist in abundance. During the six years since the settlement of the last strike, the office of union president has been filled by four different individuals. Yet the relationship has continued on an even keel. Nor is the relationship based on benefits received in a prosperous era. The parties have spent more time struggling together with adversity than enjoying the fruits of a boom. Thus the relationship has survived changes in key individuals and important alterations in the environment. It meets the logical test of being mutually satisfactory and the empirical test of outlasting important changes. It is stable.

A Postscript

The basic facts of this relationship have not changed since 1952 when the study was completed. There have been no strikes during this period, and union and management groups continue to work together constructively on their common problems. The relationship has been further tested in two ways. First, and perhaps most difficult, the volume of business for this company, as for virtually all other machine-tool builders, has declined significantly from its Korean-War peak. The parties successfully met all the typical and difficult problems associated with reductions of force and hours. Second, despite the decline in employment, a new contract was negotiated in June 1953, without undue difficulty and without any loss in the mutual confidence and trust that had been built up between the parties.

CHAPTER 17

American Velvet Company
and the Textile Workers (CIO)

GEORGE S. PAUL, *Director of Labor-Management Institute, The University of Connecticut, is author of* NPA Case Study No. 11. *His full report, condensed in this chapter, was published in April 1953.*

Suspicion, strike, and industrial unrest were the forerunners of the good relationship which exists between the American Velvet Company and the Textile Workers Union of America (CIO). This story provides a good example of how a union and a company, when faced with what seem to be insurmountable obstacles, can stop horsetrading and turn to honest collective bargaining.

A. Wimpfheimer & Bro., Inc., which owns and operates the American Velvet Company, was established in 1845. The founder and first president, Abraham Wimpfheimer, died in 1885 and the company has remained in the hands of his descendants. American Velvet Company's manufacturing operations in Stonington, Connecticut, date back to 1892. The employee-employer relationship in the early days was one prevalent in that era. The company hired mill hands as they were needed and regarded them much the same as the machinery which was necessary to manufacture its velvet. The mill operated on a seasonal-demand basis and employment of the people was also seasonal. Unions were not wanted by the company. People interested in them were considered undesirable radicals and were continually weeded out. The manufacturing end of the business seemed to be considered a necessary evil. Top management operated out of New York, the sales headquarters, and was unacquainted with the Stonington employees and the plant under normal operating conditions.

The first open labor-management conflict came the year after the

Stonington plant opened. Poor business conditions in 1893 led American Velvet to tell its weavers and warpers they would have to work for reduced wages. The unorganized workers walked out in protest; new weavers were imported and the strike was broken. One by one, weavers who had struck moved away from Stonington as the company refused to rehire them. Disputes continued to arise as efforts were made to organize the mill from time to time, or the company ordered workers to run extra looms.

There was some organization by the AFL in the 1920's, but the company apparently did not recognize the local. The Velvet Workers' Association—which came into being at Stonington in 1934 and attempted to become a national union by combining a number of local velvet workers' unions—was organized and in part recognized by the company in July 1934. However, it never was successful in obtaining a written contract with the company. American Velvet seems to have begun to accept the idea of employee representation and organization. Some people feel that the Velvet Workers' was important in paving the way for the union that followed; others believe the changes taking place in terms of a new generation and economic and social conditions were the important factor. The author believes that all these causes played some part in the development of subsequent attitudes. That there had been a great deal of change in company philosophy is evidenced by a contract signed in 1937, with the Textile Workers Organizing Committee of the CIO (forerunner to the Textile Workers Union of America).

That first contract must have seemed like great progress for it contained many of the provisions for which unions were then striving. It contained a closed-shop agreement; recognized the union as collective bargaining agent for all the employees; included a seniority clause and sections on child labor, safety, and sanitation. The contract called for an eight-hour day and a 40-hour week, with time-and-one-half pay for overtime. Eight holidays were established, with double pay for any holiday worked. A grievance procedure was established, with the fourth step being an impartial arbitrator appointed by mutual agreement. Discharge cases were made subject to arbitration, with the possibility of reinstatement with compensation for lost time. The employer agreed to deal with the shop committee and permit the general shop chairman admission to all departments. And finally, a 10 per cent increase on all existing rates of pay was scheduled for June 12, 1937. A second contract, negotiated in June 1938, was essentially the same as the first.

Despite the terms of the contract, the relationship was not happy. The parties evidently had not learned that even the best contract must be accompanied by intelligent interpretation and enlightened administration.

A critical period came when poor business conditions forced American Velvet to attempt to go from a two-loom to a four-loom system. With an already strained relationship, this attempt started a long and bitter strike, lasting from August 1938 to November 1939. At the termination of the 16-month strike, the era of industrial peace began at American Velvet.

A Good Relationship Begins

The 16-month strike was a grueling experience for the company, the union, and the workers. The striking workers had hungry families, empty fuel bins, and unpaid bills. Business was generally poor and other employment practically impossible to find. Machinery and buildings stood idle as the company lost money and worried about customers. The owners were torn between three choices: move to the South, sell out and quit, or stay in Stonington and work out a solution. All three possibilities were seriously considered.

Upon returning from one of many surveys made in the South, Clarence Wimpfheimer found that the other owners had tentatively decided to sell out. Apparently it was at this point that Clarence Wimpfheimer, contrary to suggestions made by family advisers, decided to become sole owner of American Velvet.

In the latter part of 1939, the strike-torn company and union began a new approach to their problems. The first change of attitude probably came when Mr. Wimpfheimer decided to work with and fully recognize the union itself. This change did not come overnight, but it does seem that the company had started to look upon the union with friendliness rather than hostility.

The employees and their union had a tremendous amount to learn if they were to build the kind of relationship the employer seemed to be seeking. Individually and as a group, the worker at American Velvet was hostile toward his employer. The workers felt that what was good for the employer was usually bad for them. Good production had often meant unemployment, because it had often meant high inventories, resulting in layoffs. As a result, the workers had not tried hard to keep production up, and sometimes did their best to keep it down. Despite this general attitude, a guarded willingness to meet the employer something like halfway was expressed in an effort to get back to work.

The 1939 Negotiations

The company in the 1939 negotiations talked about cooperation, peace, and good relations with the union. The union members were hungry, broke, and tired of the strike, but not convinced that the company's treatment would be different from the past. The company, too, must have had some grave doubts about getting cooperation and real production from these people with whom it had fought for years. The owner talked about and offered profit sharing. However, because of lack of confidence in the company's ability to make profits at that time, because they feared a trick of some kind, or perhaps for a number of other reasons, the union turned down profit sharing.

In November, Local 110 of the Textile Workers signed a one-year contract with American Velvet. It included a four-loom system with mechanical innovations to lessen the increased loom load. The other provisions were basically the same as those of the 1937 and 1938 contracts. But this time the parties made many adjustments.

Top management had changed basically from absentee management to a local, interested management which was in the shop working with the people every day. During the first year, there was no closing time for key members of management. The confidence of the worker had to be won and production had to be increased if the company were to stay in business. Management began asking workers and union officers for help and suggestions, and sharing its information with them. When grievances were presented, they were listened to and, if found to be legitimate, were adjusted as soon as possible. Some members of management at American Velvet would not or could not conform to the new ways. One by one, they were replaced by more progressive men and women. Many of the replacements through the years have come from union ranks.

The memories of union members cautioned them to keep their guard up; they were reluctant to have their union work too closely with the company. However, some union leaders knew that management had to have their cooperation to succeed. If the company did mean what it said, a new life was about to open for the Stonington velvet workers and they wanted to help build that kind of life. If, on the other hand, management was not sincere, the workers might live to regret full cooperation in terms of rate cuts, heavy work loads, unemployment, and in lost confidence and trust in the union.

Slowly but surely, management and the union began to trust each other that first year. Management, from the top through the ranks, was selling itself. As acceptance began to take hold, employees and the union alike began to cooperate. This was not a relationship of full trust, but certainly a tremendous amount of progress had been made.

New Profit-Sharing Plan

The 1940 negotiations were conducted in a new atmosphere. Most of the people felt that they had done a fairly good job in the past year, and many were content to maintain the status quo for the contract year ahead. The president of American Velvet, however, felt that profit sharing would do much to improve the situation. But he felt that a three-year contract must be signed to give profit sharing a fair trial. The union, on the other hand, was reluctant to sign any contract covering more than one year, and had turned down profit sharing the year before.

In spite of many obstacles, the company had made money during the first year after the strike. The turning point in the negotiations seems to have come when the company offered to share profits for the past year just as if it and the union had agreed in 1939 on such a plan. The company said it would pay each employee an additional 11 per cent of his wages for the past year as his share in the profits. Many union people could not believe this employer was willing to give them something for nothing under the name of profit sharing. Others suspected that, in some way, the promised profits would not be paid, but would be used somehow to cut prices and hurt other workers in the industry. The proposal, however, was accepted—undoubtedly to get 11 per cent of the past year's pay rather than because of any confidence in the future or in profit sharing as such.

In December 1940, the American Velvet Company and Local 110 of the Textile Workers signed a three-year contract (text of which appears in Appendix A, *Case Study No. 11*) containing a profit-sharing plan. This was the beginning, by contract, of an idea and philosophy which have meant continuous benefits for the company and the employees.

PARTNERS IN VELVET

Marked by growing teamwork, this relationship since 1940 has benefited the company and its management, the union and its members, and the community in which it exists. American Velvet has grown from a mill originally operating 25 looms and employing 35 people, to an organization now operating approximately 250 looms and employing over 400 people. Since the latter part of 1939 when the company was reorganized, there have been ups and downs, but the company has continuously grown. Starting with a net worth of less than $190,000 in 1940, by 1952 it had grown in net worth to over $1.6 million. Gross sales of a little over $1 million in 1940 rose to over $5 million in 1952. In that same period of time, it enjoyed a total net profit of over $8 million. (The growth from 1940 through 1952 is shown, by number of employees, gross sales, net profits, and net worth, in Table 1 of *Case Study No. 11.*)

The Management

The management organization at American Velvet is informal. A small company plus a conviction that informality is best make this type of organization possible. There are two main divisions of manufacturing— the warping and weaving department and the finishing, dyeing, and shipping departments—and a new plush department which is just beginning. These divisions are run as separate and distinct operations, with the respective superintendents being totally responsible for their operations, including buying, planning, hiring, and firing. While these operate separately, there is a complete exchange of information and cooperation. Most of the management people are primarily production people who know how to manufacture velvet. The big job of labor relations and public relations, Mr. Wimpfheimer reserved for himself.

One of the criteria for selecting companies to be studied in this series was that the constructive relationship could not be explained in terms of a personality. The situation at American Velvet meets that criterion, but the company's energetic and dynamic president and owner has had an important guiding role in developing industrial peace. The job of putting this company back on its feet and building its harmonious relationship with the union was certainly not done by one man. Many able management people worked alongside their president, and have contributed greatly to the company's successful relationship. But the impetus and coordinating leadership were furnished by Clarence Wimpfheimer, and his determined leadership continues today.

The Union

Local 110 of the Textile Workers has been free of "political" factions. Officers of the union stand for election every year, usually in hotly contested elections. In thirteen years there were eight local presidents. Members who come forward as leaders remain active after they leave office. An active and alert membership makes this local outstanding. Membership meetings are lively and well attended, and management proposals are intelligently questioned and debated until a decision is reached. There is no evidence that this is a company union; rather it is militant in every sense of the word. However, the union is sufficiently mature to act with responsibility and to work out problems with the employer when it is to their mutual advantage. There is no evidence that the union presses illegitimate grievances or backs an individual in an unjustifiable situation. There are no private deals between an employee and the company. Employees and supervisors alike work through union representatives. One gets the impression that the company is dependent on the union in its everyday operations.

Local 110 has been active in the business of its national and regional union, as well as in its community. Few issues come up in the Eastern Connecticut Joint Board of the Textile Workers or at other levels in the union in which the local does not participate and take its stand; in fact this local helped to form the Board. Many contributions to education have been made by the local through the years. It has donated a collection of books on labor history, economics, and labor-management relations to the Stonington Free Library; offered an annual prize to the member of the Stonington High School graduating class who excels in an understanding of the principles of democratic government; featured speakers on subjects of general interest at union meetings; been well represented at seminars conducted by the national and state CIO. And the local joins with management in public discussion of the profit-sharing plan and union-management cooperation before groups throughout the country.

The union makes a point of sharing responsibility—which involves regular donations—with the community in all legitimate endeavors. Its welfare committee is active in visiting sick members and in coupling a personal interest with the insurance for sickness and disability which the employer carries. It participated in a local cooperative store started to stimulate other stores in Stonington to begin providing satisfactory services in terms of quality, variety, and cost. The store was sold after about ten years when it had served its purpose. The local has made itself felt politically in Stonington and throughout Connecticut. A number of its members have held elective and appointive posts in the area. It starts at the grass roots, concentrating all year on getting new voters registered and on getting out the vote for elections.

The Labor Force

The work force originally was made up of German socialists who had migrated to this country. Through the years, however, it has become a thoroughly mixed group of people, in terms of nationalities and cultures.

By and large, the present group of workers represents second and third generations of American Velvet employees. Slightly over 20 per cent have been with the company over 15 years; and over 2.5 per cent for 35 years or more. The largest number of employees are between the years of 30 and 60. The number of workers and the proportions of men and women have fluctuated through the years, but more men than women have been consistently employed at American Velvet. (Seniority distribution of men and women and age distribution for both groups, for 1952, are shown in Tables 2 and 3, and the numbers of male and female employees from 1940 through 1952, in Table 4, of *Case Study No. 11*.)

People seen in the American Velvet plant or at a union meeting are earnest hard-working people. Each employee is ready to speak for himself. Not all agree on details but, in general, each is convinced he has a good job and belongs to a good union. They seem sure a reasonable solution can be found to problems which may arise.

THE RELATIONSHIP IN OPERATION

Little time is wasted in this relationship on wondering if someone is trying to pull a fast one. Everyone concerned can devote full energy to finding ways and means of doing things for the benefit of all. The company, in a positive way, welcomes the union and depends on it for help, rather than merely tolerating it. The union and its members realize that their welfare depends on the success of the company.

Without a formal suggestion system and with no monetary rewards other than a share in profits, workers are continually offering suggestions to cut costs and improve production. When a shift changes, for example, all machines are kept running, and this occurs three times every 24 hours. Without an order or suggestion from management, the workers remain until the person from the next shift is actually ready to take over.

The degree of cooperation is also illustrated by a development a few years ago. The company had made plenty of velvet but had not sold much. Inventories were high and finances low. The union offered to lend American Velvet money from its national treasury. The men and women in the plant had another idea. Showing a willingness to gamble with their company, the employees suggested a four-day week until sales picked up. This suggestion was put into effect for a short time. The employees preferred this share-the-work policy to layoffs for part of the group, and they demonstrated their concern with the economic status of the company.

Sharing the Profits

Profit sharing did not in itself cause peace at this plant. It has, however, become an important part of the relationship and one of the major factors in industrial peace. Like any other technique, profit sharing is no better than the people who operate it. To be successful, it must be accompanied by good labor relations, complete understanding of the plan by the parties, and a sincere desire by them to make it work.

American Velvet's president feels that he is entitled to all the profits he can make. He also believes that the people who help him make these profits are entitled to share with him on an equitable basis. Importantly, profit sharing at American Velvet has never been a substitute for good wages. Wages before profit sharing are at least in line with those of the industry and the community, and generally are higher. Profit sharing has come to mean more than merely doing your job and sitting back to see what the profits are at the end of the year. It is an incentive for all to contribute constantly what they can to improve the situation.

The belief in profit sharing spread to the company's salesmen, who are not part of the union and who operate out of New York, 150 miles from the plant. They voluntarily agreed to pool their sales and participate in the plan. This move tended to solidify the organization more than ever in terms of purpose and objective. Salesmen are now concerned with manufacturing, while the workers and union are deeply concerned with the activities and results of the sales department. Periodically, the salesmen meet with union and company officials at the plant to discuss plans, problems, and results.

Since profit sharing has been in effect, there consistently have been profits. The question of whether the relationship would be impaired if there were no profits cannot be conclusively answered. Both company and union feel that they would survive such a condition. The union feels it would be no worse off than without profit sharing, since profits paid are in addition to going union wages. It recognizes that if the company did not make money, the workers would suffer with or without profit sharing. It is impossible to determine what the results would have been if, in 1940, some other plan or system had been tried instead of profit sharing. At any rate, with the background of successful experience, it is doubtful that industrial peace would continue if the plan were discontinued.

The profit-sharing plan has been changed a number of times since 1940. The original plan provided that 30 per cent of net profits, after taxes, would be distributed to employees at the end of the year as additional compensation or bonus. All employees (including foremen) who worked at least 160 hours during the fiscal year were eligible to share in the fund. The fund was divided among the eligible employees in proportion to total earned wages during the fiscal year. This amount was paid in lump sum between the end of the fiscal year (November 30) and the following January 31. Top executives have their own profit-sharing plan which is in addition to and comes after the employees' 30 per cent of net profits.

In 1941, the plan was changed to 25 per cent of net profits before taxes. With this exception, the plan remained the same through 1946. In 1947, a basic change was made in the plan. The over-all amount of profits to be shared by the company with its employees was raised from 25 per cent of net profit before taxes to 30 per cent of net profit before taxes. Twenty per cent of net profits is paid to the employee in cash under the original provision of the plan for the annual bonus and 10 per cent of net profits is paid into a fund to provide for pensions. (For details, see the profit-sharing clause in the most recent contract, which is reproduced in Appendix B, *Case Study No. 11.*)

It was felt that, in effect, the employer contributed 5 per cent and the employee contributed 5 per cent to the pension plan. Some criticisms are voiced against the new arrangement. Pensions are intended as a guaranteed financial security for the old and retired worker, but tied to profits, pensions in this plan are not guaranteed. One of the company's main answers to this is that it is financially impossible to provide pensions in any other way. Also, it is felt that if there are profits, pensions will be good; if there are none, in the long run, other types of pension plans will also be meaningless. Some of the workers feel that under this arrangement, they have some control over the size of their pension, inasmuch as they help determine profits. Another weakness of the pension plan lies with the older worker's status at the time the plan was adopted. Since individual accounts are kept, there is no way for the older worker to make up credit for his years of service before the plan was adopted.

In thirteen years, employees have received almost $2.4 million as their share of profits. The size of the yearly share for each worker has fluctuated from 11 per cent to 39 per cent of his annual pay. (A statistical record of profits and profit-sharing amounts from 1940 through 1952 appears in Table 5 of *Case Study No. 11.*)

The worker in this plant who does not produce his share is in trouble with his fellow employees. The union complains to management if it does not feel things are being handled effectively and economically. Costly overtime is something that not only management worries about, but that the union also tries to avoid. The profit picture is presented to the union every month. When profits are lagging, every employee gets to work to improve the situation.

Wage Increases

Total wages before profit sharing paid at American Velvet increased from about $290,000 in 1940 to $1.3 million in 1952. Both figures are approximately one-fourth of sales for the respective year. In this same period, average hourly earnings before profit sharing rose from 60.5 cents to $1.579 per hour. (Table 6 in *Case Study No. 11* shows wages and hourly averages paid at American Velvet from 1940 through 1951; and increases effected in the past 10 years are also listed on page 28 of the original study.)

The method of wage payment is for the most part on a straight piece-work basis. The systems of wage payment and job classification have remained uncomplicated. While there are advantages in simplicity, it seems that piece rates, work load, and allowances have been permitted to get out of line. However, the union and management are trying to correct this.

Grievance Procedures

Grievance handling is informal, although the contract contains a standard four-step procedure. No grievance has ever been reduced to writing and none has reached the arbitration stage. Because of the informality, it is difficult to discover how many grievances are settled at the various levels. It appears that most are settled at the lower levels, although some have gone to the company president before all other lower steps were fully utilized. While this latter method has been welcomed by the union and has led to prompt settlement, it has the disadvantage of denying to lower levels in management and the union valuable experience in dealing with each other, and the company also has paid a price in terms of the foreman's loss of prestige. Management is attempting to improve this condition. Regular meetings of foremen have been started with the objective of strengthening their position.

Company rules and regulations are informal: "No smoking" in designated areas only is the one formal rule with prescribed punishment for violation. A large amount of self-discipline is exercised. Again, this informal, direct approach by top management has brought successful results, although some foremen feel that more authority to discipline and discharge should be delegated to them. The small size of the organization has a great deal of bearing on this subject.

Communications and Consultation

The keynote in communications at American Velvet, as in most activities there, is informality. The size of the organization makes it possible for the president and other executives to know nearly everyone by his first name. While there are a number of more formal opportunities for communication, the big job of information sharing is done as these people meet, work, joke, and talk together.

Every morning at eight o'clock, the president of the company and his top echelon go through every department in the shop. It is not a hurried trip and they do not go as a group. Workers have no fear or resentment when they see top management coming; rather, this presents an opportunity for all to talk to the boss, offer ideas, or lodge complaints. And the questions are often put by the president and other executives. Management officials operate in this same manner among themselves. There are no barriers between departments or individuals. When a problem arises, it is everyone's problem.

A unique group known as the "Pops' Committee" operates as a top adviser to both the company and union. This committee is made up of all the former presidents of Local 110, although some are now in supervisory jobs. It has no authority to make, install, or change existing regulations or conditions. Most of its members have worked in the mill for at least twenty years, and thus have a long background of varied experience on which to draw. This committee concerns itself with production, finance, labor relations, and in fact, with almost any problem that presents itself. It is not only called in on differences between the company and union, but also when there is a difference between company executives. The "Pops' Committee" has been effective and has contributed to industrial peace. Both union and company have a great deal of respect and confidence in its recommendations and opinions.

Rapid expansion and the development of new fabrics during the last ten years brought problems which expressed themselves in such things as excess overtime in some departments and none in others, piecework rates that were out of line because of changing methods and equipment, and poorly balanced work loads. When some of these basic problems multiplied, the "Pops' Committee" initiated a committee called the "Planning Board." Three members of the "Pops' Committee," who were also union members, were requested to meet with three members from management to investigate and study all of these inequities. The board is purely advisory. It makes on-the-job studies and gets the opinions and advice of affected workers and their supervisors, then it makes suggestions to the "Pops' Committee" and to the union's shop committee and management in their regular meetings. Normal labor-management procedures are followed in putting any of the board's recommendations into effect. In making use of this joint board, management feels that it is respecting and recognizing the union as an interested party, responsible enough to participate actively in establishing and developing an efficient and equitable program of production.

The union has received and distributed information to the employees or discussed and settled problems before the foremen have known about them. As in the case of grievance handling, top management has seemingly become aware of this condition. Many complainants feel that the regular meetings of foremen have already improved the situation. While these meetings, in themselves, do not correct the foremen's problems as the forgotten man, they are an important medium of communications and a potential cause of industrial peace.

The shop committee of Local 110 is the official arm of the union which meets with management. It is at these meetings that grievances are hammered out, contracts negotiated, and all the natural functions of such a committee performed. As is true in most meetings, people disagree and occasionally tempers run hot. But here, too, basic mutual trust and co-operation are present. When a difference of opinion occurs, it is not always between management and labor. Often management officials disagree with each other, or part of the shop committee is on one side of the fence and the rest on the other. The meetings provide a picture of free men and women, expressing their opinions and convictions as they see them. They seem concerned with what is right and fair, and are involved in a free exchange of information which has resulted in decisions to benefit all.

Some people undoubtedly think this company has been too submissive in its relationship with the union. Others feel that the union is too easy to get along with and has in many cases accepted responsibilities that ordinarily would remain with the company. The relationship has, in the final analysis, benefited the company, the employees, and the community.

For the Future, What?

Since profit sharing has been in effect at American Velvet, business has been good. There have been profits to share. What will happen when there are losses to share? The workers at American Velvet say, "Workers have always shared losses in terms of unemployment." Both management and labor feel that their relationship and their profit-sharing plan will survive bad times if they come.

Clarence Wimpfheimer has been so instrumental and responsible for the present relationship that one wonders if it would continue without him. Although he is the leader, it appears that management people generally are proud of their part in building the relationship and will work for its continuance. The only son of the president, Jacques Wimpfheimer, is treasurer of the company and is already carrying on in his father's footsteps. He is liked and respected not only by the employees but by his associates in management.

Another test of this relationship will come if competition forces the company to go from its four-loom system to six looms. It seems inevitable that this test will come. Some competitors are already operating on the increased loom system, and it was just such an increase that caused the major breakdown of the relationship in 1938.

This and other tests will in time be answered by the parties. It is up to management and labor, by continued application of the philosophies and actions that have built this sound relationship, to prove that industrial peace can survive the problems that the future will undoubtedly present.

A Postscript

Since April 1953, when this study was issued, the relationship between the company and union has continued to be dynamic, and the causes of peace remain the same. New problems have arisen and solutions have been worked out. A constant effort is made to better the relationship and promote general understanding at the plant by improving existing techniques and seeking new ways of working together. One example of this effort is the recently instituted plan to send production foremen out with salesmen to meet customers, so that the foremen can learn at first hand the customers' problems and needs. In return, the salesmen are brought into the plant to learn the manufacturing processes and problems. In sum, the situation continues healthy and the underlying causes of peace remain in operation at American Velvet.

CHAPTER 18

Atlantic Steel Company
and the Steelworkers (CIO)

GLENN W. GILMAN and JAMES W. SWEENEY, *both of the School of Industrial Management, Georgia Institute of Technology, are authors of NPA Case Study No. 12. Their full report, condensed in this chapter, was published in November 1953.*

A commonly held concept of right and wrong underlies the productive, steadily improving relationship between Atlantic Steel Company and Local 2401 of the United Steelworkers of America (CIO). The explanation of this stable and profitable relationship lies mainly in the fact that the union has never fought over the principle of collective bargaining as such, but from the start has viewed the union as a means to an end—the settlement of labor-management issues on the basis of a plant-wide moral code.

THE ENVIRONMENT

Atlantic Steel is located in a section of well-kept residences and schools in the heart of Atlanta, Georgia, one of the South's major cities. When ground for the plant was broken in 1901, it was in a wooded area outside of town. Today one can drive ten miles north from the plant's gates and still be within a metropolitan area. If the plant's physical environment is unusual for a steel installation, so is the city's labor relations environment different from the sort one would expect to produce Local 2401.

American Federation of Labor locals for many years have been accepted within the pattern of Atlanta's economic life, and the Railway Brotherhoods are strong. But industrial unionism of the kind which came after the Wagner Act is not indigenous to the Gate City of the South. Three large automobile assembly plants and several nationally owned packing houses bargain collectively with CIO locals. The AFL's International Association of Machinists, born in Atlanta as a craft union, has returned as an industrial union to represent the workers in a huge aircraft plant. All of these, however, represent what has amounted to transplantation of collective bargaining into the local scene by agreements arrived at in Detroit, Chicago, or Los Angeles, between top representatives of national corporations and national unions.

There are also a number of small plants that are organized under industrial unions, but they are neither individually nor collectively significant as employers of industrial labor. The two large textile mills within the city are nonunion, as are a great many smaller manufacturing concerns of various types. Organizing is ordinarily resisted to the full extent permitted under the Taft-Hartley Act, and a strike is almost always necessary (and not always successful) in getting a contract.

Only at Atlantic Steel is there an industrial local of significant size that has been essentially a native product from the beginning. It did not ride into being on the coattails of the great organizing drive of the Steel Workers Organizing Committee in 1937 and 1938, but was a grassroots movement. The existence of a healthy union-management relationship in a labor climate where the attitude is apathetic at best and more often antipathetic is not easily explained. However, certain regional influences permit understanding not only of the relationship at Atlantic Steel, but of the prevailing attitude of the industrial Southeast toward present-day industrial unionism.

The core of Atlanta's population has been drawn mainly from the Piedmont Plateau of the southern Appalachian Highlands—the industrial area of the Southeast. The Piedmont's role in the Southeast, socially, politically, and economically, has been as significant regionally as it has been unrecognized nationally. The Piedmont is part of the South; yet it is not, nor has it ever been, what the nonsoutherner thinks of as typically southern. Before and after the Civil War, it was made up of small, largely self-sufficient family-owned and operated farms. The tide of immigration, mainly from the north and west, into the Piedmont virtually ceased after 1830. Since then, five generations of living together, of solving common problems with a gradually developing set of common traditions and customs, of developing a common way of looking at the world, have led to the striking homogeneity of the Piedmont's people.

Sociologists have for many years tried to distinguish between two major types of social organization. The first grows out of the society itself; it is informal, implicit. The second, formal and explicit, is to a degree imposed upon the society. The informal type takes its particular shape and growth because of the possibility of cooperative action based on understanding, the fitting together of individual lines of action resulting from each being aware of the subjective intentions of the others. The formal type is based upon the necessity of obtaining cooperation through conformity to a set of objective rules and regulations, under conditions where mutual knowledge of individual intentions is either impossible or difficult. The informal organization tends to be dynamic; its traditions and customs are not written down, and thus change imperceptibly as conditions change. The written-down rules and laws of the formal social organization tend to assume a static character, since they must be as deliberately changed as they were deliberately formulated.

The society of the Piedmont is typically informal. The people of the Piedmont feel uncomfortable, strange, and out of context in a social atmosphere that is predominantly formal and impersonal. A second characteristic of importance to labor relations in the Piedmont has been imparted by the flavor of the frontier which still lingers. Such concepts as self-respect, self-reliance, respect for the rights of others, willingness to cooperate—praised in the folk tales and lauded in the folk songs—have become the standard against which all else must be measured, even if that standard may not always be followed by the individual. To both management and the work force, a union appears as the advance guard of an alien form of society. Management officials in the Piedmont object to unions on economic grounds quite as strenuously as they do anywhere; but the strength of their resistance lies in the fact that they and their work forces, while differing on economic grounds, tend to agree as to the undesirable role of the union. Piedmont work forces are likely to welcome the union only when the understanding that underlies the informal organization of themselves and management into a single unit disappears. The story of Atlantic Steel and Local 2401 is a story of how this came about.

The Company

Atlantic Steel Company, employing approximately 2000 employees of which 1800 are in the bargaining unit, is an independent manufacturer of semifinished and finished steel products. The majority of its stock for many years has been closely held by one family which has no other connection with the steel industry. This small company depends on versatility, service, and a quality product in an industry dominated by industrial giants.

A wide variety of operations is carried out in the company's installations, including its three 75-ton open-hearth furnaces, a new 60-ton electric furnace; a blooming and a billet mill; rod, hoop, and wire mills. The principal share of Atlantic's ingots goes into items ready for consumer use, but it also sells general-purpose carbon steel in semifinished stages. The company's willingness to make up special orders involving nonstaple stock, in quantities that would not interest larger steel companies, sometimes has meant the difference between the year's profit and loss. In addition to its own forging, fabricating, and galvanizing, the company performs these services on custom orders in a manufacturing department, and its warehouse sales division carries noncompeting basic and fabricated products of other steel companies to round out its line.

History of the Company

The Atlanta Steel Hoop Company, predecessor of Atlantic Steel, was started in 1901 by eight Atlantans—three bankers, two real estate men, one doctor, one lawyer, and one manufacturer of tin plate and metal products. As owners, they were seeking dividends, but they also were keenly interested in finding a way to keep Georgia money at home. Although equity capital was always hard to find in sufficiently large amounts, the company constantly expanded. It shared in the general prosperity during the latter half of the twenties, and with the rest of basic steel, slid into the cellar during 1930, 1931, and 1932. Even so, the financial position of the company remained sound during the depression years, and in 1933 it climbed out of the red.

Beginning in 1933, the company was able to get back on a relatively steady production schedule, though it was occasionally necessary to borrow money for payrolls while the warehouses were crammed with unsold stock. A continuing program of expansion and product diversification was undertaken, along with an aggressive search for new markets; and by 1940 production had reached 139,322 tons per year. The output of ingots did not increase greatly during the war years; but after 1945 it began to expand once more, reaching 200,826 tons in 1950. This is the limit of its open-hearth capacity. A new electric furnace, added in early 1952, is expected to increase melting potential by another 90,000 tons per year.

There has been a high degree of continuity at Atlantic Steel's top level of management. T. K. Glenn served as president from 1908 to 1922 and as chairman of the board from 1922 until his death in 1946. Robert Gregg, who succeeded Mr. Glenn as president, left Atlantic Steel in 1932.

He was followed by Charles F. Stone, who became the incumbent chairman of the board in 1947, when Robert S. Lynch, now president, assumed that office.

"Community relations" as a deliberate program was begun only in 1945, but Atlantic Steel's directors and top management have always been active in civic life. Since the company started its planned public relations program, community activities have been jointly undertaken with Local 2401. Together they assume responsibility for a particular civic or charitable project or drive and share the credit for its success. This united front has tied Atlantic Steel even more firmly into the total community, and has earned the community's respect for the Steelworkers.

The Company's Competitive Position

Basic steel is a classic example of an industry oriented to raw materials, but Atlantic Steel was deliberately oriented to markets—steel bands for cotton bales, steel hoops for turpentine casks at the start—and it has remained so. Limestone, coal, and pig iron must be shipped in from some distance by rail. This raises costs considerably over Alabama competitors which have raw materials close at hand and are almost as centrally located with regard to the regional market. Local resources in scrap iron and steel are now sufficient for the company's needs, but even here it must bid competitively against northern firms.

Since steel is an industry in which labor costs amount to almost 50 per cent of the total value added by manufacture, economies effected in the labor cost per unit of output have a considerable bearing on competitive position. For a number of years, the company was able to compensate partly for its high-cost location by a low wage differential. Since 1941, however, the wage differential, under direct and persistent attack by the union, has been considerably reduced; in many jobs it no longer exists. Atlantic Steel still performs many operations manually that are automatic in more modern installations, but it is undertaking an expensive modernization program. Reduction of unit cost by increasing production is no longer possible, since the soaking pits, blooming mill, and billet mill are bottlenecks that can be removed only by major capital investments. The ratio of labor to total cost, therefore, is higher for Atlantic Steel than for most of its competitors who have more modern plants. This means that factors which encourage the work force to use their skills to optimum advantage are of even more importance to the survival of Atlantic Steel than to its competitors generally.

The People in the Work Force

Statistical breakdowns of the work force by age groups, ethnic groups, educational levels, place of origin, and so on, are not kept at Atlantic Steel, apparently reflecting the company's policy that employees are to be treated as individuals instead of a mass to be analyzed and dealt with categorically. The attitude toward the ethnic composition of the work force illustrates this point. The writers estimated that approximately 30 per cent of the employees are Negro, and management and union officials agreed that this was probably correct, but neither showed any interest in checking its validity. They are interested in whether a particular job is held by a Negro or a white man, for the company abides by regional traditions to a degree. But on the job, a man is judged by his performance rather than by his color. While there is no mixing of whites and Negroes at the same job level within a particular work group, there is a tendency to substitute Negro workers for white workers in a mixed group, and to substitute groups of Negroes for groups of white workers, with no change in pay scales. Not only are Negroes paid the same rates paid to white men for the same work, but their pay scale is relative to the plant rather than to other lower rates in the area.

The great bulk of the employees of Atlantic Steel, white and Negro, have come from the Piedmont farms. A small but highly important nucleus of skilled steelworkers from outside the Atlanta area, who have had to be brought in from time to time, includes fairly similar ethnic backgrounds. The main difference is that recruits from neighboring farms have never worked for a steel company, or for any other company, for that matter. Most of the white and Negro workers have been brought up in Baptist, Methodist, or Presbyterian homes, and the majority are conscientious though not zealous church members. Thus they tend to resolve every situation in similar terms of what is right and what is wrong.

THE UNION

The Steelworkers Union was preceded by two short-lived AFL locals. The Amalgamated Sheet Metal Workers International Alliance in 1906 got a contract, but internal difficulties in the local and the company's failure to renew a contract in 1907 led to its demise. In 1918, the Amalgamated was revived, but again died a quick death after a strike that was not supported by the international. Apparently the company was not happy about the union in either period, but took no active steps to hinder it. The main difficulty seemed to be that there was not sufficient union sentiment among the workers to nurture a local and no real knowledge of the function of a union.

Organization of Local 2401

The great organizing drives in "Big Steel" and "Little Steel" by-passed Atlantic Steel. However, a nucleus of employees, made up largely of the skilled men who had come into the plant from outside the area, watched with interest what was taking place elsewhere; and the idea of a union at Atlantic Steel began to be talked about seriously by employees as a solution to plant problems. The company was aware of what was going on, and its opposition was somewhat more active than in the old Amalgamated's time. A staid and conservative management sincerely saw in the CIO a foreign organization that was attempting to destroy the foundations of free American enterprise.

The center of organization was in the mechanical department, which contained the highest percentage of skilled workers and outsiders, and the hoop and rod mills were also well represented. The company made several tactical errors—one when it granted a raise in the mechanical department before the workers' pending petition for it had been presented, but raised wages only for workers in that department. This gave credence to claims that the company was trying to buy off the organizers. These unofficial organizers recognized this as a strategic time to invite in professional talent to capitalize on the company's tactical mistake. Thus, late in 1940, an SWOC organizer finally arrived at Atlantic Steel.

Organization still moved slowly. An NLRB election gave the union a seven to one majority, but there were only 114 dues-paying members in the early fall of 1941 out of a bargaining unit of 1102 employees, and 60 per cent of the members were Negroes. The company was not disposed to come to terms with the union and negotiations were getting nowhere. The local decided that its only hope lay in drastic measures. Against advice that a strike without the open hearth, blooming mill, and the yard department (all strategic sections in which there were practically no members) would be suicidal, the local went on strike in October 1941. It shut down everything except the open hearth and blooming mill, which continued to operate.

Two explanations are offered as to why there was such a small membership compared with the NLRB vote. The most common reason given by management officials and workers is that most employees were in sympathy with the union, but hesitated to say so openly. One union official believed, however, that the bulk of the people were loyal neither to the company nor to the union. Relations, he said, had degenerated to "every man for himself," and many employees were hoping to cash in as strikebreakers.

Before the election the company had said that if a strike resulted from the union's recognition, it would keep the plant open. It promised to bring in food so that employees could remain inside the gate and receive pay for 24 hours a day for the duration of the strike. The company carried out this plan. Better than half the plant went out initially, but people began trickling back immediately, prepared to stay inside the gates for the duration. Six weeks later when the strike ended, nearly the entire plant was operating, manned by many employees who had voted for union representation.

The company could have broken the local had it remained adamant in its opposition. The decision to offer the union a contract seems to have stemmed from the top echelon of management. Union representatives who took part in the initial collective bargaining feel that the president was disposed to deal with the union before the strike, but that the strong antiunion attitude of the rest of top and middle management caused him to hesitate. When the strike demonstrated that a group of a little more than a hundred men could cripple the plant, the seriousness of the situation was brought home to the board of directors, dominated by T. K. Glenn as chairman. It became apparent that the company would eventually be organized. The board was more concerned with the possibly disastrous long-range economic effect of continuing efforts to break the union than with the short-range satisfaction of crushing it; and it threw its weight behind the president, Mr. Stone, rather than the other officials whose views were more in line with the personal beliefs of the board's members.

The local's membership grew slowly but steadily. Only 60 per cent of the employees were dues-paying members by 1945. By 1947, the check-off list included 75.6 per cent of the bargaining unit, and two years later the figure had increased to 86 per cent, with about 4 per cent of the members paying dues directly. At present, only 10 per cent of the employees have remained out of the union; some are the oldest employees who have never become reconciled to unionization and the others are new employees.

The Local Today

Through the years, the union leaders have proved to be remarkably capable of adapting to changing circumstances. Harry Perkerson, president of the local, and Earl Black, chairman of the plant grievance committee, were moving spirits of the early organization drive. Several years of arm's-length bargaining, from 1941 to 1945, served as a training period for the union's officers and departmental representatives. These union men who were able to take care of rank-and-file members when sharp trading and table pounding were the order of the day, have proved equally capable of cooperative action and a logical, reasonable, and nonemotional approach.

The local is democratic. All questions of any importance are brought before the membership at biweekly meetings, and opportunity for full discussion is permitted before a vote is taken. No evidence of steam-roller tactics was observed at any of the meetings attended by the writers, and every effort is made to get the membership out to meetings. A typical meeting will find only 7 per cent to 10 per cent of the available membership present, but during a three-month period probably 30 per cent of the membership will have been present at one or more meetings. Attendance increases considerably when matters of plant-wide importance are on the agenda.

The local has had four presidents since its organization, and there seems to be no desire on the part of the present officers to perpetuate themselves in power. The continuity of leadership in the union has been accompanied by a policy of encouraging younger men to become departmental committeemen, in order to provide a constant supply from which the top offices can be filled. The resulting consistency in point of view and the gradually changing top leadership give an impression, which management comments substantiate, that the union is essentially stable and responsible.

No internal "political" problems plague the local. There were opposing points of view on major issues and debate in the union hall quite often became vehement, but there did not appear to be any group that consistently aligned itself on one side or another of the issue or consistently opposed the elected officials. At election time, contests are on an individual basis; there are no slates of candidates.

The greatest problem of internal organization which the union faces is the danger that the local could split up into a number of small groups representing various crafts and trades, or for skilled men to line up in opposition to the semiskilled and unskilled workers. So far this has never developed, partly because of swift and intelligent handling of grievances that might result in cleavages and partly because the union emphasizes the importance of presenting a united front when dealing with the company.

The union does not have a race problem. The Negro members of the work force have always been strong supporters of the local. The union was firm during the early years of collective bargaining on the elimination of the Negro-white wage differential between men doing the same level of work. There is no evidence of bloc voting among the Negro members, nor of any attempt to persuade them to vote that way. Formal segregation is not practiced in union meetings, although there is informal segregation in seating, reflecting the habitual practice in Atlanta. The local accepts the policies of segregation that are practiced at the plant in deference to southern mores, but puts all its resources behind an employee who has been subjected to individual discrimination because of his color, and it works toward expanding job opportunities for Negroes.

Union Security

The union shop is forbidden by Georgia law. The contract contains only a provision that the company will present two application forms for check-off of dues to each new employee; if he wishes to sign them, one copy is forwarded to the union and the other goes into the company files. The local is satisfied with this arrangement. Actually, for the past few years the local has had what amounts to a union shop. Whereas management has not formally adopted a policy of recommending that new employees join the union, many superintendents and general foremen take it upon themselves to do so. They feel that it is better to have all the workers in the union than some in and some out, and they tell new employees to join the union because it is representing them and they should support it, and further that they should attend meetings so they will know "what's going on." They point out, however, that no one should pressure the old-timers who do not want to join.

Some new employees who come from nonunion or antiunion backgrounds remain unconvinced that they should join what they consider to be a radical organization, even after encouragement from company officials. If so, their fellow workers take over the task of converting them, and they are usually successful.

Local Autonomy

An unusual degree of autonomy is possessed by this local. Through an oversight, Local 2401 rather than the CIO's SWOC was named on the ballot in 1941 as the bargaining agent. As a result, the local rather than

SWOC was certified by the NLRB as official bargaining agent for the unit. It was not until 1950 that a new certification election was held to correct this.

Legally, Local 2401 was an independent union. The company was not required to recognize international representatives, nor to admit them to bargaining conferences, but it has always done so. The local was a member of the United Steelworkers of America, paid its per capita tax, and had the services of a field representative. But the contracts between the local and company were not subject to review by the international, and became valid as soon as they were signed by company officials and locals. The local still does not consider its contract as mere confirmation of an agreement in which the basic points have been worked out in the Pittsburgh area. Its contract is so untypical of the usual collective bargaining agreement signed in the steel industry that for the local to follow more than the broad lines of national bargaining in the industry would require a major revision of its whole contractual relationship.

The local's relation to the international is one of voluntary cooperation rather than of dependency. It answers a national strike call, not because it is taking orders, but because it believes in the necessity for a united front when important issues are to be resolved between labor and management.

Preparation for protracted annual bargaining sessions creates no problem for this local. This is because contract deficiencies are adjusted as they appear, either by side agreements, supplemental agreements, or amendments. If a problem cannot be handled as a grievance, it is bargained out over the conference table, with no consideration as to whether it must be deferred until some later, stipulated date. Both the union and the company have conducted bargaining according to the spirit rather than the letter of the contract since before 1945; but when it is impossible to stretch the contract to cover a particular problem, both parties think the reasonable solution is to change the contract. Between June 12, 1945, and August 4, 1948, for example, the contract was amended ten times and four supplemental agreements were added.

DEVELOPMENT OF THE RELATIONSHIP

Mature collective bargaining, which began about 1946, was preceded by two periods which managerial and hourly-rated people alike refer to in explaining the current relationship. One was the period of individual bargaining, from 1901 to 1941; the next the period of transition, from 1941 to 1946.

Individual Bargaining: 1901–1941

Top management, the skilled people, and the country boys built the plant together. There was no formal personnel policy, few rules and regulations. But there gradually developed an accepted way of doing things and every man had and knew his place and function. Any particular managerial decision might appear completely unilateral, but actually it was not announced until there had been a realistic and for the most part unconscious rehearsal of its probable impact upon the people. Both management and the work force were able to orient their actions in terms of their knowledge of the other's probable responses.

This continued during most of the 1920's. However, there is not unanimous agreement among employees who were familiar with the period as to the satisfactory nature of that informal relationship. This is particularly true when the question of favoritism is raised. The majority of the long-service employees say that there was little favoritism. "We were like one big family in those days," one of them recalls nostalgically. But a few men declare that favoritism was rampant. "There were always these kingpins in every department. They weren't foremen or even lead men, but everybody was supposed to kowtow to them. When management wanted to know something, they'd come straight to them. They'd take their word against anybody." Both groups are telling the truth as they saw it. The key lies in the phrase "one big family." This was the strength of the early relationship and the seed of its later weakness.

As the company grew older and increased in size, the point was inevitably reached at which family relationships could no longer encompass the entire employee group. Continuance of the highly informal, yet powerful, folk type of relationship came to mean that there was one group in the family and one outside it. It continued to be a good relationship for those who belonged. It was frustrating to those who did not.

The developing rift initially was caused by the lack of an adequate training program within the company, rather than the increased size of the company. The young country boys who started at the lowest level when they came in accepted and were accepted by the informal organization. But as need arose for highly skilled workers, there were few men available within the plant who could fill the requirements. Outside craftsmen came to the plant justly proud of their skills. They saw no reason why it should be necessary for them to kowtow to the informal leaders of the work group, to the elders of the tightly knit informal organization. But they learned that ability was not enough; for management maintained its informal contacts with the elders and relied upon their advice as to who should receive promotions. Able men, not in the family, were passed over in favor of less capable men with less seniority who belonged.

This situation, to which a number of factors were added in the 1930's, brought about the collapse of the folk relationship. First, the depression disturbed the faith of many people in their individual ability to cope with all eventualities. The company struggled to stay open. It instituted a share-the-work program, then the plant went on three days a week, and then two. Wages were cut, and cut again. For a while the plant closed down entirely, with only a skeleton crew of supervisory people remaining. The company was resolved that none of its people should go hungry or seek relief, and the personal fortunes of its owners and top management were used to help employees. But the people of Atlantic Steel did not want charity, they wanted jobs.

At the first hint that the turning point in the depression had been reached, the plant got under way again. When there were no orders on hand, production went into the warehouses. Before 1930, the president had been in the plant and, directly and through the general superintendent, had maintained an uncomplicated and effective line of communication with the people. During the 1930's, Mr. Stone concentrated on finding markets and developing more diversified products. The principal responsibility for the maintenance of employee relations fell upon N. C. Harrison, the vice-president in charge of operations.

Between 1935 and 1940, the work force doubled. Even had the workers still constituted a family, it would have been much too large for one man to keep in touch, and Mr. Harrison had less time for direct communication than his predecessors, as he dealt with an expanding firm and new products, the development of a more complicated management structure, related responsibilities. Mr. Harrison was an old-timer with the company and he turned to other old employees whose judgment he trusted to keep him informed on how people felt about things. Unfortunately, these elders grew increasingly less representative of the work force as a whole and less aware of the workers' actual attitudes. Mr. Harrison unknowingly was formulating employee policy on an unrealistic image of the work force. The old-timers felt he was fair-minded, just, and dependable. To others, his actions often seemed to be arbitrary, whimsical, illogical, and unpredictable.

An even more disturbing element hastened the breakdown of the informal structure. Not only did skilled men in the hourly-rated group come in from outside, but supervisory people at various levels were imported.

Some men were promoted from the ranks, but many of these lacked ability, experience, and proper training. The importees were competent, but were not acquainted with the existing unwritten body of policy and practice. And the people who had been brought up in the relationship were so close to it that they could not explain it or the things that made it work. The newcomers operated on the basis of policies developed elsewhere, which remained as mysterious to the workers under their direction as was the "way we do things at Atlantic Steel" a mystery to them. Thus the methods of the foremen from each group seemed arbitrary and illogical to the other as well as to workers. Almost every employee interviewed agreed that there was considerable favoritism during the 1930's, but there is not agreement as to who played favorites. There were undoubtedly some "bull-of-the-woods" foremen, but in many cases reliance on coercive measures to maintain discipline was probably the last resort of frustrated foremen who could not set up effective communication with their people along more reasonable lines.

Another factor served to atomize the work force. It was a tendency, which previously had been held in check by the unifying symbols of Mr. Glenn and then Mr. Gregg in the plant, for each department to regard itself as sovereign in a little realm all its own. "There wasn't just one company here before 1945. There were a whole lot of little companies. There were 'fences' between every department. If you happened to get outside your own department, everybody looked at you with suspicion."

Talk of a union, resulting from this atmosphere of bewilderment and frustration, for a while contributed even more to the disunity. Higher wages and shorter hours were seldom mentioned as basic causes of the unrest leading to eventual unionization. They were only something hoped for in addition to a more important objective. The clue is in the description of what was wrong before the union. Favoritism, patronage, and partiality—these words were heard over and over. The people seemed to be looking for re-establishment of a situation in which they could predict where they stood.

Top management's opposition to unionization, though forceful, seems to have been honest and open. The ringleaders of the union groups were well known and management attempted to bluff them into abandoning their activity; but the bluffs were called and discharges did not follow. The emotional content of the opposition increased in the lower ranks of management and in the work force, where there was a sizable antiunion group. The active organizers remember this as a period of intense conflict; but as the writers compare their accounts with organizational campaigns conducted elsewhere, it seems never to have degenerated to a "no-holds-barred" struggle. This is in spite of the fact that a number of organizations in this antiunion community expressed disapproval of the activities of Atlantic Steel employees who were attempting to form the local.

Transition: 1941–1946

Relations during the strike in the fall of 1941 seem to have been marked more by the expectation of violence than by actual violence. The fact that strikebreakers stayed inside the gates around the clock reduced the possibility of conflict on the picket line. The only actual violence occurred the first day of the strike, when a bread truck and a milk truck attempting to deliver food to the plant cafeteria were overturned. After that, the Atlanta police were constantly on the scene. There were fist fights and a great deal of name calling back and forth across the fence, which did not help relations afterward. But when one considers that emotions were at high pitch, and a great many of the people on either side had come from gun-totin' backgrounds, the strike was conducted with remarkable restraint. As nearly as can be gathered, this arose from the healthy respect that each side had for the other. Responsible leadership on each side seemed intuitively aware of the limits within which the conflict had to be contained.

The company demonstrated its ability to run the plant despite the efforts of the union; it made 17,000 tons of steel while the pickets were at the gates. But the union got its contract. A peace treaty had been signed by top management and union officials, but a continuing guerrilla warfare was being carried on at lower levels. A large group among lower and middle management felt that the union could eventually be shaken loose, and their policy was shaped by this belief. The union knew that it had to have the support of a majority of the work force and at least the grudging acceptance of on-the-spot management before it could relax its militant attitude.

Both management and the work force were divided among themselves. A minority group among the superintendents, general foremen, and turn foremen felt that the company should stop fighting the union and devote major attention to the business of making steel. Much more production was lost, however, because of the rift among hourly-rated workers who had declared sides during the strike. Group incentives were in use in some departments and individual incentives in others, but for both kinds of operation, informal cooperation between members of the work groups was necessary to obtain satisfactory earnings for everyone. But "the union men wouldn't help the 'scabs' make money. They'd take a short pay check themselves before they'd cooperate with the men who had stayed in." As a result, production suffered seriously from 1942 through 1945.

This continuing lack of cooperation was a spontaneous gesture on the part of the rank and file, which the union constantly battled. From the first, the union officers tried to remove animosities. They tried to attract the older men who had been sympathetic with the union until they had fallen out over the strategic value and timeliness of the strike. They worked at selling the union to the people who had been apathetic during the organizing period, and they got in touch with new employees. They fought as hard for nonunion employees as for members when they were authorized to do so.

The company appointed a member of its sales staff as personnel director, and his office was soon overwhelmed with grievances. Bargaining over these reflected the character of the relationship during this period: general suspicion, delay, horse-trading, and dissatisfaction on both sides. The company attempted to short-circuit the grievance procedure, urging aggrieved workers to carry troubles directly to their turn foremen. The union, frustrated by delays in settlement of the grievances that it presented, fell back on direct and simple methods when more peaceful means failed. Departments were shut down or slowed down for an hour or two. Occasionally, the union extended the stoppage or slowdown to the entire mill for a full shift or even for a day before the company agreed to bargain out the issue. There are no official records of work stoppages at Atlantic Steel between the local strike in 1941 and the industry-wide strike of 1946, but there were a number during that period.

The effectiveness of the departmental "quickie" or slowdown lay in the fact that the union used them with discrimination, only to back up a position when it was sure it was right. The question of what was morally right and wrong from the first was the yardstick against which the union measured company policies and practices. Union leaders had organized only because they saw injustices in the plant, and felt that the union would be a tool in correcting them. They wanted a union so they could continue to be self-respecting steelworkers. These men had little background in the formal aspects of unionism. To begin with, they had little more skill in interpreting the legalistic terms of their contract than did the rank and file. They respected their contract as a symbol of achievement, but felt much more sure of themselves in falling back upon moral principles when it came to deciding whether or not a man really had a case, and in presenting it.

This ethical approach to labor relations strengthened and solidified the union during the difficult transition years. Many nonunion workers who had suspected the union's basic motives found that the local was fighting for the same body of principles that they themselves held, and they came to believe that the union's policies were somewhat more realistic than those of the old family organization. Thus the local slowly enlisted the support of many of the men who had once been elders in the family. They were invaluable additions; once within the union, they supported it as staunchly as they had opposed it.

Reliance on the ethical code rather than upon the formal terms of the contract had still another advantage. This code was common to members of the union and management. Thus, forcing the settlement of an issue in terms of agreed-upon moral principles made it appear that principles were not involved. Discussion centered on the best policy by which these principles might be achieved, and increasingly over the facts involved in a particular case.

The Present Relationship

By the end of 1945, union leadership, though militant, had demonstrated responsibility; its officers and committeemen had become capable bargainers, and the membership had steadily grown; the parties were settling issues themselves, without the help of outsiders; they agreed generally on principles and were reaching agreements on the basis of facts; and smoldering but hidden resentments were brought into the open by the flood of grievances which were being diagnosed, if not cured.

Within eight months the company and the union undertook joint formulation of a contract provision designed for their mutual advantage. And by the end of 1946, despite the intervention of an industry-wide strike in which the union participated, it became evident that another era in industrial relations had begun for Atlantic Steel. This study—undertaken immediately after the 1952 strike in steel, and during a period further complicated by a change from two-turn and three-turn operations to three and four, and thus green crews—reveals that the accomplishments of the parties to this relationship have been solid and enduring, furnishing a substantial foundation for future labor peace.

Statistical Measures of the Relationship

Measurable results of the stable relationship are provided in four sets of data: figures on safety, turnover, absenteeism, and to a limited extent productivity. Both management and union indicate their conviction that joint efforts have brought about steady improvement in the records of these four important elements in steel, and they indicate that continued cooperation will maintain such results.

A marked decrease of the frequency and severity rates of accidents is attributed largely to the company's program of regular departmental safety meetings of workers and supervisors. These, with the union's enthusiastic support, not only are used to analyze and correct causes of accidents, but to eliminate safety hazards before accidents occur. (Table 1, *Case Study No. 12,* giving figures for frequency and severity rates for the years 1942–46 and 1950–52, shows a drop in the frequency rate from 17.12 to 4.59 and in the severity rate from 5.71 to 4.72.)

Turnover rates were affected in 1945–46 and again in 1950–51 by the changing military status of workers, but the record shows a steady decrease in the average monthly rate at Atlantic Steel during a period in which the company was increasing the size of the work force. Using 1945 as a base year, the average monthly rate had decreased by 80 per cent by 1952, while the work force had increased by 53 per cent. (Table 2 of *Case Study No. 12* presents data for 1945 through 1952.) Although many factors affect personnel turnover, a sharp drop in the rate from 1946 to 1947 tends to substantiate the company and union statements that the improvement in the industrial relationship contributed largely to this decrease. Both feel that the turnover rate will continue at about the 1951–52 levels, barring a change in the military *status quo* or in the present union-management relationship.

Absenteeism in a continuous operation steel plant, where much of the work is carried on by crews, is costly to the company and the work force. On August 6, 1946, the company and the union concluded a side agreement (incorporated into the 1952 contract) providing for the discharge of employees incurring three unexcused absences within any three-month period. This had an immediate effect. In 1945, the average weekly absentee rate was 13.62. During the last four months of 1946 after the absenteeism side agreement was made, the rate dropped to 6.86, a decrease of almost 50 per cent. The unexcused absence rate—always the most disruptive of production—of only 0.41 by 1953 represented an extremely significant increase in the efficiency of plant operations. (Table 3, *Case Study No. 12,* shows excused and unexcused absentee rates for 1945 through 1952.)

No data concerning employment productivity are kept at Atlantic Steel Company. However, since all the company's products are processed from ingot production, this is a rough measure of efficiency in the entire operation. From 1936 to 1951, no major technological changes were introduced nor were there any additions to the physical capacity of the furnaces or mills at Atlantic. During that period, any increase in the annual ingot production had to come about through minor technological changes, better scheduling and processes, and increased efficiency of the work force. Using 1940 as a base year, the annual output of steel ingots mounted steadily through 1950, with the exceptions of 1944 and the strike years of 1946 and 1949. Although it is not possible to determine how much of the increase resulted from management factors and how much from increased worker efficiency, all management persons, including Joe Girdler, vice-president in charge of operations, held that "a substantial part of the increase has been due to the improved industrial relations policy."

Catalysis for Peace

Labor relations changed with such speed, once moving, that one gets the impression of a catalytic response. The catalytic agent in this case was Robert Lynch. He came to Atlantic Steel in August of 1944 as general superintendent of operations, and by 1947 was president. Without exception, union and management people gave Mr. Lynch credit for the change which took place in labor relations between the fall of 1944 and the fall of 1946. Management people say: "He told us, 'the union's here to stay, and we might as well accept the fact and learn how to live with it.' . . . He taught us that we had to operate as an integrated company, that the finished product of one department was the raw stock of another. . . . He never made a promise he couldn't carry out. . . . He took the foremen into management. . . . He let us know what was going on; we knew where we stood."

Typical comments from people in the bargaining unit and from union officers included: "You could get a straight answer out of him; if he didn't know, he'd tell you so. . . . He figured the company was in business to make steel, not to fight the union. . . . There were a lot of times that he disagreed with us; but we knew where we stood with him. . . . He came up the hard way; he knows what a turn on the open hearth is like. We spoke the same language. . . . He told the supervisors right out that they couldn't expect the union to be fair with them if they weren't fair with the union. . . . He got out in the plant and got to knows us, and gave us a chance to get acquainted with him."

Yet despite the unanimous credit given Mr. Lynch, nearly all of management and the workers say the relationship is now sufficiently stable so that it would endure if he were to leave the company, but they stipulate that the man who replaced him would have to continue with essentially his same policies. As a matter of fact, Mr. Lynch has not had to participate actively in labor relations for the past two years; much of that work is now done by Forest Willingham, director of industrial relations.

Employees, when asked about the methods Mr. Lynch used, all agree that it was a gradual process of change, without spectacular achievements from one day to the next—no "methods," "formulas," "expert analysis," "scientific management." Apparently nothing was done that was foreign to the people or their ways, or they would have noted it and remembered; yet within a period of months people were working together who had been fighting; there was less defense of positions and more attention to problems. Many small bits of information from here and there give a picture of how this was accomplished.

"I didn't bring anything new into the plant," Mr. Lynch told one of his officials. "I worked with what I found here." During the first year he talked to everybody in the plant and tried to find out what they thought. He instituted a series of weekly conferences with the union officers, familiarizing himself with their points of view and their definitions of the nature of labor relations. Mr. Lynch considered it equally important, however, to give the people an opportunity to find out where he stood. He could not announce the details of future changes until he himself was sure of what was needed, but he could give them an indication of the general line of thinking he would bring to bear on specific cases in the future. He began to work toward the solution of problems that were of mutual interest to the company, the union, and the people.

The safety program was set up and Mr. Lynch attended the regular departmental safety meetings. "The safety meetings turned out to be mostly gripe sessions at first," a supervisor recalls. "Then, after the air finally got cleared, we began to accomplish something. I guess that was where we first began to get the idea that we were able to work together; and that the union could be helpful as well as a nuisance."

The joint attack on the next big problem, absenteeism, is often mentioned as the turning point in the relationship. Immediately after the war absenteeism increased sharply. The company tried to correct the problem in various ways, but both the company and responsible employees were suffering. The union asked for a conference with the company officials to see if some means could be worked out so that the irresponsible employees, who were losing pay for those who wanted to work, could be disciplined. The result was the August 1946 amendment on absenteeism.

Thus the union demonstrated almost immediate appreciation of the changing situation in top management. Mr. Lynch's policies were far from being unanimously supported by other people in top and middle management and the supervisory ranks, but he had the backing of the president and the board of directors. The union could begin to feel that finally it was achieving direct and effective communication with that level of the company at which policy was formulated.

When the union went out during the general steel strike in late 1946, there was a different feeling in the air. The company made no effort to operate during the strike, and Mr. Lynch saw to it that stoves were provided at which the pickets could warm themselves, and hot coffee was supplied to them from the company cafeteria. The union stayed out after the national settlement, since local bargaining could not get under way until the pattern had been set. The delay was also partly caused by a continuing difference of opinion in top management as to the necessity of accepting the union. The 18.5-cent wage increase in line with the national pattern, that was finally granted, symbolized the defeat of the antiunion element, and resignations were accepted from two of the vice-presidents. In June 1946, Mr. Lynch was elected vice-president as well as general superintendent; Mr. Harrison continued as vice-president in charge of operations until his retirement the following year. In 1947, Mr. Stone was elected chairman of the board to succeed Mr. Glenn, who had died during the previous October, and Mr. Lynch was made president.

"In 1946," an official of the company reports, "we felt that the members of the bargaining committee of the union were ready to work with us in attacking our production problems. The big question in our minds was how to get our foremen to go along." Training programs and weekly conferences for supervisory people were instituted. These conferences, too, began as gripe sessions, but ended on a more constructive note. The subject of labor relations was only one of a number of topics. The supervisors found out for the first time what was going on in the company; what kind of problems it faced; what management was trying to do about them. Mr. Lynch did not plead the cause of unionism. He merely pointed out that the men in the plant could make or break the company, and the union was their union; when management fought the union, it fought the men who were making the steel that kept the company alive.

Gradually the supervisory people too began to discover that getting along with the union entailed no change in their basic principles. A surprising number of the old supervisors were able to "retread," and in nearly every case, they did so in terms of conviction rather than mere compliance. "The union isn't much different now than it ever was," says one man in the upper level of management. "It's the company that has changed." This appears to be borne out by facts. There is no evidence anywhere along the line that the union has changed its basic policies since it signed its first contract in 1941.

As the relationship began to settle down and take shape, a new informal organization began to develop in the plant. It was not quite like the old one, for certain new techniques had been adopted. But it became evident that only the techniques, not the philosophy of mass social organization, had been adopted. This modified informal organization was not the union and its membership; *the union was the instrument* of the organization by which the people in the work force were able to maintain effective communication with management and thus again achieve reciprocal understanding.

Role of the Industrial Relations Director

The director of industrial relations, Forest Willingham, came with the company as an hourly-rated employee in 1911. He was a member of the old Amalgamated and participated in the unsupported strike in 1919. In sympathy with the union movement during the late thirties, he fell out with the leadership over the wisdom of the 1941 strike, but later was elected secretary of Local 2401 in 1943. Then he became a foreman in 1945; and in 1947 was appointed director of industrial relations by Joe Girdler, the vice-president in charge of operations.

Mr. Willingham had no instructions as to how he was to carry out his personnel responsibilities. He employs none of the standard techniques of personnel work. He knows the people in the plant and what problems of employee relations look like to the hourly-rated employee, the union officer, and the supervisor, and he has not forgotten how it felt on the lower rungs of the ladder. There are conflicting reports from employees and supervisory people as to the amount of his line authority. The matter of how much actual authority, however, is not significant, because his background and personal abilities are such that he is able to resolve disputes through a process of mediation and conciliation. He has a knack of ferreting out the basic issues in dispute, getting the parties to agree on what they are disagreeing about, and then getting them to agree on what is right and what is wrong. If a clause in the contract is useful, he refers to it, and one of his functions is to interpret the contract; but his interpretation is moral rather than legal. When there is no pertinent contract provision, he seeks a settlement by reminding the parties of pertinent factors on which they agree.

Neither management nor union regards Mr. Willingham as a company man. He is expected to base his actions on a frame of reference that encompasses both the company and the union. A member of top management, confirming this diagnosis of the director's role, pointed out that, "He must have a wide latitude if he is going to be able to function efficiently. He has to be able to take the side of the union as well as of the company. He is being paid to tell the company when it's wrong as well as to tell the employees when it's right."

Acceptance of the Relationship

Both management and the union accept the present relationship without question. Management is concerned mainly with how the union may be used as a positive force in the plant. This applies not only to areas in which cooperation of the union might be expected. A company vice-president says, "We regard the opposition of the union to a company policy or practice not as an obstacle, but as a further source of information which should be taken into consideration."

Nearly all the supervisory people are of the opinion that it is easier to maintain good employee relations with than without a union, though they generally qualified this by stating that this is true only when the union is of the responsible type enjoyed by Atlantic Steel. The few who said it would be easier without a union based their objection on only one count, the insistence of the union upon strict seniority in transfers and promotions. They also noted, however, that the union apparently appreciated management's difficulties in this respect and was trying to make seniority workable from the managerial point of view.

The union feels that its acceptance by the company is sincere: "There are still a few unreconstructed individuals around who would rather see us out than in; but they are exceptions. . . . The company may look like they're fighting the union sometimes, but usually they're just stalling until they can figure out what to do. They don't try any union-busting so far as I know. . . . This company has never had production like it's had the past few years since it stopped fighting the union. It's too smart to go back to the old way."

Both management and union people are inclined to believe that their relationship is better than in most companies, but every man interviewed on either side seemed to think the relationship could be improved. Confidence, not complacency, appears to mark the attitudes of both parties. Neither side is so confident, however, that it takes the other for granted; there is an alertness on both sides. A cooperative attitude on the part of the union can be depended upon only as the result of frank and objective delineation of the issues and problems by management. Management, too, is aware that the union is affiliated with the international, and that in certain cases issues cannot be resolved entirely in terms of the local situation.

Neither side assumes that satisfactory settlement of an issue at the policy level means that it will automatically be carried out satisfactorily. Their confidence becomes less categorical as they survey the lower levels of both hierarchies. It is significant, however, that neither the union nor the company is blamed for the deviations of the individual representing it. "If we didn't have a union, he'd be making a fuss over something else," says the company of the overzealous committeeman. The union says of the foreman who seems to have declared his own private war on the union, "He's just a punk who's too small for his job, and he thinks that if he makes enough noise, nobody will notice it."

The union is also aware that its desire to operate without a written and confining body of precedent means that it constantly must exercise vigilant control lest informal practices and private deals, detrimental to the over-all relationship, creep into the body of customary practice. The chairman of the union's plant-wide bargaining committee says, "The union will not accept as a precedent any grievance settled without union intervention."

The company is well satisfied with worker productivity under the relationship. "The man-hours per ton are higher at Atlantic Steel than they are at many new plants having heavy investments in modern capital equipment, but they have decreased steadily since 1945, up until last year. We're just about at our optimum output with the present plant," says a top company officer, and superintendents and general foremen are inclined to agree. There is no hesitancy in ascribing the high level of productivity to the spirit of cooperation now existing between the members of the work force, and the willingness of the union to go along with management on production problems.

The union is extremely interested in production and is likely to be somewhat more critical of production figures than is management. Its members feel that the company is not yet fully tapping their know-how in solving the practical production problems of the plant; and that even with present equipment, greater production is possible. The grievance sessions and negotiation meetings attended by the writers invariably turned into conferences over production problems; but the union wants a greater opportunity to help solve production problems in a somewhat more organized manner.

The union also is interested in seeing the company expand. Part of this grows out of the desire for a larger membership; part from the knowledge that an expanding plant means upgrading of jobs as new men are brought in at the bottom. But there is the additional factor of pride in the company. Employees like to say that they work for Atlantic Steel. There is a high degree of identification between the people and the company.

An important element of the present relationship (which old employees say has always been the practice at the plant) is the assumption that the employee is a mature and responsible individual who can be counted upon to run his job. The best example of this is the lack of restrictive rules and regulations circumscribing the workers. Men seem to wander off and on their jobs at will. Employees felt no need to seek permission from their foreman to take time out to talk with the writers. This lack of regimentation applies to both white and Negro workers. The explanation seemed to be self-discipline, as a general foreman explained: "These men know what their job is. . . . If we tried to ride herd on these people like they do in some plants, production would suffer. . . . You let these people know what's expected of them, white or Negro, act like you figured they had sense enough to run the job, and they'll come through for you. When they don't, there's something mighty wrong, and you better start looking for what it is."

Communications and Rights of the Parties

Communications between the parties are marked by informality and a minimum of reticence. Cost figures on every stage of manufacture are available to the union; the officers are not only permitted but are urged to study them. While there is no requirement that they do so, most superintendents and general foremen talk over proposed changes with the departmental committeemen before they are put into effect.

In bargaining and negotiation, union-management communication is greatly facilitated by the personal acquaintance of people on the two sides of the table. With amazing accuracy, both parties are able to rehearse in their own minds the other's probable responses to a proposal. As a result there is little haggling; each side makes what it considers to be a fair proposition.

Communication between the union and the company is actually better than between union officials and the rank and file, and between top management and its lower and middle ranks. Top management makes every effort to keep in touch with lower levels, particularly through frequent meetings with various groups; the union does everything in its power to get a good turnout at union meetings, but neither feels that it is getting the results it should. In the opinion of the writers, however, communication between and among all groups at the plant is superior to that of most organizations. The formal channels are more effective than most, and the grapevine is swift and reliable.

The lack of insistence on management prerogatives and union rights greatly facilitates communication between the union and management. Communication is regarded principally as a means by which problems are to be settled, rather than a way to state the respective positions of the parties. A case in point is union-management cooperation in maintenance of discipline. A supervisor, noting a particular worker indulging in an attitude or following a line of action that will get him into trouble, tells the chairman of the department or the plant grievance committee about it, and asks him to speak to the man. The union officer, if his own investigation discloses that the supervisor's misgivings are well-founded, makes it his responsibility to bring the recalcitrant worker back into line. "We're interested in making steel, not showing people who's boss," was the comment of the supervisor when asked if he did not consider this practice to be the surrender of a management prerogative. "We'd a damn sight rather keep a man on the job in the first place than put through a discharge after he's fired," was the reply of a union official when he was asked if he did not think the practice put him in the position of being a company stooge.

The rights of the parties are outlined in the contract, and there is the usual management prerogative clause. Apparently, it is there more as a formality than for any other reason, because the general superintendent said, "All this talk about losing face is a bunch of poppycock. The men who work the jobs know more about them than anybody else. It doesn't constitute any compromise with principles to accept advice from the union or the people." This attitude toward a problem that is a stumbling block to peaceful relationships in many plants stems directly from the fact that bargaining is completely centered on problems instead of principles.

BARGAINING IN ACTION

In collective bargaining at Atlantic Steel the "how" is not as important as the result; both sides are willing to change, modify, or invent procedures as they are needed to achieve a mutually satisfying end.

Grievance Procedures

In grievance processing the contract provides one informal and four formal steps. The informal step involves the complaining employee and his immediate foreman. The contract does not specify a role for the elected grievance man at this level. In practice, however, he sometimes is invited to participate. If the aggrieved worker does not receive satisfaction at the informal step, he complains to the departmental grievance committee through his sectional grievance man, and the grievance goes to the first formal step of the procedure, which involves the departmental superintendent.

The union's plant grievance committee and the director of industrial relations under the contract form the second step of the procedure. The practice in the second step, however, is to have not only the committee present at the meetings but also the aggrieved worker and his departmental superintendent with his foreman. Several of these meetings were observed. The union and management representatives would present the case as each understood it, then the director of industrial relations questioned the representatives, trying to reconstruct the case in a way which would get as much agreement on the facts as possible. He would suggest what he considered to be an equitable solution and try to persuade both parties to accept that solution or to agree on its modification. If he found that was impossible, he sent the grievance to the next step.

In spite of a contract clause requiring that the grievance committee submit a written statement, the written grievance is practically unknown at Atlantic Steel. Since the beginning of the new relationship in 1945, one grievance has been committed to writing, and that was because it involved the rate of pay under a government contract. The director at the end of each meeting between the parties writes up a résumé of the meeting and the agreement to be kept in the files. Whereas there is no body of written precedent in the light of which grievances are to be settled, precedent does play a role. Those precedents that are pertinent are recalled; those that are not, or those that would embarrass the presentation of a case, are forgotten. There is no obscuring mass of written decision that draws attention either from the problem at hand or from the search for what is right and what is wrong.

The third step of the grievance procedure, according to the contract, brings together the vice-president in charge of operations and the representative of the international union. In practice, if the grievance is not settled at the second step, it is taken up by the superintendent of the plant and the plant grievance committee and the president of the union. If agreement is not reached at this meeting, one is arranged between the vice-president and the international representative, accompanied by the chairman of the plant grievance committee or the union president. While this study was under way, one grievance went through the third step.

In that instance, involving one of the rolling departments, the meeting was held in the company auditorium and the participants in the meeting included the persons specified in step three plus the grievance men from the mill. The issue was the addition of a fourth turn in the mill, which would require moving experienced men from their old crews to form the nuclei of the new crews. Such a change, the union claimed, would result in a loss of earnings because of the reduced efficiency of the new crews. It has been customary when a grievance comes up on an important or basic issue such as this, for the company and the union to agree mutually to omit the first steps of the grievance procedure and begin at the top. Because of this telescoping, the session tends to take on the characteristics of collective bargaining, and differentiation between it and a grievance session becomes impossible.

Issues which cannot be resolved by the third step of the procedure, provided they pertain to the application of the contract, may be submitted at the request of either the company or union to an arbitrator whose selection is provided for by the contract. An arbitrator was called in only twice between 1941 and 1945, and since then only one grievance has been put to arbitration. Persons in the union and in the company indicated that the union pushed that issue to arbitration in the face of an almost certain adverse decision as an illustration to members that it could not protect them if they openly violated agreements with the company.

There was considerable feeling on the part of the company and the union that issues should never leave the plant and be put into the hands of an outsider, but should be settled one way or another within the union-management relationship. Management consistently expressed the opinion that going to arbitration with a grievance was in effect placing management's decision-making prerogative in the hands of a stranger. Most of the union people felt that arbitration was futile at least, and since only a specific issue was decided, the violation of principle which caused the grievance would go unchanged. The arbitration clause remains in the contract as a sort of safety device which each side hopes the other will never see fit to invoke.

Four general characteristics help to explain why grievances do not appear to be the hot issues at Atlantic Steel that they are in many relationships. One of these is the emphasis on speed of settlement. Grievance meetings are held almost daily, and notification of the meeting is by the simple expedient of telephoning the representatives of both sides and asking how soon they can be available for settling such-and-such a grievance, at so-and-so's office. Apparently, the first person who hears about the grievance calls the others to arrange the meeting. Another is the degree of participation by all the interested parties, and the personal relationships between the parties which permit informality and flexibility. A third characteristic is the stress on fairness to both the aggrieved and the company. The effect of the proposed settlement upon future grievances of a similar nature is considered, but precedent is not allowed to become the main criterion for accepting or rejecting a solution. Fourth is the complete absence of horse trading on grievances. Both parties emphasized that horse trading will never solve any grievance but will merely result in a greater number of grievances. Unjustness to the person whose grievance was traded, they point out, would not be mitigated by the fact that the company or the union gained by the transaction.

The Contract and How It Works

There are two unusual features in the contract. First, either the company or union may withdraw from the agreement at any time merely by formally notifying the other party of an intention to do so at least 20 days prior to the proposed termination date. Thus it may end on short notice, or it may continue in effect, with the amendments collectively bargained from time to time, indefinitely. With the thought that this might lead to instability in the relationship, the writers discussed this question at length with nearly all of the company's management, from departmental supervisors up; with nearly all the union's top officers, and with many of its rank and file. Not one person held the view that the insertion of a no-strike clause or a specified termination date would help the relationship, but on the contrary, that such a change would represent a distrust which does not and should not exist. There was a consensus that the relationship was stabilized because issues could be brought out and settled as soon as they arose without postponing action to a date when the right to strike or lockout would be effective.

The second unusual feature is the provision for continuous bargaining. One section, entitled "Day-to-day Bargaining" states:

The parties mutually realize that this Contract does not and could not feasibly purport to provide a satisfactory solution for all of the problems which will arise in the day-to-day operation of the plant and business of the Company; and the parties recognize and acknowledge a continuing obligation to negotiate in mutual good faith, from time to time as requested by either party, with respect to any and all matters affecting the terms and conditions of employment, of the Bargaining Unit employees, or any of them, whether such matters be provided for in this Contract or not.

The section further provides that: "Many such matters can be handled through negotiations between the parties hereto without need for amendments to this Contract."

A number of specific articles of the contract conclude with a provision for the company and the union to "engage in further collective bargaining, in a mutually sincere effort to solve the issue." The determination of what is an excused absence under the absenteeism section; the establishment of job rates after a trial period; the changing of work schedules initiated by either the company or the union; transfers; promotions and demotions; and all matters affecting safety—these are sections which contain clauses providing for the parties to "negotiate in good faith" concerning any disagreement related to the section or article.

For example, any supervisory employee can suspend an employee, but he cannot discharge him. Immediately upon suspension, the company must notify the union and promptly investigate the circumstances. The company negotiates with the union concerning the discharge, but reserves the right to make the decision. If the union does not agree with the decision, it can send the case to arbitration immediately or give the required 20-day notice of termination of the contract.

The contract provides for vacations up to three weeks; six paid holidays with double time for holiday work; overtime at time and a half for more than 40 hours worked in one week or eight hours within any 24-hour period. Seniority is both occupational and by department, with the occupational seniority restricted to any one department. Seniority is the sole criterion for promotions, transfers, demotions, and layoffs. However, there is a trial period for each job during which the worker does not accumulate seniority on the new job, nor does he lose seniority on the old job. If, at the end of the trial period, the promoted worker does not perform satisfactorily, the company calls a collective bargaining session.

The international representative, Charles Mathias, and the union's officials claim that they have the finest and most liberal pension and hospitalization plans in the steel industry. Neither is mentioned in the contract even though they were put into effect as a result of the industry-wide strike in 1949. Provision for these benefits is made in a supplemental agreement which terminates in 1954. When the contract was terminated in 1952, this agreement was not disturbed. In a separate agreement the company agreed to use the accumulated dividends from the plans to pay the premiums during the 1952 strike, despite the fact that it was not obligated to do so.

Because of the vast number of hourly and tonnage rates in the plant, the parties make no effort to include them specifically in the contract. The contract article on wages merely outlines briefly the settlement of the 1952 strike concerning the general wage increase of 21 cents, intraplant adjustments, and retroactivity; and deals with guaranteed daily earnings for tonnage employees, reporting allowances, and absenteeism. The unusual part of the wage article provides for continuous collective bargaining over wages. Although a wage-rate book, reputed to contain some 50,000 rates for the various jobs, is not mentioned in the contract, the company and the union have agreed that the book is the rate structure for the plant. If a rate needs changing, the union and the company bargain out each change, as well as general wage adjustments, in accordance with the wage clause.

Wages are important at Atlantic Steel, but they are not a disturbing issue for two reasons. First, Atlantic Steel follows the industry pattern in general wage adjustments. (Table 5, *Case Study No. 12,* shows comparative data for the northern and southern patterns of wage increases and Atlantic Steel's wage increases for the years 1946 through 1952.) The local has obtained an increase either equal to or greater than both the northern and southern patterns since 1946. Because of what the union considers a unique local wage structure at Atlantic Steel, the application of the collectively bargained increases has been distributed each time to meet particular wage needs in the company's wage structure. Though the rates at Atlantic Steel are still slightly lower than the northern rates, they are well in excess of the general wage level of the Atlanta area. The local reputation of Atlantic Steel is that of a high-pay place to work. Second, if an individual rate is changed, it is bargained out in the continuous bargaining process; the relationship does not have to sustain the shock of intermittent bargaining sessions, each dealing with large numbers of individual rates.

Both the company and the union consider their contract good, but by no means the cornerstone of their relationship. Nor is it accorded any sanctity as a written document. It is considered merely an incomplete outline under which the union and the company agree to conduct themselves until it does not fit a result they want to achieve; then they change the contract.

Bargaining Sessions

That collective bargaining at Atlantic Steel is truly a continuous function is illustrated by the fact that 275 bargaining sessions were held in 1950. The number of sessions, however, does not mean that an excessive amount of time is spent in haggling or is taken from productive duties. One session attended by the writers showed that the meetings are mixtures of bargaining and the swapping of information and ideas concerning production problems. The subject of the meeting was a "hot issue" —but of the total elapsed time, 10 minutes were devoted to the hot issue and 45 minutes were taken up by a discussion of a production problem. Characteristics of that session, and three others attended by the writers, were: the expeditious manner in which the bargaining was carried out; devotion of most of the time to a mutual analysis of some production problem; the absence of a written and signed statement on results, although the issues taken up were serious.

The collective bargaining function is broken down into two divisions. If the matter to be bargained concerns a major financial commitment on the part of the company, or if a new contract is being written, the bargaining is carried out by Wilbur Glenn, who represents the controlling interest of the company, with the aid of the company's legal adviser, Ralph Williams. The union is represented by the international representative, Charles Mathias, and the union's bargaining committee. Bargaining over all other issues is carried on by the line supervision of the plant; neither Mr. Glenn nor Mr. Williams participates in those sessions.

The plant-level bargaining is of three types. Many questions arising within a department are settled between the departmental supervisor and the departmental grievance men by means of an understanding. These are merely verbal agreements reached to cover a specific situation and can be terminated at any time by either party. They carry no precedent at all if the issue later involves other departments, or if a similar issue arises. At the next higher level is the side agreement, which results from collective bargaining between the line supervision above departmental superintendent and either the plant-wide grievance committee of the union or its negotiating committee. The side agreement is usually a written document signed by both parties as the result of bargaining over an issue which is either interdepartmental or plant-wide. It is considered a local agreement and does not require ratification by the international union, as do the contract and written amendments bargained at the top level. The parties do not consider the side agreement to have any legal value since either party can terminate it at any time. (An exception is the side agreement concerning the pension and hospitalization plans.) The other type of plant-level bargaining is the grievance procedure, which can result in understandings at the departmental level or, if carried higher in the procedure, a side agreement. The great bulk of the grievances settled above the departmental level result in verbal agreements, some of which are summarized and consigned to the files.

The Qualification and Training Program

The problem of obtaining qualified tradesmen in the metal and wood trades, and keeping them, has always been disturbing for Atlantic Steel, because of the high ratio of maintenance employees to production workers and the small reservoir of skilled trade workers in the Atlanta area. The union had its own problems with the trade workers. Members who were trade helpers did not relish the sight of journeymen being hired in above them and decreasing their chances of moving up. The tradesmen hired in as journeymen were not usually familiar or sympathetic with the concept of industrial unionism, which created friction in the shops. Nor were these hired-in journeymen inclined to pass on the trade to their helpers.

The company's desire to assure an adequate supply of tradesmen and to implement its policy of promoting from within led to meetings with the union concerning the possibility of a training program for the mechanical trades group. The union wanted some voice in the operation of whatever program was set up and in the selection and promotion of the apprentices. The mechanical departments qualification and training program, negotiated between the company and the union and contained in a side agreement, was put into effect in 1950. Later it was extended to the wire and nail mills, and eventually will cover many trades in the manufacturing and warehousing departments.

Under the program, it is possible for a man hired at the gate to reach the classification of tradesman in four years providing he passes the standards set up by the qualification board, which is composed of two men from the company and two from the union. This board cannot bargain or handle grievances but "can and should make recommendations to the company and union pertaining to matters for bargaining and grievances under the contract which pertain to the qualifications and advancement of employees in training." The industrial relations director is secretary of the board and maintains the files of the employees in training.

To qualify for the training program an employee must have a minimum of an eighth-grade education and pass several simple mechanical aptitude tests. The program sets up six classifications for the trainees. As they move up through the classifications, they accumulate stated increments in their pay rates, as actual helpers to journeymen. The tradesmen, to whom trainees are assigned, have had instruction on the ways the helpers are to be taught. The foremen also have been briefed and are instructed to see that the trainees get practical training and are not shunted off into holding the tools for the journeymen. From the helper classification, the trainee moves into his trade if his records prove his ability.

Both the union and the company are highly satisfied with the program. Company officials have stated that without the mechanics supplied by the program it would have been impossible to put the new electric furnace into operation within such a short period. The company's policy of promotion from within is complete. The union feels that its members now have an opportunity to get ahead without the frustration of dead-end jobs, favoritism, and lack of a chance to learn.

The procedure of the board provides an important clue to the attitudes and methods of the parties to this relationship. The union and company representatives make independent, thorough investigations, questioning each candidate's fellow workers, tradesmen who work with him, and his foreman, several weeks before his consideration at a board meeting. When the board meets and the information is pooled, there is a complete picture of the candidate, which leaves few points remaining for possible disagreement. Since the beginning of the program, every board decision has been unanimous and the parties expect this to continue. The union representatives refuse to consider a man for promotion if the results of the parallel company and union investigations do not show that he is fully qualified. The union is extremely proud of the program and it is insistent that the standards remain high. The company is fully in sympathy with these goals. They represent the union's desire to make seniority workable for the company as well as a protective device for the rank and file.

An Emerging Relationship

No stereotypes exist in this relationship. In October of 1953, the union orients its actions towards the company as it exists in October of 1953, not as it was in October of 1941; and the company deals with the real union of the present, not with a fixed picture of the union that it formed twelve years earlier and never changed.

Neither party thinks of the other as an entity whose responses are completely predictable on the basis of an ascribed and completely comprehensive set of attitudes, tendencies, characteristics, policies, practices, and so on. The company probably knows more about the union, and the union in all likelihood knows more about the company, than is common in such relationships; yet each admits that the other still remains to some degree a mystery. Not only does each party admit to a lack of complete knowledge of the other, but neither claims to be able to foretell the exact nature of the circumstantial factors that will be the determinant in any future situation.

Because of this mutual recognition of growth and change, there seems to be room for continued adjustments to new developments which may further test the relationship.

A Postscript

Since field work for the Atlantic Steel study was completed, there has been no substantial change in the relationship between the company and the union. Several important issues have arisen in addition to the normal day-to-day problems. Because the new crews for the recently added electric furnace were drawn from the open-hearth crews, a serious problem of seniority arose which is still in the process of being worked out. The relationship has sustained the problems arising from a considerable drop in sales and production with the inevitable layoffs. The company followed the national pattern of wage increase set during the summer negotiations between the union and "Big Steel," and there was no disruption of the relationship over any issue during the local negotiation. In summary, the structure, attitudes, and methods of the relationship are still as described in the study.

CHAPTER 19 _____

Working Harmony
in Eighteen Companies

and a Variety of Unions

FREDERICK H. HARBISON, *Executive Officer of the Industrial Relations Center, University of Chicago, and* JOHN R. COLEMAN, *Industrial Relations Section, Massachusetts Institute of Technology, are authors of NPA Case Study No. 13. Their full report, condensed in this chapter, was published in November 1953.*

After announcement of the intention to study the causes of industrial peace in some companies, many cases where good labor relations existed came to the NPA Committee's attention in which the parties, for one reason or another, did not want their names revealed. Also, additional studies giving important insight into the causes of industrial peace have been published by other institutions. In order to broaden its base for findings, therefore, the NPA Committee on the Causes of Industrial Peace decided to publish a report summarizing the experience in eighteen such companies. The sample is drawn from a variety of industries in this country and in England, including steel manufacturing and processing, machine-tool shops, electrical goods manufacturing, rubber, chemicals, public utilities, food processing, and mining.

These unions and companies have learned to get along in a reasonably harmonious fashion, or, as the parties most frequently described it, have developed "pretty good relations." The authors have termed this type of relationship "working harmony."

Thirteen of the companies were investigated at first hand by the writers.[1] Five are studies made by others which have been published in recent years. The five are:

[1] The cases on which this study was based have also been used as part of the basis

Studebaker Corporation and Local 5, United Automobile Workers (CIO), by Frederick H. Harbison and Robert Dubin, *Patterns of Union-Management Relations,* Science Research Associates, 1947.

Alexander Smith, Inc., and Textile Workers Union of America (CIO); Brown Instrument Company and United Electrical, Radio and Machine Workers of America (independent, then CIO); and R. Hoe and Company, Inc., and International Association of Machinists (AFL, then independent), all by Richard A. Lester and Edward A. Robie, *Constructive Labor Relations: Experience in Four Firms,* Industrial Relations Section, Princeton University, 1948.

S. Buchsbaum and Company and Local 241, International Chemical Workers Union (AFL), by Andrew H. Whiteford, William Foote Whyte, and Burleigh B. Gardner, "From Conflict to Cooperation," *Applied Anthropology,* Fall 1946.

ATTITUDES AND POLICIES

Clear-cut elements in the attitudes and policies of management and union officials were characteristic of these eighteen working harmony relationships.

Management's Approach

The approach of the companies' policy makers was to maximize the possible assets and minimize the obvious liabilities of dealing with organized labor. Management always had in mind the objectives of greater efficiency, better production, and a healthy earnings record; and was striving to prevent the union from interfering with the exercise of basic managerial functions.

All of the companies in the survey were apparently convinced that the union is here to stay. Some management leaders, recognizing that it would be impossible to break the power of the union among workers, appeared to rationalize acceptance of the union into a conviction that collective bargaining was a necessary condition for running a business and a legitimate way of dealing with their employees as a group. They said that the unions, in representing the workers' interests, were doing a job that management either could not or would not do so effectively. Policy centered on getting along with the union rather than on inventing ways to outmaneuver it.

All company spokesmen indicated a desire for businesslike relations in

---

for discussion of working harmony relationships to be found in the authors' *Goals and Strategy in Collective Bargaining,* Harper & Brothers, 1951. The general framework and point of view are the same in both reports; but *Case Study No. 13* involves more detailed examination of certain key aspects of the bargaining situations.

collective bargaining. They wanted to deal with a union which abided by its contract and guaranteed, to the maximum extent possible, the respect of union officers and of employees for that agreement. To achieve this end, there was general agreement that management had to take certain realistic measures to enhance opportunities for responsible union action. Specifically, most of these companies identified a union's responsibility with its feeling of security. Measures to promote union security varied; some agreed to the union shop, others gave the union the names of all newly hired employees, or the company president wrote personal letters advising employees to join the union. There was no evidence of any management attempt to discourage membership or to discriminate against union members. Practically all the eligible employees were union members. Some of the companies were attempting to increase the unions' prestige in their communities also, by suggesting names of union officers for membership on various civic boards. In one or two situations, there was company support for union candidates in local elections.

The company executives invariably pointed out that the main advantage of the union, its principal positive contribution to management, was in getting ideas across to and reflecting reactions of workers. Some use of the union as a channel of communication was found in almost every case. These uses included smoothing out adjustments to new production techniques and equipment, putting down rumors and thus avoiding trouble in the shop, getting across economic facts about the company's competitive and profit situation, and building trust in the fairness of the company. No company felt that the union was perfect in this respect; all pointed to such shortcomings as the filtering which necessarily took place within the union. Even so, almost all companies were reasonably well satisfied with the union as a communication channel.

A practical example of how this channel was used arose in a plant where a high proportion of the work had traditionally been done by skilled craftsmen. In 1948, this company contemplated major technological changes which were designed to convert production from the older handicraft techniques to assembly-line methods. Recognizing that the change-over would have serious repercussions, particularly among the craft-conscious workers, management brought the union in as early as possible for discussions on all phases of the program. Although there was some friction when the change-over was made, the company spokesmen unanimously agreed that success was the result of working closely with the union at all stages and relying upon the union leaders to see that affected workers understood the company's plan and the way it protected employees.

Few companies attempted to exclude specific subjects from discussion with union representatives. And in most cases, the company sought the union's cooperation in areas which lie beyond collective bargaining, such as safety and selection and training programs, although the company appeared to retain primary responsibility for planning and initiating action. Company executives pointed out that if management by-passed the union on these matters, the prestige of the union leadership would tend to rest on gains based on pure bargaining power. In seeking the union's assistance, these company officials felt that they were giving the leadership a constructive opportunity to become important.

The most representative policy found in these companies might be summarized as follows: "Pay a lot of attention to the human problems in operating the enterprise; do a down-to-earth job of negotiations with the union in the areas appropriate to collective bargaining; and try to get the union to go along in the areas beyond collective bargaining with as few formal commitments as possible."

The Union's Approach

The union attitudes and policies in all eighteen cases also had certain common elements. Relatively harmonious relations with any particular company did not seem to take the edge off a union's basic desire to drive hard bargains for its membership. But the distinctive feature about the eighteen cases was that the unions appeared to be convinced that their ability to get more, in terms of wages or job security, was closely linked with the economic health of the businesses with which they bargained. This concern with the company's ability to pay did not result in the sort of positive action which in union-management cooperation serves to increase productive efficiency; but at least there was a marked willingness under the proper stimulus—usually a threat to the jobs of the members—to eliminate some major obstructions to higher productivity.

This attitude was illustrated by the actions of a district director of the Steelworkers, who bargained with three of the eighteen companies. His reputation as a tough fighter and his bargaining record assured continuing loyal support from the membership; yet his willingness to respond to gestures of good faith and cooperation from management had won the respect and friendship of many employers. During 1947, one employer was at a distinct competitive disadvantage on a certain product. Thirty-five per cent of the working force might lose their jobs if the product's costs were not decreased by the elimination of some loafing in the shop. The district director recognized that the good contract which he and the local committee had successfully bargained for was proving too costly to the company. He told the members bluntly: "If you want higher wages, better vacations, more security, a health and welfare fund, you must, of necessity, recognize that your company cannot give it to you unless you first give it to the company. You've got to put money in the barrel if you want to take it out."

This approach common to most of the union leaders stemmed from experience with companies facing economic crises and a desire to help avoid such difficulties. In a few cases, this concern for the company's economic position seemed tied to a broader concern for the interests of the community, as stated by a member of a union bargaining committee: "There's only one big employer in town and so when we sit down to bargain with him we know we're really bargaining for the whole community. . . . If either of us acts irresponsibly, we'll have a ghost town right in our midst."

The unions' concern for company welfare, coupled with their feeling of security, appeared to produce a fairly consistent bargaining strategy. In each company, the union was still anxious to squeeze all it could from the employer in terms of wages and other work benefits. But the tactics were those of skillful negotiators who, avoiding name calling and unnecessary friction because "it costs too much and gains too little," turned to hardheaded discussions and realistic trades. Such tactics appeared possible only where the leaders were secure within their union organization.

To a large extent, the best contract in the minds of the union leaders is the one which meets their objective of job controls, and which has the strongest protective clauses on such things as seniority, discharge procedures, work assignments, and, where applicable, rate setting. Many of the union leaders sought informal job controls when their acquisition through specific contract clauses was clearly impractical because of determined company opposition. Accordingly, advance consultations with management, wherever company actions affected job content or numbers employed, were looked upon as an effective method of control. Although the companies looked upon advance consultation as a way of getting help from a union without formally surrendering their prerogatives, the unions considered it as a way of influencing and controlling managerial actions. The union leaders claimed that this kept them in the know about what was going to happen in the shop. They could analyze the union's position, prepare members for changes, and avoid being caught by surprise.

The unions appeared to have substituted the police function for the protest idea. Their primary objective was to regulate rather than to oppose management. The leadership tried to build membership allegiance to the union without destroying the workers' trust and confidence in the company. This kind of situation posed some perplexing problems for the union leaders. They were always vulnerable to charges of being tools of management unless they got a continuous stream of tangible benefits for members. When asked how they faced up to the "political" problems of a harmonious bargaining relationship, the union leaders usually replied that two factors helped solve this dilemma. First, they were able to communicate what they themselves had learned about their firm's economic position to the membership. The union officers contended that when members had the facts and figures they were willing to be reasonable. Second, they never allowed themselves or the members to be taken in by a company; their efforts were constantly directed towards policing all management's actions which had an impact upon the members' interests.

Looking for new outlets for their unions' energies, some of the leaders were pressing—several very successfully—for a broader range of matters on which to bargain with the company. Often the demands to make this or that a matter subject to bargaining seemed to be made primarily to rally the membership. Also, most of the unions were pressing forward in the field of community relations and political action. Union representatives were serving on school boards, in city welfare agencies, and in a good many local political offices. Most of the union officers saw serious limitations to collective bargaining as a means of achieving broad social and economic goals. They were determined to supplement contract gains by national welfare legislation. The passage of the Taft-Hartley Law in 1947, moreover, was a tremendous stimulus to political activity on the part of local unions.

The Nature of Collective Relations

The interplay of the union and management approaches is reflected both in the major issues in contract negotiations and in the day-to-day living under the signed agreement.

The Status-of-Parties Issues

Union security and managerial functions were of relatively minor concern in the eighteen companies, though the issues of status were not completely resolved. The union's need for formal contract protection was reduced by management's wholehearted acceptance and encouragement of responsible unions. In three companies, a formal union-shop provision was part of the contract. In eleven, management was directly or indirectly encouraging workers to belong to the union. Accordingly, the labor leaders in the latter cases, though continuing their demands for a union shop at frequent intervals, seldom pressed the matter.

To most of these company officials, encouragement of union membership was simply good business. However, the informal type of union security appealed to them for several reasons. Most professed opposition to the principle of compulsory membership. They did not wish to run counter to the stated policy of the industry's leaders on so crucial an issue. And they preferred a situation in which the company could quietly withdraw its support from the union in the event the leadership became unreasonable.

The issue of managerial functions was seldom resolved as easily as that of union security. No one settlement could once and for all define each party's rights. While the companies were concerned with guarding their right to manage, they did not want head-on clashes with the union. Their policy, therefore, was to avoid attempts to draw a line which separated union and management rights, and to concentrate on solving problems as they came up. The union leaders preferred consultation on problems to an inconclusive argument with a company over abstract principles. Company officials not only felt that to draw a definite line would invite a fight, but they were also confident of their ability to exercise managerial functions because they had a reasonable union. The consensus was that a responsible union was not a serious threat to management's ability to direct the enterprise effectively, and only rarely was there an expression of real concern over attempts by the union to extend the area of bargaining. Furthermore, there was an incentive to adopt a problem-solving approach because management often could enlist the union's support in selling the employees an agreed-upon program.

Two examples illustrate the sensible results of this problem-solving technique. A group of veterans returning to a small steel fabricating plant found that harmony had replaced prewar labor-management strife. They formed a small but militant protest group and refused to go along with the rest of the membership in giving management high production in return for a good contract. Under the contract, the company had full authority to discipline these men, by layoffs if necessary. But instead of taking unilateral action, company officials asked the union officers to help bring the veterans into line. The union succeeded in persuading them that the company needed high production to stay in business.

At another company there was a hard-hitting but basically harmonious bargaining relationship. A foundry was operating at a loss because of low productivity, and nothing the company could do through normal supervisory channels seemed to help. Finally, the company asked the union for help. The difficulty seemed to be both bad supervision and loafing. Once the two sides began their joint attack, productive efficiency improved and before long the foundry again showed a profit. Almost simultaneously, in another plant (not included in this survey) of the same company where a less harmonious relationship prevailed, another critical problem arose involving management's rights. When the company decided it no longer could keep up with competitors unless men who had been operating two machines would take on three, the local management did not consult with the union leadership. The change-over was refused by operators, who threatened to strike; the issue went to arbitration; and management was upheld. But the change-over was made grudgingly and production did not meet the company's expectations. The company had protected its right to manage, but the costs involved in doing so were high.

The Grievance Machinery

Grievances were few, efficiently handled, and discussed more on the basis of facts than in the context of union "politics" or management's power position. Furthermore, it was a common practice in some companies to view the grievance process as a springboard for union-management negotiations or consultation on a wide range of subjects.

As a result of this attitude, most union leaders were not interested in using a flood of grievances, real and imaginary, to harass the company or to build up a record of victories. In the larger companies the parties set up formal grievance-screening or appeal committees to sift out legitimate grievances and accelerate adjudication. In the small companies, grievances often were screened informally by the union committeeman and the aggrieved worker. In either case, one of the most significant characteristics of the harmonious relationships was the effort to wash out bad grievances and to settle a greater proportion of cases informally at the first step in the procedure.

In this connection, the experience in the largest company in this survey (a steel company employing approximately 14,000 employees) is significant. Prior to 1940, in each of the company's ten plants widespread unrest and accumulated dissatisfactions stemmed from a cumbersome grievance procedure. The average time required to dispose of a grievance, which could go through four stages, was estimated at 90 days, 51 days in the fourth step. Top leaders on both sides sat down to work out a less aggravating grievance machinery. These meetings, the first gesture either party had made in the direction of a harmonious relationship, resulted in the establishment of a general appeals committee. It was composed of 32 management and union people, including at least one representative of each side from all ten plants. Once a month, the committee discussed all the grievances which had advanced to the fourth stage since its prior meeting. It was not expected to settle grievances, but to assist the company executive and international representative of the union who had this responsibility.

Management and the union alike agreed that this simple machinery resulted in a drastic cut in accumulated time for grievances at the fourth stage, more calm and restrained appraisals, a decline in the total number of grievances, less dissatisfaction on the part of workers whose cases were in process, anticipation of some grievances before they arose, and virtual elimination of arbitration. The indirect effects of the committee were even more important. The success in jointly attacking the grievance problem and the periodic management-union meetings led to better understanding between the parties on many other issues and a greater emphasis on facts in negotiations.

Special Joint Committees

Twenty special joint committees were functioning in thirteen of the eighteen companies. The breakdown is: 8 general labor-management committees; 5 safety committees; 2 job-evaluation or time-study committees; and 5 miscellaneous, including one each on apprenticeship, grievance discussion and contract clarification, information program, seniority, and suggestions. The importance attached to these committees in interviews with management and union leaders indicated that some intensive analysis of these activities was appropriate. However, in several companies where there were no formal joint committees, the relationships did not seem very different because of that fact. The parties felt that extensive discussions in the regular grievance committees and informal information sharing were fully as effective in promoting stability and understanding.

The popularity of safety as a subject with which joint union-management committees dealt seemed to result from the fact that it was relatively noncontroversial and was so obviously in the best interests of both parties. There was considerable uniformity in all five of the joint safety committees studied. The usual procedure is indicated by that in the plant of an electrical goods manufacturer employing about 2000 people. Safety was part of the job of the plant's wartime labor-management committee. When that committee collapsed after the war, the joint safety committee became an independent body. Representatives were appointed by the union from each department in the plant to meet monthly with the company's safety engineer and two other members of management. Reports on all lost-time accidents throughout the plant as well as hazards observed in the departments formed the basis for discussions of ways to prevent similar accidents. And each meeting concluded with a visit to the sites of serious accidents during the past month and on-the-spot discussion of accident prevention.

A major share of the committee's energies was devoted to publicizing the importance of safety measures. The committeemen attracted considerable prestige throughout the plant and union members sought appointment. The results were spectacular in the earliest months, with a 35 per cent drop in man-hours lost. After about three years the accident rate had leveled off at an average of 60 per cent lower than before the committee began its work. Committee members found themselves less in the limelight. The company's safety engineer explored new devices to sustain the committeemen's interests. The most successful was a program of safety-training classes, through which members of the committee remained busy and interested; but the enthusiasm of most of the employees appeared to have died out. Both parties gave full credit to the committee for achieving an enviable safety record and some spokesmen contended that there was value in having workers and management get together to solve even such peripheral problems as safety matters. But beyond that they saw little continuing importance in the committee.

The two committees for time study or job evaluation included in this survey were started by companies searching for ways to promote acceptance of incentive systems. The unions, which played passive roles in establishment of the committees, were inclined to believe that their participation was a means of protecting workers' job interests under an incentive system. Available evidence indicates, however, that there was little difference between the rates arrived at by joint time study and those which management set on its own initiative. The most obvious benefit of both committees was to eliminate most grievances over the setting of individual incentive rates. In both cases, there were wider acceptance of the rates and a more effective incentive system, principally because the union had a measure of participation in the rate-setting process.

The time-study committee that seemed most effective operated in a situation where the relationship between management and labor had become quite strained during the life of the committee. The company, searching for an efficient time-study and production-methods department, and also for ways to make its incentive system mutually acceptable, invited the union's participation in running the department. Strongly supported by the union's international, the local agreed even though it was somewhat suspicious of the company's motives. Four union members were elected to serve full time on company pay in the time-study department, and after they had been trained, were assigned to serve on teams with the company's time-study men. Each job in the plant was then studied by one of these teams. The project soon ran into difficulties because the union representatives were invariably defeated in the next election, and the company had to start training new men who could not become fully competent on time study within two years. Finally, it was agreed that management would choose the union representatives from names submitted by the local and that those representatives would stay in the department as long as the union was satisfied.

The reaction of company officials toward the setup was varied. They pointed to some increases in production of as much as 50 per cent once the jobs were studied and incentive rates established. They felt that the removal of the union leaders' fears of time study had been responsible for general acceptance of the rates by the rank and file. But on the other side, the company's industrial engineer said that many of the union representatives did not have the proper educational background for training in time study, and many of the company's foremen resented the fact that union representatives often were much better trained than they in techniques of time study and job evaluation. But he admitted that the plan had saved much time which would have been absorbed in endless grievances under a management-controlled system.

The union gained influence and prestige through the successful operation of the system, and the leaders felt that they had protected members' job interests, while giving workers the opportunity to make extra money through incentive pay. However, the union saw in this plan an attempt by management to conceal points of basic disagreement in the relationship which centered about issues of personalities. For example, it claimed that the company president gave only lip service to building the union's prestige, that the minor functionaries in management were unfriendly to the union, and that there were so many changes in management personnel that the company was incapable of carrying out a consistent labor policy. For several years, a tense situation shaped up around such issues, and the authors got the impression from union leaders that a showdown was avoided only because of the desire of the parties to keep the time-study experiment going. Thus this particular joint committee stabilized a relationship characterized by mixed harmony and basic disagreements.

The 1947 contract negotiated by the United States Steel Corporation and the United Steelworkers included a clause providing for establishment of a joint committee to study and recommend on seniority practices, which became general throughout the steel industry. In a large number of cases, the committees never actively functioned, and where they did, results varied widely. The seniority committee in one of the steel companies does function. It was established by the only American company in this survey which had continued its wartime labor-management committee, which resulted largely from the enthusiasm of the company's industrial relations manager. This man's belief in joint activities caused him to welcome the clause calling for a joint seniority committee as an effective way to attack one of the most troublesome problems under the labor agreement. Management had long felt dissatisfied with the seniority clause because it was not designed to meet the specific needs in this plant and was unnecessarily restrictive in limiting management's right to shift men within the plant. The local union was not sure of what this committee was to do, but in conformity with policy recommended by its international officers, was willing to try to work out some improvements in the seniority system. Furthermore, the union's favorable experience in previous labor-management committees was an important factor in its willingness to undertake the new assignment.

In a long series of meetings, many spokesmen for both sides advanced proposals and counterproposals. Gradually there emerged an over-all plan which seemed to meet the requirements of the two parties. The plan was based upon departmental seniority for the filling of vacancies, and plant-wide application of seniority in case of layoffs. Another aspect of the agreement which appealed to the interests of both parties was a carefully outlined job-bidding procedure which meant that the employee with the highest seniority was awarded the job if, in the opinion of the company, his ability and physical fitness qualified him for it. The parties subsequently incorporated this agreement into the contract, and, before disbanding, the committee worked out lines of progression best suited to the various departments. Both parties agreed that they had benefited, not only in connection with seniority, but from the additional experience and education they had gained in jointly studying a complex problem.

The eight general labor-management committees in the companies studied operated under such titles as "labor-management committee," "works council," and "good and welfare committee." One which seemed typical was in a public utility. The employees were organized in 1940 by the International Brotherhood of Electrical Workers (AFL), following a reorganization in top management. The new company officials welcomed the union's organizing efforts and actively assisted in getting all but a few long-service workers into the union. Union officers said they had a good contract and had a high regard for top company officials. Management looked upon the union as a stabilizing force and an effective method of communicating with employees. At the same time, agreements were reached as a result of tough bargains.

The mutual-problems conference was established in 1945 on the suggestion of the union and with the ready agreement of the company officials, who had been thinking along the same lines. Every two months, in each of the four divisions of the company, three representatives of labor and three of management held all-day sessions on any problems of mutual concern. The parties rotated their delegates, although the union president and the company's director of industrial relations were always present. The agenda was open to anyone in the company who cared to have a particular subject discussed, and items stayed on the agenda until disposed of satisfactorily. The follow-up on agenda items was good, and communication of the results of meetings to the employees was effectively handled by the union in its compulsory monthly meetings and in day-to-day contacts.

After several months of operation, when the issues of greatest mutual concern had been discussed at length, the problem of assuring an interesting agenda for each session became serious. To overcome this, management promoted discussions on subjects, not necessarily covered by the contract, which were not especially crucial but were interesting problems. In this committee (as in several other general committees), contract interpretation became one of the major issues for discussion, with each side feeling that a better job was done in the quiet atmosphere of committee meetings than could have been hoped for in subsequent grievance sessions. Technically, it was within the conference's jurisdiction to discuss problems more directly associated with the production and distribution of electric power; but in practice such issues did not appear on the agenda.

A company official, summing up the contribution made by this committee, wrote as follows: "Grievances have been practically eliminated due primarily, we believe, to the splendid cooperation of both company and union in adjusting problems by either or both taking proper corrective action, when necessary." And the union president expressed a somewhat similar sentiment when he told the authors: "I feel that we've done a job in this committee. This way we get a lot of things off of our chests without having to reduce everything to writing in the form of grievances. We get to know more about what makes the company tick, and also what makes the bosses tick."

The direct results of the general labor-management committees in terms of actual problems solved seem less important than the indirect effects in building good will and mutual confidence between the parties. The general committees in these companies have been in operation for varying periods of time, four having been established before World War II, two beginning during the war, and two starting up in 1946. There are several noticeable differences between these committees and the wartime labor-management committees (most of which collapsed following V-J Day, when the War Production Board stimulus ended). Only one of the eight committees studied ordinarily discussed production questions; and in that exception, a carry-over from the war years, the discussions were vague and general. By avoiding the controversial issues touching upon questions of managerial functions and the sharing of the fruits of increased production, these committees appeared to have improved their chances of survival. All eight committees needed a continuing impetus to keep going. They were kept alive partly because of the active support of one or two persons, usually management staff officials, who believed ardently in the potential benefits of the committees and were willing to work to keep interest in them alive. The eight general committees were remarkably successful in solving the problem of follow-ups, usually by clear delegation of responsibility and by setting time limits within which progress reports were to be filed with the committee. Most of these committees were functioning in situations where relationships between the parties were relatively harmonious to start with, whereas the wartime committees were often set up in companies where management had not fully accepted the union which still functioned primarily as a protest group.

Bargaining Over the Contract

Contract negotiations in these eighteen companies were affected by other elements in the relationship: frequent and comprehensive communication between management and union; use of grievance sessions as opening wedges for discussion of broader problems; a great deal of informal day-to-day consultation. In most cases, both parties approached negotiations with a sophisticated awareness of each other's needs and with a good idea of the reactions to any given demand.

Management was usually willing, and often anxious, to give the union the facts about the company's economic position. There was, for example, little opposition to letting the union officers look at the company's books, although the local officers claimed that they were not interested in seeing the books because they could tell how well the company was doing without that. Recognizing the "political" requirements of the union representatives, management was often willing to go more than halfway on some issues when it believed that it was in the company's best interests to help out particular union leaders. In most cases, the union leaders used their "willingness to cooperate" as a strong bargaining point in making demands. Both parties defended this sort of deal making as hardheaded bargaining adapted to the environment within which they negotiated.

There was a mutual desire to discover and agree upon bargains which were good for both sides. For example, the Alexander Smith and Sons Carpet Company was anxious to eliminate from its contract with the Textile Workers a length-of-service bonus which seriously distorted earnings in favor of senior workers. To make this palatable, the company proposed a flat 12-cent increase in place of the service bonus. The union officers were able to sell the contract to the membership on the basis of a wage increase. In another case, a company was willing to give an extra 5-cent wage increase over and above 12 cents already negotiated with the union. But top management wanted to have this 5 cents left out of the contract, to capitalize on the good will it expected if the 5 cents were paid week after week while everyone knew that the company was under no obligation to do so. The union leaders decided to accept it. "It didn't hurt us any because we knew the company would go on paying the nickel and we decided that they might as well get something out of it too."

The majority of the companies operated within the framework of the economic patterns set by key bargains negotiated in their basic industries' power centers. Thus the parties began their negotiations with the wage issue partially settled and with only the fringe issues left for discussion. Where there was no acknowledged industry pattern, settlements seemed geared partly to prevailing community practice, and this tendency had a similar, if weaker, impact upon bargaining. The wage structure in all the companies appeared to be based on prevailing standards in the industry or in the community.

Through increased communications, the parties found that they were actually clearing away some of the bargaining issues before them or were testing solutions to their problems in advance of formal negotiations. In all the companies, there were examples of an increased emphasis upon informal negotiations in such areas as wage administration, with the result that the meaning of the contract was constantly changing in response to new conditions in the plant.

Finally, as in all other types of relationships, the prospects of a strike played an important part in contract negotiations. Practically all the employers continued to weigh their contemplated actions in terms of the union's ability to strike if a conflict arose. The union leaders continued to concern themselves with keeping the union membership on its toes and the union treasury in shape to support a strike if it became necessary. Yet there were few strikes in the history of these eighteen companies. Both sides had an acute awareness of how far they could go in any one direction without bringing on a strike and of how much a strike would net them. On the other hand, occurrence of occasional strikes did not seem to upset the basic stability of the situations. Instead, they sometimes seemed to clear the air and to prove that the weapon was still sharp even if seldom used.

CHANGING PATTERNS IN WORKING HARMONY

The picture of industrial relations at these companies is not complete without consideration of why the contracting parties move into the working harmony relationship, and why, in some cases, they may move back to an armed truce relationship or go on to more positive union-management cooperation. To understand these dynamics it would be desirable to observe the growth and progress of these relationships over long periods of time. In this study, the authors have had a maximum of two years of firsthand experience in looking at the individual situations. While an attempt was made to trace the history of the relationships, it was necessary to rely to a large extent on the memories of the participants as to what had taken place in the past. During the period of the study, however, it was possible to observe changes which took place in a few of the relationships. Despite obvious shortcomings in drawing conclusions from such meager data, tentative and cautious inferences may provide insight into the nature of these dynamics.

It is reasonably certain that no one action by either group led to the pretty good relations which were observed. It is just as certain that no explanation of their development is to be found in such vague terms as "trust," "good faith," "confidence," "mutual respect," and "fair dealing." Instead, working harmony appeared to result from a complex process of growth in which, over a considerable period of time, each party made successive accommodations to the other as it appraised and reappraised means for advancing its basic interests.

Dramatic conversions seem to have been rare among most of the company and union leaders. Working harmony was hammered out over a period of years. Moreover, there was no one point of arrival, for even in the relationships which seemed relatively stable there were gradations of harmony from day to day. In all the situations, changes constantly took place, and the test of stability in any one relationship was the degree to which these parties absorbed the changes without upsetting their basic understandings.

This study suggests that the instances of working harmony, while fewer in number in the American economy than the cases of armed truce, are increasing at a fast rate. But in some instances, similar relationships have deteriorated over a period of time and the parties have gone back to straight power bargaining. This happened in two of the eighteen cases analyzed in this report.

Pitfalls for the Parties

The most crucial danger in working harmony for management lies in counting the benefits of peace without due regard to the costs. For example, one company's production standards were loose after the war and labor costs were out of line with those of competitors. The company recognized the danger in this situation but did not force the issue because it did not want to upset a long no-strike record. When its market began to tighten up, management had to face the union's open defiance in order to initiate action which would allow the firm to stay competitive. Thus a policy of giving in during good times had to be amended at a psychologically bad moment, and the strain on the relationship was acute. A second example occurred in two separate plants where management's eagerness to get along with the union resulted in short-circuiting the foreman group. Following a minor rebellion by the foremen, management learned that harmonious relations were likely to be extremely costly unless enthusiastically supported by all ranks of supervision. Accordingly, it gave foremen more support in grievance cases and more authority in dealing with the workers, even at the expense of sometimes antagonizing the union.

A second and more complex pitfall which management needs to avoid is in overplaying its support for the incumbent union leadership. In one of the two cases which disintegrated during the course of this study, management sincerely believed in unionism but wanted to make sure that the right-wing element in the union stayed in office. To this end, the company openly worked to build up the prestige of these leaders, and gave them just a little bit extra to take back to the membership. So complete was management's identification with the right wing that it took only the slightest economic reverse to upset the apple cart. In 1949, the demand for the company's products was sharply reduced; the company began to make layoffs; the left wing charged in the union elections that management and the other union leaders had become so "lovey-dovey" that the workers were no longer protected. The left wing won the election and collective bargaining immediately reverted to a more militant basis.

The principal pitfalls for the unions studied centered about a possible breakdown in identification between leaders and the rank and file. Where harmony existed only between top management and top union people, the union leaders acted in response to a different set of images from those of the rank and file. Occasionally this breakdown might have been compatible with continuing stability for a short period; but the chances for the leadership to weather a crisis seemed diminished by it, particularly where alternative candidates were anxious to take over the elective offices.

Such a breakdown occurred in one local of the Steelworkers. A large number of inequities in a company's piece-rate system had sprung up in the war when loose rates presented no particular problem. Management and the union had entered upon the harmonious phase of their relationship immediately after the war. Company officials frankly wanted to sell the union on the need for rate revisions—some upward and some downward. By 1948, the union president's close association with and understanding of management's problems had convinced him that the company needed some relief, and he started negotiating changes in many rates. A union election came along and he was defeated because he was not able to "get the wave length" of the membership in discussing a ticklish management problem.

Occasionally, the unions were faced with an economic crisis in the company which posed doubts about the practicability of accommodating the union's objectives to those of the company. In their concern over job protection, the unions sometimes felt that their only recourse in the crisis was to hold on doggedly to what they had already won. The question of the union's ability to retreat as well as to advance in response to economic developments is complex. In the final analysis, the union's policy in regard to an economic crisis in the company appeared to depend on which of two expectations were greater: whether the company and union together could weather the storm if each gave up a little; or whether all that had been won in the past could be maintained if the union fought hard enough against the company.

A third union pitfall is the absence of anything for the membership to do in a harmonious relationship. Some alternative direction is needed for the members' interests and energies once the protest function of the union is played down; otherwise there is either complete apathy towards the union or a succession of made-up grievances from a disgruntled work force which feels left out of things. The survival of working harmony appears to require constant broadening of the problem-solving activities within the over-all framework of a management organization responsible for running the business and a union organization constantly policing management's actions in the interests of workers.

Stable Relationships

Both sides in these relationships were enthusiastic about developments, despite the wide fluctuations, and while unwilling to make any commitments about the future, felt reasonably certain that they would be able to maintain a relatively harmonious approach to collective bargaining. The stability in this process of accommodation appeared to have three principal roots:

1. The fact that harmony continued to pay off in terms of the advancement of the separate objectives of the contracting parties.

2. The fact that a continuing amount of accommodation fortified the identification between the two parties' interests and that they came to recognize a mutual stake in the survival of harmony as such.

3. The fact that the parties could nevertheless continue to engage in hardheaded bargaining without upsetting the relationship; their relations did not require an atmosphere of sweetness and light.

The type of relationships found in this survey appeared to represent one method by which a major share of conflicts in labor-management relations were contained within the bounds of order and stability. The direct participants in them claimed that this sort of accommodation of objectives was paying off in terms of a steady record of gains for each side, and that tough but reasonable bargaining was consistent with their respective long-run interests. For these reasons, the number of relationships similar to these may increase in the future.

APPENDIX A _____

Atomic Energy

—A Special Case

Strikes in essential industries and ways to cope with them while safeguarding individual freedom and the public welfare present one of the great American dilemmas. While outside the general assignment of the Committee on the Causes of Industrial Peace, this subject stimulated continuing discussion during the course of its work. About midway in its activities, the Committee sponsored preparation of a report on *The Development of a Policy for Industrial Peace in Atomic Energy,* which was published in July 1950.[1] The aim was to increase understanding (1) of the intensive efforts being made by management, labor, and the government to maintain democratic procedures of collective bargaining in a government-owned, privately operated plant, complicated by the need to guard national security; and (2) of the complexities of collective bargaining in other industries where strikes could create a public emergency or directly threaten the public health and safety.

In 1948, following the threat of a work stoppage at Oak Ridge, President Truman appointed a Commission on Labor Relations in the Atomic Energy Installations to "concern itself with the broad code of conduct which should be observed by management and labor in their relations with each other in the vital program." In carrying out its assignment, the three-man Commission, headed by William H. Davis, thoroughly analyzed U.S. policy as expressed in the Atomic Energy Act, and surveyed the points of view of and special problems encountered by the Joint Committee on Atomic Energy of the Congress; the Atomic Energy Commissioners; local AEC officials; the Federal Mediation and Conciliation Service; the companies operating major installations; the universities operating research installations; maintenance, townsite, and construction contractors; the American Federation of Labor; and the Congress of Industrial Organizations. (A summary of these special

[1] This brief summary is based on NPA Planning Pamphlet 71, published in July 1950, which the Committee subsequently recommended for inclusion as part of the series of *Case Studies.* The pamphlet was written by Donald B. Straus, then Executive Secretary of the Atomic Energy Labor Relations Panel, now with the Health Insurance Plan of Greater New York.

views is included in the report.) The Commission's next task was to recommend a labor policy which would harmonize these seeming irreconcilables:

1. How to safeguard the national interest against strikes.

2. How to maintain security without impeding collective bargaining.

3. How to promote collective bargaining in a government-owned plant operated by a private company on a cost-plus-fixed-fee basis.

In April 1949, the Commission recommended to the President neither additional legislation nor compulsory arbitration, but rather reliance upon voluntary acceptance of atomic labor policy without legal or administrative compulsion. The President then appointed the Atomic Energy Labor Relations Panel to help carry out the recommended labor policy.

Companies and unions in the atomic energy program agreed not to cause any interruption of production through strikes or changes in the basic working agreements without first giving the Panel a chance to resolve the differences. When one of the parties to a dispute in atomic energy feels that it has gone as far as possible in collective bargaining and still has not been able to negotiate terms which are acceptable, it then may notify the Panel. That is in tacit recognition that the right to take economic action of any kind remains in escrow with the Panel until after the impartial group has either (1) dismissed the case as one affecting a nonessential part of the atomic energy program, or (2) had an opportunity to settle it, or (3) had utilized its full procedures and had failed to settle it. In theory, at least, no strike in atomic energy is possible until the Panel has been officially notified of the dispute and has followed one of its procedural routes. Thus, the nation is safeguarded against a surprise emergency—and further protected by the deliberative processes of the Panel.

The procedures of the Panel purposely are indefinite—primarily to allow the Panel every opportunity to bring about an agreement but also to avoid letting the parties know in advance what to expect from the Panel so that they will be less eager "to relinquish their own responsibility for working out a solution." The procedures are distinguished from compulsory arbitration partly by this fuzziness of outline, and further by the fact that the Panel's recommendations are by no means an assured part of the process nor, once given, are they binding. The recommendations can be accepted or turned down by either the Atomic Energy Commission, the contractor, or the union.

By June 10, 1950, the Panel had been called in on eleven cases. Nine had been settled satisfactorily by a variety of techniques (described in the report) and two were still before the Panel.

An important factor in agreement making appeared to be the strong moral responsibility felt by contractors and labor unions to maintain atomic production. Both not only had patriotic motives, but also recognized that if the voluntary policy proves ineffective in avoiding disastrous strikes in atomic energy, public opinion will demand that work stoppages be outlawed by drastic legislation—which by extending government control over wages and working conditions, might have far-reaching effects on collective bargaining outside the industry.

A POSTSCRIPT

On March 6, 1953, President Eisenhower accepted the resignation of the Atomic Energy Labor Relations Panel's chairman and members; and later in March announced a new Atomic Energy Labor-Management Relations Panel, to be established under the Director of the Federal Mediation and Conciliation Service. He directed that the new Panel exercise substantially the same jurisdiction as that of the former Panel, but established a change in procedure on referral of cases. The Director of the Mediation Service now has the function of referring cases to the Panel, but only after he has established that parties to a dispute have fully utilized normal processes of collective bargaining and that the Atomic Energy Commission believes the dispute threatens interference with an essential part of the atomic energy program. The former Panel's report to the President, dated December 1, 1952, summarized the handling of a total of 59 cases; by December 1953, the new Panel had handled two cases.

Union and Management Experience in 138 Companies

A Summary of Responses to an NPA Questionnaire

More than a thousand nominations of companies and unions whose good relations appeared to be noteworthy were made following public announcement of the project of the NPA Committee on the Causes of Industrial Peace Under Collective Bargaining. After the Committee eliminated those situations which were obviously inappropriate for study, 400 companies still seemed eligible. In order to narrow the field to a few representative companies and unions, a letter was sent to each, explaining the project. It contained duplicate questionnaires on labor-management relations and requested that management officials fill out and return one questionnaire and union officials the other.

The returned questionnaires bore out the Committee's contention that union-management relations often are peaceful. Although only a few of these firms could be chosen for intensive, on-the-spot investigation, a summary of the information they supplied illustrates that a larger group of firms than it was possible for the Committee to study in detail were enjoying successful labor relations when the project started.

This appendix presents only the highlights of the data supplied by company and union officials—or both—who had the time, interest, and authority to fill out and return the questionnaires. It is not a tight statistical analysis, but draws together some statements based on fact and some on opinion. Nevertheless, something may be learned from the experiences of companies of different backgrounds, locations, and characteristics which in 1947 shared the common experience of peaceful labor relations.

Simple tabulations were made of the 203 questionnaires received prior to October 1, 1947. Of these, 93 were replies from unions, and 110 from management. They represent a total of 138 companies, of which a basic group of 65 had both management and union replies. Included in the 138 companies were 28 on which only the unions reported, and 45 with replies by

353

management only. In cases where it seemed important, tabulations were made both for the total number of companies reported upon and for the basic group of 65 companies.

All geographic areas of the United States were covered. More than half of the companies were located in the Middle Atlantic (33) or East North Central (38) sections of the country. The number of companies in other areas was: New England, 17; West North Central, 12; South Atlantic, 11; East South Central, 6; West South Central, 2; Mountain, 2; Pacific, 11; and more than one geographic area, 6.

Here are our questions and notes on pertinent answers, grouped according to a description of the companies, the unions, and the workers, and information on the labor-management relationship and its results.

The Company, the Union, the Workers

How long has the company been in business? . . . How many plants does it have?

Analysis of the companies showed that 75 per cent had been in business from 11 to 70 years, with marked concentration at the period of 31–50 years. Of the total, 45 per cent were one- and two-plant organizations; 26 per cent had three or four plants each; 22 per cent had from five to fifteen units. In addition, nine companies whose operations were particularly spread out, reported 22, 24, 25, 26, 31, 50, 60, 89, and 171 units. Some of the companies which operated on a multiple-unit basis reported for only one representative plant. The kind of organization which was not well represented was that where operations were scattered over the United States or the world in such a way that conditions lacked uniformity from plant to plant; where so many contracts were signed with so many unions that no one experience seemed typical. Often officials of such concerns expressed interest in the study and explained their reasons for considering their businesses ineligible.

What is the principal industry or industries with which the firm is identified? . . . What is the number of employees today? In 1939? In 1944? . . . What is the present number of wage earners? . . . What proportion of these do you roughly classify as skilled? Semiskilled? Unskilled? . . . What proportion are male? Female?

Information is largely on manufacturing concerns, with a total in the sample of 122. This group is heavily weighted by textile mill products (12 companies), apparel and other finished fabric products (12), iron and steel and their products (22), electrical machinery (14). In addition, there are 10 communication and public utility concerns, 3 in the wholesale and retail trade, and 1 each in construction, transportation, and services. In 1947, 46 per cent had 2000 or fewer employees; 25 per cent, from 2001 to 4000; 18 per cent, 4001 to 10,000; and 11 per cent had over 10,000. The largest organization had 24,000 employees in 1947. Skilled, semiskilled, and unskilled wage earners were about equally represented, but there was a preponderance of male employees.

Does the company belong to an employers' association which deals with the union on an industry-wide or an area-wide basis?

Despite expectations to the contrary, the officials of only nine firms indicated that they followed the procedure of industry-wide or regional negotiations of contracts. In contrast, it developed that companies which operated a large number of plants often signed separate union agreements at each of the plants.

When did the company first begin to deal with unions? . . . What is the principal union with which the company deals today? . . . When was it recognized? . . . Does your agreement include a union shop? Closed shop? Maintenance of union membership? Sole recognition? Other form of preferential shop? For how long?

In over half of the cases, the main union with which the company dealt was recognized sometime during the period 1937–41. About one-fifth of the unions had been recognized during the period 1932–36; and only about 5 per cent had been recognized before 1932. Some relationships with unions had started before union recognition, but most of management signified that their union dealings began during the year when recognition took place.

Union groups naturally followed closely upon industrial classifications. Of the 138 unions, at that time 48 were affiliated with the American Federation of Labor; 77 with the Congress of Industrial Organizations; and 13 were independent. Most often encountered were the United Electrical, Radio & Machine Workers of America (then CIO, now independent), which was concerned at 10 companies; the United Steelworkers of America (CIO) at 21 companies; and the Textile Workers Union of America (CIO) at 16 companies. Unions which figured six times each were the International Brotherhood of Electrical Workers (AFL); two Federal Labor Unions (AFL); the United Automobile, Aircraft & Agricultural Implement Workers of America, International Union (CIO); and the International Association of Machinists (then independent, now AFL) was named in eight companies.

About half of the union-management agreements stipulated a union shop. The union responses were: union shop, 47; closed shop, 3; maintenance of membership, 44; and sole recognition, 42. Management's responses showed: union shop, 60; closed shop, 7; maintenance of membership, 44; sole recognition, 45. Few contracts provided for other forms of preferential shops. Reporting on the date of expiration of the union-management agreement was too incomplete to merit attention.

Is your company's wage structure high, low, or favorable, compared with other plants in your industry? With similar occupations in your community?

Since answers on wage comparisons were entirely based upon opinion, they should be evaluated as such. Apparently management officials thought a bit better of their wage records than did union officials, but in both cases at least two-thirds were of the opinion that their wage scales compared favorably with those in effect at other plants in the same industry, and over one-half believed they compared favorably with similar occupations in their community. The breakdown of responses from both management and the unions for comparison with their industry is: management—31 per cent higher, 68 per cent favorable, 1 per cent lower; union—16 per cent higher, 78 per cent favorable, 6 per cent lower. On the comparison with community wage rates, it is: management—43 per cent higher, 55 per cent favorable, 2 per cent lower; union—28 per cent higher, 69 per cent favorable, 3 per cent lower.

The Union-Management Relationship

What is the scope of your collective bargaining relationship? . . . Simple collective bargaining on wages and working conditions? . . . Joint committees dealing with production, training, safety, or other problems? . . . Cooperation between union and management in eliminating waste, improving production methods, or other problems of mutual concern?

About half of the 138 companies were said to carry on simple collective bargaining on wages and working conditions—which we assumed to mean that the bargaining relationship was concerned solely with the drawing up of a contract and the enforcement of its clauses. One or more joint committees operated at the remainder of the companies. Replies did not always indicate the type of committee, but safety seemed to be the most frequent type, with some concentration also on apprentice training. Other joint committees mentioned were concerned with time study and job evaluation; wages or rates for piecework; seniority; production; accident, health, sickness, and life insurance; social and recreational activities; suggestions; operation of the contract; counseling and training; and merit rating. (A summary table appears in *Case Study No. 13,* page 26.) Over one-half of the officials replied in the affirmative to the question on cooperation between union and management in eliminating waste, improving production methods, or other problems of mutual concern, but the area of cooperation was seldom defined.

During the history of your union relations have there been strikes or lockouts? . . . Approximate length? . . . If so, when? . . . For what reason?

According to the answers, only one lockout had occurred since union recognition by the 138 companies. About 50 per cent of the companies had not experienced a strike since recognition of the union. Of those who had experienced strikes, comparatively few had more than one—7 management officials reported 2 strikes; 2 reported 3 strikes; 3 reported 5 strikes; 1 reported "many strikes"; and 4 reported sporadic, unauthorized strikes.

About one-fourth of the strikes for which duration was reported were short, lasting ten days or less; almost two-thirds were less than a month. Several strikes, however, were said to have endured for four months and others for two or three months. Of the companies reporting one or more strikes, roughly two-thirds had experienced them during the period 1944–47. This is not surprising in view of the late date at which many of the unions had been recognized and the fact that during World War II strikes were kept to a minimum so that disputes came to the surface with cessation of hostilities.

Wages alone, or wages in combination with some secondary factor or factors, constituted the chief cause of dissension (26 and 9, respectively, according to management). Some of the other issues cited are: union and closed shop, grievance procedures, ratio of first class tradesmen to helpers, job classifications, seniority rights, discharges, Sunday and vacation arrangements, and contract negotiations. There is reference also to one sympathetic and one jurisdictional strike, and three where personalities played a part in the dispute.

Where were there the fewest strikes? NPA wondered whether analysis of the information would give a clue to the kind of organization where there is likely to be a minimum amount of labor difficulty, and, in reverse, where there may be recurring friction. In order to do this, three periods were selected—1943–47, 1938–47, and 1934–47—for each of which the number of strikes was recorded: by industry, by number of wage earners, and by relative level of company's wage structure in its industry and community. Only those business organizations at which the union had been recognized throughout one of these periods were tabulated. Some points emerged from cross-correlation tables, but they are not indicative of broad trends and so are mentioned only as sidelights to our general findings.

Management officials reported one strike at only four of the 18 companies at which unions had been recognized by 1934, and two strikes at only two companies during the entire period 1934–47. Union officials reported one strike at each of eight establishments during the same 14 years. Union-management relations in these cases were well established at an early date, and progressed smoothly regardless of the economic condition of the country or the experiences of war and postwar periods. All except three of the 18 concerns employed fewer than 5000 persons in 1947. Examination of the relationship of strikes to the number of employees at a wider group of establishments during the later periods, gave a further indication that strikes occurred more frequently at large than at small establishments. (This information should be judged, however, only with the fact in mind that there were far fewer large companies than small companies included in the survey.)

In the 1943–47 period, according to reports of 110 management officials, strikes were most common in the industries concerned with iron and steel and their products, electrical machinery, and transportation equipment except automobiles. The less complete reports of 91 union officials did not contradict this, although lines were less sharply drawn. In 1938–47, the largest incidence of strikes appeared in the iron and steel industry. (Again, this finding is open to question, because 22 of the 138 companies were in the iron and steel group, which is not equally balanced by other industrial categories.)

It does not appear that industrial peace has been bought by paying higher wages. Neither from union nor management response was it evident that companies which were believed to be paying higher wages than those in the industry had experienced fewer strikes than those where wages were believed to be favorable in the industry. Nor were there fewer strikes among companies which union officials believed paid higher wages than similar occupations in the community than among those companies in which they believed wages to be favorable. However, management's response on comparable community wages leads to a different conclusion. For the three periods— 1943–47, 1938–47, and 1934–47—this response resulted in figures showing fewer and less frequent strikes among establishments judged to be paying higher than the current rate for similar occupations in the community.

Despite the scattered tendencies note in connection with this analysis, it seems to indicate that the favorable experience of companies represented cannot be explained in terms of certain industries as against others, of the size of plant, or of the relative level of wages within the community or the industry.

In your opinion, would a strike result if agreement were not reached in negotiations regarding a new or revised contract?

This question revealed somewhat more divergence in union and management opinion than others. About one-third of the union officials answered no, whereas one-half of the management officials answered no.

During the period since recognition of the union, has the labor-management relationship improved? Remained about the same? Deteriorated?

A slight difference also appears in the officials' opinions as to the history of the labor-management relationship. Labor is a little bit more inclined to see an improvement than is management. Of 93 labor responses, the replies were: improved 84, same 7, deteriorated 1, fluctuated 1; whereas 103 management replies, in the same order, were: 78, 18, 5, 2. Even so, an over-whelming number of both groups of officials reported improved relations—90 per cent of all union respondents and 76 per cent of management.

Would you classify as good, fair, or poor the relationship between top management and international union officials? Between middle management and union representatives? Between foremen and rank-and-file union members?

In diagnosing the relationship between management and union officials at various levels, management is slightly more optimistic than the unions. The relationship between top management and the international union officials is considered good by 93 per cent of management respondents and 89 per cent of union respondents; that between middle management and union representatives is thought to be good by 90 per cent of management and 81 per cent of the unions; and between foremen and the rank and file is termed good by 87 per cent of management and 68 per cent of union officials. It is worth noting that the relationship of foremen to rank-and-file workers seemed delicate. Any number of officials stressed the necessity of choosing foremen wisely and of giving them special training. Some believed that difficulty is avoided by appointing foremen from the rank and file; others, by including foremen among the union members.

Has man-hour productivity increased since union-management relations were established on a mutually satisfactory basis? . . . If so, can you estimate the percentage of increase?

Very little could be learned from responses to this question. Union officials more frequently attested to gains than management. Thoughtful replies from both called attention to the fact that opinions could scarcely carry weight because wartime conditions and changing technology—also the lack of measuring rods—were so influential in the story of productivity.

MANAGEMENT AND UNION COMMENTS ON THE CAUSES OF INDUSTRIAL PEACE

It would be unreasonable to infer that the findings of this limited analysis provide a workable formula for peaceful labor-management relations. However, the statistical analysis of answers from this relatively small group of companies does seem to imply that neither the size of plant, the kind of industry, nor the relative level of wages is the key to industrial peace in these 138 companies. It would seem that the basic causes lie elsewhere.

Some of the most interesting information stimulated by the questionnaire appeared in covering letters by management and union officials or in footnotes to the questionnaires. Although such comments reflected opinion only, and should be evaluated as such, the frequency with which they recurred lends validity to them. Granted that no two industrial situations are identical, granted that labor-management relations are influenced by the politics and the economics of the day, labor peace seems likely to be realized when such attitudes and policies as those evidenced in the comments given below are present:

Acceptance of collective bargaining and a genuine desire to facilitate smooth performance.

What do management officials say about this?

"We have always had good union-management relations. The union has always cooperated in the securing and maintaining of good productivity."

". . . Prior to August, 1945, there was practically nothing but daily trouble here and since that time an almost complete absence of any difficulty whatsoever. . . . one of the Vice Presidents of the International Union told me two weeks ago that he quite often uses this company as an example of how labor relations can change from worst to best almost overnight when the men on both sides are sincere in their desires to work out a fair and equitable program."

"It has been our experience over the past ten years that when the International officials are actively interested in a given situation and in the relations between a given local and an employer, differences are much more easily adjusted before they become real disputes and greater cooperation is obtained from local officials."

And what do labor officials say on the subject?

"Relations between the Company and the Union have been very good. This is true primarily because each side has made a fair approach to the solving of their problems. Each has honored and respected to the fullest degree their contracts signed in good faith. Each has made an honest effort to make collective bargaining work, and their efforts have been richly rewarded."

"This plant has a very unique history. . . . Relations for several years were very poor, finally culminating in a two-year strike from 1937 to 1939 over the union's demand for union security and a contract. . . . I think this would be a very good illustration of where a few years ago we had the bitter extreme of both the union and the company fighting each other almost to death, and following the two-year strike or showdown, a complete change in labor relations."

"I wish to state that considering the fact that at ———— where the work consists of hundreds of intricate operations which are paid on piece work, and hourly rates, and piece work plus hourly pay, and where styles are continually changing, plus the fact that we have many craftsmen, such as electricians, plumbers, carpenters, steamfitters, machinists, engineers, firemen, etc., all under the contract, plus the fact that we have plants in several states, I personally feel it is unusual that the company and the union get along as well as we do. But there is a reason and that reason is simple. The company honestly recognizes the union and is willing to let it be known. They are willing to work with the union and don't try to work around or undermine the union. In return there is only one answer, the union has to assume the responsibility of seeing to it that the plant runs continuously and profitably so both worker and management can profit together."

An understanding of the interdependence of labor and management and putting that understanding into practice.

What do management officials say about this?

". . . By exercising patience and understanding, we have welded confidence between labor and management. Once this is accomplished, it is no longer a question of 'Labor Problems,' but a matter of company problems to be handled jointly by management and labor."

"We believe that one of the main causes of industrial peace at ———— has been our method of conducting collective bargaining negotiations. We have constantly attempted to deal on the basis of reason and sound logic and the unions with whom we deal have responded to this approach to a most gratifying degree."

"If we were to say that there was any one reason for our successfully maintaining good relations with the unions we could sum it up as 'mutual respect and understanding of the other fellow's problems.' "

"Although the feeling between the company and the union in the first years of our relationship was far from friendly, we have in the past ten years recognized the need of mutual respect and consideration for each other in order to obtain harmony across the bargaining table."

And what do labor officials say on the subject?

"We are proud of our labor-relationship with our employer and although we have many differences of opinion, we nevertheless have resolved to settle them around the conference table and that practice is paying off great dividends."

"Local ———, its members and officers, are proud to work for an employer with a record of labor relations such as exist here. True we have had trying times, but both employer and employee were always able to iron out differences of opinion at the bargaining table. Each side knows and understands the word 'compromise.' "

"A mutual understanding is enjoyed by both parties with the thought always in mind of getting the job done with the minimum of trouble."

Appointment of capable, fair-minded, and respected persons from the union and management to negotiate contracts.

What do labor officials say of this?

"Factors which have contributed to good relations at this plant are first an active, militant and well organized local union and second top management which are labor minded in that they have fully and completely accepted our union and have convinced *all their employees* that they want our union to be a well-run and successful union."

"Management has placed in official capacity sound, fairminded individuals who have endeavored to be fair on all matters pertaining to industrial relations and Local —— has followed the same pattern."

"In negotiations with this Company it is the consensus of the Negotiating Committee that the relations existing prohibit the use of threats or any form of coercion when negotiating either for contract renewal or any other provisions or amendments to a contract."

And what do management officials say on the subject?

"The greatest asset we have been able to develop in our relations with our employees has come as a result of years of dealing together, during which each party to the dealings has become convinced of the good faith of the other party."

"We do not consider that there is any patent answer to the problem, but rather that fundamentally sound philosophies must be applied to the condition inherent in an industry and to the peculiar circumstances that develop from time to time. These philosophies must be founded on fairness and must be such as to induce an attitude of trust on the part of both parties."

"We have simply proceeded out here on the basis that honesty and fairness in dealing with the local union in an attitude of mutual respect (which has permitted the education of both sides—labor and management—in getting along with each other) is about the only intelligent and unselfish manner under which the job can be done."

Formulation of definite statements on wage scales, conditions of employment, and grievance procedures, and assurance that wage earners are thoroughly aware of them.

What do labor officials say about this?

". . . Then again, we have the workers who do not listen to a mass appeal from their union officials for action, but who are able to think for themselves after being properly informed by their leaders that no strike or work stoppage can possibly exist. It has been my experience that if workers in a plant are properly informed as to a contract, they collectively think as one in the making of a determination as to what action is proper to take in a case. However, where a worker is not properly informed he lives in fear of his job and having no complete knowledge of the problems at hand follows the line of least resistance."

"The company laid its books upon the table and frankly and honestly answered all questions from the union. Six months later the division which, over a thirty-year period had operated in the red, showed a profit. . . . The division improved so much that the company is now preparing, contrary to its previous plans to close the division, to expand it and enlarge it."

Another union official cites several instances where the union helped the company increase its contracts for work. The official also mentions the incentive plan instituted under the direction of the ———— ———— Company. "The job evaluation has brought all base rates into proper balance and that balance must be maintained. In considering wage increases, the same amount of increase must be given to every individual in the bargaining unit. This strengthens the machinery of collective bargaining and simplifies its use."

And what do management officials say on the subject?

"Our good relationship with the union is due, I believe, primarily to prompt settlement of grievances, fair treatment of all employees, and serious consideration of all grievances no matter how small."

"I would lay down as one of the first principles of good relations the requirement that important information having a bearing on the welfare of employees be passed along in an understandable and logical manner. We use a weekly letter form of distribution either on bulletin boards or more lately by delivery to each employee in the entire company. . . . This information must be free from propaganda and on an honest, sincere and informative basis."

"Management makes considerable effort to give the union as much information as it possibly can, and announces its plans sufficiently in advance to the union officials so that changes are made without friction."

"The installation of a wage rate structure, fixed by a job evaluation survey providing a fair wage basis, merit increase, and incentive rates by management and labor in joint conference" and "last, but not least, down-to-earth methods of clearing differences, disputes, and grievances between management and union" are listed as two of the "real answers as to why our relations between union and management are so satisfactory."

"If I were to try to name any single reason for successful day-to-day bargaining under the contract, it is because we have insisted on a regularized system of meetings with shop committees. Superintendents of each of our plants have a meeting once a week with the shop committee of the respective plants irrespective of the number of questions that are up at the moment. Because of the regularity of these meetings all questions that do arise on either side are kept alive until they are finally disposed of and this more than any other factor is responsible for the relationship."

"We do not 'coddle' nor do we abuse. We find that the attitude of our employees toward management is simply a reflection of management's attitude toward its employees. . . . We have had no secrets in our negotiations with the union, no 'black jacks' or 'big wheels'; we have never lost a grievance we should have won, and we have never won a grievance in a manner that would reflect any particular discredit upon the shop committee or the international representative."

Appreciation of the rights of the individual; training in ways to deal with workers; participation in joint committees.

What do labor officials say about this?

"As you move through the departments of the ——— Division you would meet in the Hand Form Department, Mr. ——— ———, Foreman, who used to operate these fixtures and knows it is a tough job. The boys say he makes a swell boss. . . . In the Punch Press Department, it is ——— ———. He operated a press for a long time. He knows that they are tricky and dangerous. He was a good active union member, and is an excellent supervisor. In the ——— department is ——— ———, former member of the bargaining committee of the union. ——— has a tough assignment, but is doing quite well in it."

"Supervisors from highest to lowest level attend an organization established a year ago, the ——— ———, for the purpose of educational, recreational and policy matters. This is in no way a company-controlled organization. Officers of the company meet with the Board of Governors of the association and its membership from time to time to discuss matters of general company interest."

"The company has sponsored a training program under a competent training director based on the principles of 'Training Within Industry' and 'Job Relations Program.' All levels of supervision and union officers and committeemen have participated. . . . I wish to emphasize the fact that all matters pertaining to successful operation of the plant and all matters of industrial relations nature are jointly considered and acted upon."

And what do management officials say on the subject?

"We have counseling committees of equal number on job evaluation, merit rating every six months and on suggestion system. It works very well. We have not had an arbitration case since 1940."

"It has been our experience that men are happier if they are doing a good job and if they have the feeling they are valuable to their company. This can best be worked out through some form of an incentive system because good earnings and high productivity are the direct result . . . union time-study men set the standards of performance and of course we find them as sincere as management men."

"Our foremen and other supervisors are trained in the Company's method and appreciate the delicate responsibility with which their positions are charged. They know that every grievance, no matter how humble the source, must be given careful attention in its incipiency."

"It was felt that by training foremen in methods of democratic group leadership, and by enabling them to study and practice *beforehand*, methods of handling responses to frustration, they could meet their day-to-day situations in human relations more successfully. Consequently, a training program using role-playing techniques was initiated. . . . As for our relations with our union, they are carried on in a cooperative, amiable atmosphere. We have actively aided the union to become strong and socially acceptable in the factory and the community."

". . . It is extremely difficult, if not practically impossible, to establish any rules or plans which are certain to lead to industrial peace and harmony, basically because the human element is involved, and when such is the case, we think that the best an employer can do is to apply common sense and sincerity in his relations with the employees."

"The inner workings of our Labor Management Committees on Accident Prevention and Safety, Employee Suggestions, and Apprenticeship Training are evidences of our joint efforts toward common goals. When company and union negotiating committees meet on a variety of plant problems, the union representatives make constructive suggestions for increasing production, elimination of waste time or materials, or other similar matters in the direct interest of the company, as often does management."

"We had our supervisory force take a coaching program designed to improve the attitude of our foremen and this proved beneficial as it induced the supervisory personnel to approach a grievance or other problems with consideration."

We are not discouraged by the size or the content of our "sample." Nor do we believe that industrial peace exists in a vacuum. Time will tell whether it is possible to maintain successful relations at these and other concerns throughout the nation. The fact that collective bargaining can be accepted, the fact that it can operate smoothly in peace and in war, confirms Clinton Golden's ideas, which prompted the original undertaking of this study on the Causes of Industrial Peace Under Collective Bargaining.

366

NPA OFFICERS AND BOARD OF TRUSTEES
Continued

NPA PUBLICATIONS POLICY

JOHN MILLER, *Assistant Chairman* and *Executive Secretary;* EUGENE BLAND, *Editor of Publications;* VIRGINIA D. PARKER, *Editorial Consultant.*

NPA is an independent, nonpolitical, nonprofit organization established in 1934. It is an organization where leaders of agriculture, business, labor, and the professions join in programs to maintain and strengthen private initiative and enterprise.

Those who participate in the activities of NPA believe that the tendency to break up into pressure groups is one of the gravest disintegrating forces in our national life. America's number-one problem is that of getting diverse groups to work together for this objective: To combine our efforts to the end that the American people may always have the highest possible cultural and material standard of living without sacrificing our freedom. Only through joint democratic efforts can programs be devised which support and sustain each other in the national interest.

NPA's Standing Committees—the Agriculture, Business, and Labor Committees on National Policy and the Committee on International Policy—and its Special Committees are assisted by a permanent research staff. Whatever their particular interests, members have in common a fact-finding and socially responsible attitude.

NPA believes that through effective private planning we can avoid a planned economy. The results of NPA's work will not be a grand solution to all our ills. But the findings, and the process of work itself, will provide concrete programs for action on specific problems, planned in the best traditions of a functioning democracy.

NPA's publications—whether signed by its board, its committees, its staff, or by individuals—are issued in an effort to pool different knowledge and skills, to narrow areas of controversy, and to broaden areas of agreement.

All reports published by NPA have been examined and authorized for publication under policies laid down by the Board of Trustees. Such action does not imply agreement by NPA board or committee members with all that is contained therein, unless such endorsement is specifically stated.

NPA issues regularly the *Planning Pamphlets* and *Special Reports* series which present the findings of NPA's board, standing committees, staff, or cooperating specialists. In addition, as committees with special assignments, such as that on the causes of industrial peace, prepare reports, these are published and distributed under regular NPA publications policy and procedures.

PUBLICATIONS OF THE NPA COMMITTEE ON THE CAUSES OF INDUSTRIAL PEACE UNDER COLLECTIVE BARGAINING [1]

CASE STUDY NO. 1. CROWN ZELLERBACH CORPORATION AND THE PACIFIC COAST PULP AND PAPER INDUSTRY. September 1948. 96 pp.

CASE STUDY NO. 2. THE LIBBY-OWENS-FORD GLASS COMPANY AND THE FEDERATION OF GLASS, CERAMIC AND SILICA SAND WORKERS OF AMERICA. October 1948. 76 pp.

CASE STUDY NO. 3. THE DEWEY AND ALMY CHEMICAL COMPANY AND THE INTERNATIONAL CHEMICAL WORKERS UNION. December 1948. 100 pp.

CASE STUDY NO. 4. HICKEY-FREEMAN COMPANY AND AMALGAMATED CLOTHING WORKERS OF AMERICA. January 1949. 100 pp.

CASE STUDY NO. 5. SHARON STEEL CORPORATION AND UNITED STEELWORKERS OF AMERICA. April 1949. 72 pp.

CASE STUDY NO. 6. LOCKHEED AIRCRAFT CORPORATION AND INTERNATIONAL ASSOCIATION OF MACHINISTS. November 1949. 100 pp.

CASE STUDY NO. 7. NASHUA GUMMED AND COATED PAPER COMPANY AND 7 AFL UNIONS. February 1950. 104 pp.

PLANNING PAMPHLET NO. 71. THE DEVELOPMENT OF A POLICY FOR INDUSTRIAL PEACE IN ATOMIC ENERGY. July 1950. 112 pp.

CASE STUDY NO. 8. MARATHON CORPORATION AND 7 LABOR UNIONS. September 1950. 80 pp.

CASE STUDY NO. 9. MINNEQUA PLANT OF COLORADO FUEL AND IRON CORPORATION AND UNITED STEELWORKERS OF AMERICA. October 1951. 112 pp.

CASE STUDY NO. 10. THE LAPOINTE MACHINE TOOL COMPANY AND UNITED STEELWORKERS OF AMERICA. November 1952. 96 pp.

CASE STUDY NO. 11. AMERICAN VELVET COMPANY AND TEXTILE WORKERS UNION OF AMERICA. April 1953. 72 pp.

CASE STUDY NO. 12. ATLANTIC STEEL COMPANY AND UNITED STEELWORKERS OF AMERICA. November 1953. 116 pp.

CASE STUDY NO. 13. WORKING HARMONY IN 18 COMPANIES. November 1953. 76 pp.

CASE STUDY NO. 14. FUNDAMENTALS OF LABOR PEACE, A FINAL REPORT. December 1953. 128 pp.

[1] For additional information write the National Planning Association, 1606 New Hampshire Ave., N.W., Washington 9, D.C.